Ruth Kara-Ivanov Kaniel
Birth in Kabbalah and Psychoanalysis

Perspectives on Jewish Texts and Contexts

Edited by
Vivian Liska

Editorial Board
Robert Alter, Steven A. Aschheim, Leora Batnitzky, Richard I. Cohen, Mark H. Gelber, Moshe Halbertal, Christine Hayes, Moshe Idel, Samuel Moyn, Ilana Pardes, Alvin Rosenfeld, David Ruderman, Bernd Witte

Volume 18

Ruth Kara-Ivanov Kaniel

Birth in Kabbalah and Psychoanalysis

DE GRUYTER   MAGNES

This book is a translation from the Hebrew original: חבלי אנוש - הלידה בפסיכואנליזה ובקבלה, Series in Criticism Culture and Interpretation, Carmel Press. Jerusalem: 2018.

ISBN 978-3-11-152057-5
e-ISBN (PDF) 978-3-11-068802-3
e-ISBN (EPUB) 978-3-11-068810-8
ISSN 2199-6962

Library of Congress Control Number: 2022933738

Bibliographic information published by the Deutsche Nationalbibliothek
The Deutsche Nationalbibliothek lists this publication in the Deutsche Nationalbibliografie; detailed bibliographic data are available on the internet at http://dnb.dnb.de.

© 2024 Walter de Gruyter GmbH, Berlin/Boston and The Hebrew University Magnes Press, Jerusalem
This volume is text- and page-identical with the hardback published in 2022.
Cover image: "Womb Soaring to the Divine", painting by Haya Ester, mixed technique 2020.
Typesetting: Integra Software Services Pvt.

www.degruyter.com

All human life on the planet is born of woman. The one unifying, incontrovertible experience shared by all women and men is that months-long period we spent unfolding inside a woman's body.

Probably there is nothing in human nature more resonant with charges than the flow of energy between two biologically alike bodies, one of which has lain in amniotic bliss inside the other, one of which has labored to give birth to the other. The materials are here for the deepest mutuality and the most painful estrangement.

–Adrian Rich, *Of Woman Born*

We seem to diverge rather far in the role we assign to intuition. Your mystics rely on it to teach them how to solve the riddle of the universe; we believe that it cannot reveal to us anything but primitive, instinctual impulses and attitudes – highly valuable for *an embryology of the soul* when correctly interpreted, but worthless for orientation in the alien, external world. –Sigmund Freud to Romain Rolland, January 19, 1930

Come and see: All those plants and all those burning lamps all shine and glow, are watered and blessed, from that flowing, gushing river, in which all is comprised, totality of all. This is called Mother of the Garden, above the garden, for Eden joins with Her, not parting from Her. Consequently, all springs issue, flow, and water in every direction, opening gateways in Her. So Compassion derives from Her, Compassion is opened in Her. Yet since we call Her Mother, Female, Gevurah and Judgment issue from Her [. . . .] אהיה אשר אהיה (*Ehyeh asher ehyeh*), "I am that I am (Exodus 3:14), and I do not fathom it." Mystery of the matter is as follows: אהיה (*ehyeh*), I am – totality of all, for when paths are concealed, not diverging, included in one place, then it is called Ehyeh, totality of all, hidden and not revealed. Once a beginning emerges and that river is impregnated, to channel all, then it is called אשר אהיה (*asher ehyeh*), that I am, meaning: "Until here I am; I am ready to convey and give birth to all." "Ehyeh, I am – meaning: 'Now I am totality of all, generality with no particular.'" *Asher ehyeh*, that I am – for Mother is impregnated and ready to receive all particulars and reveal the supernal Name [. . .] Afterward, He generated that river – supernal Mother – and She became pregnant, ready to give birth; and He said, *asher ehyeh*, that I am, prepared to give birth and arrange all.

–*Zohar* 3:65a–b (Matt, 7, 427–430)

Acknowledgements

Many people have helped to bring this project to its fruition, some by offering their most welcomed and wise counsel, others by contributing their profound insights and assisting me with their support. All of them have already been named and thanked in the expanded Hebrew version of the original publication of this book (Carmel Press, 2018) and are still most heartfeltly appreciated for their help. Here I would like to specifically thank those who have assisted me in the process of editing, translating and generally making possible this English edition for publication.

First and foremost, to Prof. Vivian Liska, the editor of the book series "Perspectives on Jewish Texts and Contexts" (De Gruyter, Berlin); Jonathan Nadav, (CEO of the Magnes Press); The ISF Grant for Book Publications; and the referees of the Gorgias Press competition who kindly decided to award me the "Peras Gorgias" for the year 2019 in the category of a book in Jewish Thought.

In addition, I would like to express my warm gratitude to: Eduard Levin, Daniel Price, Iris Felix, Elizabet Michel, Myrna Milun, Gene Matanky, Levi Morrow, Sara-Tova Brody, Levana Chajes; as well as to my colleagues at the department of Jewish thought at Haifa University; at the Shalom Hartman Institute in Jerusalem; and at the TAICP- the Tel-Aviv Institute for Contemporary Psychoanalysis.

Finally, I want to thank from the depths of my heart my teachers, friends and students for the vital and meaningful conversations we have had regarding the notion of Birth and its centrality in the Jewish myth, as well as in the existential flow of our lives.

The book is dedicated to Asi and our children: Hallel, Talya, Evyatar, Roi, who teach me everyday the mysteries of love, re-birth and growth.

Contents

Acknowledgements —— VII

Introduction —— 1
1   Psychoanalysis and Kabbalah: The Meeting of Worlds —— 2
2   An Example of the Discourse of Kabbalah and Psychoanalysis: The Layers of Creation and the Layers of the Soul —— 6
3   Cultural and Emotional Entanglement —— 8

Chapter 1
The Existentialism of Birth —— 11
1   The Two Poles: Birth and Death —— 11
2   The Fear of Not Being Born and the Sin of Not Giving Birth —— 17
3   The Trauma of Impregnation —— 28
4   Mythical and Individual Birth —— 35
5   The Birth Drive —— 38
6   Neglect of the Mother (and Birth) in Psychoanalytic Thought —— 42

Chapter 2
The Theology and Ethics of Birth —— 46
1   Motherhood and God —— 46
2   Two Mothers: *Binah* and the *Shekhinah* —— 52
3   Mother, God, and the Analyst: Parenting, Theology, and Psychoanalysis —— 57
4   Motherhood and Threat —— 60
5   The "Sawing" Mother and the Concealed Mother —— 62
6   Otherwise than Being and the Law of *Rodef* ("Persecutor," "Pursuer") —— 64

Chapter 3
The Caesura of Birth —— 68
1   Caesura: Connection or a Rending Asunder? —— 68
2   "Sitting on the Crisis" —— 73
3   Psychological Birth: Back and Forth —— 77
4   The Primeval Androgynous: The Myth of *Nesirah* —— 82
5   Caesura and Sawing —— 86
6   The Three Stages of Mythical Birth: Light, Water, and Firmament —— 90

Chapter 4
"The Womb Is a Tomb": The Imagery of the Uterus and Female Guilt and Death —— 96
1. Compassion or Harm by the Womb? —— 97
2. The Womb as a Dangerous Place —— 100
3. The Guilt and Blaming of Eve, the Primal Mother —— 104
4. Birth and Female Death —— 105
5. The Womb as a Grave —— 111
6. The Womb as the Garden of Eden and the Infant as a "Writing Tablet": Anamnesis and "Discerning What May Come to Pass" —— 116
7. The Symbolization of the Womb as the Mind and the Image of the Midwife in Ancient Greece —— 122

Chapter 5
The Double Beginning of the Zohar —— 127
1. Comparing the Introduction to the *Zohar* ("Who Created These?") with Its Opening Homily ("*Be-rosh Hurmanuta de-Malka*" = "At the Head of Potency of the King") —— 129
2. Maternal Origins ("Who Created These?") —— 132
3. Birth as Donning Garments —— 135
4. Paternal Origins ("At the Head of Potency of the King") —— 137
5. Combined Parental Figure —— 141

Chapter 6
Longing for the Source —— 146
1. Unity and Multiplicity of Source and Place —— 146
2. The Dread of the Source —— 151
3. Sunlight, Being, and Not-Being —— 157
   "As Nothing before the Light of the Infinite"- Schneur Zalman of Liadi —— 159
4. Birth as a Transition between a Closed *Mem* (ם) and an Open *Mem* (מ) —— 163
5. Nursing —— 170

Chapter 7
Birth in Lurianic Kabbalah —— 180
1. Three Stages of Mystical Birth: *Ibbur* ("Impregnation," lit., "Gestation"), *Yenika* ("Suckling," "Nursing"), and *Moḥin* ("Consciousness;" lit. "Brains") —— 180

2   The Birth of *Ze'ir Anpin* —— 184
3   Conclusion —— 189
     Appendix: The Roots of Lurianic Concepts in Cordoverian Kabbalah —— 191

Chapter 8
Redemption as Birth, Birth as Redemption —— 195
1   Redemption as Birth —— 197
2   The "Constriction" and "Blockage" of the Gazelle and the Psychoanalytical Third —— 201
3   Birth Pains and Redemption in the Teaching of R. Nahman of Bratzlav —— 206
4   Redemptive Birth in Kabbalah and in Psychoanalysis —— 216

Epilogue —— 219

Bibliography —— 223

Index —— 241

Introduction

The human being is a born creature. Birth is a moment that has taken place and that continues to take place throughout our lives.

This book addresses the experience of birth, the ontological and existential fact shared by all humans – our birth. Against the "being-towards-death" experience posed by existentialism as the central movement of life, I will attempt to examine the opposite existential pole, what I will call the "approaching-birth" experience or "being born." I will suggest that central streams in Jewish philosophy, and in particular Kabbalistic and Hasidic literature, whose roots are early and linked to the Bible, midrash, and the literature of the ancient world, and which view birth as the focus of our existence, conceive of birth both as a moment in time and as a continuing experience of internal actuality, relative to which the intuitive experience of "actual life" is measured.

The book will be devoted to a discussion of the consciousness of life derived from the experience of birth and to an examination of birth "itself." My working assumption is that the human being is a born creature who is aware of his birth. The fact of us having been born is the firmest of our known facts and is something that we think about and interpret all throughout our lives. This experience can be illuminated through a variety of tools. In the chapters that follow, I will address the existential meaning of birth and its analysis through a psychological and psychoanalytical lens and through the lens of Jewish myth in general, and Kabbalistic literature in particular, showing the similarities and differences between these perspectives along the way. In addition, I will relate the physiological and biological aspects of birth and the physical context in which it takes place, its gendered meaning, and the perception of the mother as a subject with the aim of illuminating the links between birth, sexuality, Eros, and motherhood. The mother is born when she gives birth, while the infant is not only born but also transforms she who was a woman into a mother. On the symbolic level, the mother and baby have the power to transform man into father, and, at the same time, all of these testify to divine power, which creates life and is revealed in the act of birth. Birth is a powerful "rite of passage" that is imprinted on the flesh and soul of all who experience it.

The weaving together of different points of view regarding birth into one whole will result in a mosaic-like composition that addresses the notion that man is a "born creature." This kaleidoscope, if you will, includes both tightly and loosely structured chapters of study, analysis, and contemplation. This is because birth, alongside its reality, diverges into the realm of the infinite otherness, which is outside of all order – cultural, linguistic, and symbolic. Birth is the "excess," the place in which the human "overflows," slopes downward from the borders of its being, and deviates from its finality. Birth is much more than the birth of an individual, as it is the most universal phenomenon we can imagine. On the other hand, there is no more private experience than this, for the birth of one person is unlike the birth of any other. Birth deviates even from language, and makes present the self in its connection to the other that emerges from it – as they are two distinct entities which are nevertheless linked together in a sort of mysterious and paradoxical "selfobject." I will examine birth as a continuous phenomenon and as a unique, one-time event – as a symbolic event and as a uniquely female and motherly act.

1 Psychoanalysis and Kabbalah: The Meeting of Worlds

The profound questions addressed by Kabbalah and by psychoanalytic theory intersect at critical points. Those two bodies of knowledge are concerned with the human spirit in all its observed and hidden aspects. Even though the notion of "spirit," "soul," or "psyche" – *nefesh*, in Biblical Hebrew, a term for "life-force" – has changed over historical time, there are more than a few points of linkage between the concept of one's *nefesh*, one's non-physical self, in these two conceptual worlds. The proximity of these two fields is notable in the poetic realm, in mystical symbolism, in the effort to decipher the language of dreams, in the weight attributed to the erotic experience, and in the presence of sexuality in the theosophical system and interpersonal relations.[1]

The healing and creative power of speech finds expression both in Kabbalah and in psychoanalysis,[2] and at the same time one can recognize the difficulty of describing the fullness of emotional and mystical experience using language, with its partial and limited nature.[3] Another important point of similarity between the two fields is the centrality of the body. In Kabbalah, it is reminiscent of the semiotic concept of memory and the sense of skin and envelopment, and in psychoanalysis it comes up often in the discussion of psychosomatic phenomena.[4] In the world of Kabbalah, the body constitutes an instrument of *tikkun* ("repair," "restoration") and the point of connection between the human and the Divine, which is similar to the world of therapy, in which the body constitutes a key to the psyche and its secrets.

---

1 Freud, "Beyond the Pleasure Principle."
2 Liebes, *Sefer Yetzira*; Freud and Breuer, *Studies in Hysteria*.
3 Bergstein, "Emotional Truth."
4 Bick, "The Experience of the Skin"; Anzieu, *The Skin-Ego*; Pedaya, *Psychoanalysis and Kabbala*.

Sigmund Freud brought about a revolution by pointing out the influence of childhood and "the beginning of life" on the adult person. Later on, his followers at the British school of object relations sought to focus on the stage before the Oedipal drama.[5] Theorists such as Wilfred Bion, Alessandra Piontelli, and Suzanne Maiello later explored the infant psyche and dealt with the experience of the fetus in the womb and the prenatal state.[6] These ideas echo Kabbalistic concepts of the divine origin of the soul, the stages of its descent into the world, and the shape of the soul and its parts. These connections deepen in Lurianic Kabbalah, which describes the structure of divinity in light of the secrets of impregnation and reincarnation. A full development of the theory of the soul appears in Hasidism, which suggests a transformational process in which Kabbalistic language is applied to a psychological rubric that focuses on the human being and the improvement of his character.

In medieval Kabbalah, the connection between the human and the divine is woven around the concepts of birth and creation as a foundation on which the first pattern of relationships is formed. The *Zohar* often refers to God as *Adam* ("human"), and "body,"[7] and it portrays the divinity as having been born and having grown "in the image of Man." God is the mystic's central object of reference, just as the baby sees reality and himself through the eyes of his mother.[8] Despite Freud's resistance to the "oceanic feeling," which is mentioned in *Civilization and Its Discontents*,[9] there is a great deal of similarity between mystical concepts that focus on the connection between the finite and infinite, the human and the divine, and parallel concepts in psychoanalysis such as Bion's "becoming O," which reflects the experience of faith and an awareness of the infinite.[10]

The Kabbalistic corpus, like the psychoanalytic one, grapples with the meaning of existence while opposing the rigid explanations offered by Jewish and Christian institutionalized religion. These two subversive compilations are products of creative European thought that reflected novel conceptions of the "self," and imparted significance to relationships with the Other, both human and divine. Through its discussion of the Godhead and the conceptual structure of the *sefirot*, Kabbalah offered a new way of understanding the mysteries of the human

---

[5] See below for discussion of Kleinian and Winnicottian ideas as well as those of other theorists.
[6] Bion, *Two Papers*; Piontelli, *From Fetus to Child*; Maiello, "The Sound-Object."
[7] Liebes, "Sections of the Zohar Lexicon," *Adam*=§18, §22–25, §27–28, §53, and more; *Gufa*=§ 31–35, §150, §179, and more.
[8] Winnicott, *Playing and Reality*.
[9] Freud, *Civilization and Its Discontents*, 64.
[10] Bion, *Attention and Interpretation*; idem, *Clinical Seminars & Other Works*.

soul, while psychoanalysis determined the subconscious to be the imperceptible driving force of human existence.

Despite these profound connections between the fields of Kabbalah and psychoanalysis, the founder of the research into Kabbalah, Gershom Scholem, wrote in his diary entry for 2 July 1918 that *"psychoanalysis is a dreadful thing. It's pointless to contradict theoretically because its results are correct, and then you'll have to look for a better foundation."*[11] Though Scholem avoided any overt application of Freudian theory or other psychological concepts in his study of Jewish mysticism, his writings on the figure of Sabbatai Zvi, for example, display the thoughtful use of psychological concepts and a deep understanding of borderline personalities.

The picture has changed considerably since his time. Scholars of Kabbalah and psychoanalytic theoreticians, respectively, have explored partial connections between Kabbalistic theology and psychoanalytic and gender theories. Until now, however, no attempt has been made to develop an overarching scholarly methodology and conceptual system to connect Kabbalistic doctrine with psychoanalytic and gender theory. The study of religion remains separate from that of the human psyche – a lacuna which this book aims humbly to fill.

The project of reading psychoanalysis in relation to Kabbalah is part of a scholarly turn, an attempt to reevaluate our present understanding of man. To be engaged in this project is to be convinced that the examination and comparison of the two fields is mutually enriching. It is my hope, shared with the scores of scholars who are wielding premodern texts in new ways in order to interrogate modern disciplines, that by placing them side by side and illuminating each field through consideration of the other, I will be able to elucidate the contribution of each discipline to the other. Thus, for example, Kabbalistic study helps us delve deeper into the psychoanalytic theory of the self and reveal its hidden spiritual side, while impenetrable mystical ideas are clarified through psychoanalysis and the experience derived from the therapeutic practice. Modern conceptions provide new interpretations of ancient works and enable us "to read ourselves" and even to unravel the original intentions of these texts. At the same time, Kabbalah makes possible the illumination of contemporary ideas, as well as the understanding of concepts such as birth and Eros, which are the fundamental axes of our existence.

In this book, I would like to give the reader a window into what we can gain by reading the contributions of these two fields together, indicating where concepts are complementary or similar and where they differ or at odds with one

---

[11] (Emphasis is mine). Scholem, *Tagebücher*, 264. See also Abrams, *Ten Psychoanalytic Aphorisms*, 2–4.

another. These comparative explorations will, I hope, demonstrate that, while there is no turning back from modernity, by ignoring the wisdom of the ancients we forfeit hard-won understandings of ourselves and the human condition.

Theorists such as Melanie Klein, Donald Winnicott, Wilfred Bion, Donald Meltzer, and others explored the infant's consciousness, and dealt with primal experiences and feelings of the fetus toward the mother. Emotions such as rage and aggression, destructive energies and incestuous yearning, were discoursed through the therapeutic prism of the analyst–patient bond, and their "transference" and "counter-transference" as a reflection of their mutual "birth" in this relationship.[12] The dyad of the relationship between mother and child – and between therapists and patients – can be viewed as echoing the relationship between God and human beings, as we learn from rich scholarly literature dedicated during the last decades to the comparison of Kabbalah and psychoanalysis.[13]

Both in Kabbalah and psychoanalysis, the "depth of the psyche" stands at the core of what their practitioners seek to explore. According to Freud, the parts of the self are built on a model of archeological layers: this is the division of the mind into superego, ego, and id in the elaborated "structural model" from 1920; in the earlier Freudian so-called "topographical model," the mind is divided into the conscious, unconscious, and subconscious. Similarly, in the Kabbalistic literature the Godhead is combined from *sefirot* – divine measures, instruments, and powers.

In both fields, unity does not contradict a state of multiplicity: the matrix of the *sefirot*, whether it represents God's own self or hypostases of the divinity – God's instruments and powers – testifies, even in its multiple character, to its unitary origin. The relationship between mother and child can be viewed similarly: in birth, a body emerges from another body, and from then on the baby's existence represents the idea that there are two beings that were once one. So it is with the child's own experience of self. It is precisely in the presence of the mother that the child develops a capacity to be alone.[14] The world of the *sefirot* is a world of "infinite relations," couplings, and complex interactions of dependency between each *sefirah* and its opposing quality. The individual, in the human world as in the

---

12 Aron, "With You I'm Born Again."
13 See, for example, Ostow, *Ultimate Intimacy*; Ankori, *And this Forest has no End*; Gamlieli, *Psychoanalysis and Kabbalah*; Eigen, *The Psychoanalytic Mystic*; idem, *Kabbalah and Psychoanalysis*; Aron, "Black Fire on White Fire"; Starr, *Repair of the Soul*; Garb, *Yearnings of the Soul*; Pedaya, *Psychoanalysis and Kabbala*; Kaniel, "The Impressive Caesura"; idem, "Birth – From Metaphor to Reality." Following Erikson, Lake, Fowler, and others, Helen Holmes has recently discussed uterine life as the foundation of faith and the formation of divine intimate representations. She claims that primal experience of trustability with the mother allows for the creation of feelings of hope and trust. Holmes, *Seeing God*.
14 Winnicott, *Maturational Processes*, 29–35.

divine, is perceived as "broken" and absent from the part that complements and completes it. Recognition of what is missing lends a paradoxical wholeness to each of the divine qualities.

2 An Example of the Discourse of Kabbalah and Psychoanalysis: The Layers of Creation and the Layers of the Soul

According to Freud, the parts of the psyche – superego, ego, and id – are built on a model of archeological layers piled horizontally, one on top of the other.[15] Similarly, the passages between the conscious and the unconscious represent *horizontal divisions*. In an optimal situation, a connection is maintained between the layers, while in times of illness the system loses its wholeness and experiences rupture and division between the various parts. In contrast to Freud, other psychoanalysts imagine a vertical division, such as Heinz Kohut's "vertical split," which expresses the relations between developed and regressive parts of the self and the split created in the wake of a narcissistic breakdown. Kohut questions Freud's assumptions regarding mental health, emphasizing the beneficial experiences of attachment to a "selfobject" that enable the experience of a "merger" with the idealized person. In this scenario sketched out by Kohut, the child's need for omnipotence, mirroring, healthy narcissism, the idealization of the parent, and the "grandiose" appearance finally receive their real place. When these parts remain unprocessed, a vertical "split of shame" is created, a break that divides the parts of the self.[16]

From a different perspective, Philip Bromberg suggests that the vertical split expresses "states of self" that are divided not because of a gap between the conscious and the unconscious, but rather because they are a reflection of a person's different appearances and roles.[17] Bromberg and Stephen Mitchell dispute the question of whether a constant and continuous core self exits, but they agree that the "multiplicity of the self" is a sign of mental health, so long as no dissociation arises and the person does not reject any of his parts as "not me."[18]

---

[15] On the image of the analyst as an archeologist, see, for example, Freud, "Gradiva"; idem, "Constructions in Analysis." See below Chapter 4, n. 59.
[16] Kohut, *The Analysis of the Self*; idem, *The Restoration of the Self*.
[17] Bromberg, "The Multiplicity of Self"; idem, *Standing in the Spaces*.
[18] Mitchell, *Hope and Dread*, 95–122. On the "multiple self" of the Godhead in the Zohar: Kaniel, "Matriarchs and Patriarchs as Sefirot."

Such examples of vertical and horizontal divisions can shed light on some basic ideas in Kabbalistic thought. The distinction between the paternal and masculine in the divine, identified with the power of mercy (*Hesed*) on the right, and the maternal, feminine aspect, identified with judgment (*Din*) on the left, represents a vertical division. The relationship between the upper *sefirot* and the lower *sefirot* represents a horizontal division as well as the hierarchical gradation, as hinted at in Freud's teachings. The "super-conscious" realms of the divine *sefirot* reflect the subterranean depths of the psyche and the repressed layers related to the id and the unconscious. In both instances, what is essential is concealed and placed out of sight.

The perception of evil in Kabbalah, too, reflects models of horizontal and vertical bifurcations. There, the forces of evil are called "the other side" (*Sitra Ahra*), which surrounds the *Shekhinah* and lies in wait for it and its armies, flows from the *sefirah* of *Gevurah* or *Binah*, and is even presented as a system of ritual uncleanness (*tum'a*) that parallels that of holiness (*kedusha*). The Kabbalist R. Moses de León calls the forces of evil "another cause," an epithet that illuminates the connection between the parts that a person adopts and internalizes and those that he rejects and from which he disassociates.[19] This epithet highlights the similarity between the conceptions of damage and repair (*tikkun*) in psychoanalysis and Kabbalah. While *tikkun* comes from the psychic ability to unite contradictory and opposing parts, damage comes from seeing them as divided and focusing on their disassociation. The individual is in infinite motion between integration and disintegration; in Melanie Klein's terms, this is the motion between the schizo-paranoid position and the depressive position.[20] Sometimes, it is possible to attain acceptance and integration between good and evil, and sometimes the struggle between the sides leads to a breach between the parts and psychic death.[21]

According to Joyce McDougall, every person seeks to connect and make contact between the different aspects of his self, and, as she says, "to bring forth its own Jekyll and Hyde, its own Faust and Mephistopheles, split-off but vital and necessary parts of every self." Only with the joining together of those parts can "love and hate [. . .] be reconciled, enabling the subject finally to sign the treaty of many years' silent warfare, which otherwise might lead to exhaustion and death."[22]

In the mystical world as well, one can find an awareness of the simultaneous desire to both create connections and combinations between different sides and to preserve the distinctiveness of those forces and positions, in order

---

19 See below, Chapter 1, n. 57.
20 Klein, *Envy and Gratitude*.
21 Eigen, *Madness*; idem, *Psychic Deadness*.
22 McDougall, *Theaters of the Mind*, 15.

to facilitate a productive tension between the parts of the divinity and the active elements of the human psyche. In the eyes of both Kabbalah and psychoanalytic theory, the fully formed person is one who can encompass this dialectic within himself and contain the movement between opposites, without subsuming the parts into each other or denying the differences between them.

3 Cultural and Emotional Entanglement

An additional nexus between Kabbalah and psychoanalysis has cultural, sociological, and historical causes and roots. As a youth, Freud absorbed Jewish ideas that would influence his attitude to sexuality and procreation as the founding father of psychoanalytic theory. The centrality to Jewish law of the commandment to "be fruitful and multiply," the ambivalent attitude of the Rabbis to the sexual drive, and the relationship between sublimation in the arts and the experience of the sublime in Jewish myth – he was aware of all of these elements. As many studies indicate, Freud's Jewishness and his relationship with his father crucially influenced the birth of psychoanalysis and the existence of "Jewish impressions" in key psychoanalytical theories. These researchers discuss the return of the Jewishness repressed in Freud's personal biography and in the annals of psychoanalysis. When psychoanalysis made its appearance in Vienna at the beginning of the twentieth century, it was met by opposition and presented as a "Jewish science," one that was anomalous and irrational.[23] Yosef Hayim Yerushalmi proposes that toward the end of his life Freud returned to his Biblical roots in an attempted reconciliation with his father and with his Jewish sources.[24] Through his theory of

---

23 In the book, *A Psychotherapy for the People*, Lewis Aron and Karen Starr examine Freud's repressed Jewish roots and the latter's liminal status as a Jew in Vienna, who, due to his circumcision, represented a castrated and "feminine" male as a peculiar physician who threatened the professionalism of his Aryan colleagues, and as an individual lacking a homeland, whose writings rejected any manifestation of explicit identity, since his Judaism was perceived as an expression of a savage, unenlightened culture. Lewis and, *Psychotherapy for the People*, esp. chs. 12–14 ("Freud's Anti-Semitic Surround" 228–253; and "Psychoanalysis' Jewish Identity," 254–271). They also argue that Freud's effort to impose the ego and the superego on the id was unconsciously intended to also repress the "Yid" (= Jew), while Freud's binary thought reflects the internalization of the anti-Semitic attitude toward Jews. Aron sets forth the history of psychoanalysis in light of the transition from its perception as a Jewish science that was born within controversy and trauma, to the current attempt to present it in a positive light.
24 Yerushalmi, *Freud's Moses*, esp. 1–35, notes on 113–124, 81–100. Yerushalmi places his *Freud's Moses* in relation to the entirety of Freud's cultural corpus. Incidental to his discussion, Yerushalmi asserts: "This book is not an attempt to prove that psychoanalysis is Jewish"

Moses' Egyptian origins and his conception of the totem and taboo enrooted in the murder of the primal father, Freud expresses his conflicted religious and national identity.²⁵

Leading Jewish thinkers such as Michael Eigen, Lewis Aron, Philip Bromberg, Jessica Benjamin, Irwin Hoffman, Ruth Stein, and other founders of the American intersubjective school play a prominent role in current psychoanalytical theories; most of these same thinkers highlight the influence of their origin on their therapeutic work. As with prominent British psychoanalysts such as Donald Meltzer, Michael Balint, and Melanie Klein, their Jewish origins suggest an additional focus for research that could well confirm the relations between psychoanalysis and Judaism.²⁶ In this manner, these writers' theories are broadened by their personal biographies – particularly the conflicts between their ideas and their identities and origins.

Finally, the penetration of gender theory is evident in its influence in both these realms. Current Kabbalah research offers new perspectives on the image of the *Shekhinah* and its identity as spouse, mother, and female subject, unlike previous approaches that dismissed it as an "absence" and "lack" in comparison with the fullness attributed to its partner, the divine male. Similarly, tensions between

---

(xvii), yet he also claims that "in principle, the possibility that Freud's Jewishness was somehow implicated in the formation of psychoanalysis should not be foreclosed" (116, n. 25). See also Gay, *Freud*; Bloom, "Freud and Beyond"; Santner, *Psychotheology*.

25 On the disagreement with Yerushalmi, see Feldman, "Rebecca Loved Jacob," esp. 22 n. 7. She maintains that the centrality of the "positive" Oedipal complex, namely, the one that focuses on son–father struggles (unlike the "negative," namely, desire for the mother and its threatening consequences for us), attests to the choice of the Greek homoerotic model. This contrasts with the Bible, which is concerned with models of fraternal conflicts and creates fluid and open gender identities which face divine authority. She proposes that Freud sought to fashion psychoanalysis as a mythology that intentionally distanced itself from his personal experience and the Jewish and Biblical world. For a discussion of additional studies, see Abrams, *Ten Psychoanalytic Aphorisms*.

26 Like Freud, who represented an educated and assimilated European stance (one that was in dialogue with and held an apologetic atitiude toward Christianity and secularization), for these figures, too, psychoanalysis was a sort of "new religion" from which a return to the sources of ancient Judaism was possible. This can be seen from Eigen, *Kabbalah and Psychoanalysis*; and Aron and Starr, *Psychotherapy for the People*, which begins by discussing the difference between Freud and his conflicted Judaism, and today's psychoanalytical Jewish pride in the United States. Stein, "Excess," quoted Talmudic passages in their original language and attested to her roots, while Bromberg, "Haunted House," describes in anecdotes Max's "Yiddish self," to which he could connect as a Jewish analyst, and the obsessive parents of the typical Jewish patient. Hoffman, "Death's Door," too, mentions the Bar Mitzvah of the patient's son as a seminal event in his presenting of the therapeutic case that he analyzes. The leading Jewish American psychoanalytic theoreticians also include Kohut, Stephen Mitchell, Jessica Benjamin, Otto Kernberg, Malcolm Slavin, and Jules Silberg.

psychoanalysis and gender are discussed in psychoanalytic thought and permeate feminist theories. Openness to the incorporation of the various therapeutic methods and the encounter between Freudian, Kleinian, Bionian, and Winnicottian notions, along with relativist and intersubjective approaches and the Kohutian and Lacanian schools, can be credited, *inter alia*, to the dialogue between psychoanalysis and other bodies of knowledge, such as the study of religions, literature, philosophy, and art.

Chapter 1
The Existentialism of Birth

> Action recuperated in advance in the light that should guide it – is perhaps the very definition of philosophy.[1]
> – Emmanuel Levinas

The discussion of birth poses special challenges in light of the long-standing philosophical traditions that focus on the meaning and centrality of death. From the philosophies of ancient Greece to twentieth-century existentialism, the progression toward death imparts meaning to our lives. Both religious and secular existentialism share an awareness of the end of life and of death's overshadowing importance. The only certain datum that every living creature experiences and knows is its own death, as if to say: "I am finite, therefore I exist." This chapter examines the tension between the centrality of death in western philosophy and Christian theology, on the one hand, and, on the other, the emphasis on birth and its spiritual significance in Judaism, as developed in ritual and ethics.

1 The Two Poles: Birth and Death

Birth, as the most meaningful human experience, is considered and processed throughout a person's lifetime. It is the beginning and end of what *was* before we arrived in the world, and it is the preparation for what will be after we depart it.

In the *Phaedo*, Plato's great master Socrates refuses his disciples' offer to help him escape from prison. For Socrates, death is a means for attaining the eternity of the soul. To achieve this, the body must be rejected and its cessation ignored, in order to concentrate on what continues to exist for all eternity: the soul, the deathless spirit. His approach further validates death, for "those who pursue philosophy aright study nothing but dying and being dead."[2]

In *the Nicomachean Ethics*, Plato's disciple Aristotle muses that we wish to invest our lives with meaning through death. Referring to the Athenian lawmaker Solon's advice to Croesus, King of Lydia, he observes that life can be appreciated only in light of the circumstances of death.[3]

---

[1] Levinas, "Trace," 347.
[2] Plato, *Phaedo*, 63e–64a, 222–223.
[3] Aristotle, *Nicomachean Ethics*, Book 1, Chapter 10 (1100a10). Unlike Plato, Aristotle seems to suggest that the soul, which expresses the life principle, ceases together with the body. Notwithstanding this, in his later works, the *Ethics* and *Metaphysics*, he sets forth the possibility

For Martin Heidegger, death marks "being-come-to-an-end," and the existential terror that is inherent in the face of death gives man the freedom that comes from knowing the truth.[4] Despite the differences between the fear of death depicted by Plato and the existentialist acknowledgment of death or the fear of it, we can discern the uninterrupted historical development that emphasizes the centrality of death in philosophical thought. Franz Rosenzweig, as well, begins his *Star of Redemption* with the dramatic proclamation that the substance of all philosophy can be summarized in the attempt to flee from the anxiety of death: "From death, it is from the fear of death that all cognition of the All begins."[5]

The individual will continue to live with the fear of death, Rosenzweig states, since "in his fear of death he should – stay," since "only that which is singular can die, and everything that is mortal is solitary."[6] While birth is an occurrence that requires two, in a dialogue between two bodies that are both intertwined and torn asunder from one another, with an intensity that has no equal, death is a single moment that touches what is beyond. Aspiring to die and realize the immortality of the soul, in the attempt to escape death, and in the constant awareness of the fear it instills, we must necessarily focus on death itself, that dark force ("fog"), "a pitiless something that cannot be excluded."[7]

Notwithstanding these assertions, it is noteworthy that Rosenzweig is fluent in the entire western tradition but swims against the current, that is, in the opposite chronological direction, going from death to life. The final lines of the *Star of Redemption* read: "That which is always near, the nearest; not the last then, but the first [. . .] But whither do the wings of the gate open? You do not know? INTO LIFE."[8] Rosenzweig's magnum opus searches for "a philosophy of faith," and seeks to understand the meaning of existence, in light of life. This is a pioneering attempt to propose a new philosophy, which draws our attention from the final and known pole to that of the beginning. Unlike "life" as an abstract and amorphous notion, however, *birth* is a concrete circumstance and moment, one that occurs within the body – the same body that, only individually, can die or live. The mythos of "birth" is an event that can be located on a

---

of the soul's existence even after death. According to Patrick Duncan, Aristotle does not regard birth as an end in itself, but as a principle that expresses the potential of future development. Duncan, "Immortality of the Soul."
4 On the concept of "being-towards-death" which is interwoven with "being-towards-birth," see Heidegger, *Being and Time*.
5 Rosenzweig, *The Star of Redemption*, 9.
6 Ibid., 10.
7 Ibid., 10.
8 Ibid., 447.

temporal and spatial axis, at an Archimedean point that begins in the human body, which aspires to eternal life, arrives from within the infinite, and moves toward the finite. Human birth confirms the existence of God and proves that every one of us was created in His image. Not only were we born in the divine likeness, we come into the world as creatures capable of imparting life. As Yair Lorberbaum articulates, the human who gives birth replicates the image and countenance of God (see Gen. 1:26).[9] The importance of the commandment to "be fruitful and multiply" and the centrality of procreation reflect the paradox of the image of God that is embodied in the human countenance, for the divine eternal is supported by none other than the finite and transient.

Birth is a miracle because of its fleeting and unpredictable nature. We all die in similar fashion and with absolute equality (Song of Songs 3:19), but our births are completely unexperienced. Consequently, everyone who is born must declare: "The world was created for my sake." From the moment of a person's birth, his specific world is created especially for him. As the Mishnah explains: "Therefore but a single man was created in the world [. . .] for man stamps many coins with the same seal and they are all alike; but the King of kings, the Holy One, blessed is He, has stamped every man with the seal of the first man, but none resembles the other. Therefore, everyone must say, 'The world was created for my sake.'"[10] The moment that life bursts forth is the expanse in which the person stands as "single" – unique – before God.

Despite this, the pole of death cannot easily be exchanged with that of birth. Poetry, literature, and philosophy teach that not only does death give meaning to life, but the totality of cardinal events that occur within life owes its import to death. Death gives meaning to longing, love, and desire; to the sense of missed opportunity; and to the preference of yearning over realization. It symbolizes the eternal, the unattainable. What then can the "existentialism of birth" offer the romantic consciousness, the force of which lies in the longings and lack with which it is so full, in the face of its partial and compromising reality?

Various schools in Jewish culture (like the eastern religions, which do this in a different manner) raise the revolutionary cry to centralize the present, to realize to the greatest degree possible what is, out of an understanding of the singular, one-time nature of each individual birth. Precisely because humans are born without their consent, each person must decipher the mystery of his

---

9 Lorberbaum, *In God's Image*, 224–251.
10 M. Sanhedrin 4: 5. Compare to BT Megilah 14a: "Neither is there any rock [*tzur*] like our God (I Samuel 2:1). there is no artist [*tzayyar*] like our God. Man fashions a form upon a wall, but is unable to endow it with breath and a soul . . . whereas the Holy One, fashions a form of a fetus inside the form of its mother, and endows it with breath and a soul".

birth. As the Mishnah states: "Without your consent you were born, without your consent you live, without your consent you will die, and without your consent you will in the future have to give an account and reckoning before the Supreme King of kings, the Holy One, blessed be He" (M. Avot 4:22). The Rabbis offer an alternative to lack and longing through an awareness of necessity. They openly proclaim the relinquishment required of a living person, and the consent to accept the fundamental partiality of reality. Humans did not choose to live, and in consequence our births and lives are perceived as unique.

These rabbinic traditions can be seen as a development of pre-Socratic conceptions and the doctrine of Pythagoras, who argued that "being," from the time that it exists, will never be able to return to "not being." Birth is depicted as the moment at which a person passes from the realm of the hidden and latent "not being" – in which everything is possible – to that of "being," with its restrictions and laws. Unlike, however, Parmenides, who postulated that "being" always was, with no possibility of alteration, the Rabbis maintain that "being" develops and continues to be born. The *Zohar* amplifies the notion of birth as continuous coming-into-being. In numerous expositions, birth reflects the parallel process of the descent of the individual soul to the world, and of the birth of the *Sefirot* and their descent from *Ein-Sof* (lit., "infinity," a positive appellation for the Godhead) to reality in a process known as *atzilut* ("emanation"). Aware of the paradoxical necessity of our being born, the *Zohar* conveys how the souls descend from the "treasury of souls" in the womb of *Binah* (the Great Mother and upper womb) to the mundane world in a process both tragic and stirring. This is so because on its way down the soul is clothed in the body and in the *kelipot* (husks symbolizing the power of evil), precautionary measures, and prohibitions – the vessels which are to nourish it in this world:

> So He hewed from His Throne all the souls destined to be placed within them, and He fashioned above a certain storehouse, where all the souls hewn from His Throne reside, and He called it Body of Souls. Why is it called Body of Souls? Rabbi Bo explained, "Because when all the souls depart this world, the blessed Holy One prepares for them the form of bodies – just as they were in this world – and places them in this storehouse."[11]

The Kabbalists underline that God issues a personal invitation to the soul to leave its supernal place and enter the body designated for it. This is a medieval amplification of the "treasury of souls" imagery, which is mentioned in compositions such as *Hazon Ezra, 2 Baruch,* and the Babylonian Talmud, all of which were additionally influenced by Platonic conceptions regarding *gilgul* ("reincarnation"), the eternity of the soul, and the doctrine of *anamnesis*.[12] In the description of the

---

[11] *Zohar Hadash*, 10b, Pritzker Edition, 10, 65–66.
[12] See below, Chapter 4, Section 6.

descent of the soul to the world, the Kabbalists express the anxieties bound up with birth, and correlate it with the process of expulsion and fall to a dark and threatening land, as stated in *Zohar Hadash* (46d–47a):

> Come and see: When they were created, they were garbed in a holy, supernal form of luminosity in the Upper Garden of Eden, and in another holy form in the Lower Garden of Eden [. . .] Two angels say to them, "The blessed Holy One said, 'Go you forth from your land, from your birthplace, from the house of your father, to a land that I will show you' (Genesis 12:1)." *From your land* – the Lower Garden of Eden. *From the house of your father* – the Upper Garden of Eden. *To a land that I will show you* – a dark, base land [*the human body!*]. They show him the entire Garden of Eden, and they show him palaces and houses, supernal chambers. Then they pluck him out of the Garden of Eden, traveling with him to hell, a pillar of cloud above his head accompanying him by day, a pillar of fire by night [. . .] They take him farther, showing him all the compartments of hell, and they proclaim, "All humanity shall enter here, even those who are exempt." [. . .] Come and see: Whoever performs good deeds (positive commandments), each and every commandment that he performed soars upward and stands before the blessed Holy One [. . .] But if you do not occupy yourself with Torah, and do not dedicate yourself and perform the Torah's commandments, the blessed Holy One will abandon you [. . .] After he was shown all this, and told all about it, one of the two angels – Good Impulse – says to him, "The blessed Holy One said to me that I should go with you, Evil Impulse and I. Swear to me that you will fulfill the entire Torah – to learn, to teach, to observe, and to perform." He swears to him. Afterward he says, *Go you forth, from your land, from your birthplace* (Genesis 12:1), to a lowly body, as I have instructed you. At the point that he emerges from his mother's womb, an angel seizes him by the neck – causing him to forget the Torah – and marks him on the mouth with his finger: "Do not forget the oath that you have sworn to me."[13]

Unlike other instances in which the *Zohar* talks about sexuality and the body in a positive and empowering manner, this exposition emerges from a dualistic stance that is contemptuous of and negates the material, with a bifurcation between body and soul. The call to embrace the eternal nature of the Torah and thereby improve the soul's fate relies upon harsh threats, such as the preview of Gehennom and meeting the "angel-slaughterer," who seizes the man by the neck and forces him to fulfill God's commandments. This exposition develops the idea of the soul's primal refusal to come down into the world (which appears in the portrayals of the fetus in BT Niddah and in the late midrashic text *Seder Yetzirat ha-Valad*, which is discussed below in Chapter 4) and the necessity of both forcing and enticing it to do so.

---

13 *Zohar Hadash* Ruth 46d–47a; Pritzker Edition, 11, 279–284. See Joel Hecker's comment regarding the differences in the manuscripts (279, n. 739). Compare the image of the nation as a fetus that is born from the waters of the Red Sea, which are compared to the amniotic fluid: *Zohar Hadash* Ruth 75a–b; Pritzker Edition 11, 29–33.

The *Zohar* draws a parallel between the soul's downward journey and God's command to Abram: "Now the Lord said to Abram, 'Go from your country and your kindred and your father's house to the land that I will show you'" (Gen. 12:1). This association emphasizes that, although the entry to the world is positive, it is also tragic, in connection with the loss of the unity that we experienced in our being in the realm of the *Ein-Sof*. Abram's psychological difficulty in tearing himself away from his parents' home and his land parallels the relinquishment of memories of the past and the symbiotic relationship identified with the period of nursing. This going forth requires death that enables birth, and, in Wilfred Bion's words, entails "catastrophic change."[14]

In order to enter the material world, the soul must surrender the garments of light and the Garden of Eden that enveloped it. This sacrifice illustrates the fall into the world and the concomitant difficulty in being born. Other accounts of birth show that the soul is accompanied on its descent to the world by *nefesh ha-hayah* ("the animalistic soul"), which contains the Evil Inclination, the possibility of sin, and free will. Thus, birth is a painful compromise with the hope of redemption, for the body, creativity, and realization belong only to a substantial "being." At birth, the human creature takes part in the process of divine emanation, and thereby theurgically links the most individual aspects of being with the most universal and cosmic. In the terminology of Mircea Eliade, every birth attests to the creation of the world and recreates the act of that creation, while exemplifying the principle of cyclicity and breathing life and renewal into all that comes into the world.[15] The relation between the supernal and physical worlds set forth in the mystical literature strengthens the resemblance between physical and divine birth, transforming each individual birth into a mythical one and the greatest possible revolutionary act, one to which no other experience can be compared.

We find in these sources a depiction opposed to the terror of death. This is reverse existentialism: from the intense birth experience comes the consciousness of death, which is dwarfed by birth. Death cannot exist without the significance of birth. Many expositions in the Rabbinic, Kabbalistic, and Hasidic literatures present death as a new beginning, a *hilula* (festive, holy wedding), or a second birth. These expositions develop the dictum in Mishnah Avot (4:16): "This world is like a vestibule before the World to Come: prepare yourself in the vestibule so that you may enter into the banquet hall." This Rabbinic

---

14 Bion, "Catastrophic Change." I'm grateful to Avner Bergstein for discussing this idea with me.
15 Eliade, *The Myth of the Eternal Return*.

teaching seemingly depreciates the value of life, and turns it into a dress rehearsal for the afterlife. At the same time, however, the Tannaim suggest viewing life as one long continuum that begins here and ends in the "World of Truth." The vestibule metaphor implies that the journey toward the banquet hall draws vitality from this world into the World to Come.

This notion is developed by the Hasidic masters, who picture death as a simple passage, from "one room to the next." We have, for example, the famous statement by R. Nahman before his death "that the death of the tzaddik is merely as *one who leaves one room for another*."[16] A similar tradition is ascribed to the Baal Shem Tov, who asserted on his deathbed: "I am not concerned about myself because I know clearly that when I leave through this door I immediately enter another door."[17] Similar declarations are attributed to R. Schneur Zalman of Liadi, the founder of Habad (Lubavitch) Hasidism.[18] All these statements demonstrate these masters' willingness to accept death, and allude to their continued love of life, which they take with them into the next world. In contrast with these surprising descriptions of death as a connecting bridge, birth is presented in many sources as an upheaval, a break, and a dramatic and fierce occurrence. In the Kabbalistic literature, the pain of birth is felt not only by the actual woman in this world, it also is experienced by the *Shekhinah* and by *Binah*, as archetypical *sefirot* that represent women giving birth, with the Godhead as a whole exposed to the dangers inherent in cosmic birth.

2 The Fear of Not Being Born and the Sin of Not Giving Birth

In contrast with the existential anxiety surrounding death, I maintain that the Jewish sources contain a more profound fear, that of not being born:

> Whoever speculates upon four things, it were better for him if he had not come into the world: what is above, what is below, what was before, what after. And whoever takes no thought for the honor of his Maker, it were better for him if he had not come into the world.[19]

The greatest threat for a living person is to hear that he would "not come into the world." The danger does not, therefore, lie in death, but in the absence of birth.

---

16 *Sihot ha-R"N*, 156.
17 Ben-Amos and Mintz, *In Praise of the Baal-Shem Tov*, 257. The Baal Shem Tov gave to his disciples a sign, saying that the two clocks in the house would stop at the moment of his death. *Shivhei Ha-Besht* (Rubinstein ed.), 211, 311.
18 In the Rebbe Rayatz's *Sefer ha-Sihot*, 338.
19 M. Hagigah 2:1.

Not being born is the punishment for whoever refuses to acknowledge the border that has been breached at the moment of his birth and thereby personally attacks and affronts his Maker. This boundary is meant to form a concealing wall that also envelops and shields; moreover, it is a "second skin," which separates the infinite from the finite (up above – down below, before–behind).[20] This frontier, in Bion's words, forms a container and maternal womb that allows thought and emotion within the bounds of reality.[21]

According to Bion, an infant is not initially capable of thinking by itself, since it lacks the "alpha function" that enables it to mentalize its sensory perceptions. It is overwhelmed by "beta-elements" – impressions, feelings, and experiences lacking mental meaning which, thanks to the mother's reverie, become meaningful. Bion uses the term "reverie" to describe the mother's willingness to take in the infant's fear of death. In her love, the mother transforms those elements, which lack meaning and representation, into alpha elements, which the infant becomes capable of using to create meaning. In this manner, the infant's pain and terror become bearable and open to the processes of thought and learning. By means of the mother's willingness to metabolize and return to the infant materials that signified nothing for him, the infant internalizes this function and later learns to think for itself, and to activate the metamorphosing alpha function.[22]

Bion maintains that thought processes are emotional and creative. Thought is created by contact with "O," a term representing the infinite and the unknown, yet creativity is not possible without the containment that imparts boundary and meaning to inner sensation. The above exposition by the Rabbis demarcates the boundaries of human existence, beyond which lies the chaos into which we are liable to collapse. The places from which we should avert our eyes are the walls of the container, without which thought would be impossible. These fringe experiences are the "skin" that protects us from the moment of birth to the end of our days.

The notion that it would be preferable for a person never to have come into the world is reflected in a disagreement between the Schools of Hillel and Shammai in the Babylonian Talmud, on whether or not it is better for a person to have been born:

> For two and a half years the School of Shammai and the School of Hillel disagreed. The former asserted: it would have been preferable had man not been created than to have been created. And the latter said: It is preferable for man to have been created than not to have been created. Finally, they took a vote and determined: It would have been preferable for

---

20 Bick, "The Experience of the Skin"; Anzieu, *The Skin-Ego*.
21 Bion, *Attention and Interpretation*.
22 Bion, *Learning from Experience*.

man not to have been created than to have been created. [However,] *now that he has been created, he should examine his [past] deeds* [i.e., and seek to correct them].²³

This disagreement is not mere philosophizing for the sake of argument. Underlying it is the understanding that death is not man's main source of anxiety. The Jewish mythos views the dread of not being created and the fear of not being born as stronger than the horror of death.²⁴ The resolution of the disagreement between the two schools appears to be an attempt to regulate this anxiety, since, after determining that it would have been preferable for a person not to have been born (an impossible possibility), the Rabbis give this question a completely new meaning: "Now that he has been created, he should examine his [past] deeds." In other words, this question is not a matter of choice or wrestling with the problem of whether it is preferable to have been born (which is not up to us to decide). Rather, this discussion attests to the depth of the terror of nonexistence – a fear which is the opposite of death.²⁵ The anxiety of not being born – that is, of not properly realizing one's true essence, and not actualizing the divine image imprinted on us – is what the Rabbinical directive to mend our ways expresses.

The fear of not living life to the fullest corresponds to psychoanalyst Donald Winnicott's notion of the false self. Concealing one's true self and replacing it with a defensive personality, in which "the individual then develops as an extension of the shell, rather than as the core, as an extension of the impinging environment,"²⁶ is a living death, a psychic deadness, in the terminology of Thomas Ogden, Frances Tustin, Michael Eigen, and others. The loneliness of the soul that does not live a true life but experiences emptiness and barrenness is the heavy price paid by the overly developed self that is not balanced with the true self. In line with this conception, Christopher Bollas describes the

---

23 BT Eruvin 13b (emphasis is mine).
24 In the Kabbalistic literature, we can find expressions of the fear "of not being born" in the ambivalent desire to return back to *Ein Sof* through being "swallowed up" by the upper parents, and particularly by the Upper Mother, *Bina*. Haviva Pedaya claims that the holy chaos and the wish to return to the Big Mother emphasized in the Gironan Kabbalah and Nahmanides circle, however, collapses in the Zohar and in the Castile Kabbalah tradition. While on the one hand this description hints to *Binah*'s destructive power to annihilate the divine *sefirot*, on the other hand it raises the theme of birth, death, and rebirth in an endless cyclical repetition. Pedaya, "The Great Mother."
25 Bion alludes to this in his thirteenth seminar (Bion, *Clinical Seminars*, 70), where he discusses the patient's claim and complaint that he had never asked to be born. See also Bion, *The Italian Seminars*, 2–8.
26 As Winnicott writes in his paper "Aggression in Relation to Emotional Development." Winnicott, *Through Paediatrics*, 212.

normotic illness, or normopathy, as a person functioning externally but internally allowing death to overcome life. The fear of death while alive does not result from anxiety regarding death; rather, it comes from an awareness of the difficulty in being born and in truly living one's life.

The perception of birth as separating not being from being is common to psychoanalytical thought and the Jewish mythos. Like birth by a woman, cosmic birth is also situated between not being and being, and between the wild and the civilized. In Kabbalistic terms, being represents the expanses of the *Shekhinah*, and is known as "the world of separation" (*olam ha-pirud*). From the moment that a person leaves the state of infinite potential for reality with its compromises, surrenders, and losses, he is bound to understand the reason for his existence. The longing to be infinite and to return to before-being (such as the Sages' statement that "it would have been preferable had man not been created than to have been created") confirms the existence of the abyss beneath at the moment of birth. The conclusion of the Talmudic discussion with the declaration "he should examine his deeds" demands an acknowledgment of partiality and finitude – but also explains that human existence contains the possibility of rectification and change. The acceptance of birth as a divinely ordained decree transforms it into deliverance, and clarifies the great danger and loss lying in wait for one as yet unborn who does not bring this potential to fruition.

Janine Chasseguet-Smirgel describes the desire "not to be born," and to symbolically remain forever in the maternal womb, in opposition to the reality principle and to partiality and differences (including those between the sexes, ages, and various stages of maturity). In contrast, in order to enable extrication from the archaic maternal matrix, the oedipal/genital stage includes recognition of the existence of the father as the "other" who teaches of boundaries.[27]

In the Kabbalistic world, God, too, channels Himself and is divided into different powers that are expressed in their specificity. *Din* (strict judgment) is just that, and not *Hesed* (divine mercy), while *Hesed* cannot be *Din*. *Hokhmah* (the wisdom of God) or *Binah* (the intelligence of God), and *Malkhut* (the kingdom of God) is not *Tiferet* (the beauty of God). Each of the ten *sefirot* represents one aspect of the whole divine being, and it is only the joining together of all these powers that creates the aspect of the *Ein-Sof* ("Infinite").[28] This split and separation, indeed, is one of the paradoxes of Kabbalistic thought. Although it is forbidden to separate even a single one of the divine attributes and view it as discrete in its specificity, the very presentation of the ten *sefirot* as different and

---

[27] Chasseguet-Smirgel, *Creativity and Perversion*.
[28] Scholem, *Major Trends*, 12, 208, who calls it the "Endless."

distinct from one another – and even their identification with the parts of the human body – attests to the differentiation present within the Godhead, which, in turn, leads to consent to and acceptance of such partiality. As the author of *Tikkunei ha-Zohar* writes at the beginning of his work, in a passage incorporated in the prayer book of many Jewish communities:

> Elijah began saying: Lord of the worlds You Who are One and not just a number You are the highest of the highest most hidden of the undisclosed no thought scheme grasps You at all. You are He Who pours forth Ten Tikkunim. We call them the Ten S'firot to lead through them Worlds hidden and undisclosed and Worlds manifest and known. In them are You hidden from the sons of men. You are He Who binds them, Who unites them. And since You are within them *whosoever sunders one from its mate of these Ten S'firot to him it is accounted as if he had sundered You*.[29]

The expositions in *Tikkunei ha-Zohar* are fragmentary and associative, but they all begin with the declaration that the *sefirot* need one another and maintain constant spousal relations (whether fruitful or destructive), one with the other. Man's actions, intentions, and prayers cast out the forces of evil and effect unification within the Godhead.

The concept of the "forces of evil" has its psychological counterpart in the paranoid-schizoid position and in splitting, aggressive, and destructive energies, as opposed to integrative and inclusive energy, in the spirit of Melanie Klein's "depressive position." In the former position, the infant tends to separate the mother's good elements from her bad ones (such as the good breast from the bad one), in order to defend himself from the aggressiveness of the elements that he perceives as threatening (in both the concrete world of objects and his internalized identifications). In the depressive position, the child is cognizant of the mother's unity as a whole object, and is capable of containing the duality of his attitude toward her. This position is "depressive," because the unification of the figure of the mother arouses depressive guilt feelings and anxiety, for he might have destroyed his mother in his attacks.[30]

Klein described the depressive position as central to the child's development, because his jealousy and destructive urges are accompanied by a feeling of concern for the other, love, and gratitude, along with the ambivalence of his experiences. The ability to bear contradictory feelings of love and hate attests to psychological maturity and an awareness of substantive relationships with the world, and not only introjective identification and splitting, destructiveness, and dependency mechanisms. With this said and done, the two positions engage in a

---

29 *Tikkunei ha-Zohar* 17a (Schachter-Shalomi ed. [emphasis is mine]).
30 Klein, "Envy and Gratitude."

dialectical, reciprocal relationship throughout a person's lifetime. Every time that a person succeeds in bearing a conflict and emotional complexity, without splitting the good from the bad, he reaches a developmental achievement that is, in essence, a desire to mend oneself. Likewise, the Kabbalists view every successful coupling of the *sefirot* (even if only partial and ephemeral) as a mystical-spiritual triumph, while divisiveness between them is caused by human sins.

A psychoanalytical split is comparable to the Kabbalistic notion of the forces of evil, the *Sitra Ahra* – the "other side." Like the Jungian shadow, the Kabbalists thought of evil as material that is cast out and away, that is hidden behind reality. R. Moses de León contributed to the discussion of the forces of evil the appellation of "another cause" for these powers.[31] Such terminology sheds light on the relation between the elements that a person draws close, and those that he casts off and away or splits off. This indicates the proximate psychoanalytical and Kabbalistic ideas of correction and spoilage. In both realms, correction ensues from the mental ability to draw together contradictory elements and contain denied regions; spoilage results from a segmented view of these elements and their splitting. In both, unity does not contradict a state of multiplicity: the sefirotic system, whether it represents God's essence or His vessels and powers (hypostasis), attests, in its multiplicity, to its unified source.

The mother–child relationship is similar: in birth, one body comes forth from another, and from then on the infant's existence represents two that were one – the mother and her child. So, too, this occurs in the independent existence of the child, who develops the capacity to be alone, specifically in the presence of the mother.[32] The sefirotic world is one of infinite relationships, couplings, and ramified dependency relationships between each *sefirah* and its opposing quality. The individual, in either the human or divine worlds, is understood to be "broken" and lacking the part that will make him whole. In this context, the Kleinian model clarifies the role of the mature person as one who contains within himself, in Kabbalistic terms, the divine dialectic by movement between opposites without immersing the elements within one another or negating the differences between them. The mystical attempt to separate one *sefirah* from another is called "cutting the shoots" by the Kabbalists. In the

---

[31] De León, *Sefer Mishkan ha-Edut* (Bar-Asher ed., 134).
[32] Winnicott, *Maturational Processes*, 29–35. A solely binary dyad like that between a mother and her child hardly occurs within the sefirotic system. This is a system of excess and constant coupling. Despite the "parental relationship" between *Hokhmah* and *Binah* and the seven lower *sefirot*, there are examples of role reversal, incestuous structures, and the reverse nurturing of the upper *sefirot* by the lower ones.

Kabbalistic world, no *sefirah* exists by itself, just as, according to Winnicott, "there is no such thing as a baby," only a relationship between the mother and her child. In an expansion of this metaphor, the *sefirot* cleaving to one another keeps them in an infant state of "primary maternal preoccupation."[33] This is the situation of the first months of existence, and borders on the psychotic characteristics that ensue from the mother's total dedication to caring for her baby. We can similarly state that the *sefirot* being connected to each other and to the *sefirah* of *Binah*, from whose womb they emanate, resembles an infant in a dyadic relationship with his mother, while at the same time they are in a "maternal" stance vis-à-vis our world.

Psychoanalysis, as do the Rabbinic sources, gives pride of place to the anxiety of not being. The deepest fears explored by Sigmund Freud, Melanie Klein, and their students were the key to understanding psychosis and depression: the fear of breakdown and annihilation; nameless dread; the appearance of the phantom – all originate in the desire for life, not from the terror of death.[34] The forces of destruction and splitting belong to life, and not to death. These energies are driven from the womb, from the primal, earliest source of life. Even the longing to be drawn into the before-being and to return to the womb can be understood as the anxiety of not being. This is not necessarily a death wish, as Freud understood it, but the wish to live and the desire to be reborn.

The individual's leaving of the womb is akin to the archetype of the birth of the cosmos and the cyclicity of the life and death of the universe. Thus, Carl Jung and his followers explain the desire to return to, and be absorbed within, the womb of the Great Mother and return to the uroboric state as a call to be reborn. Jung, as did other psychoanalysts, linked death with mythical conceptions of beginnings, and described the karmic act of being born as a task meant to provide the answers that had evaded the soul in its previous incarnations. These answers correspond to the Kabbalistic spiritual "rectification" of the soul. At the transitional point between being and not being, between birth and non-birth, or between one incarnation and another, lies full human potential – which is hard to abandon. Consequently, the desire to return to the womb can be viewed not only as a death wish but as a stubborn quest for life.

---

33 See below, Chapter 2, n. 43–48. On "primary maternal preoccupation" see Winnicott, *Through Paediatrics*, 299–306.

34 For the purposes of this discussion, I will define the "death drive" – that, according to Melanie Klein, includes actively destructive aspects, anxieties, persecution, and self-annihilation – as the struggle for life within life. This experience does not resemble the existential fear of death.

Rabbinic midrashim are pronouncedly aware of the uniqueness of birth and the fear of this mysterious experience that flirts with death. Numerous expositions portray birth as a destabilizing event of overwhelming powerlessness, with consequent emphasis on God's miraculous intervention. Thus, the Rabbis often identify the womb with the grave, or, as in *Leviticus Rabbah* (12:2–3), they compare the womb to a prison, a boiling pot or heated bowels, and an inside-out purse. This splitting is meant to give man the illusion of control. Everything dangerous and negative is projected onto the mother; the exegetes thereby cleanse the newborn (and themselves) of the threatening aspect of being born.

At times, Kabbalistic expositions, based on Rabbinic midrashim, portray the feminine as the "other" and as dark, as the source of danger, destruction, and harsh judgments. Notwithstanding this portrayal, the Kabbalists also find blessing in the forces of strict judgment, which derive from the *sefirot* of *Binah* and *Shekhinah* (= *Malkhut*), since only a receptacle with boundaries and forcefulness can produce offspring. Also in the cosmic stratum, which Lurianic Kabbalah expands upon, space for the creation of the world and the birth of the cosmos was created only after God contracted Himself and vacated an expanse within the realm of the infinite.

The Rabbis are vociferous in their opposition to acts that run counter to birth, such as abortion or masturbation. Some compare anyone who does not fulfill the commandment to "be fruitful and multiply" to one who sheds blood – that is, he is a murderer – while Ben Azzai asserts that such a person "diminishes the image [of God]" (BT Yevamot 63b). Ben Azzai, who could not meet the high standard that he himself had set because of his love for Torah study, claims nevertheless that those who act this way cause direct harm to the divine image.

The obligation to procreate is presented in numerous exegeses as a cardinal tenet of the Torah. In this vein, the *Zohar*, in *Saba de-Mishpatim*, the unique poetic unit located in *Zohar Mishpatim* (*Zohar* 2:94b–114a), perceives non-procreation as the most severe sin, for which a person is punished by having to be reincarnated. According to the *Zohar*, those who refuse to be fruitful and actualize their potential are punished with a return to perpetual infancy beneath the wings of the *sefirah* of *Binah*, the *sefirah* of the Supernal Mother. In this punishment, the woman who was his wife now becomes his mother. In the symbolic stratum, the individual who refused to give life is thrust into a fantasy world with the illusion of eternal infant wholeness: life with no plight or predicament, but also no mending.

R. Moses de León expresses himself similarly in his Hebrew writings:

> When a person dies and has no posterity to carry on his name, that soul shall surely be cut off, and its pain and iniquity grow within it, and it is thrust away from God and shall

not enter into the fate of the righteous. Even during daytime its sun shall set, and it has no part in the sacred degrees or in the secret of Him who is awesome in praises. It sits outside and its image is cut off irrevocably from the images inside which all images are contained.[35]

In León's harsh language, such a person damages not only the earthly world below but also detracts from the "divine world," since his image is cut off "from the images inside which all images are contained" – in other words, the *Shekhina*, which includes all the faces of humanity. The link between the worlds depends on the person who has posterity, according to León's statements that are also quoted in *Sefer ha-Rimmon*: "Therefore, the person who reveres his Master must be whole in this world so that his image will not be cut off from that world."[36]

Only a few Kabbalists see birth as merely an idea and metaphor, as did R. Abraham Abulafia, who viewed the "son" as imagery for the intellect, and "birth" as a metaphorical going forth from potential to actualization. Abulafia's notion came from his ambivalent attitude to physicality and sexuality. Unlike him, the *Zohar* and most of the Kabbalists from the thirteenth and fourteenth centuries insisted that birth is an actual occurrence, one that influences and rectifies the supernal worlds. The body, sexuality, and procreation are a focal point in theurgic, theosophical Kabbalah: the Godhead has both a male and female countenance in order to propagate; sperm is an expression of the divine abundance that descends from above; the divine dynamism is reflected in what happens in the physical world; and human offspring are a condition for the constituting of *shiur komah* (the "measure of the body") of the *Shekhinah* and the establishment of the supernal coupling.

The notion that man's actions have the ability to influence the celestial realms gained additional force in sixteenth-century Kabbalah, in which procreation was perceived as the main purpose of the upper and lower worlds.[37]

R. Moses Cordovero highlights the importance of earthly coupling as a condition for coupling and fertility in the divine realms:

> Every situation that exists between male and female refers entirely to the secret of the supernal coupling and its rectifications [. . .] because proper coupling according to the Torah's commandment, done with good intentions, will arouse coupling in the supernal attributes, and the matter of coupling in these attributes can justifiably be compared to our own coupling.[38]

---

35 "R. Moses de León's Questions and Answers from Unpublished Manuscripts," in Tishby, *Hekrai Kabbalah*, 40–63, here 58.
36 Wolfson, *Pomegranate*, 241–244.
37 Idel, *Kabbalah*.
38 R. Moses Cordovero, *Sefer Shiur Koma*, 33, 4.

This principle works multidirectionally in several systems of the divine and in conjunction with the human world. Just as the earthly union between male and female arouses the *sefirot* of the divine couple, *Tiferet* and *Malkhut*, so the coupling of *Tiferet* and *Malkhut* depends upon and is influenced by the uniqueness of the supernal parents, the *sefirot* of *Hokhma* and *Binah*. As Cordovero wrote: "Since this matter is such, we learned an important rule about the union of Abba and Ima (Father and Mother), which must be the union of Tiferet and Malkhut."[39] His follower, Rabbi Isaac Luria, asserts that, similarly, the supernal couple, *Hokhma* and *Binah*, which are called Abba and Ima, give *mohin* (a mystical attribute of supernal life) to the lower couple of the Zeir Anpin and Nukva (the *sefirot* of *Tiferet* and *Malkhut*) so that they will bring forth the souls of earthly human beings.

Safedian Kabbalah depicts procreation not as a one-time event but as an ongoing process that builds different aspects of the soul, the newborn, and the Godhead in each instance of this recurring theme. Thus, for example, for R. Isaac Luria the terms *ibbur* ("impregnation"), *yenikah* ("nursing"), and *mohin* ("intelligence") describe different ways in which each of the *sefirot* is born from another. According to R. Moses Cordovero, even during the pregnancy, when the fetus presumably already exists, there are aspects of its rebirth, along with its growth: "And see, just like the matter of union between husband and wife has two aspects, one being rebirth and the other to grow the shoots – in other words, so that the infant will emerge."[40]

The Lurianic conception ascribes great power to the act of giving birth. This force is related to, among other things, reincarnation, and is interpreted as the raising of the sparks, advancing the Redemption, and rescuing captive souls from the *Sitra Ahra*; *Kiddush Hashem* (the sanctification of God's name, specifically martyrdom); and Torah study.

The commandment to "be fruitful and multiply" is an organizing principle of the upper world, as it is of the lower, although the Kabbalists maintain that coupling is of value in its own right, and not only for the purpose of producing offspring. Moshe Idel writes: "The two forms of fertility, the human and the divine, are potent not only in their specific realms but also, according to most theosophical Kabbalists, in the way in which they resonate with each other."[41] Kabbalist doctrine infuses fertility with both concrete and symbolic meaning. The processes of being born and giving birth occur in all the worlds, and different patterns of Eros are in effect in the relationships between the human and

---

39 R. Moses Cordovero, *Pardes Rimonim*, Gate 8, Chapter. 17, 39b.
40 Ibid., Gate 8, Chapter 17, 38a. For an explanation of these terms, see below, Chapter 7.
41 Idel, *Kabbalah and Eros*, 245.

the divine. At times, the spotlight is turned to actions in the lower world and their influence on the upper realms: thus, the relationship between the *tzaddik* in this world and the *Shekhinah* arouse the Godhead; moreover, the woman's intent while coupling draws down the abundance from the supernal *sefirot* to reality. This is accompanied by a process of arousal that goes from up above to down below in God's love for His creatures or in the divine Eros resting upon sacred places or at special times (such as the Temple, the Sabbath, prayer, and others). Striking in this context are the many terms developed by the Kabbalists to describe the mutual process of fruitfulness in heaven and on earth.

Thus, for example, the "bestowal of overflow," the "ascension of female and male waters," "sawing" (*nesirah*), "union face to face,"[42] "impregnation" (*ibbur*), "suckling" (*yenikah*), "the spreading of the intelligence" (*hitpashtut ha-mohin*), and "the establishment of the faces" (*hatkanat ha-partzufim*) – these terms express the relationship between sexuality and fertility in both the supernal and earthly worlds, and bring into sharp focus the idea that birth gives man power and partnership with the Godhead. Inasmuch as we have been born, that is, bringing the potential to realization, we are obligated to create.

If this is so, then birth is not merely an optional act, but rather a unique and choice commandment that is considered comparable to the 613 commandments and equivalent to them. Perhaps for this reason, it is the first of all the commandments given to humanity, as it is written: "And you, be fruitful and multiply and fill the earth and subdue it" (Gen. 1:28). Instead of the commandment to regard the Hebrew month of Nisan, in which the Israelites were freed from bondage in Egypt, as the first month of the year (Exod. 12:2), the commandment to raise up posterity is considered the first law of Scripture.

An excerpt of a Kabbalistic midrash entitled "The Order of the Garden of Eden," which contains many parallels to the *Zohar*, reads as follows:

> It is at midnight that God comes with the righteous to listen to the voice of the turn of the firmament, and the pillar sings and the soil of the garden is elevating, and the righteous are ascending from their mansions toward their Creator, and the entire garden is filled by His glory. At that time, the male and female spirits are copulating, as it was before they had been created. And out of this pleasantness of their desire to see the pleasantness of God, all produce fruit, and from their fruit the spirits of the converts [to Judaism] emerge.[43]

This image is provided to parallel the motif of God's enjoying the company of the righteous at night, which is widespread in the *Zohar*. But here, the midrash

---

42 *Panim be-panim*, as opposed to the conception "back to back" (*ahor be-ahor*).
43 *Seder Gan Eden* (Sachs-Shmueli ed., 273).

describes a unique occurrence that takes place in the divine world at midnight. That is the time when God studies with the righteous on high, and when the souls that have not yet been born on earth engage in being fruitful and multiplying, as they did in this world before their deaths. The fruit of those unions become the spirits of converts, in light of the view that the souls of Israel were created in advance, while the converts require "new souls." This excerpt emphasizes that the spirits' desire to see the pleasantness of God is not exhausted only in study or in coupling, but wishes to bear fruit that serve the existence of the souls of the converts in the lower world. This is how the link between the dead and the living and between the divine and the human is created – through the infant, which connects heaven to earth.

3 The Trauma of Impregnation

Birth takes its central place in Kabbalah from the anxiety of not being born that is set forth in Rabbinic literature. If someone does not study Torah properly, the Rabbis threaten him with "death in life." We may say that, in a reversal of its function, his mother's placenta chokes him:

> If one learns with the intention of not practising *it were better for him had the after-birth [placenta] in which he lay been turned over his face* and he had not come out into the open air of the world [. . .] He who learns with the intention of practising will be privileged to receive the spirit of divine inspiration [*ruah ha-kodesh*].[44]

This portrait of a strangling placenta – which stands opposed to the nourishing and protecting placenta – attests to the Rabbis' disquietude regarding birth and the mysteries of the maternal body. This midrash has parallels that express the violent physical death of the fetus by the placenta, in which the individual waiting to come forth into the world will never do so. This contrast shows that the Torah can either give life to man or annihilate him. The conception of divine providence and reward and punishment is intermingled with the womb's functions. Metaphorically, the Rabbis pose a retroactive threat: these functions are dependent on how a person lives his life, and on the question of whether one's life is worthy of being called "life."

In many ways, birth is the source of all fears, even more than death, since people are most anxious about what is most precious to them. According to Melanie Klein, the formation of the self occurs during birth, along with the appearance of anxiety. Standing against the terror of not being embodied in the force opposed to birth (Freud's death drive) is the self-organization that chooses

---

[44] *Leviticus Rabbah* 35:7 (Margolioth ed., 450).

life and wrestles with the difficulty of living it. In her important article from 1957, Klein discusses jealousy and gratitude, and the connection between the life urge and the ability to love, on the one hand, and, on the other, the mechanism that splits between the good and bad breasts.[45] This linkage is a defensive measure against the fear of not being that begins at birth:

> The threat of annihilation by the death instinct within is, in my view – which differs from Freud's on this point – the primordial anxiety [. . .] (the) tendency of the ego to split itself and its objects occurs in part because the ego largely lacks cohesion at birth, and in part because it constitutes a defence against the primordial anxiety, and is therefore a means of preserving the ego.[46]

Otto Rank argued in *The Trauma of Birth* (1924) that the infant's anxiety at birth is the source and prototype of every later anxiety.[47] He maintains that birth reflects man's overcoming of the impending dangers before life begins, and expresses the idea that the infant is threatened even before coming into the world. In the stratum of mythos, Rank associated this with the oracular prophecy that Oedipus was destined to murder his father. He discusses this theme at length in his earlier work, *The Myth of the Birth of the Hero* (1914), which was influenced by Freud.[48] In this book, he examines the Oedipus story, along with depictions of the birth of Jesus, Moses, and other heroes. Rank asserts that each engaged in a struggle with his father. For the Oedipal drama, with which Freud was concerned, Rank adds this threat to the life within the womb. Overcoming the conditions opposing birth creates a primal conflict between the infant and his parents: with his mother, who brought him into the world and then abandoned him, and with his father, who threatens to castrate him.

In *The Trauma of Birth*, Rank sought to shift the spotlight from the Oedipal drama to an earlier stage: the initial bonding with the mother. This conception eventually led to a rift between Freud and his pupil. In contrast with his later positions, in an earlier article from 1910, Freud explained that:

> the act of birth itself is the danger from which he was saved by his mother's efforts. Birth is both the first of all dangers to life and the prototype of all the later ones that cause us to feel anxiety, and the experience of birth has probably left behind in us the expression of affect which we call anxiety.[49]

---

45 Klein, "Envy and Gratitude," 176–235.
46 Ibid., 190–191.
47 Rank, *The Trauma of the Birth*.
48 Rank, *The Myth of the Birth*.
49 Freud, "Special Type of Object," 173.

The understanding of birth as the basis for every anxiety is reminiscent of ideas voiced by the Rabbis and the Kabbalists. The words of the Mishnah – "without your consent you were born" and "it would have been preferable had man not been created than to have been created" – refer to the wish to be *truly* born and to truly be fulfilled. The Sages suggest that the infant engages in a struggle over his spiritual and physical birth even before the self is formed, just as God struggles to create a viable world. This notion is hinted at in the comparison between the divine giving birth and the palace established among garbage and sewers:

> When an earthly monarch builds a palace on a site of sewers, dunghills, and garbage, if one says, "This palace is built on a site of sewers, dunghills, and garbage," does he not discredit it? Thus, whoever comes to say that this world was created out of *tohu* and *bohu* and darkness, does he not indeed impair [God's glory]! R. Huna said in Bar Kappara's name: If the matter were not written, it would be impossible to say it, viz., "God created heaven and earth"; out of what? Out of "Now the earth was *tohu* and *bohu*".[50] (Gen. 1:2)

The Rabbinical declaration "If the matter were not written, it would be impossible to say it" reveals just how difficult it is to gaze upon the beginnings of all things, and how great the drama and chaos were in the cataclysm of cosmic birth. The Rabbis' identification with the divine pain of Creation is demonstrated in an additional exposition, namely, that of God's loss of worlds before creating one capable of existing: "R. Abbahu said: This proves that the Holy One, blessed be He, went on creating worlds and destroying them until He created this one and declared, 'This one pleases Me; those did not please Me.'"[51] The Rabbis locate the burning fear of not being in the memory of the Creator and His creatures. Like the birth of the individual human, so, too, the cosmos must fight to exist and be saved. The memory of the preceding destructions is imposed on the world as a threatening shadow, but also as the hope that this time the universe will succeed in existing and not collapse. This midrash implies that God weeps and remembers the worlds that were destroyed, with the imagery of the cosmic "miscarriages" that preceded the Creation. Following in this vein, the Kabbalistic literature elaborated on the mythos of the Edomite kings, who, in Lurianic Kabbalah, are the basis for the development of the *sefirot*.[52] The dead kings – mentioned in Gen. 36:31: "These are the kings who reigned in the land of Edom before any king reigned over the Israelites" – symbolize the forces that did not survive and that are like "stillborns" (*nefalim*, also

---

[50] *Genesis Rabbah* 1:5 (Albeck ed., 3). Compare to the idea, developed by Christina and Stanislav Grof, of birth as "spiritual emergency." See Grof and Grof, "Spiritual Emergency."
[51] *Genesis Rabbah* 9:1 (Albeck ed., 68).
[52] See, for example, *Sha'ar Mamarei Rashbi, Pekudei* 33a.

meaning titans) whose death was necessary to enable the Creation of the world.[53] The Kabbalistic doctrine of cosmic cycles (*torat ha-shemitot*) also identifies the cyclical reconstruction of the destruction that preceded the Creation of the world.[54] The message encapsuled in these expositions is that the memory of the creation of "nothing" is encompassed within the "something," and that the pre-birth trauma that resembles death underlies human existence.

The abyss of death and the abyss of birth are indeed intimate. Each exceeds the bounds of experiences that a person is capable, and desirous, of having. These are the two leaps greater than all, the retreats and advances of human life: entry to and departure from the world. Birth embodies the most succinct knowledge of death, but not only of future death, as many existentialist schools maintain, but also, and mainly, of the death that precedes life, that which humans know before and during birth. The Rabbis accordingly call the womb *kever* ("tomb" or "grave") to hint at the death that already was.[55] In this sense, death is bound up with birth, and *the life that is created is that after death*.

Thus, for example, the ten Edomite kings who died resonate in the psychological theme of the dead brother, a twin who died in the womb, or an infant never born – a ghost that has impacted an individual's memory and a humanizing trauma that even influences the following generations. The life that is not lived casts a shadow, and its presence is felt by all the family members and their offspring (even those who are aware of the loss only within their subconscious).[56] The deceased, even if only a fetus, functions as a sort of "unthought known," to use Bollas's terminology.[57] Moreover, the *Zohar* and R. Isaac Luria perceive the *sefirot* as "brothers" of the human world,[58] and therefore death that occurs in the

---

[53] Isaiah Tishby, Gershom Scholem, Yehuda Liebes, and others expanded on this theme. See recently Har-Shefi, *The Myth of the Edomite Kings*; Hellner-Eshed, *Seekers of the Face*.
[54] Pedaya, *Nahmanides*; idem, "The Great Mother." See also Berman, *Divine and Demonic*, 278–281.
[55] See below, Chapter 4.
[56] This issue is discussed by Prophecy Coles (who called such an appearance an "uninvited guest from the past"), Yolanda Gampel (who deals with Holocaust survivors), Patricia Poliedri, Galit Atlas, and others. See also Fraiberg, et al., "Ghosts in the Nursery." On the crossgenerational transmission of trauma, see Faimberg, *Generations*. For a discussion of cases where the living brother bears witness to the dead brother or twin, see Schwab, "Replacement Children." As Marianne Hirsch claims, this "postmemory–often obsessive and relentless–need not be absent or evacuated: it is as full and as empty, certainly as constructed, as memory itself." Hirsch, *Family Frames*, 22.
[57] Bollas, *The Shadow*.
[58] See below, Chapter 2, n. 35.

supernal world is embedded as a trauma affecting all humankind, on both the individual and cosmic levels, which humans process throughout time.

The Kabbalistic mythos contributes to psychoanalytic insights the idea that not only does trauma compel its presence, it also becomes an instrument for healing and repair. Accordingly, the death "before life" is seen as a vivifying *reshimu* ("remaining impression"), similar to the mythical kings who died, with this destruction thereby enabling the building of new life.

In a parallel track, Joanna Wilheim proposes that the prenatal trauma of impregnation that results from the very sperm–ovule encounter is imprinted within cellular memory. Along with the positive aspect of the creation of new life, the parental merging means a loss of identity and the immersion of the paternal and maternal elements within each other.[59] While developing Bion's conception of fetal memory, Wilhelm emphasizes that patients remember that their parents did not want them, or their mothers' attempts to abort them when still in the womb. These catastrophic recollections of nonsurvival and of an almost-destroyed world are not founded on a processed intellective consciousness; rather, they are present as a physiological-sensual imprinting, one that reawakens in adult life in the encounter with rejection, danger, or threat. Relying on the physiological datum that in many pregnancies (about 75 percent) the womb attempts to rid itself of this foreign body, Wilhelm suggests that the primal experience of annihilation is liable to be imprinted within all humans, and that the body remembers the struggle for survival that began with the coupling of the parents.

Not only man, but God, too, and even the world, "should examine their actions," lest they suffer from the anxiety of not being. We see this in the Biblical Flood narrative, which marks the world's return to chaos following the joining together of the upper and lower waters, which had been separated during Creation. The midrash relates that the two types of water were rent in suffering and pain: "The lower waters did not separate from the upper waters, except through crying, and it seems that they anticipate uniting and flooding the world again."[60] The water of the Flood echoes the primordial "formlessness and void" and the destructions whose recollection surfaces anew at every birth, while Noah's Ark represents the cosmic womb through which the world is saved. The Ark (*tei'vah*), as interpreted by the Baal Shem Tov, is also *the word* (another meaning of *tei'vah*), and is the illuminating saying that has the power to create life.

---

59 Wilheim, "The Trauma of Conception."
60 *Genesis Rabbah* 5:4 (Albeck ed., 34–35).

For Bion, a person's "embryonic intuition" is imprinted in primal, unprocessed experiences and in the "animalistic" remains of the time that the fetus "swims" like a fish during the months spent in the womb. The description of humans as aqueous creatures, birds, or fish recalls the mythical portraits of the "great sea monsters" (Gen. 1:21) that were among the wonders of the beginning of Creation.[61]

As I will expand upon in Chapter 3, Bion describes birth as a "caesura" and as a bridge between the unknown before life and the enigmatic nature of life coming into being. He asserts that the memory of life within the womb includes "thalamic fear" or "thalamic behavior," which spreads through the sinews and tissues – and which, at times, suddenly appears in the analyst's consulting room in the form of uncontrollable responses, blushing, involuntary instinctive sounds, or sudden paleness. Some of these behaviors indicate a primal, nonverbal fear that is like a shadow cast into an inexplicable future in the state preceding the self and its time. Tissues and bones, sinews, and the nervous system all store memories that belong to another world, one that antedates the creation of the "self." Bion compares these memories to a time beyond time, with the curtain rising on the future before the past, a future not seen from the past.[62] As he states in his caesura paper:

> The patient may express a fear of the future which has many of the characteristics of a past which one thinks he could not possibly remember; nor can he remember the future because it has not yet happened [. . .] ideas which cannot be more powerfully expressed because *they are buried in the future which has not happened, or buried in the past which is forgotten*, and which can hardly be said to belong to what we call "thought."[63]

---

[61] On the image of the fish in the water as a way of explaining the relationship between the baby and his surroundings in the womb: Balint, *Basic Fault*, 66–67: "An important example of this harmonious interpenetrating mixup is the fish in the sea . . . It is an idle question to ask whether the water in the gills or in the mouth is part of the sea or of the fish; exactly the same holds true about the foetus. Foetus, amniotic fluid, and placenta are such a complicated interpenetrating mixup . . . our relationship to the air surrounding us has exactly the same pattern. *We use the air – without paying the slightest attention to it.* In fact, the air must be there for us, and as long as it is there in sufficient supply and quality, we do not take any notice of it . . . The situation changes abruptly if the environment is altered – if, for instance, in the adult's case the supply of air is interfered with – then the seemingly uncathected environment assumes immense importance, that is, its latent true cathexis becomes apparent . . . in our relationship to the air there are no sharp boundaries. It is an idle question to enquire whether the air in our lungs, or in our bowels, is us or not us, or where the exact boundary between us and this air is."
[62] Bion, *A Memoir of the Future.* idem, *Two Papers*, 33–37. James Grotstein compares the mother to a "screen" on which the dream of the baby is projected. See in Amir, *On the Lyricism*, 21.
[63] Bion, *Two Papers*, 43.

Bion's "thalamic fear" accords with the divine pain over the worlds that were destroyed. Following Bion, Dvora Gamlieli argues that in the Lurianic understanding, in birth, as in the cosmic Creation, a rift emerges between object and subject. "The contraction of the light of *En-Sof* means the traumatic and cruel separation of the self – the individual entity – from infinite unified existence in which it had been. [. . .] [Contraction] means exposure to the fear of not being, the terror of the end, cessation."[64]

In a similar context, Winnicott distinguished between the "birth experience" of every person and the "birth trauma" borne by a part of humankind. Trauma is an unbearable situation, one which exceeds the bounds of the infant's tolerance. For a person suffering from birth trauma, every meeting with another or with reality constitutes a catastrophic threat arousing opposition. Such an individual lives with the feeling that there is no correlation between his efforts, his ability, or even his basic experience of breathing, and what happens to him in the external world. Physiological phenomena such as chronic headaches and shortness of breath can indicate the massive pressure applied to the infant's head or lungs during birth. These symptoms facilitate the reconstruction and processing of the trauma of birth, and the identification of the break in the time continuity experienced by the fetus. Between regular and traumatic birth, Winnicott adds an interim position, in which there is no trauma, but rather exaggerated responsiveness and distress that is liable to return and to be experienced in adulthood. Consequently, most births are a gate through which the infant cannot pass unscathed. These birth scars leave a deep imprint, and the labor of healing is complex: all that can be done is the amelioration of this dramatic experience through attentiveness, reconstruction, and holding.[65]

Winnicott maintains that the body of the fetus "remembers" its birth, while the emotional and physical imprints of the birth process are stored in the subconscious. A person cannot attest, in the simple meaning of the word, to his birth, but humans know – with an inner, constant knowledge – that it happened.[66] There is an impression of one's birth within everyone, and it acquires new meaning every day. Winnicott based this position on children's games that abruptly raise memories related to birth, and, together with Bion, was one of the first to speak of the importance of this event. Winnicott stressed that the infant desperately depended on breathing (air), and that it is the mother's task to hide this deep dependence from him, just as God has to conceal from man the infinite abyss lying in wait. Or as Dana Amir puts it, following Michael

---

[64] Gamlieli, *Psychoanalysis and Kabbalah*, 118, 184. On the concept of *tzimtzum*, see below Chapter 2, n. 45.
[65] Winnicott, "Birth Memories."
[66] Winnicott, *Human Nature*, 143–151.

Balint: "It is only when we are deprived of air that we realize how shockingly total our dependence upon it is."[67]

The analyst–patient relationship facilitates experiencing the traumatic birth event that occurred but was not experienced, thus somewhat remedying the stressful memory and its recollection from the remnants in the present. In the cosmic dimension, God's role resembles that of the mother and the analyst, in aiding humankind to process the trauma of Creation, and to contend with the memory of the cosmic cataclysm and recreation.

As in the cosmic Creation, so, too, in the individual birth there is a complete upheaval, from the world in the womb to that beyond it, as we learn from the exposition in BT Niddah 30b:

> What does an embryo resemble when it is in its mother's womb? A folded writing tablet [. . .] *its mouth is closed and its navel is open*. It eats what its mother eats and drinks what its mother drinks, but produces no excrement, lest it kill its mother. *Once it has come out into the world, what was closed is opened, and what was open is closed.*[68]

In addition to the exchange of the respiratory system and the heart that occurs upon birth, the Rabbis further argue that "what was closed is open" is the placenta, which was closed and protecting, but now is open and vulnerable. Likewise, the body of the fetus, which was protected and enveloped, is now exposed to the light, and is drawn out from the water. In contrast, what had been open and is now closed is the soul (that "sees from one end of the world to the other" and had learned the entire Torah [a point I will discuss in detail in the following chapters]), which now forgets that it is "closed," and it loses the spiritual qualities it possessed in the womb. Infinitude is closed and finiteness opens, which is the source of the suffering and loss that birth entails. An analogous upheaval occurred during the Creation of the universe, in the transition from the state of "unformed and void" to one in which "Let there be light" was uttered.

4 Mythical and Individual Birth

Along with the similarity between mythic birth and individual human birth, there are striking differences between them.[69] While the mythos effects harmonization between opposing symbols and ideas, the birth of the psyche and its existential consequences uncovers dichotomies and contradictions. The birth of

---

67 Amir, *On the Lyricism*, 3.
68 Emphasis is mine.
69 On the spiritual similarities, see, recently, Holmes, *Seeing God*.

the cosmos unites the contradictory and is glorious. No experience is foreign to it, and there is space for every horror and dread within it. Dialectical thought enriches the mythos, contributes to its formation, and fructifies it.[70] In contrast, describing individual birth from a gender and psychological perspective means a return to flesh and blood. Physical manifestations presume the existence of a female object, the mother who experiences her body being torn apart and who passes on this memory to future generations. Like the mother, the fetus, too, bears the birth in its memory as an actual physical event, within space and time. This is the moment that symbolizes the beginning of time and being, an experience that leaves scars: it is therefore not just a blessed event.

The terror of cosmic Creation is abstract and philosophical, while existential anxiety is concerned with the body and its pains, from the real danger of dying and the many women who die during childbirth, to the spiritual stratum in which, after this experience, the mother and the newborn do not remain as they were. The mother, especially after her first birth, is transformed from woman to "mother"; in every birth, she crosses a perilous liminal threshold, at the cusp of life and death.[71] During birth, the fetus, too, crosses worlds and becomes a person.

In its Kabbalistic and mythical sense, birth occurs within God's womb. The venue of this birth – of the universe, the earth and the heavens, and the light – is an eternal place that encompasses beginning and end. The tearing asunder it entails, the terror of the dark, is cosmic, and the memory that is engraved in its wake is abstract, what the Kabbalists call *reshimu*, like the divine light that spreads out and leaves an impression (*roshem*). This is the breakthrough that precedes physical, individual birth, and it continues in a parallel and concealed expanse, detached from human bodies. The breakthrough of the flesh and the opening of the chamber of *Binah* resonate in physical birth, but nonetheless are so different from the mother/flesh that is torn asunder in the delivery room.[72]

The mother represents the infinite just when she is most finite, during birth. This is the time when the body is unraveled, bleeding, and asunder. The infant's birth is symbolic of the mother's finitude, of the beginning of her decline.

Although archetypical birth bypasses the experience of the individual and reflects the boundless force of existence that does not distinguish between good and evil, the dangers that the birth of the world entailed are nevertheless made tangible by its moments of terror. The *Zohar* (2:34b–35a) illustrates these cosmic

---

69 On the spiritual similarities, see, recently, Holmes, *Seeing God*.
70 Neumann, *The Great Mother*.
71 Balaskas, *Active Birth*; Rich, *Of Woman Born*; Cohen-Shabot, "Labour Pain."
72 Atlas, *The Enigma of Desire*, Chapter 5.

perils by its use of the verbs *ziazea* ("tremble"), *parper* ("vibrate"), *rifref* ("undulate"), and *hilhel* ("quake"). These onomatopoeic verbs attest that it is not only light that leaves an impression, but its absence as well, and that the forces of evil are enrooted within the processes of Creation.[73] In any mythos, and certainly in that of the Creation, the memory of the light is also the recollection of the darkness. The mythical and cosmic birth entails transgression and disruption by breaching the cyclical order of time and space. This is evident in the striking similarity between the mythical and individual experiences, since birth exceeds the periodicity of time and violates the wholeness of the body, which is now rent, with the single, whole, and closed body becoming two. The Rabbis elected to identify the feminine with a liquid and sundered quality, since women are penetrated, become pregnant, and give birth – because, in the words of the midrash, their bodies are an "open door," they are capable of bringing new life into the world.[74]

The experience of individual birth corresponds to the experience of mythological birth because both entail a necessary return to the original trauma in order to gaze upon it, and to transgress the Rabbis' prohibition of reflection ("Whoever reflects upon four things, it were better for him had he not come into the world" [M. Hagigah 2:1]). Mythical and individual birth, each in its own way, invite gazing upon the forbidden expanses – "What is above? What is beneath? What was before? and What will be afterwards?" – as M. Hagigah 2:1 then details. Birth exceeds the self and brings the possibility of a new existence, the uncanny, and the unknown.[75] It invites change, due to the dialectical nature of the mythos and the singular biography of each individual. Man's desire to leave behind a memory, to be enrooted in the immortal, meets the genetic drive to propagate and the urge to overcome the boundaries of finitude.

Death occupies a central place in western philosophy, art, and literature, while birth, in many senses, becomes an event people wish to forget. In order to think about birth, a person must look back, against the flow of time, and go "back" to the place of "sewers [. . .] and garbage," in the imagery of the Rabbis, to those discarded, flawed, or "primitive" parts of human existence. Retracing one's footsteps requires meeting all the primal crises, losses, and distresses.[76] In order to

---

[73] Berman, *Divine and Demonic*, 23–24ff.
[74] BT Ketubot 9:1. Kelly, *Performing Virginity*. On the similarity of the woman's body – and especially the womb itself – to an architectural structure such as a house or building with gates, walls, rooms, *tzirim* (doors on hinges), entrances, etc., see Fonrobert, *Menstrual Purity*, 40–67. This metaphor prevails in Rabbinic sources and seems to hint at the wish to rule over and control the untamed female body. See also chapter 7.
[75] Chapter 4, n. 79.
[76] Eigen, *Feelings Matter*; idem, *The Sensitive Self*.

understand the meaning of the path we have trodden, we must acknowledge what is lacking.

The greater the proximity to birth, the deeper the necessary regression and return to the nascent dependent state of infancy. Thinking about birth requires foregoing control and power. It demands meeting the "Unthought known" and all the "dark matter" that precedes the individual's existence. Sacrificing control in order to encounter an experience so complex is a seemingly high price for an event that belongs to "the past." Accordingly, humans discard birth and forget its existence. Death is unavoidable for people, and demands – even against their will – preparation and anticipation. Birth, however, always "already was," and therefore can be left behind.

5 The Birth Drive

Psychoanalytic theory focuses on the beginning of life. It teaches that psychological feelings, symptoms, and inhibitions that come to light in adult life have their roots in primal traumas. Along with this, Freud devoted an extensive discussion to the "death drive" and its links to the libido and the life drive. In his famous essay, "Beyond the Pleasure Principle" (1920), Freud described the unseen activity of the masochistic mechanism and the desire for self-annihilation that brings a person to his death.[77] Humans want to turn the clock back, to return to the womb and be enveloped in it, while at the same time they want to move forward even as they struggle with the terror of death that lies at their doorstep. Religion (with its illusion and distortion) and culture and art (and the sublimative experience that they afford) are motivated by the attempt to forget the anxiety of our death and to protect us from the suffering that comes from an awareness of our end.[78] Freud maintains that the life and death drives are intertwined, and that it is hard to find them in their pure form: the death drive tends to hide within the fear of castration, separation, and traumatic experience. Freud suggested that if it were not for its fusion with eroticism, the death drive would evade human perception, because of its inherent muteness: "It was not easy, however, to demonstrate the activities of this supposed death instinct. The manifestations of Eros were conspicuous and noisy enough. It might be assumed that the death instinct operated silently within the organism towards its dissolution."[79]

---

[77] Freud, "Beyond the Pleasure Principle"; see also Edmundson, *The Death of Sigmund Freud*.
[78] Freud, *Civilization and Its Discontents*; idem, "Mourning and Melancholia"; idem, *Interpretation of Dreams*.
[79] Freud, *Civilization and Its Discontents*, 118.

Witnessing the destruction and murderousness that were revealed during World War I, Freud sought to understand man's desire to take life.[80] Faced by the actual war raging outside, he declared that destructiveness is an expression of hate and the death drive. He wrote:

> This aggressive instinct is the derivative and the main representative of the death instinct which we have found alongside of Eros and which shares world-dominion with it. And now, I think, the meaning of the evolution of civilization is no longer obscure to us. It must present the struggle between Eros and Death, between the instinct of life and the instinct of destruction, as it works itself out in the human species. This struggle is what all life essentially consists of, and the evolution of the civilization may therefore be simply described as the struggle for life of the human species.[81]

In the beginning of her career, Melanie Klein described the death drive in terms similar to Freud, while diverting attention to the infant's inner world. She interprets the sources of inner destructiveness, persecution complexes, and the fear of annihilation as expressions of the death drive.[82] Klein argues that terror and anxiety are powerfully at work in the infant's psyche from the moment of birth (and possibly even while still in the womb). Destructive emotions, such as jealousy, greed, and envy, result from the activity of the death drive and struggle against the life drive. These emotions are inborn in the infant, and do not ensue solely from its relations with his mother and his surroundings. Klein viewed birth, as well, as an initial expression of the death drive:

> The first external source of anxiety can be found in the experience of birth. This experience, which, according to Freud, provides the pattern for all later anxiety-situations, is bound to influence the infant's first relations with the external world. It would appear that the pain and discomfort he has suffered, as well as the loss of the intra-uterine state, are felt by him as an attack by hostile forces, i.e. as persecution.[83]

Notwithstanding this claim, she argues that the infant's (positive) libidinal attitude to his mother reinforces the life drive in his struggle against the death drive. Aggressive defenses and the paranoid-schizoid position are connected with the death drive, in contrast with the characteristic maturity of the depressive position, which wants to choose life.

Unlike Freud and Klein, Winnicott takes the discussion of the death drive in a new direction. He asserts that the term "death drive" itself is unsuitable for

---

[80] Freud, "Why War?".
[81] Freud, *Civilization and Its Discontents*, 122.
[82] Klein, "A Contribution to the Theory of Anxiety."
[83] Klein, "Some Theoretical Conclusions," 60–61.

describing infantile aggressiveness, since this is primitive, unprocessed energy that is not motivated by destructiveness or hatred, but rather fueled by the very flow of life. He writes:

> Death only becomes meaningful in the infant's living processes when hate has arrived, that is at a late date, far removed from the phenomena which we can use to build a theory of the roots of aggression. For me therefore it is not valuable to join the word death with the word instinct, and less still is it valuable to refer to hate and anger by use of the words death instinct. It is difficult to get at the roots of aggression, but we are not helped by the use of opposites such as life and death that do not mean anything at the stage of immaturity that is under consideration.[84]

Winnicott maintains that death becomes meaningful for the child only long after birth, upon the appearance of the subjective feeling of differentiation, and after the emergence of the emotion of hatred. According to him, aggression expresses the life-force, which is not necessarily destructive. Rather, its meaning depends on the infant's acceptance by his surroundings, and the mother's response to her baby. Winnicott's viewing the combined *love–strife drive* as the life-force[85] – which could be either positive or negative – is reminiscent of the Rabbis' attitude to the Evil Inclination, which midrash says is "very good," and their attitude to the Torah, which is the "elixir of life," but which is also liable to become "a deadly poison."[86]

Bion argues that the maternal inability to contain and encompass the infant's fear of death and return it to him in a processed form, one that is bearable by him, creates a dread more profound than that of death, which he calls a "nameless dread."[87] When the mother is unable to bear for him these shreds of anxiety, in his adult life he will fail in this task, with the development of a constant and pathological attempt to rid himself of his anxieties. In contrast, if the mother succeeds in transforming the infant's fear of death and in helping him to communicate his distress, projective identification facilitates the establishment of a container–contained relationship and "the beginning of thinking."

The desire to understand is motivated, according to Bion, out of curiosity, while, on the other hand, at times it represents the movement of the death drive, as clinging to the "certain," and the elimination of doubts and inner unease. These examples attest to the different models of the death drive that object

---

[84] Winnicott, *Maturational Processes*, 190.
[85] Winnicott, *Psycho-Analytic Explorations*, 245–246.
[86] *Genesis Rabbah* 9:7; BT Ta'anit 7a; BT Yoma 72b.
[87] Bion, *Second Thoughts*, 116: "The feeling (of the baby) that he is going to die has often been misunderstood."

relations theory presents, in addition to the Freudian "repetition compulsion." Indeed, Bion and Winnicott show the death drive in a different light than Freud. Following them, we can distinguish between the fear of dying and the forces of destructiveness, disintegration, anxiety, and aggressiveness, all of which express anti-life energy, but do not ensue from future "death." Rather, they derive from birth, and from the infant's experience of (endangered) life. I therefore suggest that the *anxiety of not being born*, not the anxiety of dying, is the deep, subterranean narrative of Jewish culture.

The categorical imperative that appears in Deut. 30:19 – "therefore choose life" – arouses intense anxiety, anxiety that does not come from the pole of death, but rather, and specifically, from the source of life. Human life is precious, not because people fear to die, but *because we were born*. Birth is responsible for humans' fear of discovering that they have not realized their full potential, have not lived in the image of God, and have not properly developed. Humans are especially afraid of the birth drive. People fear for their lives, since they were liable not to have existed at all.

Winnicott calls the fear of "not being" by many names, such as the "fear of breakdown" or "falling forever."[88] Since the infant is a tender infant, who does not yet possess a sense of self, his reference here is not to a philosophical-existential death anxiety, but to the opposite anxiety, the primal dread, the danger of not being, that is parallel to falling, crashing, or breaking down. This is the anxiety of a beginning that has not begun, that has no continuation. The fear of not being born and life anxiety, that is, worry about life, and the fear of not fully realizing oneself, are basic conceptions that develop in an original fashion, and in tandem, in the Kabbalistic world and in various psychoanalytic schools.[89] And I would argue that the Christian notion of resurrection and "rebirth" results from a concern about not being born. The virgin impregnation that was forced on Mary is a void that had to be filled. The lack of physicality, coupled with the declarations that Mary herself did not undergo actual birth and that Jesus was not born as a mortal, represents a basic deficiency that calls for redress.[90] The lacuna at the basis of the conception of motherhood and sexuality in western culture resonates in the yearning for resurrection. The absence of actual birth – for Jesus as infant and for Mary as mother – inevitably results in an anxiety that is more formidable than that of death. This absence seems to

---

[88] Winnicott, "Fear of Breakdown."
[89] See, for example, Ogden, *The Primitive Edge*; Eigen, *Psychic Deadness*.
[90] Mary was named "Theotokos" (Θεοτόκος), "the mother of God" at the Council of Ephesus (431 CE), but the Nestorians insisted on the independent human nature of Jesus, and thus called her "Christotokos" (Χριστοτόκος), "the mother of the Messiah." See Pelikan, *Mary through the Centuries*.

be the reason why early Jewish culture was occupied, at times in dialogue and at other times in dispute with Christianity, with the fundamental questions of whether humans "exist"; of who merits eternal life in the World to Come; and when a person is truly "born" – is it from his emergence from the womb, from the moment he is circumcised, from the time he is deemed responsible for his actions (the modern-day "Bar Mitzvah"), or from the moment he gets married?

6 Neglect of the Mother (and Birth) in Psychoanalytic Thought

The central standing that Freud gave the father is no less important a reason for the focus of early psychoanalysis on death and the latter's relative disregard for birth. He emphasized the Oedipal drama that awakens in the son–father relationship at the ages of three or four, while he relegated birth and the relation to the mother to a marginal place in his thought.[91] Melanie Klein went back to the initial relationship with the mother and the little baby's aggressiveness (even in the womb), and was followed by Winnicott, Bollas, Green, and others, who highlighted the importance of the initial object relationship. Nonetheless, birth by itself remained a paralyzing experience and one that was placed beyond the bounds of the psychoanalytical discourse. Bion was the first to explore the importance of birth. Later on, additional students such as Donald Meltzer, Alessandra Piontelli, Joanna Wilheim, Suzanne Maiello, and Rose Woo discussed womb experiences, and some also touched upon the pre-womb state, which their predecessors regarded as an incursion into the parapsychological sphere, which does not belong to the "scientific" field.

In an article singularly devoted to the perception of birth in psychoanalysis, Lewis Aron argued that it is not by chance that the area under discussion was cast off and pushed away, like the infant who is dropped at the beginning of his life. He insisted on remembering and reviving the birth discourse that was so alive in the early debates of Freud and Rank. Following Francisco Obaid, Aron claimed that

> the heated controversy within the "secret committee" surrounding Freud revolved around Rank's championing of the birth trauma as the paradigmatic key to understanding neurosis. For Freud and his followers, the emphasis on birth trauma detracted from the centrality of the Oedipus complex, repression, and castration as the nuclear core of neurosis.[92]

---

[91] For a critique of the Freudian attitude, see, for example, Sprengnether, "Enforcing Oedipus"; Moi, "Representation of Patriarchy."
[92] Aron, "'With You I'm Born Again,'" 343–346.

He suggested that "the controversy may have inhibited analysts from attending to clinical manifestations of birth imagery and symbolism, to fantasies of birth, rebirth, and related themes." Later on, those "related themes" appeared in a new light in the theories of Winnicott, Bion, and others, who shifted the focus from the Freudian Oedipus complex and castration to birth and pre-Oedipal object relations. Aron discusses four narratives of his own "metaphorical birth" as a psychoanalyst through his encounters with four different supervisors, and speaks of his patient's birth fantasies (and phantasies). Without judging any of the proposed methods, he oscillated between these varied perspectives while contemplating the essence of birth as mutual relations and its presence in the analytic dyad.

Using key psychoanalytic themes such as "holding environment," the mother's fantasies of and unconscious conflicts with the baby, the ability (and inability) to symbolize the primal scene, and "countertransference fantasies," Aron shared with us the complex relational grid and the profound attachments connecting analyst, patient, supervisor, and readers. Indeed, the new historiography of psychoanalysis enables us to "rescue" silenced and lost voices, and to give them added weight.

In addition to this conflict between Freud and Otto Rank, this allows us to explain that Freud avoids ever substantively discussing birth because birth and maternal symbols allegedly express "oceanic feeling."[93] The perception of birth as a distant or mystical experience, one which memory cannot reach, attests to the force of the elements acting to repress it. Being a human, an enlightened creature – that is, one who connects through speech – means to forget birth. Freud believed in "talking therapy," referring to the treatment method that he had developed.[94] Regression and a return to a "pre-verbal" state are quite limited in his thought. In most of his writings and his treatment techniques, he was careful not to drown in a world of mythical imagery and symbols, nor to be swept away into expanses without language.

The theories concerned with early developmental stages – prenatal life, the birth itself, and infancy – also markedly focus on the infant rather the mother. Moreover, through the history of psychoanalysis, the term "birth trauma" has indicated the trauma of the newborn, not that of the mother.[95] The discussion of the infant's needs and inner world, while disregarding the experience of the birthing mother, is extremely surprising. The creation of life is a tangible matter that

---

93 Although Freud himself was unconvinced of the veracity of an "oceanic feeling" ("Civilization and Its Discontents," 64), many of his followers developed the link between spiritual experiences and the primal mother–infant dyad (i.e., Bollas, Bion, Kohut, and Loewald).
94 Freud and Breuer, *Studies in Hysteria*, Chapter 1.
95 Ettinger, *Matrixial Borderspace*; idem, "(M)Other Re-spect"; idem, "Demeter-Persephone Complex."

involves two people: the mother and the newborn. Leaving the mother's womb, enveloped in blood and placenta, accompanied by screams and pain, is one of the most physical experiences that a human being undergoes. This is perhaps the most intimate and concealed moment of all, to which we return again and again in the hidden depths of our consciousness, and where the self is forged.

The behavior of an adult reveals his birth experience. When it comes to the birth experience, we cannot reconstruct whether he underwent a birth that was healthy or traumatic, or optimal or harmful, or whether it featured an initial bonding with a loving mother or a hostile attitude toward her – with all these attitudes and feelings having their beginnings while the infant was still in the womb. A person's movements all attest to his relationship with his mother as a subject, since, at the outset, they were two: the mother and her fetus. How, then, is it possible to ignore the fact that birth, as an event with unequivocal tangibility, occurs, first and foremost, in the maternal body and the feminine womb, from which every individual bursts forth into this world? Despite the mother's fashioning the fetus within herself, and her afterwards setting the stage for the birth drama within her body, the birth, as ritual, is seen as the initiation of the newborn alone, while the mother is afforded only partial recognition as an object that performs the task.

The tendency to disregard the mother as subject is evident throughout the entire development of psychoanalytical theory, even in the most sensitive approaches, which concentrate on the early stage of infancy.[96] In this context, we should also accentuate the complexity of Freud's approach to motherhood and female sexuality. He viewed the mother as the source of neuroses and the womb as the source of the dread and rejection that often prove stronger than the attraction to and desire for her.[97] His dread of the feminine and his relationship with his own mother are explored in the feminist literature. These studies highlight the role of Freud's "family romance" and its influence on the history of psychoanalysis.[98]

Obviously, the roots of this disregard for the mother are much deeper and earlier. In antiquity, the mother was a receptacle for the fetus, and, in consequence, making light of her life was accepted, from the Roman emperors to the commoners, whose lives took precedence over that of their mothers.[99] Greek philosophy established a clear hierarchy in which the most sublime form of giving birth was the paternal "birth" of ideas and thoughts, while women merely imitated the process of spiritual fertility, and gave birth to "base" bodies. The Christian narrative, which aggrandizes the figure of the mother and presents Mary as the object of veneration

---

[96] Palgi-Hacker, *Mother in Psychoanalysis*.
[97] See on the subject, Spiro, "The Civilization of Discontent."
[98] See note 88; Cixous, "Portrait of Dora."
[99] Carmeli, "Dead Mother."

and as representing the Holy Family, in effect distances her from any material aspect and keeps her from any maternal and sexual fulfillment. Mary is impregnated with a lack of volition on her part, the mythos lacks a flesh-and-blood dimension, and her actual motherhood is effaced. Her impregnation and pregnancy become symbols of abstinence and virginity without agency regarding her body.

The removal of the physical mother from literature and the various other branches of culture found its way into psychoanalytical readings that apparently give her a presence while actually continuing to ignore her existence.[100] Along with his important contribution to restoring birth and early childhood to the cultural discourse, Freud also cast the female aspects of birth in a demonic and harsh light. This direction gained added force in the thought of Melanie Klein and other analysts, who find the cause of the repressed aspects of dread connected with the female and maternal body. They make this connection in light of the abundance of the milk that arouses jealousy and envy, attacks on the internalized maternal body, and the dread and the contempt that the womb arouses, as well as the symbolization of life and death that are linked to the maternal figure. In recent decades, under the influence of intersubjective and feminist philosophies, the mother has increasingly been viewed as a subject. This change is supported by new conceptions of the analytic process, which is seen, *inter alia*, as an opportunity for rebirth and the restoration of the positive experience of maternal holding. These new conceptions posit a deep connection between the analyst and the patient as mirroring the mother–child relationship,[101] and note that this substitution of analyst-as-mother enables the psychoanalytical process to successfully repair basic faults.

---

100 An exception in this regard is Bracha Ettinger, who as part of a discussion of the maternal matrix focuses on the trauma of the mother, and describes the shock associated with the birth experience.
101 Already in 1933, Ferenczi described himself as a maternal figure for his patients. See Ferenczi, "Confusion of the Tongues."

Chapter 2
The Theology and Ethics of Birth

> Madwomen: the ones who are compelled to redo acts of birth every day.
> –Hélène Cixous[1]

In Chapter 1, we discussed the relation of birth to death, and used a mythic-psychoanalytic prism to examine an awareness within life of its end that results from the experiences of not being and trauma. As we have seen, death is part of the fabric of life and its concerns, and even appears in the prenatal regions, when the soul descends to the world at the time of impregnation, pregnancy, and physical birth, and also in the constant human anxiety surrounding the aspiration for full self-realization, for the image of God being attendant, and for spiritual birth.

The current chapter will focus on the Kabbalistic ideas of motherhood, as they reflect man's relationship with God. We will also explore the ethical and theological aspects of birth, along with the encounter between clinical language, on the one hand, and, on the other, Jewish thought and the mystical tradition.

1 Motherhood and God

The prism of birth clarifies similarities between the image of the mother and that of God. Just as God created the world, the mother creates life. As God makes man, the mother gives birth to an infant. In many senses, only birth is comparable to the act of Creation. This is implicit in the statement by Eve, the first mother (Gen. 4:1): "I have gotten a man with the help of the Lord." The verb used, *kaniti*, means "creating"; by saying this, Eve declares that it is within her exclusive purview to create life, like God. Ilana Pardes cites Umberto Cassuto, who writes that "the first woman, in her joy at giving birth to her first son, boasts of her generative power, which approximates in her estimation to the Divine creative power. The Lord formed the first man (2:7), and I have formed the second man [. . .] I stand together [i.e., equally] with Him in the rank of creators."[2]

Despite the common Scriptural and midrashic identification of God as father, the Rabbis state (BT Niddah 31a): "There are three partners in man: the

---

[1] Cixous, *Coming to Writing*, 6.
[2] Pardes, *Countertraditions*, 44, citing Cassuto, *Commentary*, 201.

Holy One, blessed be He, his father, and his mother." In the following chapters, we will examine the exegetical attempts to minimize the mother's place in the birth process out of concern for the father's standing and role; here, we will concentrate on mother–God relations, which take on added force in the Kabbalistic literature.

The Scriptural sources, especially Second Isaiah, prominently depict God as a pregnant and birthing female figure, while detailing the technique of the creation and redemption of the Israelite nation.[3] A frequent appellation for God in the Tannaitic literature is *(ha-])Makom* (lit., "[the] place"), a term which also euphemistically symbolizes the female genitalia (*makom, oto makom*: "that place").[4] The Rabbis clearly associate the two openings, the supernal and the physical, and this linkage reflects the mutuality of the fertility processes in heaven and on earth. The opening of heaven is the source of mercy and souls, while the opening of the womb is the source of the body of the newborn. There is similar usage of the term *makor* (lit., "source") in reference to God, which gained currency under the influence of Neoplatonic philosophy. *Makor* has varied meanings: it can refer to the energy and power within the root of the matter, a starting point from which one is detached and returns; or to a source of divine *shefa* (lit., "abundance" or "effulgence") that emanates to the worlds below; euphemistically, to the female genitalia; or, lastly, to a concrete place. The "source" is positioned at the foundation of existence, and from it all things devolve.

In the theological realm, God is the primary source and place, which symbolizes the primal mother and the opening through which humans enter the world. The psychological realm begins with the flesh-and-blood mother, however, as the source and place of all, the awareness of whom precedes the encounter with the divine. She is the "mother-goddess," to which man develops the basis of his longings and hopes. God and the mother are the objects of man's faith and dependence, since they are the figures to whom he lifts his eyes at the beginning of his life.

An additional appellation for God in Rabbinic language is *rahmana*, which illuminated the attributes of *rahamim* ("mercy," "compassion") and love as bound together in the womb. These appellations could be viewed as a metaphorical appropriation that turns birth into a male-divine function. Mary O'Brien suggests that this appropriation enables male culture to overcome its alienation from the means of reproduction and to restore the father's superiority, despite

---

[3] Gruber, "The Motherhood of God."
[4] Urbach, *The Sages*, 53–68. See below, Chapter 6, section 1; and M. Ta'anit 3:8; M. Eduyot 5:6; M. Avot 2:13.

the fact that it is *women* who actually perform the labor of giving birth.⁵ According to Phyllis Trible, on the other hand, the metaphorical relation between the womb (*rehem*) and compassion (*rahamim*) strengthens the positive bond between maternal actions and the moral and theological divine act.⁶

Individual birth is the model for the collective birth, both of the world and of the Israelite nation. As Ilana Pardes points out, the Book of Exodus compares the birth of the People of Israel to actual birth: it occurs within the waters of the Red Sea, which like amniotic fluid are rent into two, and the blood of the sacrifice that the Israelites were commanded to smear on the lintel corresponds to that of birth.⁷ Similarly, the journeys in the wilderness are depicted as part of the process of raising an infant, who is in a state of dependency and needs feeding, nursing, and holding. The anxieties of the young people reflect infantile deficiencies that are expressed in its attitude to God and Moses, as to the nourishing mother. This dependency is presented in the drama of Rephidim and Marah, where the Israelites grumble about eating the manna and the quail. The motherly imagery is conspicuous in Moses's complaint: "Moses said to the Lord [. . .] Did I conceive all this people? Did I bring them forth, that you should say to me, 'Carry them in your bosom, as a nurse carries the sucking child'" (Num. 11:11–12). Moses rejects his role as the birthing mother and bearer of the Israelite nation, and casts it back to the "mother-goddess." You conceived the people, Moses says to God, and You therefore should resolve its juvenile distresses.⁸

Scripture also uses the term *El Shaddai* (usually translated "Almighty God," but it also refers to *shad*, "breast") in reffering to God. This name, as various scholars have pointed out, evokes the fertility goddesses of the Ancient Near East, and suggests that not only did the Hebrew divinity, too, have feminine and maternal aspects, but that this sensual and nurturing presence also was at the very heart of the Holy of Holies.⁹ This appellation is also related to the conception of an inexhaustible divine effulgence. The perception of God as nursing mother is developed in the Rabbinic midrashim and the Kabbalistic literature, culminating in a portrait of the figures of *Binah* and the *Shekhinah* as nourishing the worlds beneath them.¹⁰ The transition from the depictions of God in the ancient literature to the presentation of the nursing feminine divinity at the

---

5 O'Brien, *Politics*. See also Scott, "Gender."
6 Trible, *God and the Rhetoric*, Chapter 2.
7 Pardes, *The Biography*, Chapter 1.
8 Trible, *God and the Rhetoric*, 68–69.
9 Biale, "God with Breasts." For other meanings of the name El-Shaddai, which has various interpretations in the Midrash, see BT Hagigah 12a.
10 See Chapter 1, note 23.

center of medieval Kabbalah enabled the fashioning of a new faith experience, one based on the female experience of nourishment and pleasure as an expression of the relationship between the mystic and his God.[11]

Fascinatingly, along with the dominance of these positive and intimate experiences regarding the female deity, the Kabbalistic literature viewed the mother, specifically, as the source of *dinim*, or harsh judgments, similar to God, who judges and restricts. Thus, for example, the word *tokfehah* has a dual meaning in Zoharic Aramaic as both the maternal bosom and the force of God's judgments.[12] The Kabbalists portray God's two breasts as representing opposing qualities: the right breast is associated with *Hesed*, while the left is related to *dinim*, remarkably analogous to the conception of the good and bad breasts in the thought of Melanie Klein.[13] The nursing function is connected to both the Godhead's aspects of female beneficence and the harsh countenance of the *sefirah* of *Binah* – the root of harsh judgments and the source of blood and birth. For Gershom Scholem, the Kabbalah embodies the return of the Gnostic mythos and thought that had its beginnings in antiquity.[14] Indeed, the medieval rise of the feminine element of the Godhead can be seen as "the return of the repressed" of the ancient matriarchal era.

Although Freud tended to depict God as a projective paternal figure, motherhood and divinity have additional points of similarity in the psychoanalytic literature. Psychoanalysts such as Donald Meltzer, Jean Laplanche, Christopher Bollas, and Julia Kristeva emphasize the maternal aspect of the therapeutic and religious experience.[15] An aesthetic process is aroused in the child in the presence of the mother, with the beginning of the discovery of sexuality and the fashioning of gender identity. The divine mother, like the human counterpart, has the ability to facilitate transformation and correction, and to create for the infant contexts of space, place, and time. Thought about the interconnected *sefirot* confirms the psychological claim that before the appearance of separateness the infant experienced himself as a "self in relations", and that the symbiosis with its mother constitutes the underpinning of its inner world.[16]

---

[11] Haskell, *Suckling*, 65–88; Pedaya, *Expanses*, 158–119.
[12] See *Zohar* 2:9a; 96a; 253a. Compare to Onkelos on Numbers 11:12 to the words "Carry them in your bosom" (*saehu be'heikeha*).
[13] Klein, "The Importance of Symbol Formation." See below Chapter 6, Section 5.
[14] Scholem, *Origins*; idem, *Major Trends*.
[15] For example, Kristeva, *Beginning*; Ostow, *Ultimate Intimacy*, 3–44.
[16] See Chodorow, "Gender." On mutual recognition between the mother and the baby, see Benjamin, *Bonds of Love*, 12–84; idem, "Intersubjectivity"; Stern, *The Interpersonal World*, describes the ability of the infant "to be with the other" as a highly developmental/formative achievement.

According to Jean Laplanche, the mother (like God) represents for us the enigmatic and mysterious "great other." In a seductive relationship with her, the subject develops and attempts to interpret the hidden code of her unity and sexuality. Nonetheless, the mother will always remain undecipherable – familiar, but also alien. In an analogous context, Georges Bataille depicts God as a riddle, one that does not know itself.[17] Ruth Stein expands on these approaches, and states:

> Laplanche suggesting that the enigmatic-seductive message coming from the other is, by definition, not given to reduction or to simple registration and denotation, it can only be projected and then reintrojected in a mystified or alienated way. Similar processes occur in the domains of primal seduction, paranoia, and religious revelation [. . .] from "aside" in seduction; from "behind" in persecution; and from "above" in religious revelation [. . .] Laplanche's view is far from an interactional, mutual conception of a mother-infant relationship [. . .] Rather, it talks of a psyche and body open and susceptible to being influenced, excited, and seduced into curiosity and desire, and it stresses how the deep asymmetry between mother and infant is necessary for helping to build the infant's psyche.[18]

For Donald Meltzer, the mother's beauty and mysteriousness arouse puzzlement and aesthetic conflict in a person, with the consequent frustration and awareness of one's inability to apprehend her, together with the desire to hold tightly onto her. This relationship already begins in the womb, when the fetus senses the mother's unity, greatness, and infinitude. It then becomes more powerful, specifically *in the presence of the mother*, not in her absence: "The conflict about *the present object* is prior in significance to the host of anxieties over the absent object."[19] Meltzer describes the miracle of this relationship as follows:

> No event of adult life is so calculated to arouse our awe of the beauty and our wonder at the intricate workings of what we call Nature (since we hesitate nowadays to cite first causes) as the events of procreation. No flower or bird of gorgeous plumage imposes upon us the mystery of the aesthetic experience like the sight of a young mother with her baby and the breast. We enter such a nursery as we would a cathedral or the great forests of the Pacific coast, noiselessly, bareheaded. Winnicott's stirring little radio talks of many years ago on The Ordinary Devoted Mother and her Baby could just as well have spoken of the "ordinary beautiful devoted mother and her ordinary beautiful baby." He was right to use that word "ordinary," with its overtones of regularity and custom, rather than the statistical "average." The aesthetic experience of the mother with her baby is ordinary, regular, customary, for it has millennia behind it, since man first saw the world "as" beautiful. And we know this goes back at least to the last glaciation.[20]

---

17 Laplanche, "Seduction"; Bataille, *Death and Sensuality*.
18 Stein, "Enigmatic Dimension," 602–603.
19 Meltzer and Williams, *Apprehension*, 29 (emphasis is mine).
20 Ibid., 16.

Meltzer's approach runs counter to Kleinian theory, since, according to him, the infant has a *complete, unified conception of the mother* from the outset, while the split comes about later. In this sense, Meltzer's thought resembles the Kabbalistic notion that *tzimtzum* and the breaking of the vessels came after the appearance of the primal divine light. Likewise, the aesthetic conflict echoes the inability to apprehend God, together with the thirst for *devekut* (cleaving to God) that is at the heart of the mystical literature. Meltzer does indeed link the relation to the mother with the religious experience.

In much the same spirit, Christopher Bollas describes the mother as a transformational object, who creates the foundations of emotion, thought, and being for the infant: "Because of the considerable prematurity of human birth, the infant depends on the mother for survival [. . .] she both sustains the baby's life and transmits to the infant, through her own particular idiom of mothering, an aesthetic of being that becomes a feature of the infant's self."[21]

Bollas identifies this feeling, "a psychosomatic sense of fusion," with an experience of sanctity. In adult life, a person continues to seek not only the lost mother, but the aesthetic and spiritual experiences that reconstruct the primal dyad enabling transformation. Bollas identifies the search for the aesthetic object with the experience of transformation, which in a way resembles oceanic feeling or mystical *devekut*, and adds that "the aesthetic moment is neither social nor moral; it is curiously impersonal and in a way ruthless."[22]

Additionally, Meltzer notes that a moral stance related to the ability to impart freedom to oneself and to others may well emerge from the aesthetic conflict: "The aesthetic conflict is different from the romantic agony [. . .] *Desire makes it possible, even essential, to give the object its freedom.*"[23] To experience selfhood, man, when he becomes an adult, must release the "mother" he has internalized. At times, however, in pathological instances, he wishes to penetrate, to reenter his mother's body, and to control her by means of "intrusive identification." This situation results from the frustration brought about by the aesthetic conflict, resulting in what Meltzer calls "geographical confusion," meaning a harmful blurring of the boundaries between the self and the other, between the maternal and childish inner spaces. On occasion, an adult still dwells within his mother's body. This foreign intruder attempts to invade the mother through the openings and spaces within her body.[24] The Rabbinic exposition we examined in Chapter 1 ("Whoever speculates upon four things, it were better for him if he had not come

---

21 Bollas, *The Shadow*, 13.
22 Bollas, "Transformational Object," 105.
23 Meltzer and Williams, *Apprehension*, 27 (emphasis is mine).
24 Meltzer, *The Claustrum*.

into the world" [M. Hagigah 2:1]) is a declaration meant to prevent analogous geographical confusion regarding the divine object. A person who is conscious of the boundary, and capable of bearing the unity of the other, is worthy of being born, and can imitate the divine power of Creation.

2 Two Mothers: *Binah* and the *Shekhinah*

The diversity of Kabbalistic depictions of the mother aids in shedding light on the relationship with the physical mother. Two female figures underlie the sefirotic system: the Supernal Mother, *Binah*, and the terrestrial mother, *Malkhut/Shekhinah*, with the Kabbalists focusing on the connection, and similarity, between the two. Their teachings are grounded in the desire to unite the split female and maternal roles into a whole, single countenance. Likewise, the "division of labor" between *Binah* and the *Shekhinah* allows the Kabbalists to confront the aesthetic conflict that the Godhead kindles and to approach the enigma of the divine maternal source in order to desecrate it and intrude into its sacred expanses.

Binah, like the *Shekhinah*, is a transformational object for the underlying *sefirot* and worlds. The *sefirah* of *Binah*, like the *Shekhinah*, has many names, including "the Source of Life," *Rehovot ha-Nahar* (see Gen. 36:37; 1 Chron. 1:48), "Redemption," "Repentance" (or "Answer"), "Intelligence," "the World to Come," and "Praise." Due to its relation to the Supernal Mother, the *Shekhinah* is called "Daughter," as well as "the Land of the Living" (complementing "the Source of Life"), *Bat Sheva* (complementing the *Beer Sheva* appellation of *Binah*, both relating to the number seven, or *sheva*), and *Shekhinah tata'a* (the lower *Shekhinah*, as opposed to *Shekhinah elyonah*, the upper-supernal *Shekhinah*). It signifies the second letter *heh* in the Tetragrammaton YHWH (as opposed to the first *heh*, which is linked to *Binah*). In addition, the daughter presented as the quality of partial freedom and the remission of debts of *Shemittah*, the seventh, Sabbatical year, as opposed to the absolute freedom of *Binah*, which is called *Yovel* (the Jubilee year, in which all land reverts to its original owners).[25]

The *Zohar* identifies these two *sefirot* with female characters connected with each other, mostly in the image of Rachel in the aspect of the *Shekhinah*, and Leah, as *Binah*, and at times using additional Biblical heroines who alternate between above and below on the divine tree of the *sefirot*, such as Sarah, Rebekah, Bathsheba, and others. In this manner, the *Zohar* draws the image of

---

[25] Gikatilla, *Sha'arei Orah*, Gates1 (Ben Shlomo ed., vol 1, 53–92); 8 (vol 2, 43–76); Scholem, *Mystical Shape*, 19–140.

the Supernal Mother closer to that of the earthly one, and links the Biblical heroines with the physical women who follow in their footsteps.

As we will see in Chapter 5, the introduction of the *Zohar* presents a narrative of female relationships at the core of which the mother consoles the daughter over the destruction of the Temple. The verse (Lam. 2:13) "for vast as the sea [*ka-yam*] is your ruin; who can restore you?" is understood as an expression of the relationship between "Who" (*Binah*) with her daughter "What" (*Shekhinah*), who is also called *yam*, or "sea." The climax of this narrative comes in the *Zohar*'s account: "And Mother lends Daughter Her garments" (*Zohar* 1:2a). In this picture, the *Shekhinah* bedecks herself with her mother's adornments, namely, weaponry, and even with male attire, which is revealed during the fulfillment of the Biblical obligation of "appearing" before the Lord at the Temple in Jerusalem on the three pilgrimage festivals of Passover, Shavuot, and Sukkot. *Idra Zuta* also emphasizes the connection between the two, stating that the *Shekhinah* emanates to the worlds beneath it by force of the effulgence that it receives from *Binah*:

> In this Female [*Binah*] are linked all those below. From Her they suckle, and to Her they return, and She is called their Mother. Just as another one [*Malkhut*] is mother to the body, and the whole body suckles from Her, so is this one to all those others below. It is written: *Say to Wisdom, "You are my sister"* (Proverbs 7:4). There is *Wisdom*, and there is *Wisdom*. This Female Wisdom is called 'Small' in comparison with the other.[26]

The *Zohar* (1:240b) draws a parallel between the *Shekhinah* and her mother, *Binah*:

> Solomon spoke of two arrayals of females in the Song of Songs: one of the supernal Beloved, Jubilee, and one of the Bride, Sabbatical; one, arrayal above, and one, arrayal below. So, too, the Act of Creation included both of these sites [. . .] Therefore [. . .] (*bet*), opening of Torah: an act below corresponding to the pattern above; this one [*Binah*] making an upper world, this one [*Shekhinah*] making a lower world.[27]

The connection of the two female figures in the Godhead and their relation to the real world reflects the dynamic nature of the Kabbalistic system, which is constructed on the comparison between the Godhead and motherhood. The two mothers are models of the transformation associated with a return to the source and the memory of the unification within the womb. These two represent varying levels and modes of connection and cleavage to the Godhead, along with moments of crisis that echo the tension and pain of birth.

---

26 *Zohar* 3:296a (Matt, 9, 840–843).
27 Ibid., 1:240b (Matt, 3, 467–469).

Kabbalists mainly portray the mother's generosity and effluence with the daughter, but with few descriptions of the direct conflictual relationship between the two. Yet the dichotomy between *Binah*, representing the "concealed world," and *Malkhut*, representing the "revealed world," channels the forces of strict judgment to *Malkhut*, thereby expressing the veiled tension in mother–daughter relationships regarding birth. Helene Deutsch, a psychoanalyst who pioneered modern scholarly thinking on this issue, argues that pregnancy and birth are inundated with conflicts pertaining to mother–daughter relationships, including feelings of guilt, shame, and self-hatred.[28] The Kabbalistic literature apparently tries to alleviate these harsh emotions to lessen the distance between the two mothers, and thus set forth a model of conciliated motherhood as it relates to the human world as well.

Negative and Positive Theurgy

Just as the *Shekhinah* radiates the divine effulgence upon *Binah* and the *sefirot* above it, so, too, humans – and at times, the woman, specifically – impact on the *Shekhinah*.[29] Kabbalistic theurgy maintains that man can influence and constitute God, while God, on His part, is revealed as an entity dependent upon, and in need of, the human world. The ideational radicalism of this theurgical position, which portrays the influence of the lesser power upon the greater, is also *psychological*, and not merely theosophical. This conception proposes the mutual need for healing and for extending a hand between heaven and earth.

From the historical and political perspective, the Kabbalists, who were weak and lacking political sovereignty as a marginal group within medieval Christian society, consequently developed an extreme theology that postulated God's need for them, in order to compensate for their inferior status in this world. Their role as menders of the cosmos and healers of the Godhead reflects a deceptive sense of omnipotence that was meant to turn weakness and lack into advantage.[30]

Along with the "positive empowerment" of the Godhead, the Kabbalists also discussed the possibility of weakening and harming the supernal world. This "negative theurgy" and man's destructive actions vis-à-vis the Godhead are comparable to a child's destructiveness toward his mother – and to the importance of the latter withstanding this assault. Winnicott speaks of childish aggression as

---

28 Deutsch, *The Therapeutic Process*.
29 Idel, *Kabbalah and Eros*, 247–250.
30 Lachter, *Kabbalistic Revolution*.

an expression of the life drive. In this inner scenario within the child's psyche, he says to his mother: "I love, you, because you survived after I destroyed you [. . .] I destroy you every time I think about you, because I love you."[31] In matching fashion within the mutual relationship of God and man and the intimate bond between them, the human attack of the divine creates actual damage. This havoc is also called "*kitzutz ba-netiot*" (lit., "cutting the shoots"), that is, harming the element of attachment and fundamental trust between the two.[32]

Winnicott explains that punishment, anger, abandonment, and alienation are the mother's "natural" responses to aggression, but she must make efforts to withstand these attacks and not give in to the urge for vindictiveness, in order to aid the infant in passing through this stage. By withstanding the attack, the mother teaches her infant about the possibility of experiencing correction after destruction. Acknowledgment of the actual damage that the attack can cause the mother teaches the child to encompass contradictory emotions and complex experiences. He also learns that the world of concrete objects and human subjects exists outside and alongside him. He gradually develops an awareness of his inner world, which has dimensions and depth, like the depth and space within his mother, who is in a relationship with him.[33]

This notion, that childish destructiveness comes from a combined love–strife drive, and that it is not pathological but attests to mental health also can teach us much about the theological plane.[34] Omnipotence and aggression are essential for development, and teach the child/man to assess his actual strength in relation to the mother/God, and to reveal his ability to influence the other and to compensate for the damage. The comparison between the mother–child and God–man relationships demonstrates the importance for every individual of containing parental figures, while, at the same time, exposes the dependency of the imparters of life, both the mother and God, on those to whom life was given as a gift.

According to the *Zohar*, the commandment "Honor your father and your mother" (Exod. 20:12; Deut. 5:16) refers not only to the human world, but to the relationship between the *sefirot* of *Tiferet* and *Malkhut* with their parents *Hokhmah* and *Binah*. R. Isaac Luria consequently proposes that we humans are as brothers and sisters to *Tiferet* and *Malkhut*, who, like humans, came forth from the womb of the Supernal Mother.[35]

---

31 Cf. Winnicott, *Playing and Reality*, 89; idem, "The Use of an Object," 13.
32 For a bibliography and discussion of negative theology, see Weiss, *Cutting the Shoots*.
33 Winnicott, *Playing and Reality*.
34 Winnicott, *Psycho-Analytic Explorations*, 245–246.
35 See *Zohar* 2:90a; *Sha'ar ha-Kavvanot, Derushei Shema* 6.

These expositions indicate the dual status of the *Shekhinah*: as a mother in regard to humans, but also as sister, who is subordinate to the Supernal Mother and who shares a single womb with humans. In this manner, the attachment and dependency relations between the divine and human systems gain force, and the family model enables the intense relationship with the Godhead felt by the Kabbalists. Additionally, the dual mother model enables us to observe the destructive processes on several levels of existence, and to ask whether the flaw reaches to the "Supernal Mother," or perhaps is present only in the realm of the "lower mother." In certain Kabbalistic approaches, the Great Mother, *Binah*, is protected from the forces of evil, which cannot harm her. The resilience of *Binah* suggests the desire for the healing and strengthening of the lower mother.

This dual motherhood provides an understanding of humans not only as the children of earthly mothers but also as the fruits of a divine and infinite emanation. The experience of beneficent motherhood, which is independent of passing whims, plants the hope of healing and freedom – all for the best – in humans, with these values capable of withstanding all destruction. According to Martin Buber, cited as an epigraph by Bion in the introduction to his essay on Caesura:

> Every developing human child rests, like all developing beings, in the womb of the great mother – the undifferentiated, not yet formed primal world. From this it detaches itself to enter a personal life, and it is only in dark hours when we slip out of this again (as happens even to the healthy, night after night) that we are close to her again. But this detachment is not sudden [. . .] like that from the bodily mother.[36]

Motherhood, like the Godhead, is significantly present within a dialogical spousal and family system, but cannot exist on its own, just as, in the midrashic dictum: "There can be no king without a people."[37] Winnicott argues that there is no such being as an "infant," only the mother–child dyad: "Along with the dependence of early infancy is truly a period in which it is not possible to describe an infant without describing the mother whom the infant has not yet become able to separate from a self."[38]

At times, the harm caused to God and the mother does not come solely from an external source, but may also reflect inner tensions. God, like the mother in labor, suffers harsh birth pangs when creating the world. The suffering of pregnancy and birth, as well, connects the Creator and the created even more strongly. And like the mother, who suffers from postpartum depression or who wants to

---

36 Bion, *Two Papers*, 37.
37 *Pirkei de-Rabbi Eliezer* 3.
38 Winnicott, *Maturational Processes*, "Personal View," 177. See idem, "Parent–Infant Relationship," 587 n. 4.

keep the fetus in her womb forever, God too, at times, despairs of having created humans and, in extreme cases, seeks to destroy them or regrets having created them – as, for example, after the acts of corruption and violence of the Flood generation (Gen. 6) or the sin of the Golden Calf (Exod. 32). It has been claimed that this postpartum maternal depression ensues from the loss of the infinite potential experienced during pregnancy, and the encounter with the partiality of reality.[39] The omnipotence of pregnancy is replaced by the challenging actuality of nights without sleep and caring for an infant who is totally dependent on its mother. In like manner, God has to care for stubborn humankind, and for a people that does not heed Him, who are hungry, thirsty, complaining, and rebellious.[40] The poem of "Give ear, O heavens" apparently hints at this (Deut. 32:18): "You were unmindful of the Rock that begot you." Scripture contains many verses in this spirit, which depict God as one who gives birth, and who subsequently suffers pangs and even the tribulations of motherhood. This verse emphasizes that at times even God despairs of having given birth to humans, and wishes to return the world to the primal chaos. What could possibly be stronger than this image?

3 Mother, God, and the Analyst: Parenting, Theology, and Psychoanalysis

The analyst–patient relationship should be added to the relations between the Godhead and motherhood. Despite their differences, several points of contact between these two worlds can be identified. The great power of the mother, God, and that of the analyst is the source of the threat they pose and the jealousy directed at them. Their creative force and ability to impart life arouse contradictory feelings, such as competitiveness, dependency, and a struggle for independence. The Kabbalists afford legitimacy to human destructive forces, and look upon divine wrath in a critical and daring manner. They also mark out a space for the "processing" of negative and destructive emotions, which can transform them into constructive forces. In analogous fashion, psychoanalysis uses the analyst–patient relationship to explore the regions in the individual's inner world that cause him to fail. Dealing with transference and counter-transference enables the emotional experience to be processed within the clinical relationship, and to alleviate the conflictual junctures and projective mechanisms in which the individual finds himself.

---

39 Kron, *Women in Pink*.
40 See Pardes, *The Biography*, Chapters 1–2.

The mother, God, and the analyst are the first objects of speech at which the emotional truth is directed. The very act of addressing them and the belief that there is someone to whom one can turn are part of the process of inner integration. The Jewish technique of oral recitation of Biblical exegeses during the rehabilitative process parallels the manner in which psychoanalytic technique focuses on speech therapy as a healing and redemptive tool.[41] On the other hand, despite being a means of communication and correction, at times speech is seen by the Kabbalah, and similarly by psychoanalysts, as limiting the mental experience.[42]

The psychoanalytic tenet that every significant system is representative of the unified system, as a monad that incorporates countless reflections of mental patterns, is especially valid regarding a person's relationship with his mother and his God. The force of the relation to mother and God derives from the mystery of the beginning, and it only intensifies during the course of our lives. The analytical process likewise seeks to restore, reconstruct, or correct the "basic unity" in the womb, and to give the adult the maternal compassion he may not have enjoyed as a child.[43] A parallel can be also drawn between the mother–God and mother–analyst relationships in terms of the parental experience. The mother fills a double role in regard to her infant: on the one hand, she is an "object" in a relationship with the infant, while on the other she functions as an enveloping "environment," which is the most important component of the beginning of life. By supplying the infant's basic needs, the environment-mother aids the infant in developing healthy and independent subjectivity. Winnicott underlines that this is the illusion of independence, since the mother does not reveal to her infant the degree of his dependence at the beginning of his life.[44] In much the same way, God is presented as the One who enables the illusion of finite existence alongside the infinite divine experience. In Lurianic Kabbalah, *tzimtzum* means that God "constricts" Himself and makes room for the human,[45] just as the environment-mother absorbs her needs and presence in order to provide the little infant with existence and freedom.[46] In the words

---

[41] For example, in *Tikkunei ha-Zohar* 3:124b; and *Tikkun* 21:43a; the *Zohar* is perceived as a book that rescues the nation from the Exile and brings forth redemption. The notion of "talk therapy"/"talking cure" was mainly developed by Jewish feminist thinker Bertha Pappenheim (Josef Breuer's patient Anna O., who is described in the opening chapter of *Studies in Hysteria*).
[42] Bergstein, "Emotional Truth," 29–42.
[43] Little, "On Basic Unity."
[44] Winnicott, *Maturational Processes*, 73–82; Balint, *Basic Fault*; Amir, *On the Lyricism*, 1–13. See, on the contrary, Bion's claim: "An infant seems to be 'aware' of its 'dependence.' Inseparable from this, it also seems to be aware of being 'all alone'" (Bion, *The Italian Seminars*, 7).
[45] Scholem, *Major Trends*, 260–264; Idel, "Zimzum in Kabbalah and Its Research."
[46] Winnicott, *Maturational Processes*, 179–192; idem, *Through Paediatrics*, 300–305.

of the *Tanya* (the formative text of Habad Hasidism), God offers us the illusion that "we are something that exists in its own right."[47]

A successful environment-mother is one who "holds" the infant and withstands his aggressiveness, like God who contains the ills brought on by humankind. The mother's failure as an environment and her inability to bear the child's destructiveness matches the divine failure in the role of "container" that would allow man to develop. Continuing this parallelism, the analyst must function as a holding environment for the patient. Michael Balint compares this environment to nature and the steady and self-understood power of existence of all things:

> He must allow his patients to relate to, or exist with, him as if he were one of the primary substances [. . .] he should be willing to carry the patient, not actively but like water carries the swimmer or the earth carries the walker [. . .] [He] must be indestructible – as are water and earth.[48]

He maintains that successful analysis enables the patient to experience a new beginning, as well as a mental birth that follows regression, which resembles the situation within the womb. Margaret Little, too, characterizes the analyst–patient relationship as a reconstruction of the basic unity between the mother and infant.[49] These discussions highlight the presence of maternal symbolism and the theme of birth in the analyst's office, not only on the part of the parent/God/analyst, who functions as the "Absolute Other," but the infant/believer/patient, who hopes for returning health and self-correction.[50]

Notwithstanding the similarity of these systems, they differ greatly. The physical mother is simply a human being, and her finitude is like that of ours. She gives birth as she was born, while God the Creator – in most religious approaches – is eternal, with no diminution or death. He is the prime cause and effect, around which all revolves. Even if a similar feeling initially accompanies the infant's adoring attitude toward his mother, when he reaches adulthood he must soberly acknowledge his mother's limitations as human, "regular," and finite as he is. God, in contrast, always remains there, infinite and perfect.

In contrast to a person's biological and physical relation to his mother, the analyst attempts (for payment) to be a suitable maternal substitute during fixed hours. Additionally, placing the analyst in an "omnipotent" godly role is liable

---

47 See below, Chapter 6, section 3. This idea resonates the state of "primary maternal preoccupation."
48 Balint, *Basic Fault*, 166–167. See also his citation above Chapter 1, n. 61.
49 See above, n. 43.
50 Eigen, *Kabbalah and Psychoanalysis*; Holmes, *Seeing God*.

to be disastrous, and undermine the therapeutic process. Nonetheless, since analysis creates the possibility of examining the nature of an individual's relationship with his mother as the basis for the range of relationship patterns in his life, psychoanalytic language facilitates a deeper understanding of the relations between humans' perception of the role of motherhood and that of the divine.

4 Motherhood and Threat

Despite the melding experience of conception, in which two partner in becoming "one flesh," a gap exists between the mother's experience and that of the infant. The newborn is totally dependent upon his mother, and at times her primal faults join those of the infant. The initial dyad with the mother similarly not only is bound up in mystery and pleasure; terror, too, is present. In the Kabbalistic system, this bond is the source of the latent fear coming from the left side of the sefirotic structure, since the *sefirah* of *Binah* is the root of the forces of strict judgment and the left side of the sefirotic tree, while the *Shekhinah* represents its bottom end. The substantive connection between motherhood and harsh judgments brings into sharp focus the suffering and difficulty entailed in bringing new life into the world. These harsh decrees could seemingly be understood as the Kabbalistic demonization of the mother and as testimony to an early misogynic mindset. The Kabbalistic view, however, of the mother as the source of harsh judgments is based on the assumption that the forces of *Din* are necessary, and essential, for rectification and redemption, no less than the forces of *Hesed*. Unlike the latter, which is associated with the masculine and represents confusion, liquidity, and a blurring of the boundaries, *Din* stands for the feminine, the material, and the physical, as well as the boundary and form of things.

Feminist theoreticians lash out against the identification of the mother with traits such as containing, identification, and empathy, noting the oppression inherent in their exclusive attribution to women. Instead of the "therapeutic" and submissive stance, feminists aim to return to the discourse the multifaceted nature of the mother as a complex – and at times threatening and destructive – subject. The various waves of feminism called to reestablish maternal subjectivity, and to restore to the mother's responsibility for her world and her agency. In recent decades, their emphasis has been placed, *inter alia*, on the destructive aspects of motherhood in order to forge a realistic perception of this challenging experience.

Thinkers such as Simone Beauvoir, Adrienne Rich, Dorothy Dinnerstein, Nancy Chodorow, and Luce Irigaray engaged in a trenchant discussion of mutually reinforcing patriarchal patterns of repression: the inclination to embed the "feminine" in motherhood, and exclusively so, and the tendency to demonize the mother and motherhood, while concurrently ascribing to her perfection and limitless omnipotence.[51]

Feminists assert that the aggrandizement of the mother goes hand in hand, in many senses, with her degradation and humiliation. This dual orientation likely expresses childish fantasies about the perfect mother, who is first portrayed as a divine, superhuman figure, and who is eventually attacked for her failure to fulfill this impossible mission. Also, the degradation of the mother originates in the child/man's dependency upon his mother and the attempt to overcome his fear of her. The myth of the ideal and perfect mother serves the fantasy in which the mother is to have only positive traits, while not having any other, negative, quality connected with mothering. And indeed, this myth arouses guilty feelings in mothers who cannot meet the taxing demands that they themselves help to set in motion.[52]

We could well argue that Kabbalistic literature preceded feminism in this effort by hundreds of years. It made no attempt to embellish the figure of the mother or to paint her in a completely positive hue. Her dark side is given prominence and, as Winnicott argues, a mother who is "too good" is seen as dangerous and harmful.[53] The mystical literature sets forth the mother as the source of harsh judgments, since the child learns his boundaries and limitations through her. As a true subject, the mother encompasses destructiveness, fault, depression, and pain, with which she wrestles in her relationship with her infant and with herself. For the Kabbalists, the mother is the source of building while possessing the potential for destruction and repair, darkness and light, death and birth. She has Eros and vitality that are from the energies of *Din* and the "left" quality, and blood that enables her to create life. She is the source of harsh judgments – since she knows what loss is and what death is – that are bound up with the creation of new life.

Along with the aspects of *Gevurah* (the power of strict judgment) and "fear," *Binah* is also called *alma de-dekhura* or *olam ha-zachar* (the "world of the male" or "the masculine world") exactly at the moment that she gives birth.[54] The mother's ability to bring the male forth from her body – the opposite of her feminine essence – indicates her potential for compassion, and her ties to the masculine

---

51 Beauvoir, *The Second Sex*; Rich, *Of Woman Born*; Irigaray, *Je, Tu, Nous*; Chodorow, *Feminism*; Dinnerstein, "Sometimes You Wonder if They're Human." See also Neumann, *The Great Mother*.
52 Chodorow and Contratto, *The Fantasy of the Perfect Mother*. See Thorne and Yalom, *Rethinking the Family*, 54–75; Bassin et al., *Representation of Motherhood*.
53 Winnicott, *The Child, the Family, and the Outside World*.
54 See below, Chapter 6, Section 4.

aspects of this attribute. All the powers connected with the divine name "I am who I am" (Exod. 3:14) are attributed to the Great Mother (= *Binah*), which includes the multifaceted reality.⁵⁵ Here, the Kabbalistic view of the fullness and multifaceted nature of the maternal experience meets with the feminist notion of the mother as a discrete person and subject, to gain a better understanding of the birth experience and the mother's attitude to the infant that comes forth from her body.

5 The "Sawing" Mother and the Concealed Mother

In order to delve into the dynamic nature of the relationship between the birthing mother and the individual who is born, I will set forth two models of motherhood. Each of these models is derived from a different ontic conception of birth, but both view birth as a critical experience, one which gives meaning to human life. The first model sees birth as an ongoing and developing experience, from the beginning of life to its end, while the second emphasizes the tearing away that is at the root of birth and its isolation and separateness from any other human event. In the first model, birth is a continuing and archetypical process that influences every moment of a person's existence, while the second highlights the one-time, singular nature of birth and views it as a *situation* that exceeds consciousness and understanding, cognition and language.

The first model centers on the mother, who continues to give birth to the infant in her (real or metaphorical) womb, while the second paints a picture of the mother who vanishes and "breaks contact" upon the conclusion of the act of giving birth, which is pushed away or left far in the past. The first model is that of the "eternally sawing mother," in a paraphrase of the language of the Kabbalists.⁵⁶

---

55 *Zohar* 3:65a–b (Matt, 7, 427–430).
56 As I will claim in Chapter 3, Section 4, sawing *(nesirah)* happens not only between humans, but also between the *sefirot* in the upper world. According to R. Isaac Luria, the Upper Mother, *Binah*, saw the daughter at the eternal event of her wedding with the *Tiferet*: "And now the Supernal Mother slices away *(nesirah)* the daughter *(nuqvah)* and returns her [to be] face to face" (*Sha'ar ha-Kavvanot, Kavvanot Ha-Amidah*, 3). According to R. Moshe Hayyim Luzzatto, the *Shekhinah* shares with her mate a mystical *kotel* (= shared wall that connects the divine couple) that only the mother can release. See R. Moses Hayyim Luzzatto, *Kelalim Rishonim*, 28: "*And behold the border of the distancing is back-to-back, and the edge of closeness is face to face* [. . .]. And when they are with rectification *(tiqqun)* they are back-to-back, when they do not have a brow to raise a head in front of him, and even he does not turn to them with love. [. . .] And, therefore, *Nuqvah*, even when she is back-to-back [with *Tiferet*] – *One wall (kotel) is for both of them* [. . .] And this [the rectification] is done when *Imma* (mother) departs from *Ze'ir Anpin* (Small Countenance) and enters *Nuqvah*, and slices her away from her, and builds her not through him [the male]."

5 The "Sawing" Mother and the Concealed Mother — 63

The second, on the other hand, is that of the "constantly concealed mother," who is abandoned and desired, the source of the earliest longings and impressions in the psyche, the figure who leaves traces behind only through the "signifiers of desire" that appear during the course of an individual's life.[57] The lower mother, the *Shekhinah*, might possibly be experienced more as hidden, while *Binah* is the one who continues to give birth to the body and soul in an endless process. Although *Binah* is called "the Hidden World," its constant presence is marked as actively giving birth to the *sefirot* and the worlds that derive from it.

Combining these two conceptions provides us with a broad range of contradictory experiences regarding the same event, one which is essentially paradoxical. Birth is a moment that lasts forever, but to which we can never return.

Within the context of these two worlds, the supernal and the earthly, and the two aspects of motherhood and birth, we will discuss in the following chapters the soul's emergence from the womb; the rending of the soul from the mother's body; birth from the body and birth from the soul; the infant–mother relationship; the initial birth and the second, independent and initiated birth; the burning candle and the infinite light from which the soul descends into this world; the upheaval of all things in the infant's world during his birth; and his gazing upon the "root of his soul." Most importantly, I will highlight the situation in which all is overthrown, and as the Rabbis say of the moment of birth, "what was closed is opened, and what was open is closed" (BT Niddah 30b).

This book is a contemplative essay about various aspects of the kaleidoscope of birth and the *human throes* of anguish and pleasure, challenge and pain involved in this experience. The book incorporates Kabbalah and psychoanalysis, gender studies, and midrashic theory, with manifold voices, all of which are woven into my scholarly exploration. These diverse voices reflect the divide separating such a dramatic event that takes place in the body and the inability of language to describe and interpret it: the blood, the amniotic fluid, the placenta; the cries; the holding onto the umbilical cord; the first heartbeats outside the womb; the appearance of a human; the sudden appearance of the image of God fully manifested in the human body. A complex mechanism takes shape over the course of months – and is revealed all at once. Suddenly, a soul enters the body!

Up to the present, so little has been said in scholarly research and writing about birth – that which precedes the flesh; that which unravels all meaning; that which undermines language. What are the exact words needed to speak of the secret from whence the world exists and of the most individual – symbolic – Jewish,

---

[57] Kristeva, *Black Sun*.

universal, and cosmic expansion of the beginning of the beginning? Faced with the force and complexity of motherhood, Patrice DiQuinzio calls her book *The Impossibility of Motherhood*; the difficulty of talking about motherhood pales in comparison to the daunting task of having a conversation about birth.[58] The multitude of perspectives, dimensions of language, and the deluge of ideas and material all attest to muteness in the face of the singular experience of birth and the dearth of language to describe it.

Despite the attempt to shed light on the encounter of these diverse ideas with one another, there is still a group of concepts and terms in need of deciphering. I have attempted to navigate and mediate between these different terms and concepts, and I bear sole responsibility for all that remains puzzling and imprecise, for all the patchwork that has come into being during the course of my writing, and for the many questions that remain unanswered. Taken together, all these present the richness of the most primal of all beginnings known as "birth."

As we will see in the following section, the unique theology and psychoanalysis of birth also influences morality and *halakhah* (Jewish law).

6 Otherwise than Being and the Law of *Rodef* ("Persecutor," "Pursuer")

The halakhic and moral facets of birth relate to difficult questions that pertain to matters of life and death. The Mishnah (Oholot 7:6) establishes the following:

> If a woman is experiencing arduous labor, the fetus must be cut up while it is in the womb and brought out member by member, since the life of the mother has priority over its life. If the greater part of it was already born, it may not be touched, since the claim of [one] life does not override the claim of another life.

This *mishnah* distinguishes between the "fetus," which is a collection of members and is liable to endanger his mother's life, and an infant, "the greater part of [which] was already born," and thereby a creature existing in its own right. Once the "greater part [or "its head," in other textual variants] was already born," it is already a human being, and its life may not be taken, since one life may not be taken in favor of another: his life and that of his mother are of equal worth.

---

58 DiQuinzio, *The Impossibility of Motherhood*, 142–173.

On this issue, the Talmud (BT Sanhedrin 72b) writes:

> R. Huna said: A pursuing minor may be killed to save the pursued. He maintains that a pursuer, whether an adult or a minor, need not be formally warned. R. Hisda asked R. Huna: Once his head has come forth, he may not be harmed, because one life may not be taken in favor of another. But why so? Is he not a pursuer? There it is different, *for she is pursued by Heaven*. Shall we say that the following supports him? If a person was pursuing his fellow to kill him, he [a third party] says to him, See, he is an Israelite, and a member of the covenant, and the Torah says [Gen. 9:6]: "Whoever sheds the blood of man, by man shall his blood be shed" – the Torah is saying, save the blood [i.e., life] of [the pursued] with the blood of the pursuer.

This Talmudic discussion of the law of *rodef* establishes that even if it is a minor who is chasing another person, he may be killed to save the one being pursued. R. Hisda objects to R. Huna's not drawing any distinction between a minor and an adult, and asks how the minor can be deemed a *rodef* and therefore may be killed, since, in the above *mishnah*, if the infant's head or most of his body has come out, he is not to be killed, even if he jeopardizes his mother's life. Here, for the first time, R. Hisda raises the radical argument that the fetus might have the status of a *rodef*.

The Talmud rejects his reasoning and sides with R. Huna's position that the fetus is not considered to be "pursuing" his mother's life, *"for she is pursued by Heaven."* Notwithstanding this rejection, the very presentation of this harsh picture of the fetus as a *rodef* points to the paradoxical determinism of birth, which hangs between life and death. The fetus is seen here as the subject over whose life the Rabbis are fighting. Maimonides accordingly rules as follows in the *Mishneh Torah*:

> This is, moreover, a negative commandment, that we have no pity on the life of the pursuer. Consequently, the Sages have ruled that if a woman with child is having difficulty in giving birth, the child inside her may be taken out, either by drugs or by surgery, because it is regarded as one pursuing her and trying to kill her. But once its head has appeared, it must not be touched, for we may not set aside one human life to save another human life, and what is happening is the course of nature.[59]

According to Maimonides, as well, the fetus could be the "pursuer" of his mother, but only when it is still considered to be a collection of body parts. Once it has begun to be born, it is not to be harmed. Maimonides makes no mention of the Talmud's harsh argument that the woman *"is pursued by Heaven."* It is the way of the world for the forces of destruction and pain to exist, and potential harm is

---

[59] Maimonides, *Hil. Rotzeah u-Shemirat ha-Nefesh* [*Murder and Preservation of Life*] 1:9, 196–197.

inherent from the very first moment of the world: what enables existence can also lay it waste. God, the procreator of the woman, might become her pursuer at the time of birth; the heavens that are suspended above us may fall on us in hard times. In his book *Otherwise Than Being, Or Beyond Essence*, Emmanuel Levinas describes birth from a philosophical and ethical perspective. He suggests that birth represents an exceptional experience that constitutes the moral significance of human existence. In the physiological dimension, birth concretely exemplifies the mother's prenatal commitment to the other:

> It is maternity, gestation of the other in the same [. . .] In maternity what signifies is a responsibility for others, to the point of substitution for others and suffering both from the effect of persecution itself in which the persecutor sinks. Maternity, which is bearing par excellence, bears even the responsibility for the persecuting by the persecutor.[60]

In this passage, Levinas develops the charged Talmudic idea discussed above, namely, that the fetus is liable to be a "persecutor" in his mother's innards. Levinas augments the Rabbis' conception with the notion that the inner and "natural" ethics of pregnancy teach that people willingly choose to bear the infinite demand of that "persecutor" who lays claim on his mother and, even before being born, turns her into the persecuted, the bearer of a debt. This is the only way to learn what "absolute" commitment to the other is: the mother is seen as "bearing" the burden and suffering, and as one who carries the burden of the world in her womb. In contrast with the resolution of the Rabbis' discussion and their rejection of thinking of the infant as a *rodef*, Levinas believes that the infant is an actual persecutor, while he presents the mother as the one who freely chooses to be the "persecuted." For him, pregnancy is the sole human act that enables the mother (and only her) to become cognizant, through her body, of the extraordinary experience that he calls "otherwise than being" – the mother, who is not "her," and the other (i.e., the infant), who is not "him" and who is yet to be. The blending of these impossible elements – namely, the infant who is an as-yet unborn subject and the mother who consents to her own persecution – creates the wonder of "life." Pregnancy is thus a fiery mirror of the absolute otherness of the human creature. Levinas puts it this way:

> Maternity is the complete being "for the other" [. . .] Where, beyond its immediate identity, being recognizes itself in its difference.[61]

---

[60] Levinas, *Otherness*, 75; see also Ben Pazi, "Rebuilding the Feminine."
[61] Ibid., 108.

6 Otherwise than Being and the Law of *Rodef* ("Persecutor," "Pursuer") — 67

In addition to Levinas's fascinating discussion of the ethics of procreation in the world of the Rabbis, he also fills in the missing link in the history of western philosophy, which tends, whether intentionally or not, to disregard this essential component, without which birth would not be possible: the figure of the pregnant and birthing mother. Levinas's moral position, which views the fetus as the persecutor of his mother, insists on the centrality of the physical experience in which the infant is present within his mother and comes forth from within her body, just as it had entered it dramatically. In the biological reality, the mother is indeed "persecuted," in many senses, by the symbolically "foreign" body of her fetus, which, in the Kabbalistic portrayal, "penetrates his mother from within" and takes possession of her body, together with the father, who changes her female status, from virgin and whole to that of penetrated, diffused, and dependent. In this context, we should not lose sight of the fact that not all mothers willingly consent to be "persecuted" by their fetus, especially in the cases throughout human history in which women were impregnated against their will as a result of rape or other horrific circumstances. Levinas's conception could well serve to empower women, and function as a symbolic model of morality; at the same time, these views are liable to be interpreted as justification for violence against women and for viewing them as unwilling victims.

In conclusion, importantly, from an ethical and theological point of view, the mother–fetus relationship is a microcosm of the relationship between God and the world. This relationship is a complex one, encompassing gratitude, knowing the other, bearing of the burden, the demand to take responsibility, blatant inequality, but also moving mutuality. This relationship enables us to examine the paradoxical nature of all existence: the mother imparts life, and at times is forced to pay with her life for this giving. Pregnancy expresses symbolic and actual selflessness, which exceeds the bounds of the self and has us confront our otherness.

Chapter 3
The Caesura of Birth

1 Caesura: Connection or a Rending Asunder?

In 1926, Freud wrote: "There is much more continuity between intra-uterine life and earliest infancy than the impressive caesura of the act of birth would have us believe."[1] Psychoanalysts have attempted to decipher the term "caesura," and use it to describe the bridge between life before and after birth. Toward the end of his life, Bion devoted an extensive discussion to Freud's enigmatic statement. Bion argued that every individual has fetal memory, but as adults we distance ourselves from this primitive and deep intuition, which, nonetheless, sometimes suddenly manifests itself during analysis:

> The embryologist speaks about "optic pits" and "auditory pits." Is it possible for us, as psycho-analysts, to think that there may still be vestiges in the human being which would suggest a survival in the human mind, analogous to that in the human body, of evidence in the field of optics that once there were optic pits, or in the field of hearing that once there were auditory pits? Is there any part of the human mind which still betrays signs of an "embryological" intuition, either visual or auditory? This may seem to be an academic and unimportant matter – unless we think that there may be some truth in the statement made by Freud that there is some connection between post-natal thought and emotional life, and prenatal life. To exaggerate the question for the sake of simplicity: are we to consider that the fetus thinks, or feels, or sees, or hears? If so, how primitive can these thoughts, or feelings, or ideas be?[2]

Following Melanie Klein, Bion hypothesized that the processes of internalization and projection already begin within the womb, and that the fetus has prenatal emotions and thoughts. He argued that embryological traces remain in the hypothalamic system and influence human experiences in life. These primal experiences – which were unprocessed and did not undergo mentalization – arouse subthalamic dread.

The term "caesura" derives from the Latin word for "cutting"; in literary analysis, it also denotes a "stop"; in prosody, it signals the transition from one passage to another and the connection between them. Hagit Aharoni and Avner Bergstein suggest comparing the caesura to a topographical figuration with a valley, streambed, or ravine, which, "if not successfully crossed to the other side, becomes an abyss."[3]

---

[1] Freud, *Inhibitions, Symptoms and Anxiety*, 138.
[2] Bion, *Two Papers*, 42.
[3] Aharoni and Bergstein, "Looking at the Future Born," 16. See also their profound interpretation in Bion, *Caesura*, 201.

A caesura represents a sundering or interruption – but also a continuation and connection, a joining together. It represents the tearing of a continuum and its completion: birth stops what came before, and something new begins. The biological state of pregnancy and before-birth is replaced by the inner mother–child object relationship. One body is suddenly detached – rent – from another, and then a relationship is formed between two who were once one. This experience is associated with anxiety, but also with confidence and strength: within the womb, the mother supplies all the fetus's needs through her body; anxiety is aroused within the fetus as a response to the separation from its mother. The mother, too, feels concern over the loss of her fetus, and goes through a physical and mental caesural experience during birth. Yet the danger and trauma of birth may also strengthen the body–soul ties between the mother and her baby; this is a bond that is actualized the moment the infant comes into the world.

Michael Balint describes birth as a traumatic experience that resembled death. Following Phyllis Greenacre, who engaged in the 1950s in pioneering research of birth trauma and its influence on the early patterns of infantile anxiety, Balint states that "birth means a sudden interruption of a hitherto gratifying relationship with an environment in which, it is true, there are as yet no objects, which is a kind of unstructured 'ocean.'"[4]

The British school of psychoanalysis places special emphasis on initial mental states and attachment to the mother immediately following birth. Melanie Klein and others in her school locate the roots of neurosis in early infancy, and in the traumatic transition from the embryonic stage to infancy.[5] When discussing autistic states and their initial causes, Frances Tustin stresses the earth-shattering intensity of the birth process, observing that this is a journey comparable to walking through the "Valley of the Shadow of Death" and the preparation of the individual for his death. The sharp transition from a dyadic relationship with the mother to being ripped away from her resembles our relationship with life and death.[6] Despite the lack of symmetry between the mother and infant at birth, both are flooded by the cyclicity of life and death, due to the mother's pain, her anxiety over losing the fetus, her worry for the life in her womb, and the similarity of the traumatic situations of "entry" into and "departure" from the

---

[4] Balint, *The Basic Fault*, 60–61: "In her book Greenacre gives an excellent description of the imagery which people use to express their feelings about, or possibly 'memories' of birth, which may be felt, for instance, as: 'a bridge from one mode of existence to another', 'a chiasma', 'a hiatus', 'a kind of blackout very closely resembling death.'"

[5] Klein's focus on early infancy was influenced by the attitudes of two of her teachers: Carl Abraham and Sándor Ferenczi. See the latter, "Confusion of the Tongues."

[6] Tustin, "Psychological Birth."

world. The way in which mother and fetus – each for itself and within their mutual relationship – experience the trauma of birth is critical for the rest of their lives.

The role of pain and suffering in the experience of birth can be understood as a source of feminine empowerment while at the same time possessing a destructive and oppressive element. According to Elaine Scarry, physical pain may destroy the identity and basic functions of the self, such as the ability to communicate and to verbally express your needs and desires:

> Physical pain does not simply resist language but actively destroys it, bringing about an immediate reversion to a state anterior to language, to the sounds and cries a human being makes before language is learned.[7]

Yet, Emily Martin, Sara Cohen Shabot, and other feminist theoreticians, following Adrian Rich, claim that the medicalization of birth inevitably rids women of their agency, and often leads to a series of unnecessary, harmful medical interventions.[8] In contrast, the mother's pain can serve as a primary means of restoring her subjectivity – she may even experience a unique sense of pleasure and power during the birth.[9]

From the perspective of the fetus, his body bears within itself a map of its birth, a topography of the psyche. Already in the early 1950s, Greenacre found a connection between birth trauma and the infant's psychophysical and biological structure. She wrote that birth generates an intense sensual stimulus that replaces the calm fetal narcissism that exists in the womb. The infant's brain remembers the pressure exerted on it during birth, and frequently needs a long time to recover from this experience. Greenacre suggests that one of the signs of psychophysical trauma in an adult is the chronic headache that accompanies the unconscious memory of birth, an idea that Winnicott would develop in his writings: "There can very easily be delay at a time when there is constriction round the head, and it is my definite view that the type of headache which is clearly described as a band round the head is sometimes a direct derivative of birth sensations remembered in somatic form."[10] These thinkers highlight the impression that remains of the intra-uterine bond as the foundation for the adult's relationships. Likewise, the Kabbalists are engaged with the *reshimu* that remains in the created world from the primordial matter that preceded

---

7 Scarry, *The Body in Pain*, 4.
8 On the danger of medicalization of birth, see Rich, *Of Woman Born*, Chapter 7; Martin, *The Woman in the Body*.
9 Cohen-Shabot, "Constructing Subjectivity."
10 Winnicott, *Through Paediatrics*, 186.

Creation, from the time of the great myths of the deaths of the Edomite kings (who symbolize the primal forces that collapsed; see Chapter 1). These impressions represent the destruction of the worlds preceding this one and the state of divine *tzimtzum* that enables cosmic and physical birth.

Our discussion of caesura will now travel back in time – paradoxically *before* the beginning in a study based on speculation and hypotheses that can neither be confirmed nor refuted. This direction was followed by Alessandra Piontelli, whose ground-breaking study used ultrasound scans to examine the continuity of prenatal and postnatal infant life. She found a direct link between the fetus's mental life and behavior, his first relationships and personality as an infant, and his early childhood games. Her findings concerning the reconstruction of fetal life in infancy are especially fascinating as regards pairs of twins. Thus, for example, she describes a pair of twins separated by a wall between the two separate placentas in the uterus, through which the two played with and kicked one another, which activity they continued to do postnatally: they improvised a screen or partition between them, through which they reconstructed constant contact and battle. Other twin pairs continued to fight over the narrow, cramped space in their mother's body, even when they were already outside the womb.

Piontelli's examination of the psychological treatment of children born of single fetal pregnancies is no less compelling: one who was at risk of abortion later described experiences in which he was washed away, while a fetus whose umbilical cord was tightly wound around its neck while *in utero* continued to suffer from breathing problems, and exhibited an inclination for auto-asphyxiation as an adult. Piontelli does not provide a definitive answer to the question of the respective parts of the fetus and the mother in establishing this continuity, nor does she argue that nature is of greater importance than nurture.[11] Although she formulates her findings quite cautiously, her statement that "presumably in young children one can find either actual memories of their perinatal state or at least traces of it still relatively undistorted or coloured by the accretions of later life" represents a quiet revolution in psychoanalysis.[12] According to her, these findings show that:

> despite the continuity of pre- and post-natal behaviour, however, birth was always an extremely important event, sometimes crucially so. Traces of it could be found in much post-natal behaviour, particularly in the case of children for whom it had been especially

---

11 "I do not want to assert, however, that 'nature' is more important than 'nurture.' What I think my findings do suggest is that the interplay between 'nature' and 'nurture' begins much earlier than is usually thought, and that certain pre-natal experiences may have a profound emotional effect on the child, especially if these pre-natal events are reinforced by post-natal experiences." Piontelli, *From Fetus to Child*, 1.

12 Ibid., 21.

traumatic [. . .] My findings both for the children I observed before and after birth and for those I treated psychoanalytically suggest that although it seems unlikely that children "remember" their experiences within the womb and their birth, such experiences are constantly re-lived and re-worked as they grow and develop. This was especially clear in the twins; in their constant talk about overcrowding and lack of space, as in their preference for playing games connected with pairs and couples, they seem to be forever linked by the fact of having once been together as a pair inside too narrow a space.[13]

As we have seen, Winnicott similarly argues that, unlike regular birth memories, psychosomatic symptoms appear in adult life following a traumatic birth. He stressed that what the consciousness does not know the child's body nevertheless remembers:

There is evidence that the personal birth experience is significant, and is held as memory material [. . .] In many child analyses birth play is important. In such play the material might have been derived from what has been found out by the patient about birth, through stories and direct information and observation. The feeling one gets is, however, that *the child's body knows about being born.*[14]

Winnicott stresses this idea in his later study: "From the infant's point of view, the change from the unborn to the born state is brought about *by the infant* [. . .] It was the infant's impulse *from the infant's point of view* that produced the changes and the physical progression, usually head first, towards an unknown and new position."[15] The conception of the infant as an "agent" of his own birth (even prior to delivery) is suggestive of the midrashic and Kabbalistic notions we will discuss in the following chapter. Although a person is born involuntarily, there is an element of choice in coming into the world.

The caesura of birth is not expressed solely in the meeting between the physical and the mental and in the body–soul bond forged between the infant and his mother; it is also present at the point of connection between the individual and the mythical. This connection – birth – is both an extremely private affair of physical and mental severance and unraveling that is liable to become abyss and trauma, and the most universal, natural, and "normal" occurrence – the basic condition for the continuation of human existence. For the sake of argument, we will develop the conception that the relationship between the mother and her infant does not begin *after* birth but rather continues a process that had begun in the womb (or perhaps even earlier, in the mother's fantasies prior to being impregnated, or in the stage of the soul's descent from the realm of the infinite and its formation). This model

---

13 Ibid., 231.
14 Winnicott, *Through Paediatrics*, 177, 180 (emphasis is mine).
15 Winnicott, *Human Nature*, 144.

enables us to suggest that the story of many generations of life continues to be woven throughout the birth of the individual. On the cosmic level, the fetus inside his mother bears within himself fetal memory cells of his parents, *their* parents, and their ancestors – and even the memory of the infinite number of preceding caesuras that have continually occurred since the beginning of humankind.

According to Bion, "caesuric" moments and experiences that mimic birth appear in every significant mental transition in a person's life and prepare the individual for changes and crises. The caesura is a master plan that is present at the wedding ceremony and at the moment one becomes a parent and at the hour of our death. These rites of passage emphasize how an individual's life relates to the divine and the infinite. Like psychoanalysts, traditional commentators and Kabbalists, too, ask how to lessen the terror of the spiritual moments of birth, in order to prevent the split between "fetal" mental states and the instant of emerging into the world in the caesuric experiences that recur in human life.

Following Bion, Hanni Biran differentiates vertical caesurae, which occur chronologically from one's time as a fetus to one's death and which resonate throughout the primordial layers of the psyche, from horizontal caesurae, which refer to the synchronous experiences of an adult who carries with him traces of the fetus, the child, the adolescent, etc. In addition, she discusses analytic "caesuric" moments, the appearance of trauma in treatment, as well as the function of great ideas and paradigms that have shaped human theoretical thinking.[16]

Meanwhile, in his discussion of the caesura, Avner Bergstein proposes that getting in touch with primitive mental states and with the origin of the self are aspired to not so much for discovering historical truth or recovering unconscious content as for generating motion between different parts of the psyche. The movement itself is what expands the mind and facilitates psychic growth. Bion's brave and daring notion of caesura, suggesting a link between mature emotions and thinking and intra-uterine life, serves as a model for bridging seemingly unbridgeable states of mind.[17]

2 "Sitting on the Crisis"

The Rabbis use the expression "sitting on the *mashber*" (the latter term understood as "birthstool") to portray the dual movement of birth, which is both a rending and a bridge. This wording graphically illustrates the liminal state of the

---

16 Biran, *The Courage of Simplicity*, 33–46.
17 Bergstein, "Transcending the Caesura."

woman in labor as being between worlds, in a life-threatening situation. Indeed, the idiom used by the Rabbis for giving birth literally means "sitting on the crisis" – namely, being in a place which is on the "fault line." This term might give us a sense of their understanding of "being born" or "giving birth." In Scripture, the word *mashber* denotes the part of the woman's body that is "broken" (*nishbar*) during birth, with her pelvic bones moving on their joints. In 2 Kings (19:3 [NJPS]), following Rabshakeh's declaration, Hezekiah's messengers address the prophet Isaiah: "They said to him, 'Thus said Hezekiah: This day is a day of distress, of chastisement, and of disgrace. The babes have reached the birthstool [*mashber*], but the strength to give birth is lacking.'"[18] The Bible likens the crisis (*mashber*) of birth to the historical reality of collective catastrophe and destruction in the period between the Assyrian and Babylonian exiles. This portrayal appropriates birth, which it transforms into a nationalized metaphor. This said, it also exhibits intimate knowledge of the experiences of women in labor, and especially with the transitional stage preceding the birth pangs in which despair prevails, just when the birth is close to its conclusion.

On the physical level, the *mashber* resembles the "stones" (*ovnnayim*) between which the women in labor would sit or on which they would place their legs, with the child dropping between them.[19] As the midrash describes:

> What does *ovnayim* mean? [. . .] when a woman bends to deliver a child, her thighs grow cold like stones. Another explains [in accordance with] what is said, "So I went down to the potter's house, and there he was working on his wheel [*ovnayim*]." As in the case of the potter, with a thigh on one side, a thigh on the other side, and the block in between, so, too, with a woman there is a thigh on one side, a thigh on the other side, and the child in between.[20]

The period of impregnation and pregnancy is characterized by a lack of knowledge, anxiety, and many speculations. In the emotional sense, "sitting on the crisis" imparts legitimacy to the "death" that a woman experiences during childbirth, as well as to her pain, and her powerlessness, which are bound up with bringing life into the world.

In the mythical sense, the *mashber* represents the image of a caesuric bridge that leads to the *halal ha-panui* (void) that is concealed within the

---

18 See also Isaiah 37:3; Hoshea 13:13; M. Arachin 1:4; M. Niddah 10:5. See also Ashurst, *Understanding Women*; Breen, *The Birth of a First Child*, 25.
19 Exodus 1:16. *Leviticus Rabbah* 27:7 (Margolioth ed., 639). On *ovnayim* ("stones," birthing stool) and labor in the ancient world, see Rubin, *Beginning of Life*, 34–35, 155 n. 5; Preuss, *Medicine*, 396–397.
20 BT Niddah 11b.

woman's body. "Sitting on the *mashber*-crisis" means to grasp the abyss, to flood it, but also to keep it as an impenetrable secret.

For Winnicott, the force of birth brings into sharp focus the difference between the experience of the event by the mother and by the infant, since a baby is born only once, but the mother has already been born, and now she herself gives birth. This understanding would seem to highlight the dependency and trauma felt by the infant during birth, in contrast with the mother's power and capacity.

In a differing view, Galit Atlas gives greater weight to female subjectivity and to the crisis that the mother undergoes during childbirth. She argues that the caesura is liable to lead to a fall and breakdown, but also to growth and self-discovery – a break*through*. This situation, of a break in unity, is so close to the Rabbinic depiction of *ha-mashber*, since the birthing mother experiences herself as "I" who is "not-I." As Atlas states:

> During that process of being born as a mother, the mother experiences a line of Enigmatic and Pragmatic breaks – breaks of time and space, of meaning, of continuity, and of boundaries – all related to an emotional and physical reorganization of boundaries, and therefore to the unity of the self [. . .] Breaks In Unity are an inherent part of the female structure and identity, and in that sense a way to postulate women's subjective position as a norm, and not as something exceptional, pathological or unique.[21]

She encounters a situation is which her body is rent and completely open, and seemingly penetrated from within. During the course of the pregnancy, birth, and nursing, the mother's ability to distinguish between inner and outer is blurred, and she cannot grasp what is within without it "trickling" out: "Allowing yourself to be penetrated means embracing a more fluid structure, developing an identity that is based on unsolidified boundaries, which include a certain degree of leaking out of the inside and letting in of the outside [. . .] the vagina is passive but also active, it holds the *capacity* to be wounded as well as the *power* to be wounded." These situations in which she lacks control induce severe anxiety, and are accompanied by constant physiological and mental changes (the large stomach, leaking milk, the infant from whom the mother is forced to part):

> That caesura requires integration of old and new, the rebuilding of a frame based on wholeness and where bodily boundaries are re-achieved. Those enigmatic caesuras need to be acknowledged as belonging to the newborn mother as much as they belong to her baby. In similar and different ways, both are subjects who are in the process of being created and recreated, defining and redefining their borders between inside and outside and the integrity of their own selves.[22]

---

21 Atlas, *The Enigma of Desire*, 61–75.
22 Ibid., 71.

Atlas also offers a feminist interpretive direction for the important term "fear of breakdown" developed by Winnicott. She understands this fear as the crisis memory borne by the infant as an echo of his mother's birth anxiety. While Winnicott concentrates on the disintegration that the infant experiences in his inner world, she describes this maternal fear as a *reshimu* that is imprinted in the consciousness of the fetus on its way out into the world. Even before becoming a cohesive "self" capable of absorbing its experiences, the fetus has his mother's birth trauma imprinted in it. Following Luce Irigaray, who discussed the female ability to be "more than one," Atlas suggests that birth prompts a sense of breakage – not only a "wordless break," but an opportunity for the mother's renewed feminine connection to her body and soul. This rupture is not pathological, as it sometimes is defined, but a "growing" break which contains the potential for maternal healing.

The imagery of the crisis and extrication from it is based on the intersubjective dialogue and dependency of mother and baby. Piontelli states that, "contrary to many popular beliefs, no fetus develops in pure isolation and its behaviour is also a reflection of the interaction with its pre-natal environment."[23] In this context, Balint disagrees with the idea that the infant is in a totally narcissistic state while in the womb, with no object relationships: "I think that it would be much simpler to accept the idea that relationship with the environment exists in a primitive form right from the start, and that the infant may become aware of, and respond to, any considerable change in it."[24] Accordingly, the caesura expresses the mutual dependency that continues after birth: "The individual is born in a state of intense relatedness to his environment, both biologically and libidinally. Prior to birth, self and environment are harmoniously 'mixed up', in fact, they interpenetrate each other [. . .] libidinally, the mother is almost to the same extent dependent on her baby as the baby is on her; neither of them may have this particular form of relationship and the particular satisfaction independently from the other."[25]

In the caesuric conception, the essence of analysis and the initial maternal holding of the infant necessarily begin by recognizing the strength of the birth crisis. It then aims to cross the chasm between the two discrete psyches that attempt to understand one another "from within." Both friction and joining, as well as bridging, are to be found in this process, along with the willingness to experience detachment and rejoining. As Aharoni and Bergstein note:

---

23 Piontelli, *From Fetus to Child*, 26.
24 Balint, *The Basic Fault*, 63.
25 Ibid., 67, 163.

The word caesura bears the meaning of an interruption of continuity and a sharp rending, followed by a continuation [. . .] The caesura itself is a process. Birth has duration, a continuum in time, which is not a "line," but an expanse with ends and a middle. It is a sort of "intermediate space" of paradoxical quality, and is situated between inside and out, cessation and continuity, closing and opening. Despite the force of the cut, the continuity exists.[26]

Bion's containing and contained model also suits caesuric continuity: just as the mother carries the fetus within her body during pregnancy, so, too, at the beginning of his life she continues to contain his soul within her consciousness. In a healthy or normal situation, the mother gives a name and meaning to a range of experiences, stimuli, and emotions that she experiences. In this manner, the infant learns the meaning of his feelings and thoughts. The maternal container is a bridge that expresses the pre-life relationship that had been forged between them.[27]

In a sense, the container and the contained exactly suit each other, yet they are consummately alien to one another. Already during the pregnancy, the infant is absolutely known to his mother, almost part of her body, even while he embodies the stranger, the inevitable other. The birth caesura links the foreign most closely. As Jessica Benjamin observes, every attachment is accompanied by duality and the constant tension between mutual recognition and self-assertion.[28] In any relationship, connection also entails detachment, and the unitary continuum marks its severance, just as any contact and connection accentuate the separateness between an individual and his fellow man.

3 Psychological Birth: Back and Forth

Birth can be viewed as a unique occurrence, as a collection of symbolic births, or as a protracted experience of being born. The decisive birth is the biological one, an unequivocal, one-time event which signals the transition between not being and being. This is matched by the additional psychological and spiritual births in human lives, some of which belong to the fetal life in the womb, while others come about in adult life, in the delivery rooms of the psyche, without cries, without blood, going almost unnoticed. Bion says: "I do it this way: When were you born? What was your birthplace? If you gave me the ordinarily accepted answers, I could say, 'No, that is very useful for the vital statistics of

---

[26] Aharoni and Bergstein, "Looking at the Future Born," 16–18.
[27] Bion, *Learning from Experience*; Amir, *On the Lyricism*, 8–12.
[28] Benjamin, *The Bonds of Love*.

the government who wants to know your birthday was on such-and-such a day of such-and-such a month of such-and-such a year. That would suit them fine.' But I would like to be able to say, 'Please tell me when your optic pits, at about the third somite, became functional. Tell me when your auditory pits became functional.' Of course, I know perfectly well that nobody can answer that question."[29]

Psychological birth, like the caesura, connects the gestational period with life after the departure from the womb. Winnicott writes:

> The basis for all theories about human personality development is continuity, the line of life, which presumably starts before the baby's actual birth; continuity which carries with it the idea that nothing that has been part of an individual's experience is lost, even if in various complex ways it should and does become unavailable to consciousness [. . .] Like Valdar the Oft-born, an infant is born all of various ways with the same inherited potential, but from the word Go! experiences and gathers experiences according to the point in time and space where he or she appears.[30]

Psychological birth can occur many times in a person's life, alongside the ongoing birth of the mother as a mother and as a human.[31]

Margaret Mahler discusses the idea of "psychological birth" in the context of her theory of separation and individuation, and locates its onset between the second and third years of life. This is the time when the child develops the ability to distinguish between self and other, and to recognize his parents, especially his mother, as objects separate from him. At times, psychological birth is delayed due to harsh environmental conditions or faulty genetic factors; there are instances in which children or adults never experience it.[32]

Thus, for example, Mahler compares the psychotic patient to the small infant, who is still in the "rapprochement" stages. She writes about both: "Neither seemed to have been psychologically born, that is to say, "tuned in" to the world of reality. What the youngest babies have not yet achieved, the psychotics have failed to achieve – psychological birth: that is to say, becoming a separate, individual entity, acquiring an, albeit primitive, first level of self-identity."[33] The psychotic's inability to perceive himself and his mother as separate and thereby

---

29 Bion, *The Italian Seminars*, 2–3. See also Bion, "On a Quotation from Freud," 515–517.
30 Winnicott, *Babies*, 90–91.
31 Rich, *Of Woman Born*.
32 Mahler, "A Study of the Separation-Individuation Process."
33 Mahler, "Symbiosis and Individuation," 89.

use her as a "beacon of orientation in the world of reality" leaves him in an infantile state and an illusionary symbiotic dyad.[34] How, wonders Mahler, do most infants nevertheless succeed in the transition from this liminal state of fusion with the mother during infancy to individuation as an adult? Mahler asserts that the central marker of psychological birth is connected with the energy of movement, namely, the infant's ability to physically distance himself from his mother, thereby signaling the conclusion of the process of emerging from the dyadic egg. Different forms of retrospection appear during this phase. At the start of the differentiation process, from the middle of the infant's first year, he moves away a bit from his mother and returns. Later on begins the child's cyclical process of departure and returning in a "checking back pattern."[35] Around the age of one, the child distances himself from his mother and returns to her for sensory and emotional refueling. Finally, at the age of two comes the stage that Mahler calls "rapprochement," in which the child learns the price of leaving and returning to the mother, and is willing to bear the pain of individuation.

I find that these models of drawing away and then drawing closer are analogous to the mystical term *ratzo ve-shov* ("running and returning"; see Ezek. 1:14: "darting to and fro"). The Kabbalists use this concept to describe their attitude to the divine communion with the Godhead, relating the element of *ratzo* with *ratzon* (the source of divine will), and their anchoring in the physical body and reality with the element of return. Conceptualizing the primal mother–infant attachment in the pattern of *ratzo ve-shov* enables us to understand the caesuric state as an experience that continues throughout life.

The Kabbalists' characterization of their experience as *ratzo ve-shov* addresses the tension in the mystic's soul: on the one hand, he longs for the omnipotent, distant experience of total communion with God, yet he also feels the need to return to the material world, the only one in which mystical activity can be realized and recognized, and acquire meaning.

This cyclical movement is the précis of spiritual life: to go forth to the encounter with the unknown, and then to return and discover that the mother is there for her child. In this context, Kabbalistic theory teaches that even the movement of *ratzo* actually entails return to the maternal source, since, by running away, a person returns to his inner place, which is both upper and lower, divine and earthly. The mother is to be found everywhere, like God, since "no place is empty of Him." Heaven and earth stand as a "home" for man, since the root of the distant soul is also his palace and his place. Life's progress derives

---

34 Ibid., 89 (emphasis is mine).
35 Mahler, "Rapprochement Subphase."

from the constant motion of being born and moving forward, along with going back. In a healthy state, an individual understands that there is no absolute communion. As this concept was put by the Baal Shem Tov: "Constant delight is not delight."

The term *ratzo ve-shov* first appears in Ezekiel's depiction (1:14) of the living creatures in his vision of the *Merkabah* (Divine Chariot). It then is mentioned in *Sefer Yetzirah* (the mystical *Book of Creation*):

> Ten Sefirot of Nothingness [*belimah*]
> Bridle your mouth from speaking
> And your heart from thinking
> And if your heart runs
> Return to that place.
> It is therefore written
> "The *chayot* ["living creatures"] running and returning [*ratzo ve-shov*]"
> Regarding this a covenant was made.[36]

In this passage, the *shuv* movement symbolizes the return to the divine source and the root of the soul – in other words, self-containment. An ethical and mystical interpretation of *Sefer Yetzirah* contains the knowledge of the Source and the ability to return to it. This ability is associated with silence, inner containment, and knowledge of God (who is called here *Makom*, or "Source"), in contrast with movement in other directions and the loss of the inner source.

According to Yehuda Liebes, division in thought (including the thought *of* division within the Godhead) is fleeting, before a sense of unity – which expresses the true reality of God, "to which all creatures, who are characterized by division and change, bow down" – returns.[37] This unity, veiled behind division, is highly mystical. In a metaphorical sense, we can say that it is the infant's ability to return to his mother (*shuv*), rather than his drawing away (*ratzo*), that reflects a process of maturation. The Kabbalists describe the difficulty of accomplishing *shuv* in reality, because of their hearts' desire for *ratzo* – that is, total mystical communion and detachment from this world. That the mystic chooses to return, as the infant chooses to return and gaze upon his mother, attests to the memory of that original unity which he retains, despite his separation from it. In terms of belief, the true, primal unity – between man and God, between infant and mother – is preserved, even if it would seem that separation has occurred in reality.

Indeed, unlike Mahler, who stresses the moment of separation as an individual achievement, Kohut claims that the cohesion of the self continues throughout

---

36 *Sefer Yetzirah* 1:8 (ed. Rubin, 119–120).
37 Liebes, *Sefer Yetzira*, 49–50.

one's whole life, and thus the moment of the movement of the child away from his mother turns into his desire to return. This theory suggests another interpretation of and different emphasis on the patterns of *ratzo ve-shov*.[38]

Contrasting with mobility enabling renewal and change, in some situations a person moves only in reverse, back to the fetal state. This is how Freud describes one expression of the death drive: as going backward, to self-annihilation, to the state before birth, to stasis. This idea was intriguingly developed by Sándor Ferenczi, who argued that children who are not wanted by their parents tend to commit suicide or choose death by such means as alcoholism, anorexia, depression, circulatory and breathing disorders, and impotence. He writes:

> Children who are received in a harsh and disagreeable way die easily and willingly. Either they use one of the many proffered organic possibilities for a quick exit, or if they escape this fate, they keep a streak of pessimism and of aversion to life [. . .] The child has to be induced, by means of an immense expenditure of love, tenderness and care, to forgive his parents for having brought him into the world without any intention on his part; otherwise the destructive instincts begin to stir immediately.[39]

Following Ferenczi, Hila Cohen observes that children who come into the world as undesirable guests will more easily drift back into "not being." The life-force is not innate within them, and they must make great efforts to acquire immunity from mental and physical harm.

Based on her belief in the possibility of healing severe damage, Anne Alvarez developed her theory of reclamation, which is meant to aid abuse victims, autistic children, or those suffering from severe deprivations and hurt to resurrect the dead parts within the psyche. The work of reclamation, like the spiritual work of the Kabbalists, aims to awaken the psyche and remind it of its will to live, and its consent to choose life. For Alvarez, children who were raised by mothers suffering from depression tend to develop a psychological proclivity to refuse life and a lack of faith in their ability to desire, progress, aspire, or even develop.[40]

Alvarez's notion of reclamation has its counterpart in the Kabbalistic conception of *tikkun*, which means delving into the regions of darkness and reviving the dead and abandoned parts, in both the individual soul and the cosmic and mythological sphere.[41] Reclamation, like caesura and psychological birth,

---

[38] Kohut, *How Does Analysis Cure?*.
[39] Ferenczi, "The Unwelcome Child and His Death-Instinct," 127–128.
[40] Alvarez, *Live Company*.
[41] For more on the concept of reparation in the analytic process: see Coltart, *The Baby*, 34. Coltart stresses four unique qualities which motivate the therapist: "giftedness, belief in the power of the unconscious (indeed in the unconscious itself), strength of purpose, reparativeness, and curiosity."

is described as an ongoing process, whose success is measured in the ability to move freely between the primordial state and adult life. When a person is willing to live with an awareness of the destructive and psychotic aspects of his mind, to go from a state of *ratzo* to one of *shuv*, to move between the extremities and be open to life, without controlling events, then the possibility of living a full life exists for him.

In the following sections, I will examine the archetypical model of birth connected to the depiction of *nesirah* ("sawing"), which is a central myth in the Kabbalistic literature. I will then link this to the psychoanalytic concept of spiritual and physical caesura. I will propose that the psychological process of separation is analogous to spiritual birth in midrash and in Kabbalah. In many senses, the infant's separation from his mother resembles the separation of the female from the male after the "sawing." Both models posit the existence of mutual, but unequal, relations of a hybrid nature.[42]

4 The Primeval Androgynous: The Myth of *Nesirah*

In *Genesis Rabbah*, we find the following passage:

> R. Jeremiah ben Leazar said: When the Holy One, blessed be He, created Adam, He created him a *hermaphrodite* [*androgynous*], for it is written, "Male and Female He created them and called their name *Adam*" (Gen. 5:2). R. Samuel ben Nahman said: When the Lord created Adam he created him *double-faced* [*du-partzufim*], then he split him [*nisro*] and made him of two backs, one back on this side and one back on the other side.[43]

This exposition offers an explanation for the contradictory descriptions of the creation of man in Genesis 1 and 2. In Genesis 1, God creates man and woman together, while in Genesis 2 man is created first, and woman is created later from his side. According to this midrash, Adam was created as a creature that combined both male and female, with the two parts joined together, back to back. The two halves of this entity are later separated into man and woman. The terms *du-partzufim* and "androgynous" come from the Greek.[44] Both evoke

---

42 Asulin, "Stature."
43 *Genesis Rabbah* 85:11 (ed. Albeck I, 55; emphasis is mine).
44 BT Berakhot 61a uses the term "double-faced" rather than "androgynous," indicating that the side from which the woman was built up parallels the "face" or "tail." "Face" means a part equal to the male, while "tail" means a lower, animalistic part. In contrast to the quality of *partzufim*, the perception of woman as a "tail" creates a discriminating hierarchy. Boyarin proposes that the teaching of R. Shemuel ("two-faced") is an interpretation of the opinion of R. Yirmiya b. Elazar ("androgynous"). In his view, in both instances we are told that the first

the recurring legend of the separation of the sexes that also appears in Plato's *Symposium*. According to the latter tradition, which is voiced by the Athenian comic playwright Aristophanes, human beings were created as spherical creatures that were cruelly cut in half by Zeus, who sought to weaken them:

> He spoke and cut men in two, like a sorb-apple which is halved for pickling, or as you might divide an egg with a hair [. . .] After the division the two parts of man, each desiring his other half, came together, and throwing their arms about one another, entwined in mutual embraces [. . .] And when one of them meets with the other half, the actual half of himself, whether he be a lover of youth or a lover of another sort, the pair are lost in an amazement of love and friendship and intimacy [. . .] And the reason is that human nature was originally one and we were a whole, and the desire and pursuit of the whole is called love [Eros].[45]

In contrast to the ancient legend, which views the appearance of Eros as a result of trauma and suffering inflicted by jealous gods, the Rabbinic midrash views the "sawing" (*nesirah*) as part of the process of Creation and God's gift to man. Thanks to this separation, procreation is possible, a theme that is developed in the Kabbalistic world.[46] The myth of "sawing" seeks to reconcile the two Creation narratives, and proposes that man and woman were first created as a single body fused back to back. Thereafter, woman appears before man as a side or flank made from him, "bone of my bones and flesh of my flesh." According to Karen Horney, this legend, in which woman is "born" of man, like an infant born from his mother's womb, reflects the "womb envy" of male writers and theoreticians.[47]

This myth could also be read in another way as a symbolic process whereby man discovers his "true self" and undergoes a spiritual individuation of the parts of his psyche.[48] The *Zohar* illustrates the characteristic loneliness of created humans as a back-to-back situation. Although this construction seemingly provides physical closeness, it signifies the greatest distance between man and

---

creature was bisexual – a hermaphrodite, two sexes within a single body, and like Siamese twins separated through surgery. Boyarin, *Carnal Israel*, 36–44. Moshe Idel indicates that the Kabbalists prefer the term *du-partzufim* because the halakhic discourse sees the androgynous as a damaged creature. Idel, *Kabbalah and Eros*, 98.

45 Plato, *Symposium*, 189c–193d.
46 As Idel emphasizes in *Kabbalah and Eros*, 53–103. In Plato's depiction, there are three types of creatures: all-male, all-female, and androgynous (half-male and half-female). The Sages recognize this third possibility, for it is only by means of such an arrangement that procreation could take place.
47 Horney, *Feminine Psychology*.
48 Jung and Kerenyi, *Essays*. On Philo's interpretation of Eve based on Platonic dualism, see Boyarin, *Carnal Israel*, ch. 1.

himself, and between male and female.⁴⁹ It is precisely with regard to this situation, says the *Zohar* (3:44b; emphasis added), that God says: "It is not good that the man should be alone":

> Adam was created with two faces [. . .] However, he did not engage with his female, and she was not a helper facing him, since she was at his side and they were as one back-to-back. So, Adam was alone [. . .] What did the blessed Holy One do? He sawed him, and took the female from him [. . .] He adorned her like a bride and brought her so that she would be facing him, face-to-face.⁵⁰

Here, the description of the woman as a *tzela* ("side") has the sense of a "helper" or "support" for the man. The *Zohar* emphasizes that support can be created only through healthy distance, and not between entities that are joined back to back. Each side can appreciate the personality of the other, but only when they are separate.

In a different teaching, the *Zohar* presents Eve as having been intended for Adam from the moment of her creation. This emphasis represents a polemic against a tradition rooted in so-called "Ancient Books," according to which Lilith, not Eve, was the first woman. Indeed, in the ninth-century *Toledot Ben Sira*, prior to the creation of Eve Lilith flees from Adam, since she refuses to be subservient to him:⁵¹

> When the Holy One, blessed be He, created His world, and created Adam, He saw that [Adam] was alone. He created a wife for him from the ground, like himself, and called her Lilith, and brought her to Adam. Right away they started arguing: He said, "You will lie beneath," while she said, "You will be beneath, since both of us are equal and we are both from the ground."⁵²

The midrash goes on to describe how Lilith is forced to sacrifice one hundred of her babies every day in order to gain her freedom. She remains in the cities of the sea, choosing not to return to Adam. In contrast to *Toledot Ben Sira*, the *Zohar* (3:19a, 44b) declares that only Eve, who emerges from Adam's side, is his true partner, since she belongs to him from the root of his soul, (as opposed to Lilith, who is created from the earth):

> The blessed Holy One sawed Adam and prepared his female, as it is written, "YHWH Elohim built *ha-tsela*, the side [. . .]" (Gen. 2:22). "*The* side" – as already established, as it is

---

49 For a discussion of the spiritual processes of individuation and the symbolism of the states of "back" and "face," see Pedaya, *Psychoanalysis and Kabbala*, Chapter 6.
50 *Zohar* 3:44b (Matt, 7, 272).
51 Yassif, *Ben Sira*, 63–71, 231–234.
52 Ibid., 231–232.

said, "And on the side of the Sanctuary [. . .]" (Ex. 26:20). "And He brought her to Adam" (Gen. 2:22) – adorned like a bride for the canopy. And in the Ancient Books it is written that she [Lilith] had fled from Adam before this. But we have not learned so.[53]

According to this reading, God "saws" Adam and Eve apart and transforms their connection from a static physical fusion into a spiritual union of love and attraction, one that is associated with the image of being "adorned like a bride for the canopy." This text depicts the soul, which starts off unified, as undergoing a "sawing" that parallels the sawing of the bodies, in contrast to the idea that the soul is divided from the onset into male and female halves. The notion of the spiritual androgynous and the "androgynous soul" is developed in medieval exegesis, starting with the philosophy of Saadia Gaon and continuing in the writings of the Spanish Kabbalists and the *Zohar* (1:91),[54] and it is evinced in the following excerpt:

> At the moment the blessed Holy One brings forth souls into the world, all those spirits and souls comprise male and female joined as one. They are transmitted into the hands of the emissary appointed over human conception [. . .] When the time of their coupling arrives, the blessed Holy One, who knows those spirits and souls, unites them as at first and issues a proclamation. When they unite they become a single body, a single soul, right and left, fittingly. (*Zohar* 1:91b [Matt, 2, 76–78])

This teaching describes the descent of the souls of males and females from the "treasury of souls," via the lower Garden of Eden, to this world and into human bodies.[55] The original conception of the souls is effected by an angel whose name is *Laylah* ("Night").[56] While in Rabbinical thought this angel is "appointed over human conception," in Kabbalistic thought this angel is also the one who pairs up all the souls.

In Charles Mopsik's view, these Zoharic teachings reflect the wish for unity of the soul, a desire that is more profound than that for physical unity. Mopsik emphasizes that gender and sexual identity – that is, the biological and social differences between male and female – signify the more primal and profound difference between the male and female parts of the soul, which were separated from each other. The gender distinction is not essential, but the result of primal sawing; therefore, an individual manifesting as a man or a woman constantly

---

53 *Zohar* 3:19a, 44b. Cf. *Zohar* 1:34b, where we find another tradition hinting that Lilith was from Adam's *tzela* (the term *tzela* recalling the Aramaic word for "catastrophe").
54 Mopsik, *Sex of the Soul*, 5–52; Idel, *Kabbalah and Eros*, 73–81.
55 See, for example, *Zohar* 1:91b; 2:246a; 3:43, 283b. See also the discussion in Tishby, *Wisdom*, 607–609.
56 For more on the angel appointed over conception, see BT Niddah 16b; *Seder Yetzirat ha-Valad*; Urbach, *The Sages*, 217. For the androgynous soul, see Idel, *Kabbalah: New Perspectives*, 120–126; Liebes, "Sections of the Zohar Lexicon," 459.

testifies to the androgynous source from which human beings are created.[57] This idea appears in another Zoharic teaching, which draws a connection between the creation of Adam and Eve, on the one hand, and the entire genealogical chain from Genesis through Exodus, on the other.[58]

The *Zohar*, like Plato in the *Symposium*, teaches that it is rare for one to meet up with one's destined soul mate; as a rule, humans are not fortunate enough to find their other half. Most often, people are motivated by concern "lest someone else snatch his intended consort, through prayer" (BT Moed Katan 18b). Nevertheless, every soul, without exception, seeks its completion in the other.[59]

As Moshe Idel notes, the Kabbalists view androgyny as a deficient state of being, since it offers no possibility of procreation or real Eros.[60] The process of sawing that separates the man from the woman is reminiscent of the moment of human birth and imitates the cutting of the umbilical cord, separating the infant from his mother's body. As we will see, the primeval differentiation between the sexes corresponds to the psychological processes of two entities necessarily separate from one another.

5 Caesura and Sawing

The caesura of birth archetypically connects the infant's relationship with his mother to the relationship patterns of his entire adult life. This is especially so for the spousal bond, which reconstructs patterns of that initial fusion and separation in order to facilitate adult erotic relations and procreation. In order to truly meet, the male and the female must undergo a process of differentiation that parallels the early caesuric movement.

An examination of these parallel processes, caesuric (for the infant) and sawing (for the couple), demonstrates how the midrashic structure transfers the containing–contained relationship of the mother and child (as it naturally takes place chronologically, when life begins) to that of a male and female couple. Psychoanalysts emphasize the mother–infant process as an underlying,

---

57 Mopsik, *Sex of the Soul*, 31–32.
58 *Zohar* 3:117a (Matt, 8, 250–253). See Lachower and Tishby, *Wisdom*, 867–940.
59 For more on this idea, see Kaniel, "Between Kabbalah, Gender and Law."
60 Idel, "Androgynes." As he emphasizes, in the Kabbalistic view the urge for sexual union leads to the "augmentation of divinity by procreation," and this situation unquestionably stands in contradiction to the aspiration to return to a primal unity such as the androgynous. Even an ecstatic Kabbalist like Abraham Abulafia notes that the *gematria* of the word "androgynous" equals that of "male and female" (39).

and fundamental, image, and Kabbalists emphasize the relations between the couple. *The infant is sawed from its mother, just as Eve, the archetypical woman, is sawed from her mate.*

The term "caesura" and the Hebrew *nesirah* are similar in meaning and in sound. Despite their disparate etymological roots, I propose that they create a proximate semantic field.[61] Each word communicates a continuing process, which both joins and detaches. Each word addresses the transition between various stages of birth: from the womb to the biological birth, from the biological birth to the psychological birth, and then – as the Kabbalists elucidate – from the psychological birth to the mystical one. The soul, too, must be sawed and experience caesura so that it may be born in the spiritual dimension, one which corresponds to biological and psychological birth.

Both caesura and sawing describe a slow, developing process (unlike the sharp, unequivocal movement associated with the word "cutting"). The slowness of the sawing could be either pleasurable or agonizing, depending on the conditions that enable it: the image of God, the mother who saws, or the individual experience of the sawed creature, which matches the infant who passes through the caesura.[62]

These two processes, caesura and sawing, connect the fetal state and the androgynous state. In each, the initial state is one of connection: just as the primeval androgynous soul was created joined back to back, so, too, was the fetus within its mother. Afterwards, the mother receives the infant that came forth from her womb, a situation which corresponds to the desire of the male and the female in the Kabbalistic myth to meet "face to face."

As we have seen, the separation created by the sawing allows for the transition from the symbiotic state to a meeting of two subjects. Gen. 2:21 relates: "So the Lord God *caused a deep sleep* to fall upon the man, and while he slept took one of his ribs *and closed up its place with flesh*" (emphasis is mine). The sawing is a sort of operation that God performs, while Adam is sleeping, for the separation and restoration of the parts that were joined like a mother and her fetus.

While the Rabbis are concerned with the human male and female who were sawed by God, in both the *Zohar* and Lurianic Kabbalah the sawing occurs *within the Godhead*. At first, the divine qualities pass from an alienated state ("back to back") to a "face-to-face" encounter, which is a fertile situation that

---

61 On the verb *nsr* in the Bible, see Isaiah 10:15. For a possible connection between the caesarean section and the life of the Roman imperators (*caesus*), as it appears in the *Sefer Yossippon*, see Preuss, *Medicine*, 421–426. See also M. Niddah 40:1; M. Keritot 7:2; Carmeli, "Dead Mother."
62 Aharoni, "Brit bein ha-Betarim."

produces offspring. Following this event in the Sefirotic system, the sawing is transferred to the human world, as well. The souls and bodies of this world, and not only the lower *sefirot*, are born from within the upper *sefirot*.

Lurianic Kabbalah, which flourished in the sixteenth century, situated the *kavvanot* (mystical intents) of "sawing" in the practical ritual plane. Sawing occurs in times of transition, such as the beginning of the new year or when night overtakes day. The two days of Rosh Hashanah, with its rituals, represent the sleep that fell on Adam during the Creation and the sawing of Eve from his body, as the archetype of this-worldly male–female relations and of constant birth (of Adam and Eve, and of all humans). The *kavvanot* of sawing are associated with additional rituals, such as *Tikkun Hatzot* (the prayer recited in the middle of the night, lamenting the loss of the Temple and yearning for the Redemption), the blessings recited upon arising in the morning, those connected with the seventh day of Passover, and, obviously, the Seven Blessings recited at weddings, which the Kabbalists understand as directed to the *Shekhinah*, which goes from a "back-to-back" position to standing "face to face" with its spouse. As Pinchas Giller stresses, Lurianic Kabbalah views the sawing as a repetitive process that symbolizes spiritual procreation, and he thinks that it is related to the perception of the upper *Sefirot* as parents who adorn the lower couple – *Tiferet* and *Malkhut* – with new crowns while they themselves are capable of giving birth to worlds and souls.[63]

Taking another tack, the sawing mythos can be seen as revolving around the psychological question of whether the fundamental human situation is one of being "alone" or "together." The Rabbis debate whether the side from which the woman was created corresponds to the *partzuf* (i.e., "face" or "countenance") or to the "tail." "Face" symbolizes a significant part of the male, while the "tail" is marginal, bestial, and abject.[64] If the woman was created from the tail, then the man is ontologically superior to her while remaining in his existential solitude. If both were created back to back, and the *tzela* means "face," then their faces will be equivalent, and a model of partnership and connection underlies their creation.

The relation between caesura and sawing draws a parallel between these questions and the psychoanalytic disagreement about what comes first: the unitary mother–infant dyad or the differentiation between them? Mahler and others are of the opinion that *unification precedes differentiation*, and therefore the initial fusion with the mother is the source of human confidence in the

---

[63] Giller, *Shalom*, 131–146.
[64] BT Berakhot 61a.

future. Unlike this opinion, Daniel Stern argues that the challenge is posed by connection, specifically, since the mother–infant symbiosis is an illusion. The perception of the "nuclear self" precedes any other perception by the infant, and there is no fusion between him and his mother. Stern writes:

> Infants begin to experience a sense of an emergent self from birth [. . .] They never experience a period of total self/other undifferentiation. There is no confusion between self and other in the beginning or at any point during infancy. [. . .] There is no symbiotic-like phase. In fact, the subjective experiences of union with another can occur only after a sense of a core self and a core other exists. Union experiences are thus viewed as the successful result of actively organizing the experience of self-being-with-another, rather than as the product of a passive failure of the ability to differentiate self from other.[65]

Similar to Stern's emphatic view, Irigaray asserts that, while still in the womb, the placenta separates the fetus from its mother, and signifies a paradoxical and mutually vital partition that permanently divides them.[66] Even if this is true, following those who regard the dyad as illusory, such a fantasy lies at the basis of numerous myths and facilitates viewing the womb as a protected place to which a person can always return.

The verses relating to the creation of man in the first chapters of Genesis can be read in light of Stern's differentiation theory, as well as in accordance with that of fusion. In Genesis 1 (which the Documentary Hypothesis ascribes to the Priestly source), the creation of man and woman is simultaneous and therefore nonhierarchical: "Then God said, 'Let us make man in our image, after our likeness' [. . .] So God created man in his own image, in the image of God he created him; male and female he created them" (v. 26–27). On the other hand, Genesis 2 (attributed to the Yahwist source) presents an archetype centered on a single human. This depiction constructs an unequal relationship between Adam and Eve. Many things happen between the moment when the male is created and from when God creates the female from his side: God makes grow "every tree that is pleasant to the sight" in the Garden, causes four rivers to flow (2:10), creates the animals, and, according to the midrash, finds a mate for each. The creation of woman appears only at the end of this narrative (Gen. 2:7–24).

As we have seen, the role of the male in Genesis 2 is filled in psychoanalysis by the mother. The infant is born from her body, just as the woman was created from the body of the man ("bone of my bones and flesh of my flesh"). Lurianic Kabbalah portrays the Upper Mother as continually "sawing" her children. This

---

[65] Stern, *The Interpersonal World*, 26.
[66] Irigaray, *Je, Tu, Nous*, 41–42.

mother continues to give birth to her children: the bride and groom, the *sefirot* of *Tiferet* and *Malkhut*. Thus, the sexual narrative is joined with the maternal one to form a single unitary mythos in which wedding fuses with birth.

Bion, as well, mentions that the container–contained imagery does not ensue entirely from the parental field and maternal containing, but also from the spousal bond, which he compares to the connection between "preconception" and "conception" – that is, the infant's anticipation of meeting the breast, his frustration when this expectation is not met, and his having to instead to have a "negative realization." Bion understands the term "conception" as the product of a mating process that is connected to the way in which the infant learns to tolerate frustration and to create from within it a new thought.[67] Thus, the infant's early experience provides the foundation for mating, just as, in mythical and Kabbalistic thought, the connection of the male and the female is the basis for the annals of heaven and earth.

6 The Three Stages of Mythical Birth: Light, Water, and Firmament

The psychological caesura of birth corresponds to both physical and cosmic processes. As we have seen, the *Zohar* perceives birth as a descent to a "dark, base land." The first step of the journey begins with the imperative to "Go from your country" (Gen. 12), leaving behind all that is near and familiar. The danger is that human birth will not be a connecting bridge, but a yawning chasm that lies in wait for the individual – as well as for the entire created cosmos. Opposition to going forth into the world, which finds expression in psychoanalytic and Kabbalistic discussions, is easily understood in light of these fears.

We will examine the portrayal of birth in *Zohar, Terumah* (*Zohar* 2:167a–b). The Zoharic exposition that identifies femininity with the primordial, turbid material from which life begins is based on the ancient notion that view the woman, not only as the source of life, but also as the root of death; it reflects the tensions regarding the fetus's desire to be born, even as it resists coming into the world.

---

67 Bion, *Second Thoughts*. Biran, *The Courage of Simplicity*, 57, states: "Without thinking, living is impossible. The potential for thinking is infinite: new preconceptions will always arise, becoming thoughts, which, in turn, will become concepts. As concepts become saturated, they turn static, losing their vitality."

The *Zohar* on the weekly Torah portion of *Terumah* draws a parallel between the three lights created on the first day of Creation and the three elements and phases from which the world and man were created. The *Zohar* connects the first light with the *sefirah* of *Hesed*, to which "Let there be light" (Gen. 1:3) refers; the second light, in which darkness and the *Sitra Ahra* (the embodiment of all evil) are innate, symbolizes *Din* (strict judgment), about which "and there was light" (Gen. 1:3) refers; last to be created is the light of the *sefirah* of *Tiferet* that divides and strikes a balance between the first two lights, and to which the wording "and God separated the light from the darkness" (Gen. 1:40) refers. A tripartite structure is known from the ancient world and Rabbinic literature, but the *Zohar* links cosmology with cosmogony, both of which are reflected in the creation of humankind. Man was created from the three elements of light-water-firmament, which correspond to the emanation of these three lights.[68]

The initial formation of the fetus comes from the supernal light, which corresponds to the paternal sperm. This is joined by the water – the amorphous and threatening "moisture" and the maternal material – as the body begins to take shape. Finally, when the body has been formed (in the language of the *Zohar*, "congealed"), the shape of the fetus is joined by the material known as "firmament," which gives him shape, and composes a person's countenance. *These are the three stages of coming into being*: first, the sperm is transformed into water; then water becomes skin, tissues, bones, and ligaments; and lastly, the congealed firmament becomes the fetus (and the universe). In the end of the exposition, the *Zohar* accentuates that when a person comes forth into the world, the so-called "waste matter" is separated from him and falls away.

According to this exposition, all that is positive and illuminating, glistening and white, is attributed to the sperm, life, and light, which derive from the male, the father. In contrast, all that threatens and is dangerous, frightening, and mysterious comes from the female, the mother. This conception is analogous to the psychoanalytic theories that identify the semiotic (as expressing the primal, physical, and sensual attachment to the mother that precedes the paternal function of language) and the maternal with the dark and "moist," and view the mother's womb as having a primordial quality, one which both attracts and

---

68 Berman, *Divine and Demonic*, 183–189. Berman discusses the "procreational purification" that was involved in the process of Creation. According to him, the purging of refuse is a necessary ontological and expository preparation that reflects the Zoharic "management of ambivalence" (189). On the tripartite structure of water, fire, and air, see, for example, *Sefer Yetzirah*. The *Zohar* (2:167a–b) suggests a concentric image instead of a linear development for these three elements.

threatens.[69] As opposed to male concentration and solidity, the feminine represents the "fluid" quality that enables transformation – but typifies chaos.[70]

In ancient anatomical thought, the male's superiority to the female ensued from the heat in his body, unlike the moisture and cold in that of the female.[71] This is mirrored in the contrast drawn between light and water, which are placed, respectively, to the right and the left: *Hesed* as opposed to *Din*. The female quality appears in the stage in which the sperm and the light begin to spread. The process of expansion reaches to all sides, until the human countenance and the complete body emerge from within it. This is the moment of birth itself, the third light that comes and, as the *Zohar* puts this, integrates the two other lights. The human countenance symbolizes the quality that balances between *Hesed* and *Din*, father and mother, light and water.

Although in most instances the *Zohar* associates water with *Hesed* and the male, here it is affiliated with the feminine. As matter that is immaterial, imperceptible, and amorphous, and which embodies transition, water has an inherently liminal quality. It is only when the firmament congeals that we can speak of a human being possessing matter and materiality. An additional feminine association is lent by amniotic fluid, a substance expressed by a mother's womb together with the infant. This conception resembles Philo of Alexandria's statement that the being created in Genesis 1 symbolizes pure intelligence, divorced from the material, while Genesis 2 speaks of the man connected to the female, that is, to corporeality (the body) and matter, which necessarily possesses "turbidity."[72]

Like other scientific fields, and in gynecology as well, medieval sources relied upon the classical approaches of Hippocrates, Galen, and Soranus, as well as on Aristotle's theory of basic humors, all of which agreed that a woman is an "imperfect" man, and that she is composed of "impure" matter.[73] The Zoharic exposition likewise depicts sperm as illuminated male abundance that descends from the mind and the female waters as containing turbidity, blood, and harsh judgments, which receive male and female form from within the "waste matter."

The human being appears in the liminal period between water and its congealment into firmament. An indecipherable difference between matter and spirit might already have existed within the light, but the process of differentiation

---

69 Kristeva, *Powers*; idem, *Black Sun*.
70 Cixous and Clément, *Newly Born*.
71 Barkai, *Science*.
72 Philo, *On the Creation*.
73 Preuss, *Medicine*, 374–432; Fonrobert, *Menstrual Purity*.

intensifies upon the appearance of the waters and their separation.[74] The chain of actions resembles alchemical movement, in which the thickening of the light transforms it into water, the spread of the waters produces the firmament and leads to its demarcation, and finally the congealment of fluids enables the body to close. The waste matter (the muddy water, the amniotic fluid) is then cast out, and the infant is revealed.

The separation of the waste matter matches the transition stage of physical birth, in which the pain and anxiety of giving birth cause many women to feel they can bear no more, as they undergo what seems to be a near-death experience.[75] Then comes the third, final, stage, in which the placenta and embryonic fluid emerge; the "harsh judgments" are expunged, the umbilical cord is cut, and then there is a moment of solitude and detachment leading to the meeting of mother and infant. The sound of the first crying is the caesura that is the bridge to a new beginning.

Thales of Miletus, one of the first pre-Socratic philosophers (who lived during the late seventh to the mid-sixth century BCE), stated that water is the element from which the universe was created, and therefore "everything is water." The *Zohar* correspondingly proposes that water is the hydraulic matter from which the embryo is created. Turning the water and moisture remaining in the womb into so-called "waste matter," according to the *Zohar*, represents the completion of Creation. Like a sculptor who sees a statue as an independent entity waiting to burst forth from stone, the Kabbalists regard the Creation of the world and man as a process of removing the waste, peeling away the husks, and draining the "muddy water" to allow the essential form to be revealed. Successful birth is paradoxically dependent on the *birth of the waste*. This marks the completion of the last transformation, in which the water becomes firmament and the embryo is formed and becomes a whole entity. This is the moment of caesura, of rending that connects, of hewing that imparts form.

In a Neoplatonic sense, the light characterizes a phase so early in the chain of emanation that it cannot be called a "thing." In its earliest source, with no form or shape whatsoever, this is the most attenuated of any state, completely abstract and spiritual. The qualities below the light, such as the sun and the moon, correspond to the soul under the intellect. From the first refined light emanate powers and lights with different levels of opacity from which, finally, man is created. While the Zoharic light contains turbidity and chaos, the "source" in Neoplatonic thought is whole and lacks nothing:

---

74 Pedaya, "'Possessed by Speech.'".
75 Balaskas, *New Active Birth*.

> But each thing of necessity must give of its own to something else as well, or the Good will not be the Good, or Intellect Intellect, or the soul this that it is, unless with the primal living some secondary life lives as long as the primal exists. Of necessity, then, all things must exist for ever in ordered dependence upon each other: those other than the First have come into being in the sense that they are derived from other, higher, principles. Things that are said to have come into being did not just come into being, but always will be in the process of becoming.[76]

This Zoharic exposition plainly implies that the appearance of the body compromises one's complete spiritual potential, and that the flesh-and-blood human is born upon the appearance of waste matter and the congealment of the firmament. A picture emerges of a flow between vessels, and the passage of lights: the watery state of the second day includes the illuminated state of the first day, and is eventually solidified in the container of the third day. Man is built stage by stage, and the mutual dependence of the components of Creation generates harmony between them. The light has no meaning without the water, just as the body signifies nothing without the waste matter. Man comes into being in circular processes of refinement and containment, while the role of symbolic mother is filled by the function of the preceding creation – the quality already present in the world.

Just as *bohu* means that "*bo hu*" ("the essence") is in it, in contrast to *tohu* (which possesses no such essence), so too "the waters are substantive" in relation to the light that preceded them. Likewise, the form of the archetypical embryo and its split into male and female is built on the foundation of the firmament that is separated and congealed. This and similar expositions generate an experience of being contained and of containing, along with internal upheaval and a movement of constant atomization. They seemingly wish to depict a gradual departure from the infinite – which, at the same time, means being cast out from the supernal bosom.[77] The culmination of this process consists of the emergence of the turbid water and the gender differentiation between male and female. In the conclusion of the exposition, the *Zohar* hints that the mother does not give birth only to an infant, but also to blood: the "life of the flesh is in the blood" (Gen. 9:6; Lev. 17:11), and life is also the divine strict (harsh) judgment that is intrinsically bound up with the female essence. The *Zohar* developed the ancient conception that the source of moisture and blood – and its attendant imperfection and unnerving formlessness – is the female, and applied this to the perception of the cosmos as a whole. Thus the forces of the *Sitra Ahra* are born in the universe along with the woman, and, in the words of the Rabbis, "when she was born, the Devil was born

---

76 Plotinus, *Enneads*, 2.9. See also Chapter 6, Section 1.
77 Hellner-Eshed, *River*, 321–339.

together with her" (*Genesis Rabbah* 17:6). After all, psychoanalysis did not emerge by chance from the study of female hysteria (in Greek, the meaning of the word womb, *hystera*) and from the attempt to understand the function of the womb as a home that is not a home, as an uncanny (*unheimliche*) place, one of ceaseless wandering, threat, and attraction.[78]

---

[78] See entry in Montanari, *Dictionary*, 2243–2244, *hystera; hysterikos*.

Chapter 4
"The Womb Is a Tomb": The Imagery of the Uterus and Female Guilt and Death

Birth results from the involuntary contraction of muscles of the uterine wall until its full dilation and the ejection of the fetus and the placenta. The birth process begins with the descent of the fetus's head to the birth channel, and the appearance of birth pangs. These pangs are characterized by their intensity, duration, and the intervals between one and the next. This process has three stages: the first, the opening and dilation of the cervix; the second, in which the infant exits the womb; and the third, the separation and ejection of the placenta. In the first stage of birth, pangs appear at intervals of three to four minutes, with every pang lasting forty-five to ninety seconds. When these pangs begin, the womb divides into two parts: the thick, strong upper part, which actively contracts; and the thin, expanding lower part, which remains passive. Consequently, the strong contractions of the upper part push the fetus downward, while the lower part expands, enabling the passage of the fetus from the mother's body. In order to complete the birth, the birthing mother exerts voluntary intra-uterine pressure which aids in pushing out the fetus.

With the onset of contractions, oxytocin is released in the woman's brain causing cervical effacement. Oxytocin is dubbed the "love hormone," as it is also responsible for the attachment bond between the mother and her child. The purpose of the contractions is to push the baby and bring him/her to the opening of the birth canal. As the birth progresses the sensation of pain increases and adrenaline is secreted from the adrenal gland, in response to the mother's physical exertion and stress. Adrenaline increases the mother's heart rate and raises her blood pressure. In this heightened state the body receives an influx of energy, becoming more active, as well as more alert. At this final stage of the birth process (also known as "transition") many women feel that they can no longer endure the pain. Due to the increased intensity of the pain, an experienced midwife will recognize this as a signal that the birth process is coming to its conclusion. Janet Balaskas describes this stage as involving feelings of despair and loss of faith, acute physical feelings of being torn to pieces, terror and even a desire for death.

The birth process involves areas of consciousness that are usually inactive in daily life. The active part is the neo-cortex, the thinking brain, which is responsible for rational thinking and self-awareness. In order that the birth process progresses quickly and without complications, the woman must detach herself from the neo-cortex and connect to the hypothalamus, the ancient and primitive part of her mind.

A woman connected to her hypothalmic experience is not aware of those around her, but rather she concentrates on her inner world. Her body (as opposed to her mind) leads her, moving her in a way that will help the fetus to emerge. Sometimes, her voice will produce strange and wild sounds, as she returns to a natural state of nudity. These bodily changes allow the uterus to open and the pelvic bones to move aside for the baby to be safely born. During the last stage of the intense contractions, the brain releases endorphins. Endorphins are a natural pain reliever, which causes a change in consciousness and allows for a pervasive feeling of euphoria and unity. The moment after the baby is born is described by many mothers as a feeling of ecstasy and transcendence, one that they have never felt before. This "hormonal cocktail" of endorphins and oxytocin which floods the body of the woman, and her newborn child, also holds in its sway the witnesses present to the miracle of birth.

***

This chapter will examine the diverse images of the uterus that influence the way in which birth is perceived in the midrashic and Kabbalistic literatures. Prior to the modern period, of course, the death of women in childbirth was a common occurrence, and this sad fact underlies the Rabbinic and Kabbalistic attitude toward birth. Thus, for instance, the Rabbis view the womb as a prison, a tomb, and an inside-out purse, which differs essentially from its portrayal as *aron ha-kodesh* ("the holy ark") in Cordoverian Kabbalah. All of these images reflect attempts to deal with the fear of death through the mythical symbolization and mentalization of the uterine life. The Talmud's descriptions of the womb as a "folded writing tablet" or as the Garden of Eden[1] are in stark contrast to its depiction as a place of "sewers [. . .] and garbage" or its midrashic comparison to hell.[2] Each of these images creates a conceptual clustering that offers an original illustration of the flesh–spirit connection. In this chapter, we will encounter a range of religious, gender, biological, and emotional conceptions – some depressing, others empowering – that together reflect the changes that the perception of birth underwent over the course of time.

1 Compassion or Harm by the Womb?

Mythological ideas, many of which would later be refuted, were prevalent in ancient understandings of gynecology. Thus, for example, mythology informed

---

[1] BT Niddah 30b.
[2] BT Shabbat 152a.

theories about how a woman could become pregnant with a son rather than a daughter, the side of the uterus in which each of the sexes comes into being, and descriptions of the interior of the uterus (without, of course, the benefit of confirmation by ultrasound). The arrival of the infant into the world and the precise occurrences of the moment of birth inspired conjecture and speculation. The Hippocratic school taught that birth pangs result from the fetus tearing "chords" that surround the "nest," or womb. This conception suggests that the ancients believed that the fetus actively extricated itself from the straits of the womb closing in upon it, unlike the mother who was seen as completely passive during birth and as dependent upon the infant for this process to succeed.[3]

Hippocrates's ideas found a welcome home in the thought of the Rabbis. A midrash in *Leviticus Rabbah* portrays the womb as a prison from which the fetus seeks to escape, and then adds:

> R. Simon said: The abdomen of a woman consists of many cavities, many coils, and many bands, so that when she sits on the travailing chair, she does not cast out the fetus all at once. There is a popular saying: "When one band is loosened, two bands are loosened."[4]

In this exposition, at the moment of birth the mother, in her compassion, does not cast out the infant from her womb all at once, but rather allows him to release the chords of the womb one by one. This is an example of the mother's compassion (alluded to in the connection of the words *rehem* and *rahmanut*). The midrash then describes how greatly the fetus suffers in that prison-like place, and how God helps it to be freed from its incarceration (see below for more on this theme). The Rabbis' view of the infant as an agent of his own birth is a concept that recurs in the ideas we have seen expressed by Donald Winnicott and in the "fetal memory" of Wilfred Bion and Alexandra Piontelli. Such midrashim attempt, in their own way, to portray a newborn overcoming the caesura, and thereby to forge continuity between the life of the soul in the womb and post-natal development. At the same time, this midrash reflects gender oppression through the way in which the maternal experience and the mother's agency are sidelined. The misogynistic view that birth results solely from action by the fetus, while the mother and her body are cast as being totally passive, has been critiqued by feminists such as Adrienne Rich, Janet Balaskas, and Emily Martin, who have called upon women to reclaim ownership of this experience, in which the mother's actions influence her life and the development of the fetus.[5]

---

3 Naeh, "Hippocratic Concepts."
4 *Leviticus Rabbah* 14:3.
5 Martin, *The Woman*; Balaskas, *New Active Birth*; Rich, *Of Woman Born*, 190–220.

The Bible connects the root *hvl* (the root in *hevlei leidah*, "birth pangs") with birthing, as in, for instance, the Song of Songs (8:5): "There your mother was in travail [*hiblatkha*] with you." In addition to the actions of tying and releasing, it also alludes to the relationship between birth and *habalah* ("injury"). In contrast to the notion that only the fetus is harmed during birth, in the Hippocratic and midrashic conception the infant harms *his mother's body* when it tries to free itself from the womb's membranous chords.

The motif of the womb's chords underwent a metaphorical transformation in the *Zohar*, which presents the maternal womb as a bird's nest between whose *havalim* (meaning both "throes" and "chords") the Kabbalists "nest" within the womb of the *Shekhinah*.[6] The Kabbalistic literature uses this imagery to connect the model of the mother–infant relationship with that of the relationship between God and man. Birth and the infant's/man's extrication are made possible by the symbolic actions of the mother/God, with emphasis placed on the bond and partnership between both parties. The active human self-extrication does not contradict the miraculous rescue from above, as is also indicated by the affinity of the phrases *hevlei ledah* ("birth pangs", "ropes"), *hevlei mashiah* ("pangs of the Messiah"), and *hevlei geula* ("pangs of redemption").[7] These images draw into sharp focus the paradoxical caesura of the birth experience, which could be perceived as a battlefield and prison, but also as both a swinging and protective bird's nest, and as a venue for redemption and mending.

Significantly, God Himself is depicted in the Bible as a woman in labor who actively hastens birth and redemption by means of gasps, pants, and other dramatic actions, which we will expand upon in the concluding chapter (see, e.g., Isa. 42:13–14; 66:8–9). The displacement of the physical womb by the metaphysical one is obvious: the *me'ayim* ("guts," "bowels") within the male (and divine) body is the organ corresponding to the female womb: "Is Ephraim my dear son? Is he my darling child? For as often as I speak against him, I do remember him still. Therefore *meiai* yearns for him; I will surely have mercy on him, says the Lord" (Jer. 31:19).[8]

While the creation of birth metaphors might, on the one hand, reinforce oppressive gender conceptions, those same metaphors may well enrich our understanding of this mysterious experience. The tendency to appropriate the womb from the mother ensues from its lack of accessibility and our inability to observe

---

6 Introduction to *Tikkunei ha-Zohar*. See Roi, *Love*, 170–176, 222–228; Pedaya, *Trauma*, 104–107.
7 Newman, "Birth"; Preuss, *Medicine*, 114, 394–395. See also Chapter 8 below.
8 KJV: "my bowels"; RSV and others: "my heart." MT, KJV, RSV, and others – v. 20. Preuss, *Medicine*, 114 n. 1155–1157.

what happens within it. Accordingly, the multitude of metaphors that describe the womb provide an important case study for the change over time of gendered, moral, and theological concepts. The wealth of womb imagery does not only prescribe the proper attitude to a woman and her body, it also suggests that God is responsible for human fertility.

The midrash in *Ecclesiastes Rabbah* compares the womb to Hell: "It is written, 'The grave and the barren womb' (Prov. 30:16) – what has one to do with the other? In truth as the womb yields [the child] with loud cries, so will Sheol [hell] yield [the dead] with loud cries."[9] In a similar spirit, a parable in *Genesis Rabbah* (above) has the Rabbis wondering why a king built a palace "on a site of sewers, dunghills, and garbage."[10] This theological pondering portrays the womb harshly, as a waste heap. As we shall see, this tendency intensifies in a series of threatening comparisons of the womb to a prison, a "folded writing tablet," boiling innards (*me'ayim*, bowels), and host to a plethora of dangers liable to kill the fetus.

2 The Womb as a Dangerous Place

In an expanded homily in *Leviticus Rabbah*, a midrash composed between the fifth and sixth centuries CE states:

> "If a woman conceives, and bears a male child" (Lev. 12:2) [. . .] It is only natural that if a man has given into another's keeping an ounce of silver in private, and the latter returns to him a pound of gold in public, would the former not be grateful to the latter? Even so is it with the Holy One, blessed be He. Human beings entrust to Him a drop of moisture in privacy, and the Holy One, blessed be He, openly returns to them completed and perfected human individuals [. . .] It is natural that, if a man is confined to prison with no one giving him attention, and someone comes and kindles a light for him there, would the former not feel gratitude towards the latter? So too is it with the Holy One, blessed be He. When the embryo is in its mother's womb, He causes a light to shine for it there [. . .] It is only natural that, when a man is confined in prison with no one paying attention to him, and someone comes and releases him and takes him out from there, would the former not feel gratitude to the latter? Even so when the embryo is in its mother's womb, the Holy One, blessed be He, comes and releases it and brings it forth from there [. . .] In the usual way, if a person holds a bag of money with the opening downwards, do not the coins scatter? Now the embryo has its abode in the mother's womb, but the Holy One, blessed be He, guards it that it should not fall out and die [. . .] It is the way of a beast to walk with its body in a horizontal position, and its embryo in its womb in the form of a bag, whereas a woman walks erect while the embryo is in her womb, and the Holy One, blessed be He, guards it that it should not fall out

---

9 *Ecclesiastes Rabbah* 3: 1–2.
10 *Genesis Rabbah* 1:5 (Albeck ed., 3).

and die [. . .] Nature has placed the udders of a beast where her womb is, and her young suck where [also] her pudenda are; but a woman has her breasts in a beautiful part of her body, and her baby sucks at a dignified place [. . .] If a person were to stay in hot water for one hour, would he not die? Now a woman's womb (*me'ayim*, bowels) is at boiling temperature, and the embryo is in the womb, and the Holy One, blessed be He, takes care of it so that it should not turn into a shapeless fetus or after-birth, or sandal-like fetus [. . .] If a man should eat one portion after another, would not the second expel the first? Yet, however much food a woman may eat, and however much liquid she may drink, this does not expel the embryo.[11]

A series of radical symbols stand at the heart of the *derasha*. These Rabbinic expositions present the womb as an unsafe place, a confining prison, or a carelessly held purse. While the mother is a passive figure who is incapable of aiding the fetus, and is even identified with destructive, fatal forces, God alone saves the life of the newborn. He rescues the infant from its prison, and He guards the womb from the dangers posed by the woman.

The first example underlines how the Rabbis mistrust the mysterious, unknown interiors of the female body: all that happens within the dark and dirty places of the female body arouses shame and guilt.[12] The infant is compared to silver that is raised in value or saved from loss, or to dirt that becomes a "new soul." In the first metaphor, the fetus is compared to a speck of dirt that is miraculously transformed into a fine soul, with birth accordingly reflecting an alchemical process: in those murky places, God turns the materials of embryonic existence into gold. This charged metaphor also degrades the womb, by presenting it as a purse in which "mere silver" is deposited but in which a "*litra* [i.e., measure] of gold" suddenly appears.

Following this metaphor, the Rabbis lean heavily upon the notion of the mother as irresponsible and her body as fundamentally flawed. Her womb, they claim, is an inside-out purse, whose coins are liable to scatter on the ground. According to this imagery, only a miracle saves the fetus from falling from his mother's body.[13] An additional, and extreme, illustration of their mistrust of the mysterious and "flawed" female body is their comparison of the infant a mother carries in her womb to a prisoner in jail.[14] Finally, they liken the woman to an animal – who, we learn, is superior to the woman! While the latter walks "erect" and thus abandons her baby to its fate, the animal walks on all fours, and carefully guards its fetus in a protected sack.

---

11 *Leviticus Rabbah* 14:2–3.
12 On shame at birth, see Cohen-Shabot, "Domesticating Bodies."
13 This image might reflect a latent fear of the *vagina dentate* (the vagina with teeth). See Cixous et al., "Medusa"; Millett, *Sexual Politics*, 90–92; Irigaray, *Speculum*.
14 Metaphors of the body as a jail were prevalent in Hellenistic literature, such as the texts of the Philonic corpus. writings. See Boyarin, *Carnal Israel*, 40.

This comparison portrays the woman as inferior even to a beast, and sets forth her bodily structure as destructive and fatal, were it not for wondrous divine intervention in the process of gestation and birth.[15]

These midrashim reflect extreme misogyny: a woman's womb is a prison or an inverted purse that harms the treasures within it. Rather than portraying pregnancy as the preeminent protection of the embryo to ensure its health and maturation, the images conjured by these midrashim instead speculate that it is the mother's nature to harm the fetus, to abort or kill it. The woman's innards are a cauldron, she eats and drinks to her heart's delight, and almost expels the fetus from within her. Birth is a process that, as these midrashim have it, runs *counter* to nature.

And what about the father? His absence from the first midrashim in *Leviticus Rabbah* 14:2–4 implies that the Rabbis seek to ignore or conceal the father in their depictions of the entire procreation process. Rather, reproduction is given over to two opposing forces that struggle against each other: the injurious mother and God, the rescuer. By leaving the father absent, the midrashim highlight the praise of God and intensify the binary comparison. In place of the well-known contrast of nature (woman) with culture (man), the midrash distinguishes between damage and destruction (feminine) and a "wondrous" miracle (the divine).[16]

The presentation of the maternal body and the womb as a source of shame and guilt is meant to lessen the exegetes' embarrassment at their having come forth from that same place, which they portray as filthy and drenched in blood, and yet mysterious and alluring.[17] The place "where her pudenda are" (*bet bosheta*, lit. "the place of her shame") is revealed here as the locus of the Rabbis' shame, as is indicated by the verse that is the starting point for all the exegeses in *Leviticus Rabbah* 14: "If a woman conceives, and bears a male child" (Lev. 12:2). The word "male" refers to the child that is born, and not to the father, whose absence highlights the binary relationship between the divine and the female. The Rabbis patently use this verse to ask the question: *how could the apex of human creation – the male – come forth from that filthy place, and how could they – the Torah scholars – have been born from there?* In the face of the unknowns of

---

15 Compare to the description in BT Bava Bathra 16a–b of the doe who wishes to kill the fetus in her womb by throwing it off a cliff, as well as the myth of the gazelle bit by a snake near her womb. Both animals symbolize negative and dangerous aspects of motherhood and femininity, hence divine intervention is needed in order to protect procreation from the "mother's demonic nature."

16 Ortner, "Female to Male."

17 As it is said later in *Leviticus Rabbah* 14:9 regarding the woman's womb being constantly full with blood. On this homily, see Kessler, *Conceiving Israel*, 99–103, n. 70.

pregnancy and birth, distinguishing between God as "the good womb" and the mother as the "bad womb" serves as a sort of bulwark against anxiety.

When the Rabbis channel all of birth's negativity and project it onto the woman – while associating the male (who is born) and God (the rescuer of the fetus) with the pure and the positive – they are actually wrestling with the inexplicability of this threatening experience. Moreover, birth obviously arouses their anger toward and jealousy of the woman, who has the power to bring life. Karen Horney has noted the phenomenon of womb envy, arguing that this is of matching, or even greater, force than the Freudian concept of penis envy.[18] Simone de Beauvoir maintains that maternity, which is associated with finitude and death, is the reason for the anxiety toward their mothers felt by many men. This generates a tension between the desired female partner, who represents erotic, seductive experiences, and the mother, who is perceived as the source of danger and threat to the life of the male, who seeks to be extricated from her grasp.[19] Carl Jung and his followers, especially Erich Neumann, explored the symbolism of the womb of the Great Mother as a stage in the hero's journey and the individuation and integrative processes that he undergoes.[20]

To besmirch the mother is to control her, then, but also to assuage human powerlessness in the face of the death that lies in wait during labor for both mother and fetus. Thus the Rabbis express their hidden anger against God and the injustice that exists in the world. Through these expositions they evince the unresolved conflicts in their souls regarding their mothers, their wives, and, above all, their own births.

In addition to the imagery that compares the womb to an inverted or open purse, a prison, or the sack of an animal, we also find vague anxiety around the similarities between the ways that women and animals give birth. Thus, the exegetes create a dual hierarchy: first comes God, who is above the humans who are dependent on His mercies; second comes birth by a woman; and third comes birth by an animal.[21] A series of rhetorical questions (e.g., "would the former not be grateful to the latter?") concludes, again and again, with the words of the Biblical verse "You have granted me life and steadfast love" (Job

---

[18] Horney, *Feminine Psychology*.
[19] Beauvoir, *The Second Sex*.
[20] Neumann, *The Great Mother*; Jung, *Psychotherapy*; idem, *Psychology and Religion*.
[21] The midrash differentiates between a woman and an animal, through differentiation between the female's womb and her breasts, in order to present breastfeeding as a "purified act," unlike birth itself: "A woman has her breasts in a beautiful part of her body, and her baby sucks at a dignified place." On Rabbinic images of breastfeeding, see Chapter 6, Section 5; Haskell, *Suckling*, 15–37.

10:12). This shows that the birth of a person is an act of marvelous love, and emphasizes the essential damaged quality of the mother. As the second-century CE physician Galen claimed: "Just as man is the most perfect of all animals, so also, within the human species, man is more perfect than woman."[22]

3 The Guilt and Blaming of Eve, the Primal Mother

Suffering begins with birth, and thus is unavoidably bound up with human existence. On both the individual-ontogenetic and phylogenetic levels, both culturally and universally, encounters with incomprehensible experiences spur man to search for the "cause" of existential pain. The ancient religions have always tended to blame the mother for a distressing reality, and to find motherhood responsible for human pain and sorrow.

As usual, though, blaming the mother cloaked a deeper and weightier anxiety, and indicated the search for an explanation for phenomena that could neither be comprehended nor processed. Theodicy, that presumes that God directs His world in accordance with the principle of reward and punishment, runs counter to phenomena that lack meaning, events in which man is punished through no fault of his own. Thus, for instance, the question arises: why do so many mothers and infants die in childbirth? The premise that God acts justly (theodicy, from the Greek *theos*, "god," and *dike*, "justice") compels believers to find meaning and an answer to this question elsewhere. It should come as no surprise, then, that the mother is charged with her "crimes," for which she must pay during childbirth. God's responsibility for the faulty world that He created is redirected to the human figure who gave us life.

In the history of the monotheistic religions – Judaism, Christianity, and, later, Islam as well – the mother is doubly guilty: she bears responsibility for the suffering of birth and for existence itself, which is partial and finite, and she is censured for her sexuality and desires. The Garden of Eden narrative has Eve violating a divine command and sweeping Adam up along with her transgression; *she* talks with the serpent and tempts Adam (the midrash accordingly adds that Cain is the "serpent's son").[23] Eve sins against the entire array of cosmic forces, living creatures, God, and even against her future offspring.

The Book of Ben Sira, which belongs to the apocryphal wisdom literature (alternately named Sirach and Ecclesiasticus), postulates a similar principle,

---

[22] Galen, *Parts of the Body*, 14.6.7.
[23] *Pirkei de-Rabbi Eliezer* 21.

which connects Eve's sin with all flesh-and-blood women: "From a woman sin had its beginning, and because of her we all die."[24] The guilt of the first mother, "the mother of all living" (Gen. 3:20), who thereby represented *all* women, prevailed in Christian theology and in the Patristic literature, which portrays Mary, the "second Eve," as the only one of her sex not blemished by the sin of the serpent and the flaw of sexuality. As Adrienne Rich argues in *Of Woman Born*, in the history of religions, female suffering during birth pangs and birth itself symbolizes Eve's punishment. Consequently, for centuries the Church forbade women from taking medication to alleviate the pain of birth, since these painkillers prevent the woman from bearing responsibility for the original sin.

I will now turn to the literature that links birth to punishment and death, using the motif of blood and the depiction of the womb as a source of anguish and suffering.

4 Birth and Female Death

The attribution of *dinim*, "harsh judgments" and negative imagery to female nature is not an abstract idea; rather, this concept made its way into everyday practices, folklore, and ritual. Since ancient times, birth has been viewed as a time fraught with peril. Charms, incantations, *amulets*, and prayers were attempts to protect the mother and fetus from destructive agents capable of acting at this hazardous time.[25] However, the anthropologist Arnold van Gennep mentions that, in addition to shielding the mother during pregnancy and childbirth, at times *she herself* is perceived as impure and harmful, and is therefore sent away from the camp.[26] The Talmud (BT Berakhot 54b; and Rashi, s.v. "*Holeh*"), too, describes the mother in labor as a "sick person" in need of special protection. These approaches regard the natural processes of pregnancy and birth as a period in which the woman is foreign to society. Nonetheless, the Sages allow that birth is a sensitive time for the woman, as is the postpartum recovery, which is when the new mother is in a transitional state following the trauma of birth.[27]

As an event in these societies, birth was considered a transformative rite of passage, and acquired rituals meant to protect against destructive agents and evil spirits. Tribal societies conducted ceremonies that imitated birth (Couvade Syndrome),

---

[24] Ben Sira 25:24 (NRSV); see Kohlenberger, *Parallel Apocrypha*, 479.
[25] Rubin, *Beginning of Life*, 52–76. On *even ha-tkuma*, "preserving stone," as an amulet and source of protection during pregnancy, see Preuss, *Medicine*, 384–386; Scholem, *Devils*, 60–101.
[26] Van Gennep, *Rites of Passage*, 41–49.
[27] Usually postpartum recovery is considered to last until four to six weeks after birth.

with the fathers simulating the pains of childbirth and being temporarily banished from the camp.[28] According to Mircea Eliade, this syndrome symbolizes the bisexuality of giving birth. Men take from women metaphors of birth and initiation, and at times even experience women's aches of pregnancy and their cries of birth pangs. In exchange, women in labor are given "male" powers, such as hunting skills, shamanic spells, and techniques for ascent to heaven and ties with the world of the dead, which aid them as mothers in raising their children.[29]

In certain tribes, new mothers were banished for one hundred days, a phenomenon analogous to the Biblical conception of impurity following the birth of a daughter, which lasted for eighty days.[30] The Rabbis instituted a prohibition against leaving a new mother alone, and ruled that she must be guarded for a period of up to a month. After giving birth, the new mother recited the blessing traditionally performed after delivery from a dangerous situation ("who bestows good on the unworthy, who has bestowed on me much good"), as did men after their safe return from dangerous journeys – by ship, for example, or from a trip in the wilderness, or upon release from prison.[31]

Deterministic suffering is at the heart of the Rabbinic conception of birth, as can be seen from this midrashic statement: "To a woman sitting on the birthing stool (*ha-mashber*) and she is in birthing pains, they say [to her]: 'May he who answered your mother, answer you'."[32] The Rabbis allude to the combination of blessing and curse that birth entails. The birthing mother's pains are cast in the light of her own mother's suffering, in a never-ending cycle forced on every mother in every generation. The wordplay between the Hebrew terms "response" (*ma'ane*) and "torture" (*in'ui*) points to God's role in the system of reward and punishment as an expression of the guilt of Eve and her daughters. The identification of the womb with a tomb (see the expansion in the following section) indicates both the relationship between birth and death in midrashic theory, while also vividly portraying the grim reality for women in antiquity, many of whom died during childbirth.[33]

---

[28] Van Gennep, *Rites of Passage*, 41–49.
[29] Eliade, *Rites and Symbols*, 80.
[30] Leviticus 12:4–5. See also Van Gennep, *Rites of Passage*, 46; Rubin, *Beginning of Life*, 35–36; Preuss, *Medicine*, 399–402.
[31] BT Berakhot 54b.
[32] *Deuteronomy Rabbah* 2:11.
[33] In the Biblical literature, Rachel (Gen. 35:16–19) and the wife of Pinhas (1 Sam. 4:19–21) died during childbirth. To these heroines, the midrash adds Esther's mother (BT Megillah 13a) and Michal, the daughter of Saul (BT Sanhedrin 21a). See also Nahmanides on Genesis 38:3 on the suffering during birth of Tamar and the mother of Ya'abetz. According to the Sages, the suffering that birth entails starts already at the stage of pregnancy. Moreover, the Matriarchs

As *Leviticus Rabbah* (27:7) relates:

> From the hundred cries which a woman bleats when she sits upon the birth-stool, when it is a case of ninety-nine chances of death and one of life [. . .] They call her three names, *hayetha, mehabbalta, mitbara*: *hayetha*, because she is nearly dying but revives (*hayah*); *mehabbalta*, because she is given in pledge in the hand of death; the same words that you spoke to one, you spoke to the other: "If ever you take your neighbor's garment in pledge" (Exod. 22:25). *Mitbara* [means] she was broken and faced death.[34]

The birthing mother is given three names here: *hayetha, mehabbalta*, and *mitbara*. The first appellation, *hayetha*, illustrates the miracle of the new mother coming back to life, similar to the third, *mitbara*, which references a mother's body healing after having been "broken" while giving birth, as it reinforces the suffering and death brought about by the birth process. The second name, *mehabbalta*, is connected to the "birth pangs" (*hevlei ledah*) concept and adds a new semantic field to the chords imagery. For the Rabbis, the woman is "given in pledge in the hand of death," but remains alive. This idea is based on a surprising prooftext regarding the laws of one who takes a pledge: "If you take your neighbor's garment in pledge."[35] We would have expected the Rabbis to expound on the birthing mother's condition from other verses which relate to birth pangs, such as "Under the apple tree I awakened you. There your mother was in travail (*hevletkha*) with you, there she who bore you was in travail (*hiblah*)" (Song of Songs 8:5).[36] Instead, they associate the birthing mother with one who takes a pledge (*hovel*), and pregnancy with causing harm (*habalah*).

The *hovel* is a lender, to whom his comrade pawned his garment. The lender must return this item of clothing to the borrower every morning, since the latter has nothing to wear in its stead. The Rabbis offer an analogy: while it seems to us that the birthing mother imparts life, in actuality her life is in danger, and it is restored to her after having given birth. Just as the lender is subservient to God, so too the pregnant woman turns to Him as the lender of souls, while the infant is compared to the money of the loan that comes from heaven.

---

were barren because God heard their prayers and crying. See *Genesis Rabbah* 45:4; *Midrash Tanhuma, Vayetze* 7. See also *Preuss*, Medicine, 428–431.

34 For variations in the manuscripts, see *Leviticus Rabbah* 27:7 (Margolioth ed., 639); Sokoloff, *Dictionary*, 198.

35 Exod. 22: 25. MT; RSV – v. 26.

36 *Habilat* in Arabic means "to become pregnant." On the connection between the word *hiblah* and the umbilical cord, see *Song of Songs Rabbah* 8:1–5; *Exodus Rabbah* 1:12; *Song of Songs Zuta* (Buber ed.) 8:5.

These expositions aim to highlight the wonder of birth and the necessity of divine intervention in the procreative process. Without divine providence, the "natural process" of birth could not take place.

The motif of the mother's death and rescue recurs in many midrashic sources, as in the exposition on *ovnayim* ("stones," birthing stool): "What does *ovnayim* mean? [. . .] when a woman bends to deliver a child, her thighs grow cold like stones."[37] This midrash deals with the real death of many women during childbirth. Yet, on the theological and symbolic levels it also reflects a connotation of female death as a condition for divine rescue. The image of the mother's thighs becoming frozen stones references the vitality and gentleness that she must sacrifice in order to bring life into the world: in order to contend with her pain and survive, she must become stone, she must die, and she must then be resurrected together with her fetus. The connections between a pledge given, suffering pain, turning into stone, death, and burial are all implied by these statements. Such Rabbinic dicta come together to paint a picture of the birthing mother as one who returns from the world of the dead.

God thereby saves two souls in each birth: the life of the infant and that of the mother, since she, too, comes back to life, as the parallel midrash in *Ecclesiastes Rabbah* (3:2) expounds:

> "A time to be born, and a time to die": when a woman is at the time of childbirth they call her *hayetha*. Why do they call her that? Because she is nearly dying but revives (*hayah*). And why do they call her *mehabbalta*? Because she is given in pledge in the hand of death, as the word is used in the sentence, "If ever you take your neighbor's garment in pledge [*havol yahbol*]".[38] (Exod. 22:25)

The midrash paints a complex tableau of the relationship between the woman and God. At first glance, the two are alike in their ability to create life, but the Rabbis' words also imply a latent dimension of struggle and the undermining of authority. The Rabbis seem to be saying that the mother presumes to usurp the place of God the Creator. To chasten her for her hubris, she must deliver her soul to the Creator, and be recreated by Him. Just as the lender must return the pledge – his garment – to the borrower, so, too, the woman must return her soul to the Lord upon each birth. In contrast with her, God is portrayed as a generous owner of souls, which He loans us every morning, beginning with the definitive morning of human life – the moment of birth. Even if we were to interpret the word *mehabbalta* as a passive description and the birthing mother

---

37 Exodus 1:16; BT Niddah 11b. Compare *Exodus Rabbah* 1:14; *Midrash Tanhuma* (ed. Buber), *Tazria* 5; *Leviticus Rabbah* 27:7 (Margolioth ed., 639). See also above, Chapter 3, n. 19.
38 Compare *Genesis Rabbah* 60:3 (Albeck ed., 643); Lieberman, *Tosefta ki-Feshutah*, 34.

as being given in pledge to death (and not as the owner of souls), it appears that it is *God* who brings the Angel of Death to account and rescues by virtue of His compassion.

The perception of the birthing mother as sinner is manifest in the following midrash: "For three transgressions women die in childbirth: for heedlessness of the laws of marital purity, the dough-offering, and kindling the [Sabbath] light."[39] Guilt and accusation underlie this dictum: the mother, who brings about human birth, is responsible for our death, and therefore birth is the time for her punishment. In another approach, the woman is deemed to be a sinner because she takes a "false oath" during childbirth, vowing that she will have no further intercourse with her husband. The Rabbis comment that at that moment she must pay for other sins that she committed during her lifetime. Similar guilt is the backdrop to midrashim that depict Eve as "having extinguished the light of the world," "transgressed through the chambers of her womb" (BT Shabbat 31b), and even, "shed the blood of the Holy One" alluding to the pollution of the serpent that was inserted within her. All women become "carriers" of the original sin of Eve, the first mother, and each generation must pay for her transgression by means of the three female commandments: family purity (*niddah*), the dough-offering (*challah*), and kindling the Sabbath light (*hadlakat ha-ner*).[40]

The moment of birth is a perilous and liminal time, and so it is just then that the woman is to beseech atonement for her life.[41] This can be seen, for instance, in the prayer:

> May it be Your will, the great, mighty, and awesome God, that the merit of this poor woman, who will tremble and cry out in her pangs, be recalled before You. If she has any iniquity, forgive and expunge it because of what she suffered in the pain of birth pangs. May her sound of her cry ascend to the Throne of Your Glory, and silence her accusers. May all who speak well on her behalf gather before You, as is Your attribute to be beneficent to those worthy and unworthy. May You take pity on her, for You answer in time of trouble, merciful King who is merciful to all, redeems, saves, hears, and answers.[42]

The prayer versions attributed to R. Isaac Luria, too, ascribe special prayer abilities to pregnant women and new mothers. Even if birth itself is not thought to be an offense, we cannot overlook the linkage these midrashim posit between the suffering of birth and the sin of the Tree of Knowledge, and the latter presentation as a female sin that passes from generation to generation. Additionally, the tie between

---

39 M. Shabbat 2:6.
40 Fonrobert, *Menstrual Purity*, 20–35.
41 On feminine shame and guilt which often lead to postpartum depression, see Kron, *Women in Pink*.
42 *Shevet Mussar* 24.

the womb as the source of life and the earth, to which humans return, raises the dread of the unknown that is present in the natural and bountiful experiences of birth and death. Confronting the reality of the many births that ended with the death of the mother and fetus, the Rabbis sought to offer a rational explanation for this recurring phenomenon. They asked themselves how the natural and consummately positive actions of pregnancy and birth could end in death. Their resolution of this quandary found women's sins to be responsible. If the mother is a sinner, then there is a logical reason for her death or that of her infant at the precarious moment of birth. Lacking such an explanation, death becomes an enigma, one that fills us with dread.

In addition to its realistic description and its documentation of the difficulty that bringing life entails, the Rabbinic dictum could also attest to pregnancy jealousy and the attempted male appropriation of the birthing process or its attribution to supernal forces. Faced with the powerlessness connected with birth, the exegetes offer an attempt to control the woman and the mysteries of her body by means of language. To this end, the Rabbis, *inter alia*, compare the birth process to animal parturition. We saw in the exegesis of the inside-out purse that the animal protects her cubs to a greater degree than does the human mother. Other, contrasting, midrashim, however, find similarities between the beast and the birthing mother, since the following applies to both:

> The blood is decomposed and turns into milk. Since this is an anomaly, therefore even the milk from an unclean animal should be permitted. [However,] it has been established that this would indeed be the case according to the view that the blood is decomposed and turns into milk. But according to the view that [there is no menstruation during the nursing period because] her limbs become disjointed and she does not become normal again for twenty-four months, what is there to say?[43]

The similarity between the two lies in the cries of the female in labor, who bleats and screams like an animal (as in the above midrash: "from the hundred cries which a woman bleats [*ha-poeh*; also used for the sounds uttered by animals] when she sits upon the birth-stool"). Additionally, like a beast, the new mother recovers from her having given birth over the course of two years; both undergo a similar process in which their blood is transformed into the milk that nourishes the newborn.

The blood motif connects the vision of death with the dread of birth, and is reflected in a common scholarly disagreement regarding the essential nature of female blood. One scholarly opinion views menstrual blood and the blood of

---

[43] BT Bekhorot 6b; BT Niddah 9a; BY Niddah 1:4; *Midrash Tanhuma* (ed. Buber), *Tazria*. On similarities and differences between women's birth and animal labor, see Preuss, *Medicine*, 378–410.

birth as a signifier of death and impurity, while others point to the specific ties between blood and life.[44] A study of the tribal conceptions of blood in ancient societies, and of the status of blood in the laws of familypurity and the Biblical notion of impurity, highlights the paradox of this elixir of life: that which unites (blood relatives) also separates one family line from another, male from female, the sacred from the mundane, and birth from death.[45]

Unlike psychoanalysis, with its emphasis on the needs of the infant and lesser attention paid to the mother as subject, the ancient Rabbinic sources broadcast their concern for the fluid female body which bleeds and decomposes, even if their concern was cloaked in judgmental and critical guise. This midrash declares that a woman needs two years to recover from birth, and equates her thanksgiving blessing with that for the resurrection of the dead. Death is portrayed in this midrash as an existential reality shared by woman and beast alike. The picture of decomposing body parts, even more than the stone-like stiffening of the thighs, attests to the paramount fracture and traumatic caesura of birth, not only for the infant, but also, and especially, for his mother. Many infants and mothers did not survive birth, which society as a whole thereby associated with death, given the latter's frequency. At times, this death was terminal, while in other instances the woman and the baby were able to be revived and transformed – like a larva before it turns into a butterfly.

5 The Womb as a Grave

The heroines of Genesis present motherhood as an experience existing on the threshold of death and the grave. Rachel cries out to Jacob (and to God): "Give me children, or I shall die" (Gen. 30:1), while, on the other hand, Rebekah, contending with "too many" children within her, screams despairingly about her pregnancy: "If it is thus, why do I live?" (Gen. 25:22). Both link their female selfhood as subject with pregnancy and motherhood, and consequently with death. The paradox of motherhood begins with birth: an impossible experience without which life is not life.

Many feminists contest the identification of femininity with motherhood. Thus, Simone de Beauvoir argued that a woman must forgo being a mother in order to realize her femininity, or, taking a different tack, Adrienne Rich drew a distinction between motherhood, as a feminine, personal experience, and its subservience to a patriarchal-institutional ideal, which sees women as a technical

---

[44] Douglas, *Purity and Danger*. For another reading, see Biale, *Blood and Belief*, 28–43.
[45] Levi-Strauss, *Kinship*.

means for procreation. Rich maintains that the idea that a woman has no identity without motherhood and children has been passed down from generation to generation, causing harm to women and to the possibility of their choosing motherhood as an empowering experience.

In light of these arguments, it would be interesting to reexamine what the Biblical matriarchs say, and to note that only God hears their cries, while the males (such as Jacob, who hardens his heart to Rachel's barrenness, or Elkanah, who tells Hannah "Am I not more to you than ten sons?" [1 Sam. 1:8]), are insufficiently sensitive to this female distress. These men could take an additional wife to give them children, as was the ancient custom, according to which one wife was ornamental, while another produced offspring (e.g., Adah and Zillah).[46] The self-identity of women resounds in the cries of Rachel and Rebekah, who choose to become pregnant and give birth, and who declare that their individual self would be canceled, and even annihilated, without motherhood. This could be viewed as the internalization of a national ethos of fertility, or alternatively, as a rare moment of subjectivity that links the deficiency of barrenness with death.

We learn in the continuation of the Rachel narrative that, ironically, it is the birth – not its absence – that is the cause of her death. Likewise, Mary, the mother of Jesus, wants to die at the moment she gives birth, according to the tradition appearing in the *Quran* (19:23; trans. Arberry, 332): "And the birth pangs surprised her by the trunk of the palm-tree. She said, 'Would that I had died ere this, and become a thing forgotten!'"

These exclamations of the Biblical mothers and of Mary show an awareness of the death bound up with the bringing of life, both the danger of actual annihilation and the symbolic knowledge that the child represents the mother's decline and end. This can also be seen in the common phenomenon of postpartum depression, which is related to the feeling of loss experienced by the mother, who is separated from the one who developed within her. In the psychoanalytic realm, as well, it seems that the analyst and the patient can no longer survive together, and that one of the two must "die."[47] The death of the mother or the fetus in birth emphasizes the bond between life and death, as Job attests when he says: "Naked came I out of my mother's womb, and naked shall I return thither" (Job 1:21; KJV). This link denotes the inability of language to describe that place ("thither") and the uncanny (*unheimlich*) power of the womb and the grave.

Job and Jeremiah lament the day of their birth as the day of their death, thus demonstrating the perception of the womb as a grave. It is Jeremiah, who was set

---

46 *Genesis Rabbah* 23:2 (Albeck ed., 222).
47 Carmeli, "On Being Cut." O n the symbolic death of Rachel, see Rojtman, *Forgiveness*.

apart and chosen for his mission even before he was formed in the womb, who turns to God as the "womb of the world" (*l'origine du monde*) and protests: "Cursed be the day on which I was born! [. . .] because he did not kill me in the womb; *so my mother would have been my grave, and her womb big [with me] for all time*. Why did I come forth from the womb?" (Jer. 20:14–18).[48] Job, too, after having lost all, addresses God with intimacy mixed with outcry and protest: "Why did you bring me forth from the womb? Would that I had died before any eye had seen me, and were as though I had not been, *carried from the womb to the grave*" (Job 10:18–19).[49]

Rabbinic midrashim frequently introduce the identification of the womb with the grave, primarily in connection with halakhic and presumably technical descriptions, such as the following passage from tractate Shabbat, within a discussion of whether the Sabbath may be violated to relieve the suffering of the woman in labor:

> From when is the opening of the uterus? – Abaye said: From when she sits on the seat of travail. R. Huna son of R. Joshua said: From when the blood slowly flows down; others state, from when her friends carry her by her arm. For how long is the opening of the uterus? – Abaye said: Three days. Raba said in Rab Judah's name: Seven; others maintain: Thirty. The scholars of Nehardea said: A lying-in woman [has three periods: from] three [days after confinement], seven [days], and thirty [days].[50]

It is noteworthy that this passage goes beyond the identification of the womb with the grave, and uses the word *kever* (lit., "grave") for "uterus."[51] Incidental to this discussion, the Rabbis reveal differing notions as to when the birth process begins, including the physiological (from when the blood flows) and the emotional and sociological (from when the woman needs the help of her fellow women), along with various ideas on the process of the opening of the womb and its closure after the birth (three, seven, or thirty days). The womb–grave relationship reveals their fear of the mother and her engulfing, deadly womb, alongside the glorification of the source of life, in light of the cyclical mother–earth connection.[52]

The statement "the womb is a grave" compares a living body and an actual organ, the source of life, to the source of death. The Rabbis might have thought that the grave, unlike the womb, is a familiar symbol, which could be used to concretize the mystery of birth. Along with its negative aspects, the grave also represents the

---

48 Emphasis is mine; trans. draws on NJPS. Compare to Jer. 1:5.
49 Compare to Job 3:3–12. See Preuss, *Medicine*, 114, 387, 397.
50 BT Shabbat 129a (ed. Soncino). See also M. Ohalot 4:7; BT Bekhorot 22a; Preuss, *Medicine*, 120; Abrams, *Female Body*, 103.
51 The Soncino translation of the Babylonian Talmud on this discursive unit directly renders *kever* as "uterus" and sees no need for any explanatory note.
52 Neumann, *The Great Mother*; Róheim, "Fairy Tale."

relationship between life and death. Like the womb, the grave represents an actual place of habitation: the former, before birth, and the latter, after life. Thus, the Rabbis employ this similitude to acknowledge the difficulty in deciphering the very beginning, as well as the end. They try to come full circle, in which death and birth generate meaning in relation to each other. By attaching the womb to the grave, they claim that the beginning of life can be understood only by means of death – especially female death.

As Phyllis Trible writes, Biblical poetry and narrative identify the *female* womb with the divine one; God avenges and punishes by closing wombs, or rewards by opening them.[53] What is the price of this appropriation, and does attributing the womb to God downplay the significance of the womb–grave identification? By making such a close association, were the Rabbis attempting to transfer sole responsibility for birth and death to God, and thereby somewhat lessen the woman's "guilt"?

The imagery of the womb as grave appears in an exposition on the three keys held only by God: "There are three keys maintained in the hand of the Holy One, which were not transmitted to an intermediary. The key of rain, the key of childbirth, and the key of the resurrection of the dead (BT Ta'anit 2a)." This imagery is based, *inter alia*, on the enigmatic verse in Proverbs (30:16) connecting *Sheol* with the womb: "Sheol, the barren womb, the earth ever thirsty for water, and the fire which never says, 'Enough.'"

The grave is not an abstract idea like death, but a defined and distinct object. Like the womb, the grave has a connotation of containment. Each is a vessel of death and a vessel of life; a vessel of blood, and of flesh. The womb, in psychological terms, is a "home," "container," and "transitional space."[54] The womb and the grave are therefore a single, cyclical, container. They bound the extremities of human existence, beyond which lies the abyss.

Ecclesiastes Rabbah speaks of the bond unique to these two extremities, while developing the metaphor of the womb as the portal of death: "A time to be born, and a time to die (Eccl. 3:1). What then is its meaning? Happy the man whose hour of death is like the hour of his birth; as he was pure in the hour of his birth so should he be pure in the hour of his death." The moment of birth and the moment of death give a person the opportunity to purity himself. In the symbolic stratum they are the holding space of atonement, and the cleansing of guilt, splitting, and falsification. These are the liminal moments in which the

---

[52] Neumann, *The Great Mother*; Róheim, "Fairy Tale."
[53] Trible, *God*, 36–38 n. 10–11.
[54] Bion, Winnicott, Kohut, Stern, Milner, and others discuss the function of the mother and the therapist as "transitional space" that allows the baby/patient process of growth and repair. See Milner, "Communication."

individual stands pure before his Creator. This notion enables us to understand the cry bound up with the entry to and exit from these places: "Why is the grave mentioned next to the womb? To tell you that as [the child] is brought forth from the womb with loud cries, so will [the dead] be brought forth from the grave [at the resurrection] with loud cries."[55]

Along with their pre-existentialist conception of the soul, the Rabbis hint that death has already occurred; consequently, the womb symbolizes the grave that preceded the fetus's entry to the world. Death is intertwined with birth, and therefore the life that is created is *the afterlife*. During the birth, the mother, as the infant, experiences a caesura and crisis which are a taste of actual death, analogous to Winnicott's fear of breakdown that "has already happened" but was not experienced. Birth, too, is experienced during the course of life by means of the awareness of death. Accordingly, the imagery of the womb as *Sheol* or the grave does not necessarily reflect a misogynic and critical attitude, but an existentialist stance, of humility and wonder in the face of the numinous, that exceeds the bounds of rational comprehension.

Additional Rabbinic tableaux indicate the resemblance between one extremity of life and the other, such as the Mishnaic dictum (M. Avot 4:22) "Those who have been born [are destined] to die, and those who are dead, to be revived," while the *Zohar* lists three crying voices that are never lost: the sound of a woman in labor; the sound of the person when the soul escapes its body; and the sound of a snake when it sheds its skin.[56] These three voices combine bestiality, death, and feminine vitality, and all set man to give an accounting before God.

In midrashic and Kabbalistic thought, even God is presumably subordinate to the determinism of birth and death, within which He has a task to fulfill. We can conclude our discussion with an exposition that portrays the birth–death relationship in light of the verse (Eccl. 5:14) "As he came from his mother's womb he shall go again, naked as he came." Even more so than indicating the importance of death, the following passage from *Ecclesiastes Rabbah* is meant to hearten man while he still lives:

> It has been taught: As a man enters [the world] so he departs. He enters it with a cry and departs from the world with a cry. He enters the world with weeping and takes leave of it with weeping. He enters the world in love and takes leave of it in love. He enters the world with a sigh and takes leave of it with a sigh. He enters the world devoid of knowledge and

---

55 *Ecclesiastes Rabbah* 3:1–2.
56 *Pirkei de-Rabbi Eliezer* 33; *Zohar* 3:168b: "three voices that are never lost: the voice of a woman in labor.. the voice of a human being when he departs from the world; the voice of a snake when he sheds his skin – that voice sweeps from one end of the world to the other" (Matt, 9, 111–112.)

takes leave of it devoid of knowledge. It has been taught in the name of R. Meir: When a person enters the world his hands are clenched as though to say, "The whole world is mine, I shall inherit it"; but when he takes leave of it his hands are spread open as though to say, "I have inherited nothing from the world."[57]

Man's entry into the world matches his departure from it. The Parable of the Fox in the Vineyard conveys humans' blind spots, and the need to return to the primal state in order to "succeed in dying." Humans enter the world naked, thin, and hungry; after we grow up and gain weight, we find it hard to leave it like the fox who was stuck in the vineyard and was forced to become lean once again in order to extricate himself from it. We learn from this that a person must forgo all that he has achieved in the world when he leaves it. He must spread forth his hands and say: "I have neither taken nor inherited anything from this world."

The Rabbis discussed the meaning of life through their conception of death. They asked themselves how a person should live, while taking responsibility for his birth, "and repent one day before your death" (M. Avot 2:10). They examined birth as the factor most influential to the experience of living, deeming it to be the constitutive force driving human vitality. Their distinction (M. Avot 4:22) between "without your consent you were fashioned" and "without your consent you were born§" indicates their concept of two different planes of existence: life as a general idea, and the dramatic moment of birth. In this spirit, their dictum "Who is wise? Who discerns what may come to pass [*ha-nolad*]" can be understood as seeing who had already been born (*nolad*, in the past) and not as "who will be born [in the future]."[58] In the continuation of this discursive unit, the Rabbis ask: "What shall a man do to live? They replied: Let him kill himself. What should a man do to kill himself? They replied: Let him keep himself alive." We understand that we were born while being directed to spiritual life in this world, along with the awareness of human finitude.

6 The Womb as the Garden of Eden and the Infant as a "Writing Tablet": Anamnesis and "Discerning What May Come to Pass"

In the preceding chapter, we saw a Zoharic (and also Hegelian, in essence) description of birth: the fetus is formed from three qualities – light, water, and firmament. The fetus is composed from the father, as semen that represents infinite potential; from the mother, who represents the partiality, expansion, and fluidity of blood

---

57 *Ecclesiastes Rabbah* 5:14.
58 BT Tamid 32a. Aharoni and Bergstein, "Looking at the Future Born," 12.

and milk; and finally, the setting of the body's boundaries and the spreading out of the firmament that separates the different qualities and the cleansing of judgment from *Binah*. Like the separation of potential from realization, and the distinction between the female and the male, the Kabbalists also distinguish between the essential and the incidental, core and husk, body and waste. The difference between the body that congeals and the firmament corresponds to that between good and bad. At this point the embryo acquires form, encounters the broad outlines of surrounding reality, and is exposed to the mechanisms of projection and identification, to his inner and external figures, within him and without. Destructive and aggressive forces within the infant are projected onto his mother and return to him as an echo, reflecting his anxiety that the mother will retaliate for his destructiveness. Feelings of guilt and jealousy are transformed by the mother, who wants only the best for her infant, to become forces that aid the adult to integrate the split parts of his psyche. All this is dependent on the mother's ability to withstand the assault, and her enabling the infant to see "light," that is, to remember the good and to believe in its fundamental quality that takes precedence over the water and the coalescence of the judgments.

Memory of primordial unity also includes memory of the unraveling and detachment. Water remembers the light, and firmament remembers water. As we have seen, Bion describes the experiences of uterine anxiety or primal bodily responses that are imprinted within humans from the fetal (the earliest) stage.

Tacking another tack, Freud compared analytical work to that of the archeologist, who reconstructs ancient structures and wall paintings within ruins:

> [The] analytic work of construction, or, if it is preferred, of reconstruction, resembles to a great extent an archaeologist's excavation of some dwelling-place that has been destroyed and buried or of some ancient edifice [. . .] just as the archaeologist builds up the walls of the building from the foundations that have remained standing, determines the number and position of the columns from depressions in the floor and reconstructs the mural decorations and paintings from the remains found in the débris, so does the analyst proceed when he draws his inferences from the fragments of memories, from the associations and from the behavior of the subject of the analysis.[59]

This portrayal highlights the importance of the work of collecting memories in the mental archeology of the individual, paralleling the mythical recollection in Kabbalistic doctrine. Each of these worlds, the psychoanalytic and the Kabbalistic, exhibits an awareness of the dialectical relationship between recollection, on the one hand, and, on the other, forgetting and repression, and of the possibility of constructing a magnificent edifice from the archaic unraveled matter within the ruins.

---

[59] Freud, "Constructions in Analysis," 259.

We will now turn to an examination of the writing tablet metaphor and the depiction of the womb as an idyllic source that resembles the Garden of Eden before the expulsion. The following exposition relates to the conception of anamnesis and the memories that accompany it from the womb. Plato's writings and Rabbinic midrashim offer up the notion that the soul originally knew all, but that humans' knowledge is forgotten upon birth. This idea is set forth most forcefully in a Talmudic exposition that presents the infant as a "writing tablet" in which the Torah that it learned while in the womb is inscribed:

> What does an embryo resemble when it is in the bowels of its mother? Folded writing tablets [. . .] Its head lies between its knees, its mouth is closed, and its navel is open. It eats what its mother eats and drinks what its mother drinks, but it produces no excrement because otherwise it might kill its mother. As soon, however, as it sees the light, the closed organ opens and the open one closes, for if that had not happened the embryo could not live even one single hour. A light burns above its head, and it looks and sees from one end of the world to the other [. . .] And do not be astonished by this, for a person sleeping here might see a dream in Spain. And there is no time in which a man enjoys greater happiness than in those days [i.e., *in utero*] [. . .] It is also taught all the Torah from beginning to end [. . .] As soon as it sees the light an angel approaches, slaps it on its mouth, and causes it to forget all the Torah completely.[60]

This Talmudic exposition connects physical and metaphorical birth narratives by focusing on the divine, infinite source of the soul, which it describes as encompassing the world with its mystical knowledge ("A light burns above its head, and it looks and sees from one end of the world to the other"). This passage also recalls the image of the fetus as a complex structure, in which major functions, or *"in utero* organizing principles," are reversed. The Rabbis hint at the wondrous standing of the fetus, which is portrayed as a Torah scholar, or even as a prophet. This portrayal also alludes to the meditative technique that enables the fetus, like the mystic, to attain perfect knowledge of the Torah.[61] And this is not all: the fetus is not only compared to the sage and the prophet, but, by means of the light above his head, to the high priest, who trims the lights of the candelabrum in the Sanctuary or Temple. The imagery of the light and the *pinkas* denotes the world of writing. The word *pinkas* (usually rendered as "writing tablet") is actually derived from the Greek *pinax* – a series of connected tablets linked to one another in an accordion-like fashion. This thus suggests that the fetus is a written book at the beginning of its life. Following the Aristotelian conception of the intellect and

---

60 BT Niddah 20b; *Leviticus Rabbah* 14:8; Kessler, *Conceiving Israel*, 6 n. 22, 72 n. 45; Urbach, *Sages*, 218.
61 Fenton, "Meditation," 20.

knowledge,[62] and the Platonic doctrine of anamnesis concerned with the history of ideas, the Rabbis maintain that the infant does not come into the world as a blank slate, but rather as a *tabula rasa* – one that has been wiped clean. He therefore must undergo a process of recollection in order to return to his primal knowledge. This knowledge is necessarily bound up with the ideas (in the Platonic sense) that are engraved on the tablets of his consciousness.[63]

In this discursive unit in BT Niddah, the Rabbis add to the "*pinkas*-writing tablet" metaphor the declaration that "there is no time in which a person enjoys greater happiness than in those days." The womb is compared here to the Garden of Eden, and the Rabbis attest to the longings for the inter-uterine period, which enables passage to wondrous and distant places such as Spain: "And do not be astonished by this, for a person sleeping here might see a dream in Spain." The desire to return to the embryonic stage only intensifies when the angel slaps the fetus, and causes it to forget all that it knows. This description also accords with Bion's concept of subthalamic dread and his idea of embryonic intuition. As he suggests, sometimes in clinical work the analyst encounters a primordial fear and "nameless dread" that could have originated only in the womb. In their discussion of the fear of "not being born," the Rabbis offer a nostalgic interpretation of the embryonic stage, which they describe as an ideal place.[64]

A later midrashic work that emerged from Rabbinic traditions known as *Seder Yetzirat ha-Valad* (*The Order*, i.e., *Book, of the Creation of the Fetus*) develops Kabbalistic ideas concerning intra-uterine knowledge, infantile forgetting, and recollection. According to this midrash, the spirit of the fetus negotiates with the angel who prepares it to come into the world. The spirit initially opposes entering the world, and therefore needs to be persuaded, tempted, and even punished:

> The Holy One, blessed, be He, immediately conveys to the angel appointed over the souls, and tells him, Bring Me spirit so-and-so [. . .] he [i.e., the spirit] immediately comes before the Holy One, blessed be He, and bows down before Him. Then the Holy One, blessed be He, says to him, Enter this drop immediately. The spirit immediately opens its mouth, and says to Him, Master of the universe! The world in which I have been since I was created suffices for me. If it be Your will, do not enter me into this putrid drop, for I am holy and pure.[65]

As this midrash has it, the soul's consent to enter into its future life is conditional on its forgetting all that it saw, so that it can discover its path anew. Thanks to

---

62 Aristotle, *De Anima*, 429b.
63 Compare M. Avot 4:21.
64 See Chapter 3, above.
65 *Seder Yetzirat ha-Valad*, Version I, 153. Urbach, *Sages*, 217–220. Compare *Tikkunei ha-Zohar*, Tikkun 70, 136b.

this, a person has the capacity to decide whether to be righteous or wicked. Despite free will, the infant also has knowledge of the future, as is indicated in the continuation of this midrash, in which the angel leads the soul through all the places where the person will pass:

> He [the angel] goes about with him [the soul] from morning to evening, and he shows him every place where he will set foot, the place where he will dwell, and the place where he will be buried. Afterwards he shows him the world of the good and the bad. Towards evening he returns him to his mother's bowels, and the Holy One, blessed be He, makes for him doors and a bolt [. . .] It is written [Isa. 51:16], "And I have put my words in your mouth, and hid you in the shadows of my hand." The Holy One, blessed be He, says to him, This far you shall come, but no more [. . .] When his time came to come forth, this angel comes and tells him, Come out, for your time has come to come out into the world. He [the fetus] responds, But I already said before the One who spoke and the world came into being that I am content with the world where I dwell. He [the angel] says to him, The world into which I bring you is a fine one. Furthermore, you were created against your will in your mother's bowels, and without your consent you will be born and come forth into the world. He immediately weeps. And why does he weep? Because of the world in which he had been, for when he sets him down and strikes him below his nose, extinguishes the light over his head, and brings him forth against his will, he forgets all that he saw. Upon his going forth he weeps. Why? Because seven worlds pass before him then.[66]

Voices emerge from this midrash of choosing life, along with those that oppose the birth and that ensue from the death drive, from the desire for not-being, and the longing to return to the womb. The angel's blow is responsible for the infant's cry at the moment of birth, along with the worlds that pass before him at that moment. This point in time is depicted as a trauma that has its beginnings in the soul's very consent to come down and enter the world. Unlike the emphasis on learning and knowledge in tractate Niddah, this midrash focuses on the infant's seeing and visual experience. All that he saw and knew is imprinted in the soul's subthalamic memory, and these visions arise from within it at surprising moments. The midrash devoted special attention to the ethical issue: not only does the infant know all that will happen to him in the future, already in the womb he understands the question of reward and punishment. On the one hand, heaven shows him all that will befall him in the future, so that he will consent to come out into the world; on the other hand, he is left room to choose regarding moral questions and deciding between good and evil.

Disremembering is a protective mechanism against the injustice in human existence, like in the process of dissociative amnesia. This mechanism is at work in situations in which a person cannot think and contain a certain thought. If the

---

[66] Ibid., 154.

individual were to think, that is, to be conscious of those thoughts, the burden of this trauma might lead to his collapse. In a way, this process resonates with Christopher Bollas's "unthought known." Even though according to Bollas the term does not neccessarily deal with only traumatic events, but rather with pre-verbal knowledge and with non-formulated information which will later achieve verbalization and mental representation in the process of psychotherapy. Yet the known is perceived as "unthought," until the moment that the person is capable of thinking about it, in other words, to "remember" that matter and to consciously contain it: "This is a form of knowledge that has not yet been dreamed or imagined because it is not yet mentally realized."[67]

Although the soul knows all that will happen to it in the future, such "unthought known" cannot be thought until the person lives his life and makes his choices. The Rabbis hint here to a causal connection between growing processes and the ability to forget and repress. Only the fetus can "bear" everything; from the moment that it crosses the threshold and is born, it is subject to the influence of reality and its crises, and accordingly needs to process the world slowly and delicately. In the continuation of this Rabbinic exposition, the infant is compared to "a nut placed in a cup of water." This metaphor reveals the fragility and liminality of the transition from the protected life in the womb to the storm raging outside.[68]

In the following discussion, we will examine the concept of spiritual birth for Plato and in Hellenistic philosophy, while comparing it with the Rabbis' doctrine of remembrance. In contrast to Plato, who maintains that the material world is inferior, the Rabbis realized that the divine image within man is conditional upon the entry into the body and the entry into the material world. Nevertheless, there are important points of similarity between these two corpora. Plato establishes a hierarchy of the inferior bodily birth and that of ideas taking place in the "womb," which he identifies with the mind.

---

67 Bollas, *The Shadow*, 166. Compare to Bion, *Second Thoughts*, 110–119. Yet, it must be noted that Bollas while using the term "unthought known" not dealing with traumatic or repressed events, rather with pre-verbal knowledge and with non formulated information which will later achieve verbalization and mental representation in the process of psychotherapy.
68 BT Niddah 31a.

7 The Symbolization of the Womb as the Mind and the Image of the Midwife in Ancient Greece

Plato, whose philosophy was central to the development of western thought, invokes the theme of birth in his two major dialogues, the *Theaetetus* and the *Symposium*. In the former, he describes a meeting between Socrates and Theaetetus, in which they discuss Socrates's mother, the "noble and burly midwife, Phaenarete." Socrates compares his "art" to that of midwives like his mother, whose "function is less important than mine." As he explains to Theaetetus:

> All that is true of their art of midwifery is true also of mine, but mine differs from theirs in being practised upon men, not women, and in tending their souls in labour, not their bodies. But the greatest thing about my art is this, that it can test in every way whether the mind of the young man is bringing forth a mere image, an imposture, or a real and genuine offspring. For I have this in common with the midwives.[69]

Likewise, through Diotima's speech in the *Symposium*, Plato boldly postulates a hierarchical relationship between women birthing children and men birthing ideas. Allowing that "all men are pregnant [. . .] both in body and in soul," Diotima distinguishes between the search for "immortality" by "those who are teeming in body betake them rather to women, and are amorous on this wise," and what she termed "pregnancy of soul." Through Diotima, Plato clarifies the hierarchy of male creation over the female creation of children, for the former results in

> prudence, and virtue in general; and of these the begetters are all the poets and those craftsmen who are styled *inventors*. Now by far the highest and fairest part of prudence is that which concerns the regulation of cities and habitations; it is called sobriety and justice [. . .] Every one would choose to have got children such as these rather than the human sort – merely from turning a glance upon Homer and Hesiod and all the other good poets, and envying the fine offspring they leave behind to procure them a glory immortally renewed in the memory of men [. . .] In their name has many a shrine been reared because of their fine children; whereas for the human sort never any man obtained this honour.[70]

This oration by the wise woman, Diotima, indicates the human desire for immortality: all humans wish to reproduce, but while the lower form of reproduction expresses itself in flesh-and-blood offspring, the higher form is a mental and creative activity – thus, obviously, a *male* realm, much like the poetry of Homer and Hesiod, or the laws of Solon. Plato's ideas would later influence Aristotle, who perceived women as *matter*, subordinate to the male *form*.

---

69 Plato, *Theaetetus*, 149c–150c, 34–35.
70 Plato, *Symposium*, 206a–209e, 190–191, 198–201.

Despite the denigration of female procreation in these narratives, we cannot ignore the fact that in them such knowledge and insight emanate from two wise, beloved, and authoritative women – Socrates's mother, Phaenarte, and Diotima. They are the ones responsible for teaching Socrates the metaphorical and corporeal meanings of the act of birth. Although both passages lead to oppressive and even misogynic conclusions, they nevertheless hint at the centrality of the image of birth in ancient thought.

The theory of anamnesis appears in a few Platonic dialogues.[71] The process of "remembering" and "recollection" in Plato's dialogue known as the *Meno* adds an additional image to the analogy of human birth and the birth of ideas by implying that thoughts are like fetuses, waiting to be born and reborn in the mind.[72] Their birth signifies the transformation of thought from its liminal stage of "not existing" to the revelation of what already "was almost known" but not yet clearly expressed. In Greek mythology, thought originates in the head, which, tellingly, is symbolized as "the womb of the psyche." As Philo shows, the Latin *conceptio* also means "rumination," just as the Hebrew *herayon* ("pregnancy") resonates with *hirhurim* ("cogitations," "thoughts").[73] It parallels the Greek *syllepsin*, which bears the double meaning of physical impregnation and of fertilization with "ideas." These notions from Greek philosophy developed into modern philosophical concepts, with imagery from the realm of conception and pregnancy transformed into "the birth of thoughts." Bion, as we have seen above, similarly suggests that creative thought is born out of the meeting between preconception and conception, and represents the amalgamation of opposing components that fertilize one another.

The symbolization of the mind as womb relates to the theme of "pregnancy jealousy" that was noted by Karen Horney.[74] Hesiod gives expression to this theme by relating the narrative of the birth of Athena, who emerged from the head of her father Zeus, after he swallowed his first wife, Metis, and kept her in his belly. In Aeschylus's play *Eumenides* (*The Kindly Ones*) Athena declares: "There is no mother who gave birth to me, and I commend the male in all

---

71 Plato, *Phaedo*, 72–3; *Phaedrus*, 248–9.
72 Plato, *Meno*, 81c, 302–303. As we learn from Plato in this dialogue, thoughts are born and reborn forever, since the soul is immortal: "The soul is immortal and has been born many times, and has beheld all things both in this world and in the nether realms, she has acquired knowledge of all and everything; so that it is no wonder that she should be able to recollect all that she knew before about virtue and other things" (81b).
73 See Liebes, *Sefer Yetzira*, 109–110. Compare to the psychoanalytic perspective of Spezzano, "Home."
74 Horney, *Feminine Psychology*.

respects (except for joining in marriage) with all my heart: in the fullest sense, I am my Father's child."[75]

Despite the many centuries that have passed since the time of the ancient Greeks, we still face these same polarized notions of birth: a subordinate, female, corporeal *reproductive* function – and a superior, male, *conceptual* one.[76] Behind these different conceptions lies a male sense of oppression, the fear of the powerful "Great Mother," or the residual memories of the terrifying birth experience itself. The mythical narratives of a male giving birth, which appear in Greek mythology and philosophy, as well as in Genesis 2, may be an attempt to present a human male's miraculous ability – one that is similar to the divine power to create worlds. Men's jealousy of women might be caused by their exclusion from the most monumental event in the lives of the baby and mother. Given the ancient world's limited understanding of reproductive processes, men's fear of birth was connected to their negative fantasies about mother–fetus relations *in utero* and the incestuous attachment of the two.[77]

Although we cannot postulate Plato's direct influence on the Jewish sages, we can assume that they had been exposed to these philosophical and mythological ideas through the Hellenistic and Roman civilizations. Therefore, instead of attempting to determine the direction of influence regarding perceptions of birth, it would be more productive to explore the commonalities and parallels that arose in that contemporary cultural atmosphere.

The Rabbis combined the theory of anamnesis with ideas about the subordination of physical birth to metaphorical birth, and with other concepts such as the idea of the miraculous conception. Indeed, inasmuch as they were around at the time of nascent Christianity, paradoxical hermeneutic attitudes evolved in the midrashic world: there were radical critiques of and polemics against the Christian narratives, even as they were influenced by and in dialogue with them.[78]

---

[75] Hesiod, *Theogony*, 886–900; Aeschylus, *Eumenides*, 735–738.
[76] Gilbert and Gubar, *The Madwoman*, suggest a feminist critique of this theme. For a discussion of female symbolic writing – "with milk" instead of the male and phallic "ink" – see Cixous and Clément, *Newly Born*. Cixous, an Algerian-French-Jewish feminist writer, herself a daughter of a midwife who witnessed many real births, testifies to the influence of this physical and emotional experience on her development as a writer (Cixous, *Coming to Writing*). In this context, we might add to the myth of the "birth of the hero" (explored by Freud, Rank, Campbell, Dandes, and others) the description of the mother as a midwife and the imprint of this skill on the character of her child, the hero/heroine, as we know from the accounts about Socrates, Moses, and other important historical figures.
[77] Meltzer, *Aesthetic Conflict*.
[78] For a polemical reading of the virginal conception in the Talmud and *Sefer Toldot Yeshu*, see Schäfer, *Mirror*; Biale, "Counter-History." In addition to this position, I suggest that the

Thus, for example, the concept of the virgin birth of Jesus alludes to the notion of thought forced on – "impregnating" – a person. Also, the conditions by which Jesus was conceived by his mother, Mary's "immaculate conception," attests to the pure thought of the Savior's mother.[79] The complementary concept of the pure birth from the Father attributed to Jesus underlies the term *de utero Patris*. It also underlies the Creed of the Eleventh Council of Toledo in 675 CE, which states: "For neither from nothing, nor from any other substance, but from the womb of the Father, that is, from His substance, we must believe that the Son was begotten or born."[80]

Rabbinic homilies often preserve and even expand the hierarchy we have seen as foundational in Greek and Roman thought. In one instance, the Rabbis portray the mother's contribution to the fetus (blood) as subordinate to that of the father (semen):

> His father supplies the semen of the *white substance* [. . .] his mother supplies semen of the *red substance* [. . .] and the Holy One, blessed be He, *gives* him the spirit and the breath [or, soul].[81]

As Gwynn Kessler argues, while both Galen and Hippocrates viewed the mother's contribution of blood (the female component) as a vital substance transformed into nurturing milk and as necessary as the male semen, the Rabbis, in contrast, saw the womb as an insecure, even dangerous place. In a more general sense, Kessler finds the womb to be a central locus for the construction of Jewish identity in Rabbinic literature. She maintains that the Rabbis, despite their acquaintance with Greco-Roman writings on embryology, emphasize the primacy of God's role in procreation, at the expense of the biological parents, and in particular at the expense of the mother. As the Talmud states: "There are three partners in man: the Holy One, blessed be He, his father, and his mother."[82]

By comparing the womb to a purse that exposes all its money, bowels, and a filthy place (see above), the Rabbis reveal their ideological, political, and religious polemics with the Hellenistic and Christian worlds, as well as their

---

Sages were also influenced by this narrative. An example of such influence can be found in the statement adduced by the Rabbis concerning Lot's daughters in *Genesis Rabbah* 51:8. Indeed, God himself is the supreme father who impregnated the older daughter of Lot. Consequently, the Jewish Messiah symbolizes the *Divi Filius* ("Son of God"). See Kaniel, *Holiness and Transgression*, 130–140, 227–230.
79 Koren, "Sarah."
80 Idel, "Womb."
81 BT Niddah 31a (emphasis is mine).
82 BT Kiddushin 30b. See Kessler, 67–84, 91–100.

profound fear of birth, and the uncanny feelings related to the womb's darkness and mystery.

Plato and the Rabbis were not the only ones to stress the centrality of the imagery of procreation. The first-century Jewish-Hellenist philosopher Philo of Alexandria set forth the connection between pregnancy and thoughts:

> For when the mind bestirs itself and receives an impulse towards some object belonging to its own sphere [. . .] it becomes pregnant and is in travail with its thoughts.[83]

Philo was influenced by Platonic philosophy and sought to advance Jewish ideas by means of allegory. He asserted that thoughts are conceived within man's consciousness but are actualized only upon their becoming words and sounds uttered by the mouth, like an infant who comes forth from his mother's womb.

Current technological advances enable insemination without the father's direct involvement. Nonetheless, even in the twenty-first century, in most cases a person is born not only from the mother, but from the father, too. The struggle between female and male procreation demonstrates textual compensatory attempts by men in the face of the bodily empowerment of female birthing. Jealousy of the womb and pregnancy leads to the development of many models of being born from the father, which in myths represent spiritual birth, reaching maturity, the birth of ideas and thoughts, and mental growth.

---

[83] Philo, "That the Worse," 286–287. See Liebes, *Sefer Yetzira*, 109–110.

Chapter 5
The Double Beginning of the Zohar

According to Gershom Scholem, prior to the expulsion of the Jews from Spain the Kabbalists focused on the beginning of Creation while abandoning national and historical issues in favor of "primordial history."[1] Their writings, most notably the *Zohar*, concentrated on the esoteric *Ma'aseh Bereshit* ("Account of Creation") and *Ma'aseh Merkavah* ("Account of the Chariot"), and so enabled the mystics to remain in their embryonic "inner homeland," which essentially comprised the symbolism of the worlds of *beri'a* ("creation") and *atzilut* ("emanation"), rather than focusing on Messianic ideas and eschatological motivations:

> Kabbalistic doctrine developed apart from eschatology because in its original setting it concentrated less on the end of the world than on the primordial beginning of creation [. . .] The Spanish disaster was the beginning of the "messianic birth pangs."[2]

Isaiah Tishby similarly asserts that "the eyes of the kabbalist, searching for the highest and most recondite origins of being, were fixed first and foremost on the divine area in the act of creation, while the origins of the external world entered into his calculation only as a secondary phenomenon, bound up with the emanation of the *sefirot*."[3] According to Scholem and Tishby, then, the first Kabbalists focused on the "myth of origin" rather than on realistic, historical, and developmental processes of existence.[4] For the first generations of Kabbalists, the link between the human world to the supernal world was rooted in the riddle of origins, the mystery of "emanation," and the understanding of the primal source of beginning.

Indeed, the word *bereshit*, or "beginning," is variously interpreted in the *Zohar* as a reflection of the psychological and spiritual self-perception of its authors. This approach was expanded upon in the early fourteenth century by the author of *Tikkunei ha-Zohar*, who suggested seventy interpretations for this word.[5] For example, *bereshit* is hermeneutically interpreted as referring to the creation of a poem or a love song (*bara-shir* or *shir-taev*);[6] to the designated

---
1 Scholem, "The Messianic Idea in Kabbalism," 38–39.
2 Scholem, *Sabbatai Sevi*, 15, 18.
3 Lachower and Tishby, *Wisdom*, 549.
4 For other attitudes, see Idel, *Messianic Mystics*; Liebes, "The Messiah of the Zohar."
5 See Giller, *The Enlightened*; Roi, *Love*.
6 *Tikkun* 10, 24b.

goat (*bara-taish*);[7] to the double element (*bara-shtei*); or to the creation of the primordial pits that connect earth and the abyss (*bara-shit*). In addition, the author suggests that the word may hold other creative meanings, such as indicating the ritual of Havdalah through the combination *bara-trei-esh*, which means "created two lights."[8]

Through skillful midrashic techniques, *Tikkunei ha-Zohar* ponders the question "Whence do we come?" As a composition written one generation after the *Zohar*, it aims to elucidate the riddle of origins not only as a mythical endeavor, but also as a poetic self-reflective task that turns back to the urtext of the *Zohar*.

The mystical writers understood that creation has a myriad causes, and that the mystery of birth cannot be wholly or unequivocally interpreted. The sermons of the *Tikkunei ha-Zohar* acknowledge the parallel process that happens both at the depth of the Godhead and in the individual's own psychological contemplation, as he uncovers his own origin and creates himself.

Let us now turn to two unique Zoharic narratives offering answers to the riddle of origins based on gender differentiation. The first is from the introduction to the *Zohar*, and the second is from the opening passage of the *Zohar* on Genesis. The first deals with the way the *sefirot* – as symbolic "divine children" – constitute the Upper Mother *Binah* ("Understanding"), while the second examines the concept of the Upper Father, the *sefirah* of *Hokhma* ("Wisdom"), as the source of divine will (*ratson*), impelled to create the worlds. Psychologically, both cases involve an attempt to look backward to the primordial Creation and to solve the riddle of the universe's and people's origins.

I suggest that the combined version of these two Zoharic homilies enables the reconstruction of a "combined figure" of divine father and mother. Indeed, later on, the author of *Tikkunei ha-Zohar* will interpret the word *bereshit* to refer to the coupling of the sefirotic parental pair, the *sefirot Hokhma* and *Binah*, symbolizing two primal entities, by means of wordplay: "two beginnings" and "two heads" (*bet-reshit*; *bet-rosh* = "head").[9] In a wider sense, the parallel analysis of these texts allows us to explore the riddle of birth through a mythical and Kabbalistic prism.

---

[7] *Tikkunim Tinyana* (second part), *Tikkun* 2, 139a.
[8] Ibid., *Tikkun* 6, 143b.
[9] See, for example, the opening of *Tikkun* 55, 88a: "*Bereshit bara* – two heads, and they are father and mother."

1 Comparing the Introduction to the *Zohar* ("Who Created These?") with Its Opening Homily ("*Be-rosh Hurmanuta de-Malka*" = "At the Head of Potency of the King")

The opening lines of any literary work may serve as an enigmatic code that provides a key to understanding it. In the case of the *Zohar*, the section known as *Hakdamat ha-Zohar* (*Introduction to the Zohar*, hereafter *Introduction*), was printed in Mantua, Italy, in 1558, on the opening page of the edition. The *Introduction* (*Zohar* 1:1a–15a) opens with the image of the rose and the feminine symbolization of the *sefirot* of *Binah* and *Shekhinah* (the Upper Mother and Upper Daughter), through discussion of the verse from Isaiah (40:26) "Lift up your eyes on high and see: *Who created these*?" This portion focuses on maternal qualities and the act of birth from the upper mother's womb.

By contrast, located at the formal beginning of *Zohar Bereshit* (Mantua edition, *Zohar* 1:15a–b) is the phrase *be-rosh hurmanuta de-malka*: "At the head of potency of the king." Unlike in Mantua, the printers of the *Zohar Cremona* (which was printed in 1559) begin their version of the *Zohar* with the homily on the power and potency of the male king which focuses on the emanation process (*atzilut*) and the emergence of the divine measures, *sefirot*, from the source of the Upper Father, *Hokhma*.

Unlike the homily "At the head of potency of the king," which appears in all manuscripts and in the first two printings of the *Zohar* (in the Mantua edition some fifteen pages later), the section of the *Introduction* does not appear in some manuscripts, and in others it appears in different locations (for instance, in the Cremona edition it appears without any special marking in the middle of *Parshat Bereshit*).[10]

Daniel Abrams, examining why the *Introduction* is not mentioned in major Kabbalistic works of the fourteenth and fifteenth centuries, suggests that it is a separate composition, apparently written only after the main "body of the Zohar" (*guf ha-Zohar*) was composed.[11] According to Abrams, printers in the sixteenth century gave the *Introduction* its name and its canonic status as the ceremonial gate to the whole Zoharic composition. It might be that several authors were involved in its composition; its authorial identity remains a riddle.[12] Here, I would

---

10 *Zohar Cremona* 1:29a–b, row 17.
11 Abrams, "Eimatai Hubberah ha-Haqdamah"; idem, "The Invention of the Zohar." Based on the connections between the introduction and the sections of *yanuka*, Jonathan Benarroch suggested that both texts represent the "intermediate layer" between the *Zohar* and the *Tikkunim*. See Benarroch, *Sabba and Yanuka*.
12 Mayer, "The Introduction to the Zohar."

like to stress the difference between the masculine perspective of the opening passages of *Parshat Bereshit* in the *Zohar*, and the feminine myth of the homilies in the *Introduction*. If, indeed, the *Introduction* was a later composition, we might hypothesize that its writer attempted to correct the absence of feminine and maternal birth in the masculine opening passages of the *Zohar*. Thus, the cluster of the homilies situated at the beginning of the *Introduction* focus on the upper womb, which is also called "holy of holies," "hechal," and the "palace of *Binah*."

The narrative of the *Introduction* opens with a homily presented in the name of R. Hizkiyah. At its center stands the mother–daughter relationship. Unlike the feminine and uterine myth of Creation, the opening of the *Zohar* is attributed to an anonymous source, in the spirit of the *Tosefta* units, reflecting a pre-verbal, pre-relational realm, wherein the godhead exists alone, without even the absence of any others who could potentially be present.

The *Introduction's* homilies offer the name *Elohim* as an appellation for the *sefirah* of *Binah*, and discuss her relationship as a "mother" with the sefirotic "daughter," *Shekhinah*.[13] Stylistically, the *Introduction* exhibits clear poetic similarities to the central framing narratives of the *Zohar*, such as *Saba de-Mishpatim*, *R. Metivta*, and the *yanuka* stories. The author of *Tikkunei ha-Zohar* was familiar with the introduction and based on it some of his homilies (for example, the ceremony on the staff of Moses). Later on, in the sixteenth century, the printers of *Zohar Mantua* contributed to its canonical placement by locating it at the opening pages of the *Zohar*.

Like many homilies in *Zohar Bereshit*, both the *Introduction* and the formal opening of the *Zohar* on Genesis expound upon the opening verse in the Bible: "In the beginning God [= *Elohim*] created the heaven and the earth" (Gen. 1:1). However, unlike the feminine reading, which illuminates the bond between the Kabbalist and the Godhead through the word *Elohim* as an appellation of *Binah*, the masculine interpretation addresses the *sefirah* of *Hokhma* (which it terms "head") and stresses the word "beginning" in the first verse of Genesis. Such an awakening of divine will to create a universe, following upon the decree of the male king, differs profoundly from the description of the birth of the worlds in the *Introduction*.

Reflecting stereotypical gender differentiation, the *Zohar* has a feminine and a masculine narrative. The feminine narrative deals with relationships and the attachment between the mother and the daughter (*herstory*) while the masculine narrative deals with the mystical origin of emanation and utterance of

---

[13] The centrality of the *Shekhinah* and its relationship with the Upper Mother is intensified in *Tikkunei ha-Zohar*; see Roi, *Love*, 13–39, 68–69; Liebes, "The Zohar and the Tiqqunim"; Pedaya, *Expanses*, 139.

the father-king and the sources of the divine sperm (*history*). "At the head of potency of the king" is a metaphorical and metaphysical account of Creation resonating with philosophical and Neoplatonic concepts, while the *Introduction* exploits hermeneutically the mystery of the letters of the Hebrew alphabet, the constructions of Eros, and the use of wordplay in the spirit of Rabbinic midrash, in order to focus on the human gaze that constitutes the Godhead.

The division between a "masculine" and a "feminine" narrative parallels, in a way, the division between chapters 1 and 2 in Genesis. Chapter 1 represents a linear story of Creation, which is structured and "masculine," while chapter 2 is arranged as a circular, "feminine" myth, which contains the struggle between good and evil, the figure of the serpent, sexuality, sin, and human tragedy.[14] I suggest that the author or redactor of the Zoharic introduction wanted to reverse the relations between the chapters and stories in Genesis, and to privilege the maternal myth of birth over the masculine, paternal account. In the Cremona printing, however, it may be that the arrangement of the homilies was in accordance with the Biblical structure.

Indeed, the verse "In the beginning God created" was understood by the Kabbalists in a radical way. According to one reading, the father (*reshit*), *Hokhma*, created the feminine God *Binah* (*bereshit bara et Elohim*). This interpretation indicates that the constellation of *sefirot* was not created "out of nothingness," but rather "out of something."[15] Another interpretation of the same verse teaches that *Binah*, known as *Elohim*, gives life to the divine son (Aramaic: "son," *bra*). The son, in turn, representing six *sefirot*, creates the mother and invests her name with meaning – *Elohim*. This reading echoes the psychoanalytic notion that the boy perceives his mother as a goddess containing all worlds, possessing even various androgynous (i.e., male and female) features.

Following this discussion, I will now concentrate on the languages of giving birth in the *Introduction* as opposed to the opening passages of *Zohar Bereshit*. Although in the process of emanation (*atzilut*) *Hokhma* precedes Binah, I will begin the discussion with female birth and then paternal birth; finally, I will look at these two beginnings, in the *Introduction* and the *Zohar Bereshit*, as a form of connection between "divine parents," providing a combined solution to the riddle of the worlds' origins.

---

14 On *gynocritics*, see Showalter, "Feminist Criticism." For a discussion on the difference between feminine and masculine narratives (*history* vs. *herstory*), see, for example, Gilbert and Gubar, *The Madwoman*; Gilligan, *Different Voice*.
15 Gottlieb, *Studies*, 18–28.

2 Maternal Origins ("Who Created These?")

The *Introduction* of the Zohar opens with the image of a rose among the thorns (*Zohar* 1:1a). Inspired by the Beloved in Song of Songs, the rose is a stock image in Rabbinic midrash for the people of Israel and its tribulations in exile.[16] By mentioning the word "rose" twice, the *Zohar* bestows the female character with ambiguity, between red and white, law and mercy, *Binah* and *Malkhut*.[17]

The statement "*esh shoshanah ve esh shoshana*" is indicative of the relationship between the two feminine *sefirot* from which all worlds descend. The erotic image of the rose is projected onto the *Zohar* as a whole, as a dynamic composition in constant flux, dependent upon the mystic's deeds and responsive to his courtship. Later on, the *Zohar* describes the mystery of the value of letters and of the names of God: from the first occurrence of the word "*Elohim*" to the second, there are thirteen words symbolizing the attributes of mercy, like leaves encircling a rose; the next five words until the following occurrence of *Elohim* symbolize the protective *gevurot* ("judgments") around the rose. The homilist moves on to the describing ritual of raising the hand holding the wine goblet, as is the custom while reciting the blessings of Kiddish and Havdalah, as appearing like a flower and its petals. These images set up the rose as a key to the entire Zoharic composition, like a rosetta or mandala holding the entire constellation of the Godhead, and as the feminine dyad imaging all worlds.[18] The homily teaches that the blessing of the rose – that is, the people of Israel – depends on its being among the thorns and the nations, growing ever stronger as a result of their pressure and persecution.[19]

In this homily, *Binah* is called *Mi* ("Who") while her daughter, *Malkhut*, is called *Ma* ("What"). The dyad of the feminine attributes represents here questioning words that simultaneously serve as "answers." The connection between these two spreads downward the configuration of *sefirot*, branching out from the top to the bottom, from the head of infinity (*Ein Sof*) to our world, which is identified as the *sefirah* of *Malkhut*. At the same time, the Zohar posits a relationship between human and divine in the reverse direction, through the movement of the mystic's gaze raised upward following the cry, based on the verse from Isaiah (40:26): "Lift up your eyes on high and see: Who created these?"[20]

---

16 *Song of Songs Rabbah* 2:2.
17 The image of two lilies/roses appears in *Tikkunei ha-Zohar* 26, yet this double Zoharic formulation is missing in *Or-Yakar* of R. Moses Cordovero. For more on the ambivalence of the female character in the Zohar, see Liebes, "Bride"; idem, "Shekhinah Is a Virgin?".
18 Elqayam, "Lily"; Abrams, *Female Body*, 60–63; Fishbane, "Rose"; Hellner-Eshed, *River*.
19 Cf. *Zohar* 2:189b.
20 On this homily, see Wolfson, *Speculum*, 330–345; Liebes, "Zohar ve'Eros," 67–68.

> When Concealed of all Concealed verged on being revealed, it produced at first a single point, which ascended to become thought. Within, it drew all drawings, graved all engravings, carving within the concealed holy lamp a graving of one hidden design, holy of holies, a deep structure emerging from thought, called מי (*Mi*), Who, origin of structure. Existent and non-existent, deep and hidden, called by no name but Who. Seeking to be revealed, to be named, it garbed itself in a splendid, radiant garment and created אלה (*elleh*), these אלה (*elleh*) attained the name: these letters joined with those, culminating in the name אלהים (*Elohim*). Until it created אלה (*elleh*), it did not attain the name אלהים (*Elohim*). Based on this mystery, those who sinned with the Golden Calf said " אלה (*elleh*), These, are your gods, O Israel!" (Exodus 32:8). Just as מי (*Mi*) is combined with אלה (*elleh*), so the name אלהים (*Elohim*) is constantly polysemous. Through this mystery, the universe exists.[21]

According to the *Zohar*, the letters of the alphabet continue the process of autogenesis. Following that same process, the *Zohar* strengthens the feminine mother–daughter bond between *Binah* and *Malkhut*: the daughter receives from her mother "garments" and "adornments"; and like her, she learns to create worlds and souls. It is then that the *Shekhinah* transforms from the letter *heh* into the masculine letter *yod*, as it is said further in the introduction to the Zohar:

> For מה (*mah*) was not so, is not composed until these letters – אלה (*elleh*) – are drawn from above to below, and Mother lends Daughter Her garments, though not adorning Her with Her adornments. When does She adorn Her fittingly? When all males appear before Her, as is written: *[All your males shall appear] before the Sovereign, YHWH* (Exodus 23:17). This one is called Sovereign, as is said: *Behold, the ark of the covenant, Sovereign of all the earth* (Joshua 3:11). Then the letter ה (*heh*) departs and י (*yod*) enters, and She adorns Herself in masculine clothing in the presence of every male in Israel.[22]

The *Zohar* presents an original description of the image of the adornment of *Shekhinah* in the three pilgrimage festivals. Whereas according to the Biblical command only Israelite males must appear in Jerusalem three times a year, the Zohar stresses that the *Shekhinah* is involved in this ritual, not only as a decoration and as a passive bride waiting for her husband(s)'s arrival, but also as the central figure who directs the activity taking place inside the Temple. As Daniel Matt comments, this commandment "implies that the masculine power of the *sefirot* must be drawn down to *Shekhinah*, the Sovereign. Through the ritual of pilgrimage, *Shekhinah* is

---

21 *Zohar* 1:2a (Matt, 1, 9–10, n. 58–64).
22 *Zohar* 1:2a (Matt, 1, 9–10). See there, n. 58–64. Here the letter ה (*heh*) signifies the feminine, and the letter י (*yod*) signifies the masculine. When the masculine powers of the *sefirot* reach Shekhinah, she is transformed from feminine to masculine, from מה (*mah*) to מי (*mi*). Then she rules the world.

adorned. During the three festivals the *Shekhinah* is like *the ark* housing the *sefirah* of *Yesod, the covenant*, a union that reflects the upper binding of the *sefirot*."[23]

Here, the *Shekhinah* clothes herself in male clothing and in adornments she receives from her mother, the *sefirah* of *Binah*, as well as from all the men who gather before her during the three festivals and adorn her face, as we learn from the verse "before the Sovereign, the Lord" (lit., "before *the face* of the Sovereign, the Lord"). The scene of adornment has received extensive scholarly attention, but this attention usually focuses on its theological meaning rather than on its gender context. An exception is Elliot Wolfson, who claims that this text (like many other Kabbalistic sources) expresses the idea of the assimilation of the feminine into the masculine and the transforming of the *Shekhinah* into the phallic corona (*aṭeret ha-yesod*).[24]

I suggest another reading. I believe that the mother prepares her daughter for this tough, male-centered, and phallic world by dressing her as the ultimate "alpha male." King David is regularly used in the *Zohar* to present the active part of *Shekhinah*'s face (as we learn also from the play on the word *melekh* "king," and *Malkhut*, the name of the *sefirah* attributed to him). As I have claimed elsewhere, in terms of national identity, that the figure of the *Shekhinah* represents the fragile reality of the Jews, who were deprived of political sovereignty. The fantastic realm of the divine *sefirot* gave them a sense of power and an imaginary kingdom. Thus, *Shekhinah* is both active and passive, and can thus easily shift between her different masks and performative roles.[25]

In addition, this homily is based on the notion that the Patriarchs symbolize the three legs of the Chariot, with David serving as the fourth. Although David is a male hero, the *Zohar*, which is interested in the subjectivity of the *Shekhinah*, uses him as an affective feminine figure of *Malkhut* by emphasizing his feminine aspects: his poetry, his dancing before of the ark, and even his sins. The idea that the Upper Mother lends her daughter divine garments, and adorns her with frills, indicates parallel processes of birth for both of them.

The gift of birthing is shared by the two female emanations.[26] *Binah*, however, is awarded the name *Elohim*, due to her ability to give birth to *sefirot* and divine emanations, while *Malkhut* is not of equal status, since she gives birth to attributes

---

23 Matt, *The Zohar*, 1, 9.
24 Wolfson, *Circle*.
25 Kaniel, *The Feminine Messiah*.
26 However, *Zohar Vayeḥi* (1:246a–b) indicates an essential difference between these two feminine images: *Binah* is called *Olam ha-Zachar* (the world of the masculine) when she is giving birth; *Shekhinah*, on the other hand, imprints female qualities on her offspring, and they are considered female and called "feminine" even though they are males. See below ch. 6 n. 51–52.

that are not "above the heavens" but only powers that located "under the heavens." The meeting point of the two feminine aspects is the holy pilgrimage ritual. This picture completes the glorification of the rose, the ritual of raising the hand holding the Havdalah wine goblet, at the beginning of this textual unit.

In the above-discussed *Introduction*, birth is presented as an image of multi-generational fertility. The children "give birth" to their mother, transforming her from "question" to "answer"; they reverse her essence and adorn her, just as she gives birth to them and dons them as garments. Such images resonate on an emotional and psychological level: at first, the mother is "above the heavens," among the stars and upper firmament; ultimately, she descends and is revealed here, on earth, through her offspring. As noted in the *Zohar*, the mother appears not only at time of birthing or at the ritual of the pilgrimage: she is present also in pain and suffering, as we learn from the verses of Lamentations, Isaiah, and Proverbs that are woven into the text. The feminine experience of destruction and crisis heightens the daughter's need for her mother to rescue her, as we find in the homily itself:

> Yet if you say you cannot endure or be healed, then "[What can I say for you, to what compare you, O daughter Jerusalem? To what can I liken you, that I may comfort you, O virgin daughter Zion? For vast as the sea is your ruin] *Who will heal you!*".
>
> (Lamentations 2: 13)

The *Introduction* regards Creation as a quintessentially feminine phenomenon, stemming from the desire for adornment. Binah, "[s]eeking to be revealed, to be named [. . .] garbed itself in a splendid, radiant garment." Later, *Malkhut* follows her and is revealed through producing offspring and creating this world. The quintessence of giving birth, according to the *Zohar*, is donning splendid garments. Indeed, in the Kabbalistic writings, the name of God Himself is seen as a garment of glory and beauty, while they present the *sefirot* as stars embroidered on this radiant garment.[27] Paradoxically, the desire to be revealed is expressed by covering up, while giving birth, the most intimate moment of nakedness, emerges here as an act of donning clothes.

3 Birth as Donning Garments

Psychologically, birth is defined as separation and individuation, the imposition of a clear-cut border between the self and the other. Clothing symbolizes the enveloping of the skin that differentiates the body from non-corporeal. The skin is meant to delimit and protect the psychological vessel. Similarly, the garments of the

---

[27] Schneider, *The Appearance of the High Priest*.

emanations of *Binah* and *Malkhut* constitute a kind of "Skin-Ego" that protects the divine light enshrined within the vessels.²⁸ The divine garment has erotic and playful qualities, but also references the tragic garment of vengeance (*purpera*) which God embroiders with the memory of the martyrs. Following the *Zohar*, the term *hitlabshut* develops in Hasidic teachings: the donning of garments expresses the imprint of the divine presence (*reshimu*), even when the primal source is concealed and hidden. To quote *Ha-Tanya*: "It is, by way of illustration, like one who embraces a king. There is no difference in the degree of his closeness and attachment to the king whether he embraces him when the king is wearing one robe or many robes since the king's body is in them."²⁹

God seeks to reveal himself through his garments, and contact with the Godhead takes place through the garment, as an allegory for the envelope symbolizing the most intimate of encounters between the Godhead and the human being. In the words of Gershom Scholem, "Everything needs clothing, for that which has no clothes cannot be revealed."³⁰

As we have seen, the *Introduction* teaches that Binah wishes to display the beauty that is encapsulated in her offspring, the *sefirot*; she therefore adorns and decorates herself with them, as with a garment. Thus, garments are an expression of emanation, of protective presence; likewise, it is a phase in the descent of offspring and the worlds. The *Tikkunei ha-Zohar* also considers the *Shekhinah* as encompassing all worlds and their adornments:

> And the *Shekhinah* is an image (*ṣiyyura*) of the higher and lower [ones], all the icons (*diyoqnin*) of the *sefirot*, and all their names are imaged (*meṣuyyurim*) within her. And within her are carved souls, angels, and holy living creatures (*ḥayyot*). And within her are carved those, which concerning them it was stated: "And their faces were the face of a man."³¹
> (Ezek. 1:10)

According to R. Moses Cordovero, the Upper Mother adorns her body not only externally but also internally by engraving her offspring upon her womb.³² Thus, the discussion of putting on garments opens up new expanses for understanding the birthing experience. Donning garments, in the *Zohar*, reflects a twofold process of revelation and concealment, an encounter between potential and manifest, a connection between past and future, for future offspring and all their doings are dressed and engraved in the mother's body even before their creation. To give

---

28 Bick, "The Experience of the Skin"; Anzieu, *The Skin-Ego*.
29 *Tanya*, "Sha'ar Hayichud ve-Haemunah," 1, 4.
30 Scholem, *Sabbatai Sevi*, 27.
31 *Tikkunei ha-Zohar*, Tikkun 22, 65a; Roi, *Love*, 47–65.
32 Cordovero, *Pardes Rimonim* 23:1; Hellner-Eshed, "Mythical Midrash."

birth is to be revealed, to cover up the infinite concealed nakedness of the past, and to realize its potential in the future. Just as donning garments is an act of self-exposure – both of the mother who exposes what had been hidden inside her, and of the infant who is now revealed in her body – so too the adornments of the feminine personae of the Godhead – *Binah* and *Malkhut* – reveal by concealment.

In Neoplatonic terms, to don garments is to descend into the material world, moving away from the single absolute source. The paradox of donning garments and the experience of revelation is expressed in mystical and philosophical language in describing the process of emanation: donning garments is related to exposure, nakedness, and distancing oneself from the pure source. Embodiment and the donning of garments entail obscuring, and are identified with materiality.

4 Paternal Origins ("At the Head of Potency of the King")

As we have seen, the relationship between the Upper Mother (*Binah*) and the Upper Daughter (*Shekhinah*) stands at the heart of all the *derashot* in the introduction of the *Zohar* (the *Introduction*). Now, I will turn to another archetype of paternal creation:

> At the head of potency of the King, He engraved engravings in luster on high. A spark of impenetrable darkness flashed within the concealed of the concealed, from the head of Infinity – a cluster of vapor forming in formlessness, thrust in a ring, not white, not black, not red, not green, no color at all. As a cord surveyed, it yielded radiant colors. Deep within the spark gushed a flow, splaying colors below, concealed within the concealed of the mystery of *Ein Sof*. It split and did not split its aura, was not known at all, until under the impact of splitting, a single, concealed, supernal point shone. Beyond that point, nothing is known, so it is called ראשית (*reshit*), Beginning, first command of all.[33]

The homily "At the head of potency of the king" deals with primordial formation, with the unseen chaos movement from the *Keter* to the Upper Father, the *sefirah* of *Hokhma*. While *Binah* is the divine womb, temple, and "treasury of souls," where the *sefirot* are given form and shape; *Hokhma* is the first beginning of thought and a formless stage of existence.

Unlike the psychoanalytic division, which attributes law and language to the father and the semiotic and pre-verbal stage to the mother, in Kabbalistic thought *Binah* represents limits and law and is connected to the symbolic stage

---

[33] *Zohar* 1:16a (Matt, 1, 109–110).

(as we have seen in many homilies linking *Binah* to the ten utterances from which the world was created). In addition, *Binah* validates divine law and judgment. The Upper Mother delimits the *sefirot* and endows with meaning words and souls that emerge from her womb. She is identified with the birth of language, law, and order. By contrast, the father, *Hokhma*, is presented at an earlier stage of the chain of emanation and is identified with the beginning of seed and the pre-verbal stage. *Hokhma* is the source of the attribute of *Hesed* ("Mercy," "Compassion") in its inchoate, undifferentiated form.

This homily positions the *sefirah* of *Hokhma* in a state of consciousness with no distinct, unequivocal words, akin to the psychological experience of "negative capability" (in Wilfred Bion's words), which refers to the willingness to sustain doubt and uncertainty.[34] This experience is associated with reality lacking differentiated forms, colors, and sounds; at this level, chaos reigns, approximating a primordial, embryonic existence.

The *Zohar*'s language in this text indicates that it drew inspiration from ancient Jewish sources such as the mystical composition *Sefer Yetzirah*. In *Sefer Yetzirah*, the process of Creation is founded upon the following two elements: "He hewed, as it were, immense columns or colossal pillars, out of the intangible air, and from the empty space."[35] The *Zohar* employs the poetics and symbolism of *Sefer Yetzirah*, striving to grasp what cannot be grasped, or, in the words of the *Introduction*, to grasp the indisputable, or, in Zoharic terms, "what is not standing to question."

Birth, according to the *Zohar*, means returning to the primordial chaos of undifferentiated elements. In many senses, these primal elements parallel the psychoanalytic concept of the "unrepressed unconscious." Unlike the "repressed unconscious" which preoccupied Freud, the *unrepressed* unconscious (i.e., that which never underwent mentalization and therefore cannot be repressed) remains primitive material. To use Bion's term, there are "beta-elements" of the psyche. Similarly, the personal and cosmic experience of birth remains outside verbal experience and beyond the dimensions of existence that can be grasped verbally. In Julia Kristeva's thought, the *chora*'s maternal, semiotic quality is chaotic, while in the *Zohar* chaos is associated with the paternal figure.[36]

The homily "At the head of potency of the king" elucidates the first part of the first verse in Genesis 1:1 – "In the beginning when God created the heavens and the earth" – in light of its latter part – "The earth was a formless void and darkness

---

[34] Bion, *Two Papers*; Bergstein, "Emotional Truth."
[35] *Sefer Yetzirah* 2:6. See www.sefaria.org.
[36] Kristeva, *Powers*.

4 Paternal Origins ("At the Head of Potency of the King") — 139

covered the face of the deep." By joining together hermetic, incoherent readings, it creates a primordial world of birth that threatens to engulf our familiar language in darkness, wind, and the abyss. The birthing experience is nicely illustrated in the hermetic phrase "a cluster of vapor forming in formlessness, thrust in a ring, not white, not black, not red, not green, no color at all." While the meaning of each individual word is clear, the Zohar seems to leave the phrase in its entirety intentionally incomprehensible and chaotic. It is nonetheless clear that this homily deals with the revelation of the Godhead from the head of the infinite, the *Ein Sof*, and the awakening of the divine "will" to create the universe. It focuses on the essence of *Hokhma*, called here *reshit* ("beginning"), which symbolizes fatherhood in the configuration of the *sefirot*.

The passage abounds with alliteration and *colors*; it traces primordial experience by means of rare, polysemous, and unique words, many of which appear nowhere else in Zoharic literature. Such words as *butzina*, *meshiha*, and *hormenuta* are juxtaposed with such mysterious and unique expressions as "a cluster of vapor," "engraved engravings in luster on high," "spark of impenetrable darkness flashed." It would seem that the homily's linguistic obscurity reflects a primal, preverbal phase. To this may be added the authorial anonymity of the passage, which is presented as a kind of vision uttered by a heavenly voice announcing the creation of the worlds, as in other homilies in the Zoharic sections of *Matnitin*, *Tosefta*, and *Sitrei Torah*.[37] Reading this homily activates deep, concealed psychological layers demanding to understand the beginning of the process of Creation.

The homily addresses the *Hokhma* as a "first point" which bursts forth downward toward the *sefirot* and worlds beneath. These movements simulate birth and the realization of divine potential; however, in contrast to the homilies said in the name of R. Shimon bar Yohai or R. Hizkiyah, in the *Introduction* the anonymous passage under discussion presents birth as yet without distinct characters or relationships. This Creation is unknown, other, which as yet does not know itself.

It is in this downward move that the *Zohar* locates the awakening of the divine will to create worlds; this is now regarded as an archetype of every creation and birth. The symbolic and psychological significance of moving from *Ein Sof / Keter* to *Hokhma* raises a question: at what moment does the Godhead or a human being expand beyond themselves to create new reality?

What is the nature of that "first will" and what transpires within it? The image of *Hokhma* as Divine Wisdom and as "first point" can be explicated by drawing on psychoanalytic theory. This *sefirah* represents the concentration that spreads into forms and colors, thereby indicating a "transformational ability" that is evidence

---

[37] Gottlieb, *Studies*, 163–169.

of well-developed container–contained processes. An individual who is connected to his "embryonic self" is capable of having the psychological flexibility to be reborn again and again from that "first point." To achieve this, according to Michael Balint, one must believe in a "new beginning" and must be able to return to infantile dependency and regression in analyst–patient and transference relations.[38]

Identified with the figure of Supernal Father, *Hokhma* is first consciousness and thought. Thus, the image of him as "beginning" alludes in Kabbalah to a conception of the father as "head" (*rosh-reshit*) of the *sefirot*. Early movement, the beginning, comes from the head, impacting the entire system, in a mystical as well as therapeutic context. The *Zohar* in this homily emphasizes the king's head and the emergence of His will and speech.

Like the Greeks and Talmudic sages who viewed speech as born of thought, so too Freud considered "the talking cure" to be a method with the power to change patterns of existence and bring healing to the human psyche through speech.[39] Influenced by Kabbalistic views, Hasidism developed mystical techniques of guided speech, and concentrated on the letters of the prayers as vessels for theurgic intent as well as for meditation, turning inward, and self-healing.[40]

In the view of the Kabbalists, the male seed, which leads to birth, comes from the head and descends from the *mohin* (consciousness, lit. "brains") to the netherworld. The Creation of the worlds begins with the connection between the thing, the object, the will, and divine speech. Influenced by antiquity, Kabbalah views Creation as a process which takes place first and foremost through language. Thus the closing words of the Zohar's first homily, *maamar kadma'a le-kola* ("utterance precedes all"), allude to the first words in the Torah ("In the beginning God created") and to the first words in the Zohar ("At the head of potency of the king"), and to ten other utterances through which the world was created.[41]

At the center of "At the head of potency of the king" is a model of paternal birth. Even at the moment of conception, the father's part is implicit, seen only with the infant's birth. Yet precisely from the father's inconsequentiality during pregnancy arises the need to enhance his role on the poetic and mythical stage, to reverse nature and symbolically remove women from the action of birth. Thus, for instance, Alan Dundes claims that the "birth" of Eve from Adam's rib (Genesis 2) expresses Couvade Syndrome, womb envy, and a model of "male birth" in light of

---

38 On the contrary, Abrams, *Female Body*, 63–66, claims that the introduction to the Zohar as well as its opening homily ("*be-rosh hurmanuta de-malka*") contain *both* erotic *and* feminine elements, a technique that aims to negate the phallic symbols in Creation.
39 On the "talking cure," see Freud and Breuer, *Studies in Hysteria*. See also Chapter 2, n. 41.
40 Idel, *Between Ecstasy and Magic*, 273–315; Pedaya, *Psychoanalysis and Kabbala*, 100–176.
41 M. Avot 5:1.

the rib-phallus symbolization.⁴² In the same manner, Ellen Haskell deals with images of masculine suckling, such as the midrash about one of the sages for whom a "miracle was performed on his behalf, and he developed breasts like the two breasts of a woman, and he nursed his son," or about Mordechai nursing Esther.⁴³ Some monks in the Middle Ages perceived Jesus as a beneficent, nurturing mother, a view which Caroline Bynum has proposed, challenges the way Christianity views the female body by expanding paternal birthing and nursing.⁴⁴

In the Jewish mystical context, Elliot Wolfson suggests that every birth in the Kabbalistic configuration of the *sefirot* is a male act, since the source of the mother's strength derives from the father's seed. *Binah* depends upon *Hokhma* for giving birth; likewise, *Shekhinah* depends upon the *Tiferet* – in accordance with the Kabbalistic principle that anyone receiving is "female" with respect to whoever is endowing from above.⁴⁵

I claim that all of these descriptions that focus solely on male birthing may thus reflect womb envy, due to the mother's boundless power to bring forth life.

5 Combined Parental Figure

The first verse in Genesis interpreted by the *Zohar* in a subversive and radical way. Instead of providing a passive and neutral description, the *Zohar* suggests that *Hokhma*, the father (or beginning), creates and gives birth to the *sefirah* of *Binah*, the mother, who is called also *Elohim*. The verse consequently is read as follows: "At the beginning, *Bereshit* created *Elohim*." This reading combines the image of the androgynous of Genesis 1 with Eve's creation from Adam's rib in Genesis 2: 21–22.

In the following section, I will combine the homilies "At the head of potency of the king" and the introduction to the Zohar (*"Who created these?"*) in order to suggest that, together, these texts attempt to restore the notion of the "combined parental figure," as discussed by Melanie Klein and expanded upon by Donald Meltzer and his followers. Indeed, the concept of the combined parental figure might shed light on the unique Kabbalistic portrayal of the upper parents *Hokhma and Binah,* who are regarded in the *Zohar* as " two fellows that are forever inseparable" (*trein rein de-lo mitparshin*).⁴⁶

---

42 Pardes, *Countertraditions*, 50.
43 BT Shabbat 53b; *Genesis Rabbah* 30: 9. Haskell, *Suckling*, 29–30, 87–89.
44 Bynum, *Jesus as Mother*.
45 Wolfson, *Circle*, 98–106.
46 See, for example, *Zohar* 3:4a; 267b.

In her discussion of the primal scene, Klein addresses the infantile aggressive wish to penetrate the mother's body, in which the father is in perpetual intercourse. According to Klein, the combined parental figure is perceived by the child as "a two-backed beast" engaging in dangerous, violent sexual union – a negative reflection of the mythological two-faced creature. In a pathological state, this figure takes control of the child, who is jealous of his parents' love because he is excluded from it.[47] At times, this experience accompanies the mature individual as well, impairing his ability to form healthy relationships and develop mature sexuality. By contrast, in a balanced psychological state the child develops the ability to "separate" his parents from each other and to see each of them as a complete, real object.

Unlike Klein, Meltzer emphasizes the nurturing, protective aspects of the combined parental figure, regarding it as the basis for adult creativity and sexuality. For him, the parental chamber is a sacred, mysterious space, whence inspiration can be drawn from a respectful distance. In this shrine, the two parents dwell as the cherubim clinging to one another. Entry into the holy of holies is barred, symbolically, by the gatekeeper, that is, the father protecting the mother's body from the child's attempt to penetrate her and return to her womb.[48] Meltzer associates the combined parental figure with religious experience and the ability to shelter under the wings of the *Shekhinah*. He terms the mother's breast a "Nuptial Chamber" belonging to an integrated parental figure which combines the feminine "hill" with a phallic nipple.[49]

Indeed, Kabbalistic theories of the union of *Hokhma* and *Binah*, like the example of the father "giving birth" to the mother and then, according to the *Zohar*, copulating with her in order to create worlds, is closer to Meltzer's reading than to Klein's destructive portrayal of the parental figure. In the *Zohar*, the "lower pair" in the divine family, *Tiferet* and *Malkhut*, pursue the relationship by separating and breaking apart, unlike the unified upper couple *Hokhma* and *Binah*. Nevertheless, the Kabbalist views the lower pair as eternally united as well, as we learn from the mystical formula recited before observing the commandment

---

[47] Klein, "Infantile Anxiety Situations."
[48] BT Yoma 54b; Meltzer and Harris, *Apprehension*, Chapters 4–6, 8.
[49] As Meltzer states: "Out of this evocative imagery there arises in the mind the image of the Nuptial Chamber, whose privacy and mystery need to be guarded only by the love and respect of those outside [. . .] [The] inner world structure, which has always been imaged in the architecture of religion [. . .] this is the "heart of mystery" where meaning is generated. The place of this creative intercourse, so prosaically called the parental bedroom, is the locus of awe and wonder in the internal world. Or more correctly, here is where the alpha-function takes place, where the creative act of symbol formation quietly proceeds through the night." Meltzer and Williams, *Apprehension*, 82.

phrase *"le shem ihud kudshe-brich-hu-u-shchintei "*("for the sake of the unification of the holy one, blessed be he and his *Shekhinah*").⁵⁰ This mystical concept mirrors a basic psychological wish to see one's parents as eternally united, since the child himself is a combination of his parents.

Moreover, the *Zohar* interprets the sin of incest (*gilui arayot*, lit. "uncovering nakedness") as the separation of the parental union. Unlike in the Bible, forbidden sexual relationships in the *Zohar* include prohibitions against separating an existing union and preventing a union that should take place. According to this idea, revealing parental nakedness is forbidden on both the metaphorical and physical level, since upon the separation of the parents their nakedness is revealed, exposing to the individual's eyes a reality he was not supposed to see. The *Zohar* explicates the verse Proverbs 16:28 as follows:

> Rabbi Hizkiyah said, "From here: A slanderer separates an intimate" (Proverbs 16:28) – that is, separates the King from Matronita, as is written: "Your father's nakedness and your mother's nakedness you shall not expose" [. . .] for the King separates from Matronita, and Matronita is distanced from His palace, so there is nakedness of all.⁵¹

In this context, Kabbalists use the term "*kitzutz ba-neti'ot*," meaning "cutting the shoots" or "causing heresy," and define it as an unforgivable sin.⁵² The Kabbalist's theurgic role is to construct the union of *Tiferet* and *Malkhut* in perpetual intercourse, like the endless union of *Hokhma* and *Binah* in order to avoid the sin of splitting apart coupled parents. While *neti'ot* – lit., "saplings" – symbolize a potentially fruitful union, cutting them down is akin to separating forces and exposing their nakedness. Incest and *kitzutz ba-neti'ot* are parallel sins which damage the bond between the *Shekhinah* and her partner. These acts are considered the ultimate "negative theurgy," for the damage to the divine world brings in its wake damage to the human world, too.

Like the Oedipal myth, the Kabbalistic myth is based on a wish to cross transgressive borders and fulfil incestuous desire. Whether the primal scene is a child actually witnessing the sexual congress of his parents, or whether it is a fantasy arousing fear and curiosity, and kindling creativity and sublimation, the very discovery of the parental union belongs to the realm of mystery, never to be known or comprehended.

In psychoanalytic terms, exposing the nakedness of the parental couple symbolizes an inner split and disbelief in the internal parental union. Causing harm to that combined parental figure is slashing and cutting away at the very

---

50 Hallamish, *The Kabbalah in Liturgy*, 45–70.
51 *Zohar* 3:74a (Matt, 7, 500–503); Hellner-Eshed, *River*, 335–340.
52 *Tikkunei ha-Zohar, Tikkun* 56, 86b–90b; *Tikkun* 34, 77b, and so on.

base of the child's existence. One is therefore obliged, despite the difficulty, to look upon one's origins and imagine one's own primal beginnings; at the same time, as Meltzer stresses, one must protect and preserve the parental figure in its sacred shrine. In the child's consciousness, the mother is perpetually connected to the father, so developing healthy eroticism is possible vis-à-vis the parental figure without invading or defiling it.

Human birth symbolizes the perpetual parental union and the existence of the primal scene in the body of the infant they created. In this sense, birth is the first and the most perplexing riddle of existence. The wish to know the essence of "how we were created" occupies humanity on the mythic as well as the personal level. This enigma continues to challenge human beings in profound and repressed ways, deriving from the difficulty of turning our gaze to that wondrous, threatening past of the combined parental figure. The magical ties of our origins are bound up with the mystery of birth, and in a healthy situation they indicate a well-developed state of relief and protection.

The Kabbalists describe states of consciousness bordering on psychosis or hallucination as being related to "basic unity," since – like Winnicott, Balint, Bion, and Little – they believe that only through a regressive return to the "first point" (like the conceptualization of *Hokhma* in the homily of "At the head of potency of the king") can one be reborn in a new reality. Birth of this kind is not perceived by the *Zohar* as pathological or destructive; nonetheless, it signifies construction and repair. Likewise, as suggested by Lewis Aron, the primal scene is of great value, since it teaches us how to accept contradictive values and paradoxical combinations:[53]

> Psychoanalytic theory and practice needs to avoid the dual errors, first, of condensing these realms or collapsing them one into another so that only one aspect is highlighted. This is the error of premature synthesis, which is modeled on the combined parent figure, which collapses what should be two distinct elements. It needs to avoid the other error of splitting off contradictions and ambiguities, separating them from each other so that they are thought to apply to different developmental stages or different diagnostic groups.[54]

Mircea Eliade claims that the androgynous signifies wholeness by virtue of maleness and femaleness residing in a single entity, like the Godhead, which is similarly

---

[53] Aron, "The Internalized Primal Scene."
[54] Ibid., 220. Arons says: "I focus on the need to move not exactly toward integration but, rather, toward an acceptance and celebration of multiplicity [. . .] While people certainly need a cohesive and integrated sense of self, they also need to accept, tolerate, and even enjoy confusion, contradiction, flux, lack of integration, and even chaos in their sense of who they are" (202–203).

constituted of opposites. It may be said that the return to the beginning of emanation reawakens the incestuous wish associated with intergenerational relationships (as in the Oedipal model) and that it reflects the desire to unite with both parents (perceived as a single figure, with a single source). Indeed, the myth of the androgynous links the perpetual union between the father and the mother in the infant's consciousness.

In the words of the Kabbalists, birth, besides embodying the process of emanation, also symbolizes exaltation and a return to the primal source, to the crown (*Keter*) from which all forms derive. The combined parental figure is signified in the *Zohar* by the first point, which alludes to the potential union of the upper parents and their reciprocal impregnation. Thus, the two homilies – the *Introduction* and the opening of *Parshat Bereshit* – describe parallel processes of emanation from both the womb of the father and the womb of the mother. These homilies, "At the head of potency of the king" and "Who created these?" address the riddle of the move from infinite to finite, from absence to presence. In each of them, the *Zohar* traces aspects of chaos and creates a shrine of parental fecundity.

Chapter 6
Longing for the Source

> How from the One, if it is such as we say it is, anything else, whether a multiplicity or a dyad or a number, came into existence, and why it did not on the contrary remain by itself, but such a great multiplicity flowed from it as that which is seen to exist in beings, but which we think it right to refer back to the One. —Plotinus, *Enneads* 5.1.6.

1 Unity and Multiplicity of Source and Place

In an individual's birth, as in mythic birth, all begins and ensues from a single source. This chapter will examine various aspects of the term "source," looking at it in he contexts of gender, philosophy, Kabbalah, and Hasidism. The relationship between the emanating source (Plotinus: "the One") and its derivatives is a fundamental issue in Greek philosophy, Gnosticism, and Christianity, all of which ask: how does the "one" become "many," and what is the relationship between the derivatives and the supreme idea, the primal source, God?

Plotinus compares the chain of emanation to births: the supreme source is God, from whom the Intellect is derived in a second birth and Beauty is derived in a third birth. He has the following to say on the source–derivative relationship:

> It is because there is nothing in it that all things come from it: in order that being may exist, the One is not being, but the generator of being. This, we may say, *is the first act of generation*: the One, perfect because it seeks nothing, has nothing, and needs nothing, overflows, as it were, and its superabundance makes something other than itself. This, when it has come into being, turns back upon the One and is filled, and becomes Intellect by looking towards it. Its halt and turning towards the One constitutes being, its gaze upon the One, Intellect.[1]

Unlike the entities below it, the primal One is not beholden to one form, and therefore everything can issue forth from it. Actuality and corporeality run counter to the philosophical model, which views the very act of procreation as testifying to the wholeness of the source:

> And all things when they come to perfection produce; the One is always perfect and therefore produces everlastingly; and its product is less than itself.[2]

---

1 Plotinus, *Enneads* 5.2.1. Despite the differences, in this chapter I take the Neoplatonic idea of "generation" to be a parallel idea to human birth and reproduction in the natural world.
2 Ibid., 5.1.6.

For Plotinus, the source is necessarily superior to that which derives from it, but this is not the case regarding human nature: in the human world and in the animal and vegetative kingdoms, birth does not cause the mother to exist forever or to have primacy over her children.

> For since it was perfect it had to generate, and not be without offspring when it was so great a power.³

The natural source is not detached from what it brings forth, nor does reproduction attest to the mother's superiority and perfection. In contrast with the philosophical model, human beings'
uniqueness stems from the fact that man – together with his parents, who endow him with body and spirit – is a partner in his own creation.

Kabbalah presents an important encounter between, on the one hand, Neoplatonian philosophical ideas and, on the other, Rabbinical conceptions which prioritize an understanding of the body as divine image and which emphasize the sanctity and essentiality of sexuality.⁴ In Kabbalah and Hasidism, these apparently contrasting notions connect the ritual with the mystical and the psychological. Unlike medieval Jewish philosophers, who tended to stress God's perfection and immutable unity, the Kabbalists highlight the dynamic nature of the Godhead and its need for completion and aid from the human world. The act of giving birth, then, results from a divine coupling that seeks to fill lack and absence. *Lack*, and not perfection, motivates the divine Source to beget.⁵

The danger of being consumed and the fear of a return to the chaotic state "before birth" is inherent in the quest for the Source, which represents the wish to return to a lost unity. The Source is the root of good which is expressed in the very act of emanation but which is also liable to become a consuming force that harms its offspring.

Both Kabbalah and psychoanalysis are markedly concerned with the mysterious and mercurial power of the "Source" (however defined). Both seek to decipher the hidden beginning. This search takes place in different levels of consciousness:

---

3 Ibid., 5.1.7.
4 Lorberbaum, *In God's Image*; Boyarin, *Carnal Israel*; Idel, *Kabbalah and Eros*. Harold Bloom, in the introduction to one of Moshe Idel's books, defines Kabbalah as "fascinatingly fused prose poems that uneasily amalgamate Neo-Platonic psychologies and Gnostic mythologies." Idel, *Enchanted Chains*, i–ii.
5 R. Moses Cordovero allegorizes the Infinite (*Ein Sof*) as a father: "The Infinite (*ein sof*) *causa causarum* (*ilat kol ha-ilot*) rectified, emanated, imprinted, and garbed his son, which is *Keter*, who is his effect (*ha-alul mimenu*) like a son is the effect of his father (*ha-alul me-aviv*)." (*Peirush to* Sifra de-Tzniuta, Section Shiur Komah 3: 88). On the dialectical and dynamic concept of the *Ein Sof*, see Idel, "Androgynes"; Valabregue-Perry, *Concealed*.

like scientific experiments that are designed to understand the structures of the universe, the nucleus of the living, and the vegetative, and thereby to draw conclusions regarding their creation, psychoanalysis is preoccupied by fantasies about the moment of coming into being and the primal scene. Beginning with Freud, who viewed the Oedipal complex as the *shibboleth* of psychoanalysis and as a developmental stage that links the personal and the collective (ontogenesis and phylogenesis),[6] theoreticians such as Otto Rank, Melanie Klein, Donald Meltzer, and others explore the enigma of man's origin and the consequences of the drama of birth. A similar quest emerges from the Rabbinic theories of Creation; their expositions on God, the Creator and Destroyer of worlds; and Kabbalistic myths such as the death of the Edomite kings (see above, Chapter 1). All of these reflect mystical attempts to arrive at the beginning and the "nullification of thought" (*afisat ha-mahshavah*) and to draw upon the infinite Source, which cannot be understood but which can be perceived only through its derivatives.

The metaphor of the flame arising from the ember, which first appears in *Sefer Yetzirah* and was developed by the nascent Kabbalah, illustrates the difficulty of embracing the Source and fully comprehending it. R. Isaac the Blind formulated this point in his commentary to *Sefer Yetzirah*:

> All that emanates (*she-mitpashet*), all are from the source, and if the source should cease, all cease [..]. For many threads are drawn from the burning coal that is one, and the flame is unable to exist independently; rather only through something else.[7]

The root will always remain elusive and unresolved. Notwithstanding this lack of resolution, at times the place where it emerges and the manner of its influence can be revealed. As described by the thirteenth-century Kabbalist R. Isaac ben Samuel of Acre, man can attain the "connection of the light":

> When his thought will ascend and he will direct it upwards via the beginning of the light, which he began to attain, it will go via this light in his thought, *until it arrives at the root of the entry of the light*, as a twisted thread and a flame on a burning coal [. . .] And only that he should not pull. For the more a person pulls on a twisted thread, the more he is distanced from it.[8]

R. Isaac of Acre adds a warning to the mystic that he should not draw, "for the more a person draws the bulb, the further it moves from him."[9]

---

[6] "The shibboleth that distinguishes the adherents of psychoanalysis from its opponents." Freud, "Three Essays," 226 n. 1.
[7] Translated by Gene Matanky.
[8] Emphasis is mine.
[9] R. Isaac of Acre, "Commentary on a Book of Creation," 32.

1 Unity and Multiplicity of Source and Place — 149

It is not by chance that the Tannaitic literature uses the appellations *makor* ("source") and *makom* ("place") for both the maternal and divine bodies. The Rabbis keep a "safe distance" when describing the uterus and the vagina, but they never refer *solely* to a specific, individual, physical body. Rather, the Rabbis transform the private uterus and female body into a general metaphor representing the cosmos and the transcendental experience of existence. The divine appellation seemingly covers the female genitalia, conceals the corporeal with language, and effaces all that the Rabbis wish to keep hidden and opaque.

The relationship between mother and God, in light of the partnership between the "source" and the "place," highlights how central a concern the body and sexuality was to the Rabbis, as well as their aversion to and exclusion of the mother. Similarly, it points to moments in which erotic literature appears in – or is excluded from – midrash. Additionally, the ambiguous meaning of the term "place" explains the development of the conception of the Godhead from Rabbinic literature to the medieval Kabbalah. According to Ephraim E. Urbach, the replacement of the Tannaitic appellation of God (*ha-Makom* [the "place"]) by the Amoraitic "Holy One, blessed be He" was meant to repress any corporeality or Gnostic conception of God; it was similar to the substitution of the appellation *Shamayim* ("Heaven") by *Shem Shamayim* ("Name of Heaven").[10] In contrast, Arthur Marmorstein maintains that the abandonment of the former appellation *ha-Makom* signifies the desolate state of the Land of Israel after the Bar Kokhba Rebellion and the attempt to turn the relationship between God and a certain location into the notion of the divine as sanctifying any place.[11]

The Rabbinic dictum about (the male) God "He is the Place of the world, and the world is not His place" is not applicable to the Kabbalistic concept of the *Shekhinah*, which is often identified specifically with the world and the human condition.[12] The detailed description of the *Shekhinah*'s members within the *shiur komah* (the "measure of the body" [of God]) tradition demonstrates the formation of a conception of the *Shekhinah* as an actual place, one that is described by means of its maternal and erotic quality.[13]

Furthermore, the Tannaitic term *makom* ("place") eventually led to the Hasidic idea that "there is no place void of Him (*leit atar panui minei*)." As Biti Roi shows, this formulation is implanted in the rite of the *Shekhinah* and in the *Tikkunei ha-Zohar* literature, and reinforces the relationship between the worldly body and the worship of the *Shekhinah*. In Kabbalistic thought, "that place" not only indicates

---

10 See, for example, M. Ta'anit 3, 8; M. Eduyot 5:6; M. Avot 2:13; Urbach, *The World*, 53–68.
11 Marmorstein, *Doctrine*, 92–93.
12 *Genesis Rabbah* 68:9; *Pesikta Rabbati* 21; Margolin, *Inner Religion*, 238–241, 274.
13 Asulin, "Stature"; Roi, *Love*, 311–398. See there also on the *Shekhinah* as "Image of All images".

the connection between the Godhead and the flesh-and-blood world, it also makes one conditional upon the other. The *Zohar* declares that whoever is not married, in this world, is incapable of joining with the divine Source.[14] The Kabbalists view the *Shekhinah* as a gate to the divine world, and as analogous to the female sexual organ. The identification between the supernal and worldly sources appears in numerous expositions, following the principle that "all women are in the image of the *Shekhinah*." Thus, the two openings – to Heaven and to the female body – unite around the threshold of birth, and it is possible to say of the *Shekhinah* that "He is the Place of the world, and the world is His place."

The "source" and the "place" signify the heart of the holy, the place of the Altar, the heart of the world, Jerusalem, the Holy of Holies, the opening to heaven – and the opening to the female womb.

The connection to the mother's womb is imprinted in the navel of every human born. It is a scar, a testimony to the intimate point of connection with our mothers' bodies. Like the source of the womb, the navel is the bodily member that grasps all the extremities and contains all the opposites. When discussing the meaning of dreams, Sigmund Freud compared the navel to a region forever undeciphered. After discussing all the meanings, a concealed element, one that cannot be explained, still remains. The "navel" of the dream contains both terror and pleasure. This, according to Freud, is the hidden wish of the dreamer *and of the dream itself*:

> I had a feeling that the interpretation of this part of the dream was not carried far enough to make it possible to follow the whole of its concealed meaning. If I had pursued my comparison between the three women, it would have taken me far afield. There is at least one spot in every dream at which it is unplumbable – a navel, as it were, that is its point of contact with the unknown.[15]

Joshua ben Samuel Nehemia similarly stated that the *Shekhinah* is like a navel "because it fits exactly in its place, like a fetus in its mother's womb, and in it the Sages know the secret of *ibbur* that is given over to them. It receives the *shefa*, and gives in abundance to all creatures, for just as the fetus receives food through the navel, so, too, she receives, and she is the navel of all the world."[16] It is not surprising that the great mysteries of Kabbalah – *gilgul* ("reincarnation") and *ibbur* ("impregnation") – are linked to the navel, the point of connection for the meaning of dreams. Even when this meaning eludes us, as it is beyond reality, its "unresolved" existence still leaves an impression.

---

14 Liebes, "Zohar ve'Eros," 99; Yisraeli, *Interpretations*, 175.
15 Freud, "The Interpretation of Dreams," 111. See also Felman, *Sexual Difference*, 68–120.
16 Idel, "Arayyot," n. 200.

Indeed, the first dream of any creature is to return to the most individual and secret source, the maternal womb, which symbolizes the very belief that one can dream. This belief is based on a sensual and physical experience: the knowledge that mother is here, holding us, even before we knew how to ask for the ability to dream, even before we learn to speak. According to William James, a similar bond is forged between man and God, one that he calls a "leap of faith." God's existence can never be proven, but we leap toward Him, skip over the hurdles of the incomprehensible and the unknown – and then God is revealed and leaps toward us.[17]

2 The Dread of the Source

Unlike the Rabbinic expositions that debate with Hellenistic and Christian positions and that reflect a positive attitude to sexuality and the female body,[18] other midrashim represent radical asceticism; they reject not only the body, but the very institution of marriage. These latter conceptions would likely portray the womb as a grave, or the woman as "a pitcher full of filth and her mouth full of blood" (BT Shabbat 152a) and the vagina as "the most soiled and sullied of all the parts of the body," as *Tanna de-Ve Eliyahu* puts it:

> A story is told of one of R. Akiba's disciples who ranked first among twenty-four thousand disciples. Once he went into the Street of the Harlots where he saw a harlot with whom he fell in love, and so he had a messenger go back and forth between him and her until evening. In the evening she went up to the roof and saw him seated like a commander of hosts at the head of the disciples with Gabriel standing at his side. She said to herself: Woe unto this woman to whom all kinds of Gehenna's punishments are bound to affix themselves! And he – such a distinguished man who looks like a king! – shall this woman respond to his desire and, as a result, when she dies and ceases to exist in this world, inherit Gehenna? If, however, he is willing to accept her refusal [of him], she will save him and herself from the punishment of Gehenna. So when he came to her, she said to him, My son, why are you willing to lose life in the world-to-come for the sake of one hour in this world? But his passion was not dismissed until she said to him, My son, the part which you desire is the most soiled and sullied of all the parts of the body, the odor whereof no creature is able to endure. Still his passion was not diminished until she took hold of his nose and put it as [her cleft whence there came an odor as of] the grave. When he smelled the odor, the female organ became so repulsive to him that he never married. Thereupon a Divine Voice was heard, declaring, Such-and-such a woman and Such-and-such a man are destined for life in the world-to-come.[19]

---

[17] James, "The Will to Believe"; idem, *Varieties of Religious Experience.*
[18] Boyarin, *Carnal Israel*; Rosen-Zvi, "Evil Impulse."
[19] *Tanna de-Ve Eliyahu*, 471.

Mary Douglas examines the understanding of the female body as polluted and despised in her writings, beginning with tribal cultures and their attitude to menstrual blood as the source of contamination. Julia Kristeva, following Douglas, describes the aversion to the mother as ensuing from the symbolic "abjection" of her body, with its fluids, smells, and threatening and consuming sexuality.[20] Kate Millett discussed the conception of the female sexual organ as a wound and a cut, and as the source of shame in the history of religions. Her approach was expanded by Esther Fuchs as regards Biblical depictions.[21]

The aggadic passage in *Tanna de-Ve Eliyahu* ends with the total repression of physicality and sexuality, when its heroine the harlot convinces the Torah scholar to curb his lust. As Rella Kushelevsky, Tali Artman-Partock, and others have shown, most of the harlotry narratives in the Talmud end with happy marriages, the woman's repentance, and both spouses mending their ways.[22] This narrative, in contrast, teaches that prostitution is concealed behind every seduction. In the words of the exegete, man's rectification lies solely in complete abstention from women. In antiquity, as today, men are not alone in fearing "that place" and the encounter with the source of life. Here, the woman herself besmirches her body, and in the end the man surrenders to her extreme stance, thereby intensifying the narrative's misogynist orientation; it cultivates asceticism, even as it casts women as the worst agents of repression for viewing their own bodies as sources of shame. The harlot, who represents the entire female sex, feels that she is entirely impure and the source of "Gehenna" (= "hell"). She is not merely a sex object, she is a woman doubly exploited: initially, because of her role as a harlot, and later due to the way in which the authors have her express utter contempt for her body *and* soul.

According to Kushelevsky, this narrative is influenced by the model of Christian abstinence, but it appears to reflect long-standing anxieties, prevalent since the ancient world and continuing on to the present. Does it reflect not only a fear of women but also an opposition to their very existence? In nature, sexuality and reproduction are clearly intertwined with and embrace one another; this may be why many religions attempt to separate sexuality and reproduction and to delude their believers into considering them as disparate, unrelated axes of existence.

The tendency to differentiate between maternal and sexual roles, and between the harlot and the mother or virgin, has characterized humankind from its very

---

20 Douglas, *Purity and Danger*, 83–115; Kristeva, *Powers*. See also: Ettinger, Matrixial Borderspace.
21 Fuchs, *Sexual Politics*; Millett, *Sexual Politics*, 90–97.
22 Kushelevsky, *Penalty and Temptation*, 169–180; Artman, "Tale Type."

beginnings. In almost every culture, these distinctions seek to control women through the compartmentalization of the various aspects of their being.[23]

Many Kabbalistic works, first and foremost the *Zohar*, offer a different conception, in which worldly existence is a condition for communion with the Godhead. Maternity and the processes of impregnation and giving birth are the central traits of the *sefirah* of *Binah*, from whose womb the worlds emanate. Despite the partition separating the worlds, many Zoharic expositions link human sexuality with the divine. The former bares itself and is seen to be like its divine counterpart through countless countenances. In an especially daring depiction in *Zohar* 1:150b, Jacob's ladder dream (Gen. 28:12–17) is interpreted as referring to the male and female sexual organs, as corresponding to the coupling of *Yesod* ("basis," "foundation") and *Malkhut*, and as connecting "the house of God" with "the gate of heaven":

> Since Jacob was not married, nothing more is said explicitly [. . .] After he married and engendered, this is said to him explicitly – *From here we learn that whoever is incomplete below is incomplete above* [. . .] Immediately, He was awestruck, and said, "How awesome is this place!" (Gen. 28:17) – He said, "This is none other than the house of God!" (ibid.) – this must not stagnate; this must not exist alone. Its fulfillment is none other than the house of God, performing with it, creating fruit within it, pouring blessings into it from all smooth members of the body; *for this is the gate of the whole body*, as is written: this is the gate of heaven! (ibid.) – gate of the body, indeed! Gate through which blessings pour below – fastened above, fastened below.[24]

In the Kabbalistic system, union with the forces of evil connotes taboo and filth, while all other pairings are regarded favorably. The essence of this system is connection and not division, since its motive, Eros, unites the mutually dependent divine source and the human. A cultural and gender-focused reading enables us to state that any division, by its very nature, is harmful. So, too is the differentiation between motherhood and sexuality that, as Adrienne Rich observes, creates a confusing emotional experience of both attraction and aversion to the mother's body. This differentiation is followed by a male takeover of the woman's most private experience: motherhood. Or, as Simone de Beauvoir and others emphasize, male authors differentiate between the desired partner and the mother, who is perceived as dangerous and threatening to the male, who seeks to be extricated from her womb.[25]

---

23 For a bibliography on this issue, see Kaniel, *Holiness and Transgression*.
24 *Zohar* 1:150b (Matt, 2, 334–336); Liebes, "Zohar ve'Eros" (emphasis is mine).
25 Rich, *Of Woman Born*; Beauvoir, *The Second Sex*.

In analogous fashion, splitting the worlds, divine and human – while aggrandizing the former and denigrating the latter – drives a wedge between sexuality and the maternal body, on the one hand, and, on the other, the theological significance of fertility and Eros. The psychoanalytical literature, too, describes splitting as a survival mechanism for the self in times of distress, but its force could also cause great harm. In contrast to the array of disconnects and splits, movement between the various experiences and roles inherent in motherhood and feminine sexuality enable this dialectic to be contained, and to create balance and cohesiveness. Thus, for example, by making a relationship with the Godhead conditional upon marriage to a woman in this world (in the spirit of the above Zoharic passage) and emphasizing the intents of the couple at the time of sexual union (as is indicated by a classic text such as Nahmanides's *Igeret haKodesh*), one enhances the value of sexuality and motherhood, and accentuates the link between the divine and female sources.[26] Additionally, these intents and marital practices strengthen the ties of all humans, men as well, to the this-worldly maternal source.

The tendency to differentiate between motherhood and giving birth, on the one hand, and, on the other, Eros and sexuality might be one of the causes of the sweeping abstention from discussing birth and the stress placed on death

---

[26] The text is attributed to Nahmanides, but according to Gershom Scholem it was authored by R. Joseph Gikatilla. See Scholem, *Mehkarei Kabbala*, 225–235. For more on the composition, which represents a genre of Kabbalistic literature that deals with sexual *kavannot*, see, for example, Biale, *Eros and the Jews*, 101–112; Mopsik, *Sex of the Soul*. See also Gottlieb, *Studies*, 526–528. Although this medieval Kabbalistic treatise is distinguished by its exceptionally positive evaluation of properly conducted sexual intercourse between husband and wife, effectively elevating it to the status of sacrament, it allocates distinct theurgic functions to each of the two partners. As Ada Rapoport-Albert claimed (in a private conversation), nowhere in *Igeret haKodesh* is the *Shekhinah* said to be represented by the earthly wife during coitus. Rather, the text employs the classical Rabbinic notion of the *Shekhinah* as the divine presence, which comes down to rest between the virtuous husband and wife during intercourse, thus becoming their partner in the creation of the fetus (ed. Cohen, 5, 111). Moreover, in the process of procreation, the respective roles of the partners are defined in conventional Aristotelian terms: she provides the fetus with "matter," while he endows it with "form" (3, 79); she is the "receiver" while he is the "giver" (2, 59). While the Patriarchs had the capacity to draw down the light of the supernal realms, there is no similar statement attributed to the Matriarchs. Indeed, Biale concludes that "the husband is not expected to turn his wife into a Kabbalist; her intention is sufficiently pure if she possesses the appropriate 'fear of heaven.' The Gnosis (*sod*) of intercourse remains the monopoly of the male mystic" (*Eros and the Jews*, 107). Yet, according to Moshe Idel, Charles Mopsik, Yehuda Liebes, Biti Roi, Leore Sachs-Shmueli, and others, the *Zohar* as well as compositions such as *Igeret haKodesh* emphasize women's enhanced theurgic role. On special notions of the feminine impact on the divine in the theurgic and theosophical Kabbalah, see Idel, *Kabbalah and Eros*, pp. 247–250.

in human culture. An authentic discussion of birth requires connecting all that has been separated and split by exegetes and thinkers throughout the centuries. It is much easier, in comparison, to talk about death. A discussion about death has a single goal: to perceive the absence of motion rather than the dynamics of life; annihilation instead of dialectic; the absolute end and cessation of desire rather than the paradoxical.

In order to understand the birth experience on all its levels, we must therefore reconnect all these ties while simultaneously studying the texts that show their dread of and contempt for the female body. These works cannot be rejected on the grounds that they reflect an ancient phenomenon that exists only in legends and midrashim. Rather, in order to decipher this misogyny, we must examine its "sources." In this context, Kristeva argues that rejection of the maternal source is a precondition for development of the self, an inherent part of the initial narcissistic experience, and a tragic possibility for detachment from the amniotic fluid and placenta that accompany human birth: "Even before being like, 'I' am not but do separate, reject, ab-ject. Abjection, with a meaning broadened to take in subjective diachrony, is a precondition of narcissism."[27]

The mother is the source of threat and danger; she is the object that is "rejected" specifically because of the birth "death" that arouses hatred. As Céline puts it: "Those females [. . .] can wreck the infinite."[28] Kristeva notes that rejection of the mother takes precedence over any awareness of the self, and that this attests to the undeniable influence of the maternal source. Paradoxically, the mother is the refuse we must remove in order to construct our identity. Abjection is what guards the individual's limit and his survival: "Self-giving birth ever miscarried, endlessly to be renewed, the hope for rebirth is short-circuited by the very splitting: the advent of one's own identity demands a law that mutilates, whereas jouissance demands an abjection from which identity becomes absent."[29] Consequently, our mourning for the already lost mother is indeed our mourning for our very birth and finitude:

> Abjection is a resurrection that has gone through death (of the ego). It is an alchemy that transforms [the] death drive into a start of life, of new significance [. . .] The abject is the violence of mourning for an "object" that has always already been lost.[30]

Kristeva emphasizes the point that dread of the laboring mother is shared by the entire human race. Men and women, however, have different survival

---

27 Kristeva, *Powers*, 13.
28 Ibid., 157.
29 Ibid., 54.
30 Ibid., 15.

techniques when faced with the primal body from which they emerged. Due to their identification with the mother figure, women have a tendency for masochism and self-destruction. Men, however, are captivated by the illusion of individuation, and so employ the method of symbolically murdering the mother or the other as a condition for their selfhood.[31]

Nathaniel Berman expands upon the connection between Kristeva's notion of abjection and the role played by the forces of evil in the Kabbalah as spilled waste and as a catalyst for the purification of the supernal world. He highlights the danger posed by these forces, given their ability to cause the collapse of the self, even as these conditions are needed for the constitution of the subject. His discussion aids in understanding the Kabbalists' ambivalent attitude to the Godhead that creates and that is the source of all souls:

> It follows from Kristeva's portrayal that all constructions of subjectivity are precarious, due to the fact that they depend on the abjection of elements from which the subject both must, and cannot, fully separate itself [. . .] The proliferation, over the generations, of kabbalistic discursive and ritual practices aimed at either assimilating or destroying the demonic can be apprehended as attempts at grappling with the abject in the face of its ever renewed resurfacing, bringing with it persistent anxiety about the collapse or corruption of human and divine subjects [. . .] Kristeva's portrayal of subjectivity thus provides a powerful framework for reading the dynamic unfolding of divine/demonic relationships in Zoharic and related texts: from the expulsion of primordial refuse from the sphere of primordial undifferentiation; to the consolidation of divine structures and personae facilitated by this expulsion and the simultaneous crystallization of the refuse into diabolical structures and personae; to the ongoing and dangerous divine/demonic relationships of desire, nurturance, and impersonation.[32]

Following Kristeva, we must stress that the dynamic of divine relationships in the *Zohar* is gender-oriented, since the refuse is mainly attributed to the feminine. The "abject," or that which is disgusting and disagreeable, is always feminine – by design. Kabbalistic literature presents an empowering image of the divine consort, the *Shekhinah*, and stresses the bond between heavenly and earthly sources. Yet this literature is also replete with singularly misogynous portrayals. Thus, for instance, at times, the *Shekhinah* is depicted as a Lilith-like figure, one who is seductive and dangerous, with long nails, red hair, and lips like a rose – who transforms into a violent, murderous man. Other sources contain images of a menstruating woman, a serpent coiled within her innards, who causes the *Shekhinah* to separate from her husband and his sexual union

---

31 Kristeva, *Black Sun*. See also Millett, *Sexual Politics*, 88.
32 Berman, *Divine and Demonic*, 54–55.

with the handmaiden.³³ These tableaux give voice to differing modes of female abjection.

A comparison of the attitudes of psychoanalytical language and mystical language to the maternal and divine sources draws into sharp focus the parallels, and differences, between the two systems. Each language puts emphasis on the dread engendered by the womb and the female body. Along with the harsh message broadcast by the perception of the mother as the source of "abjectness" and impurity, we must also recognize the courageous attempt by both Kabbalah and psychoanalysis to understand the attraction to and repulsion from her body. Both these worlds observe the movement between aversion and attraction to the mother, as the self's constitutive core and as the basis for the ability to bear contradictory experiences such as love and hate, and splitting and cohesion. The Kabbalists' positive portrayal of the *Shekhinah*'s womb reflects their attempt to refine this negative conception of the flesh-and-blood female body. Using mystical language, they sketch a supernal counterpart to the maternal womb, and emphasize the beneficial place of the Godhead that gives birth and contains. These depictions tone down the primal dread of the source common to all religions. They do so while casting light on the teleological purpose of "that place," which – like the Freudian dream navel – represents a concrete member of the individual body, as well as an abstraction, a metaphor, and a displacement, enabling the realization and tempering of the discourse of desire and procreation.

3 Sunlight, Being, and Not-Being

Let us return to the Neoplatonian imagery of the source and its derivatives. In this view, every individual "being" seeks to be drawn back to the supernal source. The higher the level of its turbidity, the greater the distance between the "being" and its source, and the nearer the source, the greater the purification and discarding of materiality. The chief metaphor in the Neoplatonic and Gnostic worlds that clarifies the source–derivative relationship is that of the relation between the sun and its rays. Neoplatonic authors likewise depict the process of "drawing out the breath" to God, imagery that has been discussed by Alexander Altmann, Shlomo Pines, and Moshe Idel. In the Kabbalah of Girona and in the *Zohar*, the imagery of drawing out expresses the return of the souls

---

33 *Zohar* 1:138a–b; 3:79a. Liebes, "Zohar ve'Eros"; Koren, *Forsaken*, 192–251; Asulin, "Flaw"; Berman, *Divine and Demonic*, 130, 203ff.

of the righteous to their origins at the moment of their death, and a theurgic act in which the commandments are perceived as a pledge that the soul will return to the supernal source. The idea of drawing out at the time of death emerges from a Gnostic source portraying Jesus as the sun to which the rays returned at the end of life:

> If we appear in this world bearing him, we are the rays of that one, and we are grasped by him until our setting, that is, our death in this life. We are drawn to heaven by him like rays by the sun, and we are not detained by anything.[34]

These approaches indicate that, to the extent that the nature of "being" will allow, the source seeks to be gathered to and absorbed in, as seen above.

Birth, by its very nature, is seemingly the opposite: it is not based on "drawing out," but rather on "ejection," on a dramatic distancing from the source. Concurrently, however, when the newborn emerges into the world it still grasps the source of all souls, into which it has the potential to be drawn back.[35] This notion accentuates the connection between birth and death. In these threshold moments, the soul holds onto the supernal treasury of souls and expresses a special relationship to the source. During life's course, in contrast, humans spread the sun's light specifically due to our distance from the source.

Paradoxically, the moment when humans are cast forth into the world and are ejected from the source is not only the most *spiritual* moment in people's lives, it is also the most *material* instant in life. An individual is never so focused on material needs, so in need of nourishment, of holding, as they are in the minutes and months after birth. In this sense, human birth echoes the Gnostic myth of Sophia, the female Wisdom, who is cast far from the male source.[36] The soul, which was in the uppermost realms, in the treasury of souls, is suddenly cast forth into the turbid "being" of this world. As the *Zohar* (2:95b) states, "*If the daughter of a priest is married to an alien man* – holy soul, drawn from a supernal place, entering the recess of the Tree of Life." Like Neoplatonian emanationism, the newborn who is distanced from his source thirsts to return to and suck from it. The human mother differs from the supernal emanator, since at the moment of childbirth she, like the fetus, is in the fleshiest and bloodiest moment of her being. Nonetheless, the Neoplatonic metaphor aids us in understanding the mental powers active at childbirth,

---

34 *Treatise on the Resurrection* 45.28–39. The translation is from Smith, *Valentinian Christianity*, 157. See also Idel, "Light of Life"; Afterman, "Philo to Plotinus."
35 Wolfson, *Circle*; Pedaya, "The Great Mother"; idem, *Nahmanides*, 380–389; Art Green claims that the Gironan Kabbalists refrained from using birth images, which had apparently flourished in the generation of the *Zohar*. Green, "Virgin Mary," 24.
36 Liebes, "Pool"; Hellner-Eshed, "Engravings."

especially the exalting attitude of the newborn to his mother: the images of turning one's gaze upon the sunlight, the moments of abnegation vis-à-vis the source, the wish to return to the womb and be absorbed in it. Unlike this desire for self-annihilation, the material "being" insists upon seizing the reality and being molded from it. At this moment, bodily needs take decisive precedence: the first cries, the burden of weight and movement, and the need to be nourished.

The life-force of the newly born infant wants to burst through the door of life while it still glows from the primal illumination embedded within it. Just as the infant's body is small at this stage, so, too, his spiritual "tools" have yet to mature, and they are too constricted to contain the light. In consequence, each person, at the beginning of his life, undergoes a sort of "breaking of the vessels" which diminishes his lights and forces him to adapt to reality.

During the course of life, humans learn to "keep their distance" from the source, but also to remain connected to it, to achieve balance within the double experience of "not-being" and "being." The experience of "not-being" depends upon an awareness of the distance between the person and the infinite Source, while the "being" experience indicates self-realization in this world. We learn that psychological "elevation of the sparks" means acceptance of the loss of the light with which we came into the world and our consent to distancing ourselves from the moment of birth – since this distance is the only way to realize the potential concealed within.

The connection between these forces seems to be contradictory, in terms of philosophical thought. While in Neoplatonism "being" is revealed by its intellectual recognition, for Kabbalists and Hasidim this recognition enables moments of "not-being" to be contained within "being." Thus, the quality of the primeval light and of the prenatal experiences enters the present experience of human life.

People become increasingly corporeal, but at the same time the process of coming of age facilitates a knowledge of the light that is implanted within us, whose source is intangible. Actually, a person's affinity to the source increases by degrees the farther he moves away from it, both chronologically and consciously, and the more he develops his spiritual and intellectual ability.

"As Nothing before the Light of the Infinite"-Schneur Zalman of Liadi

In developing a common Neoplatonic picture, the founder of Habad Hasidism, who was also the author of the *Tanya*, R. Schneur Zalman of Liadi, compares God to "the body of the sun." Unlike humans (who have been created, and who represent the light produced by the sun's rays), the sun and its source cannot be perceived by the human eye:

> However, there in its own place, this reliance is considered naught and complete nothingness, for it is absolutely non-existent in relation to the body of the sun-globe which is the source of this light and radiance, inasmuch as this radiance and light is merely the illumination which shines from the body of the sun-globe itself. It is only in the space of the universe, under the heavens and on the earth, where the body of the sun-globe is not present, that this light and radiance appears to the eye to have actual existence. And here, the term *yesh* ["existence"] can truly be applied to it [. . .] Therefore, it appears to our eyes that the materiality, grossness, and tangibility of the created things actually exist, just as the light of the sun appears to have actual existence when it is not within its source.³⁷

The relation between the parable and the moral of this metaphor is seemingly straightforward: God is to man as the sunshine is to its spreading lights. According, however, to the *Tanya*, the reason why the intended meaning is not identical to the expressed meaning is because those created are as nothing before the sun's fierce light, while humans, in this world, are not as nothing before the light of the Holy One, blessed be He. In response to the question: Why in reality is their existence not nullified in relation to their source, R. Schneur Zalman responds at length in the following chapter of the *Tanya*, the "Sha'ar Hayichud ve-Haemunah" ("The Gate to [the Understanding of] God's Unity and the Faith"):

> For the life-force conceals itself in the body of the created being and [it appears] as though the body of the created being has independent existence and is not [merely] a spreading forth of the life-force and spirituality – as the diffusion of the radiation and light from the sun – but an independently existing entity. Although, in reality, it has no independent existence [. . .] this [concealment] is the very Restraining Power of the Holy One, blessed be He, Who is Omnipresent, to condense the life-force and spirituality which issues from the "Breath of His mouth" and to conceal it, so that the body of the created being shall not become nullified. And it is not within the scope of the intellect of any creature to comprehend the essential nature of the *tzimtzum* and concealment [of the life-force].³⁸

This discourse discusses the illusion of existence. R. Schneur Zalman maintains that only the "absolute *yesh*" – God – exists.³⁹ So that humans can nevertheless exist alongside Him in this world, we must believe "as though the body of the created being has independent existence." If we examine this conception through the lens of the experience of birth, a similar statement could be made about the

---

37 *Tanya*, "Sha'ar Hayichud ve-Haemunah," 3, 293–296.
38 Ibid., 3, 299–300.
39 Elior, *Unity of Opposites*, 29, 79–89. Compare to the conceptualization of illusion and truth, in the well-known Parable of the Barriers and Walls, told in the name of Baal Shem Tov by his grandson: R. Ephraim of Sudilkov, *Degel Machaneh Efraim*, Parashat Ki Tavo. These Hasidic homilies might also be a response to Plato's Allegory of the Cave.

mother–infant relationship. The perception of both as discrete creatures results from the mother's efforts to provide the infant with space and freedom, despite his dependence on her at the beginning of his life. And even during the continuation of his life, a person is always linked in numerous ways to his mother's body, as if his umbilical cord is still attached to her womb.

In Lurianic Kabbalah, God constricts and limits His infinite light so that the Source will not overpower those created and blind their existence. In analogous fashion, the mother's ability to vacate a space and identify with the newborn's anxiety and dependency allows him to receive nourishment and vitality from her. Once he has come into the world, the mother moves aside from her central importance, and functions instead as a containing "environment," which both protects the infant and fosters the illusion of his independence. Accordingly, the infant develops within the maternal container; later on, the illusion of his separateness becomes the actual reality, from which he can move forward.[40] Donald Winnicott describes this paradoxical relationship as follows:

> The mother identifies with the infant in a most complex manner, thereby expressing her feeling such identification, while yet remaining an adult. The infant, in contrast, identifies with his mother in the quiet moments of connection. This should not, however, be seen as an accomplishment of the infant, it rather is an achievement of the bond that the mother maintains.[41]

Winnicott writes that, as far as the infant is concerned, at the beginning of life the whole world is concentrated on him: he is all that exists. This experience is reminiscent of the passage in the Tanya that stresses the divine effort in creating the illusion "as though the body of the created being has independent existence," and as though nothing exists besides ourselves. The illusion of independence and freedom depends upon the willingness of the mother, like God, "to condense the life-force and spirituality which issues from the 'Breath of His mouth' and to conceal it, so that the body of the created being shall not become nullified." The mother consents to diminish her light, to prepare a room for us in her body, to "rent" this space to us for our initial existence, and, afterwards, to release us, to sever the umbilical cord.[42]

---

[40] See Chapters 1 and 2; Bion, *Attention and Interpretation*.
[41] Winnicott, *Babies*, 22. Jessica Benjamin claims that the mother holds a dual disposition: on the one hand, she identifies with the pain of her child, yet on the other hand she bestows upon him an outsider perspective that helps him overcome his pain. Benjamin, "Beyond Doer." See also Aron, "Analytic Impasse"; Britton, "Subjectivity."
[42] The divine constriction (*tzimtzum*), as well as the mother's consent to diminish her light, based on the quality of "being" rather than of "doing." On "being" and "doing" in psychoanalysis and Lurianic Kabbalah, see Gamlieli, *Psychoanalysis and Kabbalah*.

Additionally, the sun metaphor alludes to the way the outer covering of the body serves as a protective fortress – both against God and against the mother – so that the light of the Infinite will not swallow it. The body is the door through which God cannot enter; Job (38:11) expresses a similar thought: "This far shall you come, and no farther." Therefore, we "appear to have actual existence." The body is a home for the human, but also a sign for the mother, a negative container, that shows where self-constriction begins. Similarly, the human body signals to God the boundary of His infinity, on the one hand, and, on the other, the beginning of the human's free will and moral responsibility. The human body demarcates the constriction (*tzimtzum*) that God imposes on Himself so that man can exist, and whatever lies beyond is infinite and absolute like Him.

Man is formed within bounds, as flesh and blood, not only as an expression of God's lovingkindness, but also to protect Him from human finitude. This boundary marks the encapsulation space that shields the finite from the infinite. This "pocket" conceals within itself two well-kept secrets, namely that God "fills the earth" and existence alongside Him is impossible, and, in parallel, that the mother and the infant are distinct one from the other, while the latter is completely dependent upon her for his early existence. Concealment of these secrets, and the illusion of separateness, enable the creation of new life.

Unlike the psychoanalytical conception of encapsulation as attesting to a failure to contain, in mystical and Kabbalistic thought we have a different understanding of concealment and secret.[43] Indeed, the illusion that a human being has "independent existence" is built on an ongoing deception in which God / the mother conceal the attempts at constriction while deceiving the human / infant. Yet, a distinction can be drawn between the positive concealment of the truth, which is linked to protecting selfhood and privacy ("incommunicado") and pathological secrecy or harmful encapsulation.[44]

The Kabbalistic imagery of sunlight views as illusory the infant's separateness and independence while regarding unitary symbiosis and assimilation as the absolute truth. Certain psychoanalytical schools, however, find the symbiotic connection between mother and infant deceptive, since, even while in the womb, the fetus is a separate creature. As we have seen above in Chapter 3, Daniel Stern, Luce Irigaray, and others maintain that the placenta and the

---

[43] Hellner-Eshed, *River*, 157–188.
[44] On secrecy, hiding, encapsulation, and the concept of the "incommunicado element" in the theory of Winnicott, as well as those of other thinkers, see Margolis, "Secrecy"; Aharoni, "Hidden Secrets"; Brodsky, "Secrets."

uterus walls are a barrier separating the mother and the infant, signaling that the fetus is an independent entity.[45]

In contrast, and more in line with the passages in the *Tanya*, other conceptions view the unity of infancy as the basis for the continuing physical and mental attachment between the mother and her child. Feminist thinkers speak of the empowering force of the mother and child attachment while leveling criticism at the "autonomy" model that calls for a total break from the source. For Nancy Chodorow and others, "autonomy" is a male ideal which actually inflicts loneliness and isolation on the child.[46] The mother as subject is faced with maternal difficulty in separating from the newborn and her body's subsequent loss. In reality, at times the mother is more attached to the infant who has left her womb than the newborn is to her. She is unwilling to part with the infant, more than the infant desires a symbiosis with her.

Like God, the mother is disposed to give life to her child, and to allow him to leave her, even as her soul cries out for his return to her bosom. However, the fetus, from the instant of its creation, kicks, moves around, and tries to sever the womb's cords, in order to be extricated therefrom – to be born. But it also fears its absolute freedom, the rending of the umbilical cord, and at times seeks to be returned to the source.

4 Birth as a Transition between a Closed *Mem* (ם) and an Open *Mem* (מ)

Kabbalistic literature associates motherhood with the letter *mem* and the word "water" (*mayim*), which includes both open and closed letters. It thus hints at the movement of the fetus and the mother toward each other, reflecting the soul's journey toward its divine source. The image of the letter *mem*, which is suggestive of pregnancy, begins to develop in an early midrash entitled *The Alphabet of Akiba ben Joseph*, which reads as follows:

> *An open* mem *and a closed* mem, *a king who opens and a king who closes.* Why does the head of an open *mem* face the ground while its arm extends heavenward? This is because it points at the Ruler of the World, *to whom dominion belongs,* with its finger, as it is written (Psalms 22:29): "For dominion is Mine," and its arm extends downward to show what David said: "For all comes from You" (1 Chronicles 29:14). *A closed* mem *whose place no one knows.*[47]

---

[45] Stern, *The Interpersonal World*, 26; Irigaray, *Je, Tu, Nous*, 41–42; see also Gamlieli, *Psychoanalysis*, 118.
[46] Chodorow, *Reproduction*.
[47] *The Alphabet of Akiba Ben Joseph*, Version B, letter *mem*, 110.

This midrash implies the nonbinary character of the letter *mem* by using the terms *melekh* ("king") and *malkhut* ("dominion"). Following this, *Sefer ha-Bahir* (the first Kabbalistic work from the late twelfth century) examines the question of the open and closed *mem*, and proposes that the open *mem* is androgynous while the closed *mem* is exclusively female. Yet *Sefer ha-Bahir* qualifies this statement immediately: the difference between the two letters is not all that much, since "[t]he closed *mem* is *made like a belly from above*," and it clarifies the term "from above" as meaning "outward," unlike the letter *tet*, which turns inward on itself: "But Rabbi Rahumai said that the belly is like the letter *tet*. He said it is like a *tet* on the inside, while I say that it is *like a mem on the outside*."[48]

What is the significance of the open and closed *mem* in this homiletical interpretation? Despite the difficult language of *Sefer ha-Bahir*'s author and the many errata and differences between the manuscripts,[49] it is evident that the closed *mem* is actually not completely closed, since it has a part that protrudes outward, signaling its masculinity. It follows from this that neither version of the letter *mem* – open or closed – can be considered exclusively female, since both of them are shown as androgynous letters which include mutually the mother and the infant. Through this interpretative lens, *Sefer ha-Bahir* describes the embodiment of birth and copulation in the form of the filled (or "pregnant") or empty letters:

> What is *mem*? Do not read *mem* but rather *mayim* ["water"]. Just as these waters are moist, so the womb is always moist. Why is open *mem* comprised of masculine and feminine and the closed [*mem*] masculine? To teach you that the essence of *mem* is masculine. The opening [of *mem*] is added for the sake of the feminine. Just as the male does not give birth through the opening so the closed *mem* is not open, and just as the female gives birth and is open, so the *mem* is closed and open.[50]

We might conclude that this interpretation constitutes an appropriation of the maternal and feminine attribute into the masculine world ("to teach you that the essence of *mem* is masculine)." Yet alongside this tendency, the miraculous force in birth – an experience that crosses gender consciousness – prompts the Kabbalists, who also identify with the feminine aspect and the image of the maternal *Shekhinah*, to describe a dynamic process involving the transition between open and closed, between male and female – and so they choose the double letter *mem*.

---

[48] *Sefer ha-Bahir*, 57 (ed. Abrams, 151–153). The letter *mem* in the ancient Hebrew script had a little line protruding outward, just as the letter *tet* had a little line moving inward.
[49] Compare to the changes in other manuscripts (Ms. Vatican, Munich, and First Print 1651) (Abrams ed., 230, 272).
[50] *Sefer ha-Bahir* 57 (Abrams ed., 151–153).

4 Birth as a Transition between a Closed and Open Mem

Following *Sefer ha-Bahir*, the *Zohar* sees the mother – precisely at the time she gives birth – as demonstrating "the world of the masculine [*olam ha-zachar*]" as a font of abundance and a granter of life to the worlds beneath her:[51]

> Rabbi Shimon began: "Naftali is a hind let loose which yields lovely fawns" (Genesis 49:21). After all, it is said that the upper world is a masculine world. Since this statement rose from the Assembly of Israel [the *Shekhinah*] and upward, all is masculine. How do we know this? From the *olah* ["offering"]. Why is it called *olah*? Because it rises [*olah*] upward from the female. [. . .] Because of this, it is called the *olah* offering – because it rises from the female to the male, and from there [the *Shekhinah*] upward, all is masculine. And from the female downward, all is female, and we have already proven this. If you say: The feminine also exists "above" [referring to the *sefirah* of *Binah*], then the end point of the body shows that the entire body is male. The head of the body is female, and when you descend to the end point and the end point becomes visible, all becomes masculine. But here [the *Shekhinah*], the head and the end are feminine, since every *tikkun* ["development"] of her body is female.[52]

The term *olam ha-zachar* ("the world of the male," or "the masculine world"), is unique to the *Zohar* and to the writings of Rabbi Moses de León.[53] It seems that these sources claim that the child defines his mother's body. Thus, the homily says that the son is "the finishing point of the body," the male reproductive organ. But at the same time, we manage to hold on to the elusive and androgynous symbol of the Great Mother from whose womb the son emerges as an "other" to define and establish her maternal state.

Indeed, I suggest that the concept of *olam ha-zachar*, which is attributed to *Binah* at birth, should be interpreted not as the assimilation of the mother into the father, but as the ability to contain the "other" and to be called by his name during pregnancy. Birth is not perceived here as only a one-time event, but as a period of time that sentences us to life not only from the moment we leave our mothers' bodies but also from the time we descend from the upper womb of the "Great Mother" through to the limited existence in "the world of the male."

In this context, Bracha Ettinger presents a new way of thinking about the critical moment of birth, the duration of pregnancy, and the relationship between life and death. In her discussion of the "matrix language" – a language that touches all areas of life and accompanies us everywhere we go – she proposes that the mother and fetus emerge together.

Ettinger sees in the matrix meeting a potentially intimate connection between several individuals, and one that occurs even during pregnancy: the

---

51 See, for example, *Zohar* 2:127 and below.
52 *Zohar* 1:246b (Matt, 3, 509).
53 See Kaniel, "Gender."

mother, who meets the "non-I" that the baby represents for her, and the fetus, a "pre-subject" who meets the co-emerging "I" and the unknown "non-I." This co-emergence facilitates a renewal of psychic impressions and the creation of symbols on the individual ontogenetic level, but also in the broad and cosmic dimension that Ettinger calls a "subjective trance." Through the topos of pregnancy and birth, she explores the dimension of psychic transformation and the mutual emotional influence that can result from, and exist within, sacrifice for the sake of another. She defines the matrix as a space where there was never a "one," but always a multiplicity as well as the appearance of subjectivity linking the incipient fantasy of the mother to the emerging "I" of the fetus:

> If the Matrix points to that which is not reducible to the one and does not yearn for the one, it is because it never was One. Its lost objects are partial and multiple; they never had a single value, and they do not stand alone in the Unconscious. [. . .] This concept has implications both on the invisible ontogenetic level and on the level of a broadened Symbolic, which includes subsymbolic processes of interconnectivity. [. . .] The mother-to-be's phantasy life is also transformed by the prenatal encounter with the postmature infant with whom her/their particular matrixial subjectivity co-emerges.[54]

The transformation of the mother from the closed letter *mem* who, through birth, becomes open resonates with Ettinger's statement that "the mother grants the fetus's request to be born and accepts the call, and the sundering, willingly." She does not experience the baby's emergence as an attack upon her wholeness. Instead, she experiences two modes of existence that complement one another, just like the double essence of the letter *mem*.

Symbols are born and leave a phylogenetic stamp that continues to develop over the generations, sometimes in a subsymbolic, hidden, preverbal manner; so too the symbols of the "Great Mother," as the open and closed *mem*, resonant of water, might reflect other primordial and mythical representations of birth.

Birth is the broadest metaphor, and at the same time it is the most confident way of being, given to us by the individual maternal body that brought us into this world. Yet birth also testifies to a trauma that has already taken place, and provides sure evidence that from the beginning, from a long time ago, we have known how to exist as two together, one inside the other.

On the mythopoetic level, we might suggest that just as the Kabbalists theorize the encounter between the "I" and the "non-I," so too they divide the world into the "male" and the "female." The greatness of the mother is therefore rooted according to them in her ability to "be herself" even as she allows her offspring to imprint upon her an "other" essence. In the Kabbalistic literature, the mother

---

[54] Ettinger, *Matrixial Borderspace*.

always reflects this diversity of experiences that she knows through her womb; she is always "two," signifying the paradoxical relations between God and the being He has created: from one source emerge two separate entities.

An additional metaphor of motherhood appears in the Parable of the Bucket in *Sha'arei Orah*. The focus of the exposition is *Binah*, which is called "the World to Come" as an expression of a world in the process of formation, which "always comes" and begets itself and its progeny anew. *Binah* is also called *Teshuvah* ("Return" or "Repentance") and "the World of Freedom," since these elements enable a person to return to the place/source and start all over.[55] Although *Binah* is the source of judgments, the Zoharic literature and Castilian Kabbalah identify it mainly with beneficial and constructive maternal aspects. In the Kabbalah of Nahmanides, however, it also includes the characteristic of annihilation, as the treasury of souls to which they are drawn in order to be reborn.[56]

Kabbalists devoted considerable attention to the return to the supernal source in order to begin anew. The three uppermost *sefirot* are located in an expanse beyond the reach of cognition, of which it is said: "Seek not things that are too hard for you, and search not out things that are hidden from you. The things that have been permitted you, think thereupon; you have no business with the things that are secret."[57] This is especially so for the two uppermost *sefirot*, *Keter* and *Hokhmah*, which are identified with will and the beginning of thought. The liminal point is *Binah*, which is at the border of the transition between the concealed and the revealed, which is why it is identified with the "Great Mother," who is capable of becoming pregnant – of concealing – and of actualizing.

By expanding the symbols of *Binah*, the thirteenth-century Kabbalist R. Joseph Gikatilla proposes a discussion of the Kabbalistic process of return as an experience of returning to the womb and being revived with its assistance. According to this exposition, the process of return (*shivah*) to *Teshuvah* (= *Binah*, lit., "Return") is similar not only to rebirth, but also to drawing water from within the *sefirah* of *Hokhmah* ("Thought") and all that is above it.[58] The process of return transforms *Binah* into a vessel; thus humans, who are associated with *Malkhut*, can ascend to our supernal source, and effect mending by means of this extraction:[59]

---

[55] Gikatilla, *Sha'arei Orah*, Gate 8 (Ben Shlomo ed. II, 61, 64–65). On the concepts of repentance and *teshuva* in Kabbalah, see Tishby, *Wisdom*, 1499–1510.
[56] Pedaya, *Nahmanides*, 380–389.
[57] BT Hagigah 13a (following trans. Soncino), citing *Ben Sira* 3:19.
[58] Tishby, *Wisdom*, 1502.
[59] On the upper womb as a vessel and a tool, see Idel, "Womb."

> And no one can contemplate them, for they are known as the *omek ram* ["deep heights"], meaning that they emanate from *Keter*, which is the highest of high. No one has access to their contemplation except for the one who draws water with the bucket from the deepest well that has no end. The one who draws the water does not enter himself; only with the bucket does he draw the water from the well. Thus no creature can contemplate the essence of *omek hamachshava* ["depth of knowledge"] except through the sphere *Binah* ["Upper Mother"], which is like the bucket that enters to draw the waters from the deep well of thought while the one who draws remains outside.[60]

On the symbolic level, this parable relates to blocked situations in which there is neither access to the source nor a clear understanding of human existence and the moment of birth. We do not know from whence we came, and therefore have difficulty answering the question of where we are going. In such moments, the reality into which we have landed becomes fragmentary and unconnected, marked by its incompletion, disintegration, and lack of continuity from beginning to end. This is an existentialist depiction of human experience in the world. What must an individual do to give birth to himself, for "the prisoner cannot release himself from the prison"? R. Joseph Gikatilla presents *Binah* as the primal womb that is eternally accessible.

In the psychological sense, the mother becomes the key to revealing the beginning of "thought" and self-awareness (*Hokhmah*), from within which a new structure can be erected. As adults possessing consciousness and choice, humans can build on the first birth and the mother as the source of *Binah*, which means "understanding [i.e., inferring] one thing from another." Likewise, *Teshuvah* appears for the first time as an "answer" (yet another meaning of the Hebrew word) to the question of human life. It could be argued that this portrayal objectivizes the mother and turns her into a mere vessel. Nonetheless, according to some theories the mother must first undergo a process of alienation and objectivization in order to become the "other" whose existence we recognize.[61] From object to subject, from a figure that fills the entire space and a consuming source which unifies all, the mother slowly becomes a separate entity which is no longer in the dyad from which the individual emerged. Once a person acknowledges his limits, the mother becomes a spiritually nourishing resource, a "bucket" which brings forth "water," which aids in comprehension and attests to the recognition of her separateness. Only after recognition of the "source" is it possible to stand facing her as self confronting self, face to face.

This exposition brings together several archetypical pictures: Gikatilla maintains that the mother aids in the process of recollection, and draws forth the ideas

---

60 Gikatilla, *Sha'arei Orah*, Gate 8, *sefirah* of *Binah*.
61 Palgi-Hacker, *Mother in Psychoanalysis*, 16–84.

from the hidden place where they are sequestered. This imagery might also be interpreted in light of the difficulty of extracting the fetus from the depths of the womb in which it hides. Then the "bucket" becomes a mythical vessel meant to assist the mother in drawing forth from the womb above. The bucket as a "birthing instrument" is reminiscent of alchemical notions of the "krater" or "mortar," a vessel that symbolizes rebirth by the processing of primal mental raw materials. For Carl Jung, Gnosticism contributed to culture "the primordial image of the spirit as another, higher god who gave to mankind the krater (mixing vessel), the vessel of spiritual transformation."[62]

The krater facilitated reaching a higher level of awareness, just as the Kabbalist seeks to draw "water" from the "well" of thought with the understanding that it is more elevated than his own self, and that to this end he must reach the mystical state known as the "nullification of thought."[63]

Modern medical developments enabled the invention of gynecological instruments meant to aid in extricating the fetus during childbirth. The feminist literature views such instruments as tools of repression, which are convenient for men while creating hardship for women giving birth. These instruments, such as forceps and the vacuum, harm the woman's ability to believe in her body and her capacity for giving birth on her own.[64] In contrast, the bucket parable is concerned with spiritual birth and with the supportive female vessel, which can assuage the primal dread. Although the birth recedes further and further from us, together with all that preceded our existence, Gikatilla offers access to the shrouded realm of human origins. In this parable, the mother becomes a vessel that is plucked out from the depths of consciousness, from the wrappings of the primal memory, and from the forgotten membranes of the womb. She represents a mysterious force that extracts from the primordial depths experiences that predate existence – even the existence of the mother herself. Delving into the primordial and amniotic fluid enables us to be reborn from her womb.

Additionally, the bucket parable elicits the mother's relation to us through the "umbilical cord." As Joseph Campbell suggests, the myth gives us a rope that will link us to a riddle that is ourselves.[65] Without access to the bucket that draws and

---

[62] Jung, *Memories*, 201. He adds that "the krater is a feminine principle which could find no place in Freud's patriarchal world."
[63] Pedaya, "Possessed by Speech"; Garb, *Manifestation*, 74–91; Abrams, *Female Body*, 108 n. 197.
[64] Rich, *Of Woman Born*, chs. 6–7; Ehrenreich and English, *Witches*. For another perspective on male intervention in the medical birth process in the sixteenth and seventeenth centuries, see Bar-On, *Seeing*, 145–148, 233–234.
[65] Campbell *Myth*, 80.

the well at the rim of which we stand, we cannot descend to reach the "first point" (i.e., the *sefirah* of *Hokhmah*) – that is, to meet the source and be reborn.

5 Nursing

The nursing experience constitutes a continuing, flowing bond between the newborn and the maternal source from which he emerged. By nursing, the mother imparts to the newborn her very life-force. As Melanie Klein observes:

> The breast is instinctively felt to be the source of nourishment and therefore, in a deeper sense, of life itself [. . .] It may well be that his having formed part of the mother in the pre-natal state contributes to the infant's innate feeling that there exists outside him something that will give him all he needs and desires.[66]

Winnicott adds to this theory the omnipotence felt by the infant, who, as it were, "creates" the breast whenever he needs it. As Winnicott emphasizes, the experience of nursing requires two: the infant, who is ready to receive from his mother, and the mother, who is psychologically capable of nursing. The readiness of the two is connected to the birth experience, and its occurrence at exactly the right moment for the mother and the fetus.[67]

The Biblical, midrashic, and Kabbalistic literature transfers the imagery of nursing to the theological realm and uses it to reflect the relationship between man and God. As Ellen Haskell stresses, the Zoharic depictions enabled the Kabbalist to undergo a spiritual transformation that facilitates sensing the intimate relationship to the nursing Godhead.[68] The suckling sensation of the lower *sefirot* results in the production of milk, and restores to this world divine abundance, blessing, and nourishment. Milk is a metaphor for this world's influence on the supernal one, and an example of the linkage between a sacred text and the conception of the body as holy.[69]

---

[66] Klein, "Envy and Gratitude," 178–179.
[67] Winnicott, "Birth Memories." On the infant who "creates" the breast whenever he needs it, see idem, *Playing and Reality*.
[68] "The Zohar's reader is provoked into a contemplative and transformative internal act that reorganizes his understanding of the universe and his place within it"; "[this text] provides its reader with a richly textured and deeply coherent model for redefining his relationship with God." Haskell, *Suckling*, 11–13.
[69] Ibid., 69–88. Compare to Berman, *Divine and Demonic*, 208–220, who deals with the dark side of nursing and the negative "suckling" in the *Zohar*. On phallic aspects of nursing in the *Zohar* (regarding to the theory of Elliott Wolfson), see Abrams, *Female Body*, 123–139.

The Babylonian Talmud applies Proverbs 5:9 to Torah study: "Why were the words of the Torah compared to a breast? As with a breast, however often the infant sucks at it does he find milk in it, so it is with the words of the Torah. As often as person studies them, so often does he find relish in them."[70] Torah study is the ultimate desire of the Rabbis, and is an expression of erotic and Oedipal pleasure. The Torah is both spouse and nourishing mother, whose breasts provide constant abundance and refreshment. Following in this vein, the *Zohar* compares the mystical experience to nursing and to bathing in the river of milk that flows unceasingly:[71]

> Eyes of the head are different from other eyes [. . .] and the providential eye of the Ancient One is above them. When that cover lifts, He appears as one who awakens from sleep. His eyes open and see the open eye and are bathed in one whiteness of the good eye as is written "bathing in the milk" (Song of Songs 5:12). What is meant by *in milk*? In the white of the primordial eye. During that time, compassionate providence prevails.[72]

Just as the infant is swallowed within his mother's eyes, so too *Ze'ir* unites with *Atika* and is absorbed in the white light of *Keter*. Thus the Kabbalist "bathes" and "cleanses" in the Godhead and melds with it. Bathing in milk has an erotic nature, which at the same time is infantile and pre-Oedipal. At times in the Zoharic sections *Idra Rabba* and *Idra Zutra*, not only does the upper *sefirah Keter* bathe the son (*Ze'ir*) in the rivers of milk, but the *sefirah* of *Binah*, the Great Mother, does so too:

> "Eyes of the King – supervising all, supervising above and below; all those masters of supervision are called so [. . .] Eyebrows is the name of the place that conveys supervision to all those colors, masters of supervision. These eyebrows, downwards, are eyebrows of supervision from that flowing, gushing river – a place drawing from that river, to bathe in the whiteness of the Ancient One, from the milk *flowing from Mother*. For when *Gevurah* extends and eyes flash in red, the Holy Ancient One shines its whiteness and kindles Mother, *who is filled with milk and suckles all, and all the eyes bathe in that mother's milk, flowing forth constantly,* as is written: bathing in milk (Song of Songs 5:12) – in Mother's milk, flowing constantly, ceaselessly.[73]

This washing enables constant self-birth within a protective "bosom" while allowing the experience of pleasure and abundance. *Idra Rabba* (the "Greater Assembly") stresses that *Atika* is called "One," since it has one eye instead of two, and this eye is overflowing with compassion.[74] This portrait is based on the

---

70 BT Eruvin 54b.
71 See, for example, *Zohar* 3:289a; 283b, and below.
72 *Zohar* 3:136b (Matt, 8, 392).
73 Ibid., 2:122b (Matt, 5, 105–153; emphasis is mine).
74 Ibid., 3:130a. See also Sobol, *Transgression*, 125–127.

intimate mother–infant relationship. *Atika*'s face corresponds to the face of the mother, who, for the sake of her child, is willing to remove all covering, to be exposed, "without eyebrows." In poetic terms, the *Zohar* depicts the infant's perspective. From the angle created by eye-mouth-breast, the mother's face is concentrated into a single point, and her two eyes appear as an always smiling "single illuminating eye." As Melila Hellner-Eshed writes: "The lengthening of Ze'ir Anpin's face thus refers to its transformation into a Long-faced or Patient One (*Erekh Apayim*)." She continues: "Here, the term *erekh* (length) is interpreted to mean *arukhah* (healing) [. . .] This face-to-face gaze heals both *Ze'ir Anpin* and the cosmos."[75]

Moreover, the description of this (cyclopean) focusing contrasts a human's plurality of (split) eyes with the divine unity, thereby alleviating the newborn's feeling of confusion. The sensory overstimulations and contradictory, destabilizing experiences undergone by the infant from the moment he leaves the womb are balanced by the mother's milk-eye, which nurses him with constant, uninterrupted light.

The metaphor of awakening from sleep compares birth to ascending from the regressive reality within the womb (like the world of the *Idra*) to the excessive wakefulness of reality. At this first juncture, "man" is compared to the newborn infant. This is the *sefirah* of *Tiferet*, which is called *"Ze'ir Anpin"* (lit., "Small Countenance"). This "countenance" expresses impatience, quickness to anger, and difficulty in containing complexity and pain. This is where the mother is needed, as the container who transforms "beta elements" and intolerable experiences into thoughts and emotions that can be contemplated, and which return to the infant/adult as "alpha functions." This is also the task of *Arikh Anpin* (lit., the "Great Countenance"): to impart to the infant, the "small one," patience and inner peace.

In the literary context, these metaphors reflect the moments of divine illumination in the *Idrot* as part of an initiation rite involving R. Shimon bar Yohai and his disciples, who gather together with him in order to correct the worlds. This Tanna, in effect, begets his pupils and "enlarges" (i.e., heals) their countenances just before he takes his leave of them and ascends to the upper realms.

The Zoharic combination of the experiences of nursing-feeding and illumination-visibility-seeing reverberates in psychological theories that portray nursing as the continuation of intra-uterine life, during which mother and fetus were connected and one nourished the other. Here as well, the Torah and God nurse the infant-pupil-Kabbalist with milk-like abundance, from which they

---

[75] Hellner-Eshed, *Seekers*, 63.

can draw warmth and vitality at any time. The Talmudic exposition with which we began this discussion (BT Eruvin 54b) presents the Torah as a maternal breast that satisfies at any time, but also as a hind, whose womb is narrow and is "loved by its mate at all times as at the first hour of their meeting." Thus, a single exegesis unites maternal and erotic relations between student and text. The link between the spousal model and the maternal one generates a relationship between the container and the contained, who continually exchange roles. The reader of the text, who infuses it with meaning, is both the nourishing mother as well the infant who nurses from her, and aids in the production of the milk from which he himself is nourished.[76]

Unlike the birth experience, which tears the mother and the infant from each other, nursing unites the two into a new entity with two subjects who do not completely meld together in symbiosis. In the *Zohar*, and, following it, the Lurianic Kabbalah, the two breasts symbolize the two aspects of the Godhead: strict judgment and compassion, the draining of the evil and the channeling of the good to the Godhead. This conception resonates in the Kleinian splitting mechanism. Klein argues that in his first months of life, the infant uses this splitting as a defense against anxiety; he attributes the pleasurable and satiating aspects to the "good breast" and the negative and frustrating ones to the "bad breast," until the stage in which he is capable of regarding his mother as a "whole object" which comprises both these aspects.[77] Klein, who emphasizes the activity of the death drive and infantile aggression, nevertheless writes: "This mental and physical closeness to the gratifying breast in some measure restores, if things go well, the lost prenatal unity with the mother and the feeling of security that goes with it."[78] When everything is as it should be, maternal nurturing enables the infant to move between the opposing poles of love and hate, to adapt to the external world, and to construct satisfying close relations with others. Klein calls the breast the "source of life," the exact same appellation used by R. Joseph Gikatilla when he portrayed the connection between *Binah* the Mother and her son, the *sefirah* of *Tiferet*.[79]

In an additional exposition, the *Zohar* uses the metaphor of nursing to present the Messianic era of Redemption, when the infant will become the "mouth" that will kiss the Mother:

---

[76] Showalter, "Feminist Criticism"; Ashur, "To Read and Write."
[77] The concepts of the "good breast" and the "bad breast" first appear in Kleinian theory in 1936. See Klein, "Weaning."
[78] Klein, "Envy and Gratitude," 178.
[79] Gikatilla, *Sha'arei Orah*, Gate 5, 8 (Ben Shlomo ed. 2, 21, 63).

> As is said: *On that day, fresh water shall flow from Jerusalem, half of it to the Eastern Sea and half to the Western Sea* (Zechariah 14:8) [. . .] O holy one, O holy one! – a child's voice was aroused outside. This was the child who studied and presented his learning in the presence of a pillar of the world – the son of Rabbi Yehudah, who you raised [. . .] "That child opened, saying, '(*Ba-yom ha-hu*), On that day. *Ha-hu*, That – which one is not known. But everywhere on that day indicates *the last day* [. . .] When this day will arise, from the lattices of the courtyard will rise a flow of waters, and this flow will be from the Primordial Sea. Like a mother whose son is between her arms, and from the abundance of milk that he sucks, filling his mouth and swelling, he empties milk into his mother's mouth. So, half of it to the Primordial Sea. The Head of the Academy grasped him and kissed him. He said, "O life of this world, holy son! This is how they established it in the Heavenly Academy, and it is certainly so. *The Final Sea* – Her last rungs."[80]

This passage sets forth a state of overflowing abundance so great that it actually nourishes the source from which it came. In psychological terms, this is an attempt to express the child's gratitude for the bounty bestowed on him, while for the mystic, the imagery of the infant who feeds his mother represents the relation of the lower *sefirot* to the upper ones. The "Eastern Sea" symbolizes the Great Mother, *Binah*, and the "Western Sea," *Malkhut*, the reality of this world. The tableau of nursing connects *Yesod* (the child) with *Binah* (the mother), and *Malkhut* (the daughter and the bride). The child, the *yanuka* (lit., "infant"), receives the divine abundance from the mother, and then passes it on to the *Shekhinah* (= *Malkhut*), thus filling the "Western Sea" of *Binah*, which is connected to the Redemption. In like fashion, Klein describes the situation in which "the good breast is taken in and becomes part of the ego, and the infant who was first inside the mother now has the mother inside himself."[81] Even if Klein does not theorize that the mother is nourished by the child, we have here a container–contained relationship that develops in the inner world, similar to the infant's desire "to give birth to the mother" and create her from his body. According to Klein, this is a megalomaniacal defense, but this wish can still be seen as a positive, creative stage.

Redemption is characterized by what Victor Turner referred to as *communitas*, that is, conversion and the undermining of existing orders and the mixture of generations in order to create a new and proper one.[82] This situation reverses statuses, roles, and powers. At times, *communitas* is expressed in gender reversals, or by the son becoming a sort of "nursing mother." The Zoharic passage does not only contain a parent–child reversal; in the state of Redemption, the

---

80 *Zohar* 3:171a (Matt, 9, 128–132).
81 Klein, "Envy and Gratitude," 178.
82 Turner, *Ritual Process*.

teacher becomes the pupil, and the pupil, the teacher, since the exposition is learned from the words of the infant (the *yanuka*) to his teacher, R. Metivta (who obviously symbolizes the mother who is nourished from her son).[83]

More than any other experience, nursing is comparable to dyadic unity and the mystical connection between the Kabbalist and the Godhead. In an additional portrait in *Idra Zuta*, mother and daughter engage in mutual, cyclical multigenerational nursing: "From Her [*Binah*] they suckle, and to Her they return, and She is called their Mother. Just as another one [*Malkhut*] is mother to the body, and the whole body suckles from Her."[84]

The depiction of the *Shekhinah* as a nursing goddess joins her portrayals as a gazelle (*ayalah*) on the hilltop who feeds all the animals, and the morning star (*ayelet ha-shahar*) whose light bursts forth every morning (see below, Chapter 8). The miraculous nature of the metaphorical act of nursing is marked in these expositions: it is specifically the *Shekhinah* who is the poorest, who "has nothing of her own (*leit la-mi-garmah kelum*)," who imparts abundance to all the world.[85]

The imagery of birth and nursing especially engaged R. Moses Cordovero, R. Isaac Luria, and the sixteenth-century Kabbalists.[86] Thus, for example, Cordovero regarded the removing of the Torah scroll from the Ark during prayer services as simulating birth and the removal of the fetus from its mother's womb, and returning the Torah scroll to the Ark as returning the infant to his mother's bosom for nursing.[87]

For Cordovero, nursing is a concealed process that takes place "in the mother's innermost self," meaning the elevation of the infant and his return to the source. Just as the father's sperm originates in the mind, so too the maternal milk issues from the supernal world. Elsewhere, Cordovero draws a parallel between the *rehem* ("womb") and the 248 (in Hebrew numerology – with the same letters: *resh-mem-het*) positive commandments, and declares that the blessings recited with the proper intent prior to performing any commandment cause divine insemination and impregnation. In his book, *Pardes Rimonim*, he compares *devekut* (communion with God) and the interdependency of the worlds to the act of nursing:

---

[83] On father–son and teacher–pupil relations in the context of messianism and *communitas*, see Kaniel. "To Write or Not to Write."
[84] *Zohar* 3:296a (Matt, 9, 840–843). See Abrams, *Female Body*, 124 n. 236.
[85] See, for example, *Zohar* 1:181a; 233b; 249b.
[86] Scholem, *Major Trends*, 244–286; Fine, *Physician*, 196–205, 150–167; Tamari, "Discourse of the Body"; Meroz, "Redemption"; Weinstein, Break the Disges, 315–406; Giller, *Shalom*, 131–146. For more on these themes, see below, Chapter 7.
[87] R. Moses Cordovero, *Tefilah le-Moshe*, 134b–137a.

> Thus, *Shekhinah* is in the lower realm for a higher need. [. . .] The allegory (*mashal*) for this is a nursing woman. For when her son is alive, and he is willing to suckle, the milk in her breasts will increase. And when she has no son to suckle and flow (*le-hashpi'a*) upon him, then the milk will be lacking from her breasts.[88]

His description stresses the mother's dependency on her son, corresponding to his reliance on her, based on the principle that the *Shekhinah* (and the earthly reality associated with it) is *tzorekh gavoah* (lit., "higher need," referring to the influence of the *Shekhinah* on the upper worlds). Milk is the adhesive that links the two; it increases when those in the lower world need the supernal realm, and address it in prayer, petition, or blessing.

R. Isaac Luria (the *Ari*), who studied Cordovero's writings, compared Cordovero's teachings to the milk with which he nurses his students. In *Toledot ha-Ari* (*The History of the Ari*), the teacher compares himself to a mother whose desire to nurse is greater than that of the calf; out of concern for his students, he only gives them milk drop by drop:

> When I open my mouth to say to you some secret of the Torah, the overflow (*shefa*) increases in me like a flowing stream. And I seek some kind of tactic through which I will open for you a thin and small channel so that you may carry. For if I increase [the flow] upon you, you will forfeit everything, like an infant who chokes due to the large amount of milk that comes to him at once.[89]

Although this is an example of the appropriation of the female experience and its transference to the metaphorical realm of teaching, Luria's precision in describing the physical experience of nursing, to the degree of mentioning the narrow channels in the woman's body, is nothing less than astonishing. Similar traits were ascribed in the medieval period to Jesus and to Bernard of Clairvaux, who were depicted as nursing their flocks with milk.[90]

In a lengthy exposition in the book *Etz Hayyim*, by Luria's disciple R. Hayyim Vital, the act of nursing leads to *Ze'ir Anpin* standing on its own and the forming of its two legs, which until this stage existed only potentially. Luria compares *Ze'ir Anpin* to a youth "who already has thighs and legs but cannot walk on them until he nurses." Even though the newborn infant has all his limbs, a maturation process is needed for him to actualize them. The legs symbolize the son's sexual independence, and nursing enables him to "walk" from the mother and part from her womb in a process corresponding to *hamtakat ha-dinim*, the "sweetening" (i.e., cancellation) of harsh judgments:

---

[88] R. Moses Cordovero, *Pardes Rimonim* 8:20 (Trans. Gene Matanki).
[89] Benayahu, *Sefer Toldot*, 164.
[90] Bynum, *Fragmentation*; idem, *Jesus as Mother*, 131–133.

> The secret of the milk is the name *Ehyeh* in [the *sefirah* of] *Binah*. Behold, when *Imma* [Mother] suckles the sons, then she is called *El Shaddai*, due to the breasts [*shaddayim*] suckling them. And when she ascends upwards and withdraws atop the sons, for their suckling has ended, then *Imma* is called *El Elyon* ["Supernal God"], bestows [*gomel*] acts of kindness, which we recite in the blessings of the Patriarchs [in the Eighteen Benedictions prayer]. And "bestow" [*gomel*] is etymologically related [*me-lashon*]: "The child grew, and was weaned" [Gen. 21:8], for the time of nursing has ended. And the secret of *El Elyon* is *Binah* when she ascends upwards and *Shaddai* is when he suckles at her breasts [. . .] The breasts [*shaddayim*] are also called "breasts" [*dadim*], and they are the secret of *Elohim* ['*LHYM*] that is in *Binah*, which is *El* ['*L*] from the right, *Mi* [*MY*] from the left, *Heh* [*H*] in the middle. Join *El* that is on the right with a breast [*dad*] [*DD*] and it is Eldad; join *Mi* from the left with a breast [*dad*] [*DD*] and it will be Medad.[91]

According to Luria, the mother nurses her son with milk whose color is white, which represents the quality of compassion. Her role, as the source of life, is to transform the blood and judgments into beneficial and constructive powers. For Luria, the supernal meaning of milk is the essence of the hidden names of God.

The exposition is a complex numerology that exemplifies how the two breasts represent strict judgment and compassion in balance with one another. In the first part of the exposition, Luria maintains that the maternal name "I will be" (*eheyeh*, composed of the letters *alef-heh-yud-heh*) embodies the child's growth potential, since it has the numerical value of 948, which is equivalent to that of "milk" (*halav-het-lamed-bet*). This numerical value is obtained by adding together the numerical values of each of the letters in these words, spelled out. Thus, instead of the simple numerology of *eheyeh*, with the four letters coming to a sum of 21, he totals the values of each letter in the names of the letters: for example, the letter *alef*, instead of its usual value of 1, becomes *alef* = 1 + *lamed* = 30 + *peh* = 80, and so on. The two breasts connect right and left, compassion and judgment, with the attribute of *Tiferet* in the middle.

In the end of this complex exposition (the details of which would exceed the purview of my study), Luria discusses the dual symbolism of the breasts, in light of the narrative of prophesying by Eldad and Medad in Numbers 11:26. Luria maintains that this balancing process is expressed by the letter *heh* that remains from the divine name *Elohim*. When the initial *El* is removed from "Eldad" and the final *Mi* from "Medad," in each name the word *dad* remains, alluding to *shaddayim* ("breasts"), while, beginning in thirteenth-century Kabbalah, the name *El* represents *Hesed* ("Compassion") and the name *Mi* represents *Binah* and the source of *dinim* ("judgments").

---

91 R. Hayyim Vital, *Etz Hayyim*, "Sha'ar ha-Klalim" 3 (secrets of nursing).

The correspondence of the breasts to two Biblical characters is based on the Rabbinic exegesis in *Song of Songs Rabbah* (4:13): "These two breasts: these are Moses and Aaron ... Just as the breasts are full of milk, so Moses and Aaron filled Israel with Torah."

R. Isaac Luria's exposition is also based on the *Zohar*, and on the connection between the two *dodim* ("beloveds," i.e., the act of love) and the supernal *dadim* ("breasts").[92]

The portrayal of the two breasts as the figures of Moses and Aaron in the Sanctuary could be interpreted as an attempt to appropriate for male leaders the most feminine of all actions, and thereby to offer the Torah as a symbolic male conception. R. Isaac Luria was influenced by this line of thought, and suggests a parallel to Moses and Aaron – namely, Eldad and Medad. But this is not all. In contrast to the metaphorical language of the Rabbis, and the restrained implication of the Zoharic text, Luria creates a developed mythos of nursing. He does so by detailing the relations between the *sefirot*, a description of the fleshing out of the legs of the *Ze'ir* (see below, Chapter 7), and the influence of nursing on his growth. This nursing becomes a recurring phenomenon, which occurs within both the human and divine bodies.

Moreover, the conclusion of the exposition adds a ritual-liturgical aspect by depicting the *Avot*'s ("Patriarchs'") blessing of the *Amidah* prayer as a transition from the state of *Ze'ir*'s nursing to his weaning. In this process, *Binah* (which is called *Shaddai*, or "the Almighty"; here, in the role of nursing, *shed* = "breast") returns to its supernal place and becomes *El Elyon* ("God Most High"), which is a more elevated name. As the end of the exposition has it, every person, every day, by means of the intents of prayer, experiences the order of impregnation and nursing. Like the above-discussed exposition of R. Metivta, which represents the infant as nursing the mother in the time of Redemption, Luria sets forth cyclical processes of nourishing between the worlds, processes that occur with ritual periodicy each and every day.

Unlike the beneficial process appearing in the *Zohar* and the teaching of R. Isaac Luria, other presentations focus on the distortion that is liable to be created during the nourishing process. The desire to destroy the source of milk, or to turn one's back on the divine parent, corresponds, in the psychological realm, to the jealousy and greed that the infant feels toward the omnipotent mother/God figure. As Klein emphasizes, the mother – like God – can be experienced by the infant as the source of life but equally, when nursing is disrupted,

---

[92] *Zohar* 3:155b; *Zohar Hadash* 68b.

as the object of jealousy and cause of destruction, due to the infant's frustration at his dependency upon the mother's breast and the abundance of her milk.

The Bible frequently depicts situations in which God's desire to impart is not accepted, and His milk is seen by the people as "poisoned" and "spoiled." The Israelites' behavior after the Exodus from Egypt, in the manna and quail narratives, shows contempt for divine abundance. In comparison with the bounty bestowed on other peoples, for whom the infant/people pines, the divine milk is considered worthless. It is not for nothing that Egypt, the mighty power that caused disillusionment, is called "that broken reed of a staff" (2 Kings 18:21), to express the uselessness of such a seeming substitute for God.[93]

Negating the value of the divine milk projects a psychological defense against the suffering caused by the mother's unavailability, which is not precisely fulfilling the wishes of the people. In his 1916 essay "On Transience," Freud spoke of the tendency to protect oneself from the pain of finitude and death by depreciating the worth of things.[94] He argued that at times a person is incapable of enjoying the blossoming of a flower, and instead is occupied by thoughts of its withering, so as not to know the pain of its loss. But lessening its value does not prevent suffering.

Similar to the male sperm, the maternal milk is perceived by the Kabbalists as the abundance that reaches all the worlds when they are deserving of it. Stopping the flow of the milk is an expression of crisis and exile, resulting from turning away from the good breast and the sources of nourishment and vitality. The *Shekhinah* – as the lowest rung in the sefirotic system, and as "the Mother of the world" – assumes responsibility to cry out for the state of drying up, and to symbolize it with her body sickness, detachment, struggle, and failure. At the same time, it is the *Shekhinah* who has the task of mending and creating the bridge that will reunite the world of the child with its divine and parental source.

---

93 Pardes, *The Biography*. See also Eigen, "Toxic Nourishment."
94 Freud, "On Transience," 305–307.

Chapter 7
Birth in Lurianic Kabbalah

Following the discussion of breastfeeding in the previous chapter, this chapter elucidates feminine, biological, psychological, and spiritual aspects of procreation in sixteenth-century Sefadean Kabbalah. In the corpus of Lurianic Kabbalah, birth is a dramatic, perpetual process of the creation of bonds between the human and divine realms. In the writings of Moses Cordovero and Isaac Luria, we find bold images of the "anthropomorphism of birth" which not only affirm the soul's corporeality and sexuality, but its journey prior to its corporeal birth in this world.

This chapter will discuss spiritual and mystical explanations of physical and psychological events, such as the emergence of the infant from the narrow opening of the mother's body, the mystery of the coupling of the celestial parents, and the experience of breastfeeding and nursing. Since the earliest days of Kabbalah, accounts of birth have been associated with basic notions such as redemption, creation, and emanation (*atzilut*). In Lurianic Kabbalah, however, these concepts are charged with new meanings: martyrdom, the elucidation of prayers, the attenuation of halakhic law, and the study of Torah. As we can learn from the appendix to this chapter, R. Moses Cordovero served as an essential link, mediating esoteric knowledge for the generation that embraced Kabbalah as everyday devotional practice as it gained widespread acceptance. Indeed, many ideas in Lurianic thought are rooted in the Cordoverian school, as recent studies by Bracha Sack, Moshe Idel, and others have shown.[1]

1 Three Stages of Mystical Birth: *Ibbur* ("Impregnation," lit., "Gestation"), *Yenika* ("Suckling," "Nursing"), and *Moḥin* ("Consciousness;" lit. "Brains")

"Impregnation, suckling, and consciousness" is a Lurianic model of formation of the Godhead corresponding to a newborn's physiological and psychological development. These three phases and conditions, which persist throughout one's life, signify a "continuity of being," to use Donald Winnicott's term, which precedes all human action. Continuity of being begins in the womb and endures throughout

---

[1] Sack, *The Kabbalah*; idem, *R. Moshe Cordovero*; Idel, *The Privileged*, 77–102; idem, *Kabbalah and Eros.*

adulthood. Luria associates these phases with specific stages of gestation and infancy (seven, nine, and twelve months), from embryonic development through infancy to the advent of consciousness. Whereas "impregnation (gestation)" and "suckling" are familiar terms from physiological reality (as stages of pregnancy and nursing), "consciousness" belongs, rather, to the psychological and spiritual dimension. Luria apparently borrowed the term *moḥin* from the *Zohar* in general and the literature of the *Idrot* specifically. In the *Zohar*, consciousness is associated with the *atarot* ("crowns") of the divine parents *Hokhma* and *Binah*, as well as with the figures of the Patriarchs Abraham and Isaac in their relationship with Jacob, as *Sefirat Tiferet*, who is called *Ze'ir Anpin* (lit., "Small Countenance").[2] In the midrash, the Sages teach that one's parents represent illumination and protection, attributing to Jacob the words of Psalms (121:1): "I lift up my eyes to the hills – from where will my help come." According to the midrash, Jacob says:

> Following verses: "A song for ascents. I lift my eyes to the mountains (*harim*)." (Ps. 121:1), I lift my eyes to my parents (*horim*, instead of *harim*) who taught me and guided me."[3]

This reading resonates with psychoanalytic models of the internalized parental figures which are addressed by Melanie Klein, Donald Meltzer, Lewis Aron, and others. Following the ideas discussed above in Chapter 5, we might suggest that the Lurianic third stage of development, that of *moḥin* and "consciousness," represents a process of maturation. The crowns with which the parents first adorn the son are eventually internalized by the latter, and their illumination is perceived as the radiance of the child himself.

Certainly, this psychological process reflects the growth of *Ze'ir Anpin* – the male divine figure, who initially receives parental "aura" and radiance; and whose inner light, as he develops, shines outward. Luria was preoccupied with this process, which he considered the apogee of spiritual growth. Psychologically, "consciousness" reflects a healthy attitude to internalized parental figures and the ability to shelter under their wings. To use Hans Loewald's term, this is a possibility of experiencing life-givers as "ancestors" – as beneficial sources of inspiration rather than as harmful "ghosts."[4]

As Mordechai Pachter emphasized, the climax of the transition from "impregnation" to "consciousness" and from childhood to maturity lies in the ability to engender offspring, given the theurgic impact of human mating on the supernal world. Furthermore, the male aspect represents the transition from

---

[2] On the function of the Son in the divine world, see Idel, *Ben*.
[3] *Genesis Rabbah* 68:2.
[4] Loewald, "Therapeutic Action."

immaturity to sexual maturity. During the phases of "impregnation" and "suckling," *Ze'ir Anpin* possesses some "consciousness," but it is that of a child, increasing into maturity only with spiritual growth.[5]

The advent of "consciousness" takes place at the same age as the Oedipus complex theorized by Sigmund Freud, which is around three to four years of age. Such "consciousness" changes during each phase, and the process of growth and transformation becomes evident in the shifts of *Ze'ir Anpin* from the measure of judgment (*midat ha-din*) to that of kindness (*midat ha-hesed*).[6]

This arrangement transpires not only in the case of divine *sefirot* and certain exceptional figures such as Moses and Joseph, who undergo a process of spiritual growth and transformation. According to Lurianic belief, every individual goes through the process, in accordance with the Zoharic principle that the soul of Moses is contained in the souls of all pious men and the righteous heroes of every generation, and actually in the souls of all Jews: "Moses has an aspect of smallness (*qaṭnut*) and greatness (*gadlut*), and so are all the souls. All of them are models of *Ze'ir Anpin*, which has an impregnation (*ibbur*) of smallness and of greatness."[7] As Gershom Scholem noted, the processes of "impregnation, suckling, and consciousness" reveal the theogonic myth in Lurianic Kabbalah. This view boldly suggests that God Himself – as *Sefirat Tiferet* – was born, like a mere mortal, from the union of His parents, *Hokhma* and *Binah*. Moreover, according to this view, the development of the divine personality depends upon human procreation, sexual union, and the development of repair and redemption. As Gershom Scholem states:

> The process in which God conceives, brings forth and develops Himself does not reach its final conclusion in God. Certain parts of the process of restitution are allotted to man [. . .] The intrinsic, extramundane process of *Tikkun*, symbolically described as the birth of God's personality, corresponds to the process of mundane history.[8]

Such cosmic and personal processes of growth include phases of regression and death, which allow for the rebirth of the individual and the divine persona. Numerous descriptions of birth in Lurianic Kabbalah highlight the centrality of this experience in its various mystical manifestations, such as (1) levels of nurturing and nursing; (2) varying lengths of pregnancy (seven, nine, or twelve months);[9] (3)

---

[5] Pachter, "Katnut," 171–210, esp. 176–184.
[6] Tishby, *Doctrine*.
[7] R. Hayyim Vital, *Likutei Torah*, Vilna 1880, 91b–93b; Liebes, "Two Young Roes of a Doe."
[8] Scholem, *Major Trends*, 273.
[9] In Lurianic Kabbalah, pregnancy can last seven, nine, or twelve months. Each period symbolizes a different stage of mental, psychological, and spiritual development. For the duration of pregnancy according to the Sages, see *Preuss, Medicine, 383–384*; *Zohar 3:65b*; *Sha'ar ma'amrei Rashbi* 53b; *Sefer ha-Derushim* 228:3.

different types of "consciousness" and "spiritual entities"; (4) encircling and inner "consciousness"; (5) distinctions between "first impregnation" and "second impregnation"; (6) smallness and greatness; (7) passing from the world of dots (*niqudim*) to the world of countenances (*parzufim*);(8) garments (*levushim*) in contrast to Tetragrammatonic permutations (*shemot havayah*); (9) exiting a state of "three within three (*tlat bego tlat*)"; (10) gestation impregnation; and (11) reincarnation.[10]

Cumulatively, such references attach themselves to the actual, individual body, describing the changes it undergoes. Scholem, however, was uncomfortable with the corporeality of birth imagery in Lurianic Kabbalah. As he adds:

> The origin of *Zeir Anpin* in the womb of the "celestial mother," his birth and development, as well as the laws in accordance with which all the "upper" potencies are organized in him, form the subject of detailed exposition in the system developed by Luria's followers. There is something bewildering in the eccentricity of these over-detailed expositions – the architecture of this mystical structure might be styled baroque.[11]

In my view, Scholem's discomfort with these concepts is due primarily to the unprecedented reification of the maternal body in Safedian Kabbalah. I am not referring only to the latter's technical accounts of fertility processes but especially to its vivid, detailed anatomical descriptions of feminine internal organs, accompanied by discussion of the changes the mother's body undergoes during pregnancy, childbirth, child-rearing, nursing, and so on. More importantly, these homilies address the trauma of giving birth as well as the joy and unique bond between the mother and newborn; however, they also deal with postnatal depression and the death wish of the mother who has relinquished an essential part of her body in childbirth.

Whether in homilies delivered by R. Hayyim Vital, or those originally attributed to Isaac Luria himself (such as his *derashot* on saying "Shema," or that about *nefilat apayim*, the ritual of "falling on the face"), most of these texts feature a female figure undergoing childbirth. While the protagonists in these representations are mainly the two female *sefirot*, *Binah* and *Shekhinah*, not necessarily maternal *human* figures, it is nevertheless obvious that we are encountering the constitution of a female subject who reflects the experience of childbirth, thereby endowing it with a presence in both human and divine worlds.[12] Due to theurgic affinity of the two worlds and the physical similarity of parturition in them, there emerges,

---

10 For a psychological reading, see Gamlieli, *Psychoanalysis*. On reincarnation and *ibbur*, see Fine, *Physician*, 434.
11 Ibid., 270–271; Scholem, *Major Trends*, 270.
12 Jacobson, "Aspect."

despite everything, a sense of competence and agency in the attempts to describe "what a woman experiences in childbirth."

It should be noted that in the Zoharic literature we usually find more amorphic descriptions of birth than in the Lurianic corpus. While the Sefadian Kabbalah contains psychologically graphic, personal descriptions, in the *Zohar* we more typically find metaphors such as the image of the doe which is able to give birth only with the assistance of a snake's bite.[13] Indeed, this myth might constitute an example of "obstetric violence," an emerging concept termed by contemporary feminist critics. "Obstetric violence" is the physical or emotional abuse of a woman during childbirth, which wounds her sexual organs and exploits her weakness and vulnerability.[14] In Luria's homilies, however, the snake does not merely strike the doe – he also has sexual intercourse with her, perhaps an attempt to alleviate the harshness of the Zoharic and Talmudic scenes. Generally, in this corpus the mother is depicted as a "real subject," not merely a figurative symbol or metaphor, a tendency that resembles other mythical and corporeal perspectives in Lurianic Kabbalah, a subject that has been discussed by Yehuda Liebes, Asaf Tamari, and other scholars.[15]

This motherly figure is replete with contradictions: her figure emphasizes both her physiology and spirituality; her sexuality is not separated from her motherliness; the mother's multiplicity of selves is in flux as the mythical and mysterious become linked to psychological and physiological.

2 The Birth of *Ze'ir Anpin*

To illustrate my argument, I turn now to a homily dealing with the birth of *Ze'ir Anpin*, which focuses on the female experience of childbirth as the mother progresses along with the son through the phases of "impregnation, suckling, and consciousness." This homily connects the cycles of life and death with birth (both as a symbol and a real event), Torah study, and the transformation of the force of law into kindness. As *Ze'ir* develops, the celestial mother changes as well: *Shekhinah* is renewed and gives birth to righteous souls in similar fashion to *Binah*. The earthly woman, hinted at in the background, is another reflection of the apparatus of birth: this expresses the Zoharic principle that "all women are created in the image of the Shekhinah."[16]

---

[13] I will expand on this metaphor in the following chapter.
[14] Cohen-Shabot, "Loud"; Sadler et al. "Disrespect."
[15] See, for example, Les, "Myth"; Tamari, "Human Sparks."
[16] See for example, Zohar 1: 228b; 2:101a; 3:124a.

2 The Birth of *Ze'ir Anpin* — 185

This homily is based on the description of the birth of the male divine figure (*Ze'ir Anpin*), the primary male aspect of the divine persona, who is the son of the Father (*Abba*) and Mother (*Ima*). *Hokhmah* and *Binah* are higher personae and an upper "divine faces" (*parzufim*), who give birth to *Ze'ir Anpin* and nurture him.[17]

In *Eṣ Ḥayyim* R. Isaac Luria states:

> Now we will elucidate the birth. How did the Supernal Mother birth *Ze'ir Anpin* and *Nuqba*? And behold in the elucidation of the prayers concerning the reading of *shema*, it was explained there the matter of the Supernal Mother birthing *Ze'ir Anpin* and *Nuqba* though the mystery of the six words of *Shema Yisrael* [*YHWH Eloheinu YHWH eḥad*] [. .] And the mystery of the matter is that *Ze'ir Anpin* is the fetus found in the [stage of] impregnation of the mother's intestines, the impregnation is nine months, and when the nine months of impregnation are completed then he is born and goes out. And indeed, there is an aspect of birth whether in *Ze'ir Anpin* himself or in the aspect of his *mohin* (consciousness) of the time of expansion (*ha-gadlut*) [. . .]. For they are in the aspect of spirituality (*ruḥaniyut*) and the souls of the *mohin* of *Ze'ir Anpin*. And both aspects are equal. For it has already been explained that [the *sefirot*] *Neṣah, Hod, Yesod* of *Imma* are always entering and investing (*mitlabshin*) and divesting (*mitpashṭin*) themselves within *Ze'ir Anpin* himself, whether in the aspect of the time of impregnation, in the aspect of smallness, which is the time of suckling (*yeniqah*), or in the time of greatness, which is called by us *moḥin de-gadlut* (expanded consciousness) that is the spirituality of the *moḥin*.[18]

The homily opens by depicting *Binah* as a mother who continues to birth her son at different stages of his growth (gestation, nursing, and various stages of consciousness). *Ze'ir Anpin*, *Tiferet*, does not stand on its own but rather is attached to *Nuqba*, *Malkhut*, via his back, and the two slowly emerge from within the Great Mother via the "sawing" process discussed in previous chapters. The gestation stage, which lasts for nine months, parallels human pregnancy. The Lurianic model of nursing parallels physical human nursing, and means that the lower *sefirot* emerge from within the upper *sefirot*. Thereafter, the expanded consciousness appears, primarily in the form of the birth of *Ze'ir* and the female who separates from him, allowing him to stand independently. In the initial state, the female was not visible as a separate figure, existing in a potential, "gestational," form. This oedipal homily echoes the primordial connection of the son contained within the mother's womb while simultaneously expressing

---

[17] On the divine faces, (*parzufim*) in Lurianic Kabbalah, see Magid, *Metaphysics to Midrash*, 24–29; Scholem, *Major Trends*, ch 7; Fine, *Physician*; Giller, *Reading the Zohar*, 78–79.
[18] *Eṣ Ḥayyim* 20:3. Translated by Gene Matanky as were all the other Lurianic sources in this chapter.

the need for separation and "sawing," both between parents and children as well as between male and female.

In *Sha'ar ha-Kavvanot*, Luria describes a parallel between the transition from "gestation" to "consciousness" and the mystery of the reading of the Shema and the six words uttered therein. In the process of speaking the intentions of unification, the supernal parents, *Hokhmah* and *Binah*, are connected once again, thereby sustaining the whole system anew. The homily takes pains to depict not just the experience of the baby – who receives consciousness from its parents at various levels of his existence – but also that of the mother, who pushes the fetus out of her body amid harsh contractions and the real threat of death.

The homily compares *Ze'ir*'s birth from *Binah* – as with human birth – to the Exodus from Egypt and to redemption from subjugation to freedom. The Bible describes the women of the Exodus as "animals" (*hayot*) (Exod 1:19), and Luria develops this physical image into the spiritual idea of a lessening of vitality (*hiyut*) in the fetus. In line with classical Rabbinic homilies, Luria depicts an exaggerated threat to the Supernal Mother identical to that facing a human woman in childbirth. The birthing stool upon which women gave birth in antiquity here reappears in the image of the mother's thighs hardening like stones, conveying the force she must exert in order to push the child out of her, as well as her close call with death and paralysis. This depiction may also draw on the *Zohar*'s conception of the mother as representing the "world of the male" during childbirth. The physical crisis brought on by the narrow, blocked womb represents a spiritual crisis that ultimately leads to "sweetening" and rectification.

In the next stage, the light within *Binah*'s belly increases to the point where it must necessarily exit outwards. This depiction parallels other Lurianic homilies which describe the ascent of the lower three *sefirot* (*Netsah*, *Hod*, and *Yesod*) during the gestation and nursing stages, from *Binah*'s legs up to the level of her womb, until the light fills both her body and that of her baby. This beautiful homily depicts birth as a process of *the birth of light*, similar to the Biblical depiction of the Creation of the world through the utterance "Let there be light." This mechanistic description highlights the role of pressure as a physical force within the homily: the lights of the baby – here referred to as "guest" – combine with the lights of the mother – here referred to as "master of the house" – and the increased pressure forces them to erupt out of the mother's body.

Pressure, pain, bursting, erupting, and the threat of death combine to create a spiritual experience. The homily renders this experience as "the birth of lights," the creation of souls, and the crowning of the son with diadems. Seen through the lens of psychology and gender, the homily depicts a mutual process whereby the mother and the fetus undergo a trauma that also contains an experience of illumination. The baby emerges into the world together with light, and then must grapple with its new reality, one which is fundamentally opposed to its former experiences within the womb, as the Sages describe in the Talmud:

> [The embryo in the womb's] head lies between its knees, its mouth is closed and its navel is open, and it eats what its mother eats and drinks what its mother drinks but produces no excrements because otherwise it might kill its mother [. . .] but as soon as it comes into the world, *everything which had been closed opens, and that which was open closes, otherwise the child could not exist for a single hour.*[19]

Luria's homily wonderfully depicts what Freud called "the impressive caesura of the act of birth," which is what Bion saw as the foundation of all transitional experiences, as discussed above in Chapter 3.

The trauma of birth is both private and shared, belonging to both the mother and the baby. Later in the homily, Luria explains that the pressure of the lights within the mother's belly fulfills two functions: it brings the fetus forth from the womb, and it fills the fetus with consciousness during the gestation stage as well: "For through their ascension the lights are multiplied there and they push the embryo out."

According to Luria, consciousness and lights enter *Ze'ir* before birth, increasing his body mass and combining with his own internal lights, as alluded to in the Rabbinic legend of the lamp that emits light for the fetus from one end of the world to the other. Parallel texts connect these lights to the mythical Edomite "dead kings," themselves associated with the "shattered vessels" and the "scattered sparks." Luria describes the fetal growth beginning from *Arikh Anpin*'s initial collapse into himself. Thereafter, the fetal positioning and the lower *sefirot* ascending is repeated along the length of *Abba* and *Ima* (*Hokhmah* and *Binah*), as well as *Ze'ir* and *Nuqba*. Indeed, the male divine persona is constructed from the "fallen" lights of the upper "faces" (*parzufim*).

From the lights of "broken vessels" (*Zohar* 1:10b) of the kings that perished, *Ima* and *Abba* and *Ze'ir Anpin* and *Nuqba* are created, from the refined and subtle to the crude and dense. This explains why *Ze'ir Anpin* has "his lights" within the womb (*beṭen*) of the mother, for these lights of the kings belong to him. To put it differently, *Zeir* represents the kings in their rectified forms. The *moḥin* ("consciousness") and *aṭarot* ("diadems") come to him following their dilution and emendation, for – following *Idra Rabba* ("The Great Assembly") – Luria clarifies that it was necessary to change the kings' names, for only with "their other names" are they able to subsist. Thus, for example, Husham and Hadad are renamed *Ḥesed* and *Gevurah*. As Haviva Pedaya has elucidated, psychologically

---

19 BT Niddah 30b (emphasis is mine).

speaking the death of the kings symbolizes underdeveloped, immature forms of consciousness which are "connected to subsumptive, non-individuated stages in the world of the subject."[20]

Ultimately, the divine male develops these "fallen" lights, just as, in an ideal situation, a human child succeeds in growing and developing on the basis of the pre-existing crisis preceding his birth. Throughout a person's life, she or he will be required to continue to work through, process, and "sweeten" the pre-birth experience of death.

This homily depicts the fetus as both enveloped in light and carrying lights within him. Initially, his "vessels" are too small to contain these lights, and thus he must undergo "a dilution of lights" before being born. Three types of lights come together in order to make this possible: the light that becomes the force that pushes him out of the womb, the light that becomes the baby's consciousness, and the light that helps the mother's blood transform into milk in order for her to be able to nourish him.

This homily constitutes a uniquely impressive depiction of spiritual birth as an almost physical process the laboring mother must undergo: she moves from contractions originating in the contracting of the womb, to pressure pains which appear in the final stage to aid in pushing out the fetus. Luria interweaves the medical and psychological meanings of birth. Every birth is bound up with death: the death of the symbiosis of mother and fetus (the singular dyad of a woman and the fruit of her womb), and the death of the life lived within, which now develops independently, in the outside world. Taking as inspiration the Biblical verse "When a person *dies* in a tent" (Numbers 19:14), and the Rabbinic maxim that "Torah is not sustained except through *one who* (mi) *kills himself* over it," Luria then compares *Binah* (also referred to as *mi*) in the process of birthing to a woman who sacrifices her life for her child. *Binah* acts in this moment as the *Shekhinah*; she is Rachel ("as her soul left her, for she died" [Genesis 35:18]) when she gave birth to Benjamin.

Thus closes the circle of life and death which is constitutive for birth: the mother gives her life for the newborn, granting him all her lights as they issue forth in the form of light, body, and milk, and she then draws new life from the power of the Torah to which she has given birth. (*Ze'ir* represents the Written Torah while *Nuqba* – the female, joined to *Ze'ir* – represents the Oral Torah.)

Just as *Binah* kills herself for *Ze'ir Anpin*, the *Shekhinah* sacrifices her life to give birth to the souls of the righteous. The righteous restore her life to her by raising up feminine waters for her and through their martyrdom. She dies for

---

20 Pedaya, *Psychoanalysis and Kabbala*, 301.

the sake of the newborn, *Ze'ir*, but also for the sake of the Torah, which is sustained only by those who kill themselves over it, and it gives birth to her, as it did the mothers, *Binah* and the *Shekhinah*. The homily began with the gestation stage, and ends with the joining of the nursling and consciousness, the milk, and the spiritual nourishment of the Torah.

Through the lights' ascent, the blood (associated with judgment) turns into milk (associated with grace). In this way, the mother's very body is "sweetened" after she has undergone the near-death experience of birth.[21] Luria's homily presents the mother as capable of keeping the child's needs in mind throughout: initially she constructs him within her womb and contains his lights, then she pushes him out of her body, she feeds and sustains him with consciousness and milk, and finally she dies and returns to life in advance of the next stage of the "gestation."

While also idealizing maternal victimhood, the homily demonstrates an awareness of the real costs of pregnancy and birth, adumbrates spiritually the experience of postpartum depression, and even meditates on the growth of the mother as a spiritual subject. Her lights, which come from within her, grow more intense within her womb and emerge into the world, thanks both to her and to her children.

3 Conclusion

In conclusion, we can highlight multiple parallels between Luria's tripartite "gestation-nursing-consciousness" model, psychological models of the individual, and the historical development of psychoanalysis. Freud studied childhood psychology, object relations theory focused on nursing, and fetal studies focused on fetal life and its impact on maturation.

The Lurianic model depicts a recurring, cyclical process. After maturation is achieved, each *sefirah* returns to the gestation stage so that it can continue to be born anew, going through the whole gestation-nursing-consciousness process yet another time. Psychoanalysis similarly charts back-and-forth movements between different developmental stages. As Melanie Klein, creator of object relations theory, notes, "analysis makes its way from adulthood to infancy, and through intermediate stages back to adulthood, in a recurrent to-and-fro movement according to the prevalent transference situation."[22]

---

21 Preuss, *Medicine*, 381.
22 Klein, "Envy," 178.

The distinctions between the different stages can often be unclear. Just as the caesura binds womb life to life after birth, so too does nursing continue the process that began with gestation, claims Luria, making manifest what until now had been mere potential. It is difficult to pinpoint whether *Ze'ir*'s limbs appear in the gestation stage or in the nursing stage. The Kabbalistic and psychoanalytic understandings of regression provide an example of the interrelation of gestation and nursing. Just as many psychoanalysts argue that the key to psychosis lies in the early nursing stage, so too does the shattering of the vessels and the catharsis of evil take place in the early stages of emanation. The removal of the husks and the intrusion of the forces of judgment (*dinim*) into the gestation and nursing stages parallel the deep, primordial breaks caused by insufficient divine-maternal strength.[23]

The object relations school of psychoanalysis theorizes regression as enabling rectification and repair. Balint referred to this as a "new beginning," while Margaret Little referred to it as a "basic unity."[24] According to these theories, regression transforms a patient's uncogitated experiences, which would otherwise not be given to healing through the "talking cure." Luria similarly describes regression as a return to the gestational stage, which he refers to as "three within three" or "three contained in three," referring to the upper three *sefirot* folding over the lower, as a fetus rests within its mother's womb. The gestation stage can recur at any point in time, just as consciousness already exists within the fetus and the nursling. Like the analysts, the Kabbalists emphasize that regressing to the gestation stage enables growth and change. Luria's personal biography makes it clear that this regression means death and self-annihilation, which create the possibility for "a new birth." In many contexts, Luria describes his own return to "gestation," and says that even God returns to this state before growth and rectification.[25] Both discourses, that of the Kabbalists and psychoanalysis, valorize something evasive and hard to pin down, which they call spiritual and psychological birth – a space wherein biology and mental-mystical maturation meet. As Winnicott claims: "The individual's psychological life is not exactly adjusted to the time of birth [. . .] The

---

23 Bion, *Second Thoughts*; Winnicott, *Maturational Processes*; Eigen, *Madness*, 9–16. For a psychoanalytic reading of these terms as stages of self-construction, see Gamlieli, *Psychoanalysis and Kabbalah*.
24 Balint, *Basic Fault*; Little, *Psychotic Anxieties*.
25 See, for example, *Sha'ar ha-Kavvanot* 79c; Passover Discourse, Exposition 1; *Etz Hayyim*, Gate 40, Exposition 4. See Liebes, *The Words of God*, 107. Mark notes that R. Nahman followed Luria in seeing gestation as a pre-life state enabling new birth. See Mark, *Mysticism and Madness*, 206–211.

Psychoanalyst is forced to the conclusion that the rigid time for birth in the psychological sense is the full-term moment when physiologically it can also be said that the time has come for the child to leave the womb."[26]

Appendix: The Roots of Lurianic Concepts in Cordoverian Kabbalah

1 R. 1. Moses Cordovero, Introduction to *Shiur Komah*, Reḥem I: 77, 174–175

a. The Mystery of the Upper Womb

In the mystery of the womb (*reḥem*), which for the female is additional [in contrast] to the man, impregnation, and birth. And two doors (*delatot*) and two axes (*ṣirim*). The matter is that the mystery of the masculine member, it is the [*sefirah* of] *Yesod* for example. And there is no existence for this dimension/attribute (*middah*) in [the *sefirah* of] *Malkhut*. Although she integrates all the attributes, but this attribute is not included, for they are male (*zakhar*) signs, and *Malkhut* is female, and it is not proper that one should see signs of the male in her. And in place of the light of *Yesod*, she has [the] aspect of womb. Meaning, [this is the] mystery of "Though angry, compassion (*reḥem*) may You remember (*tizkor*)" (Habakkuk 3:2).

b. *Reḥem* = *Ramah* (248 Limbs of the Body)

And all are contracted within *RM"Ḥ*, the mystery of the womb, in order that these lights will grant reality of 248 limbs to each Tetragrammatonic permutation, for it becomes from above in this female, and these lights, they are within her when they receive the mystery of the light of *Yesod* and these 248 lights will egress (*yitpasheṭ*) and overflow in them the mystery of the light sown for the righteous (*le-ṣaddiq*) [i.e., *yesod*]. And they are the mystery of *Adonai* (*AND"Y*), for the channels of the doors, they are the straight light (*or yashar*), which are concealed and the doors that are opened to have enter and exit they are *dalet*

---

26 Winnicott, *Babies*, 54.

[and] *nun*, for they are certainly [the] female letters in this name, and thus they are doors that turn on their axes.

c. The Great and the Little Animals (*Ḥayyot*)

And the reason that impregnation is nine months – it is nine permutations (*havayot*), for there are two donors (*notnim*). One is in the mystery of the small living things (*ḥayyot*) and one is in the mystery of the great living things (*ḥayyot*) and concerning them it is written, "living things (*ḥayyot*), small and great" (Ps. 104:25). The small ones are the permutations that exit from *Malkhut* for she is the "small sister"; and the great ones exit from *Binah*, for she is a female, a great woman (*ishah gedolah*). And the impregnation of *Binah* is from the great living things and the impregnation of *Malkhut* is from the small living things. And the impregnation of the great living things is twelve months, for until they will receive the light from the supernal permutations, which are the twelve rectifications of the supernal beard – the thirteen sources of *Keter*. And after they will enlighten her with all the sources with the source that includes all, *then the same permutations are ripened and rectified to be born into an existing reality, and they do not fall, heaven forbid.* Indeed, below are the rectifications of *Ze'ir* [*Anpin*]'s beard, which are nine. And the impregnation of the female is nine months until she receives being (*havvayah*) and power from the light of the nine rectifications, nine supernal permutations, *and then she exists and does not fall.* And the *Tikkunim* explained the matter of nine months, which are nine *sefirot* in actuality (*mamash*) until they come to *Malkhut*. And that is, that she descends ten levels and it is possible after all there is in each rectification that enlightens her, she descends one level from her levels and all ascents in one path.

d. Israel the Firstborn (*Peṭer Reḥem*) of *Binah*

And according to what has been explained, it is easy to understand that there is a matter of a womb in the supernal point, which is *Binah*. And, therefore, the firstborn (*peṭer reḥem*) is in the mystery of *Binah* and, thus, Israel is called the firstborn of Israel and enough. And the mystery of the womb is certainly the mystery of the stomach (*me-beṭen*) (Job 38:29). M"Y (*mi*, lit. "who"), meaning the *Binah*, and there is within her an aspect called stomach, and that is "exits the ice" (ibid.), meaning the *Tiferet* in the mystery of mercy (*raḥamim*), for he is the firmament (*raqi'a*), a kind of awesome ice, "who (*M"Y*) gives birth to the frost from the heavens" (ibid.), that is after he egresses (*mitpasheṭ*), "who gives birth," meaning after the impregnation, the birth. And that is the supernal permutations, which are simple mercy there.

2 Chambers (*Hadarim*) of the Upper Womb and Impregnation of "New Souls": *Pardes Rimonim* 8:17

In his *Pardes Rimonim*, Cordovero describes how the woman's womb is singular, so that even twins are carried in one womb; however, he explains that a women's womb comprises seven chambers (*hadarim*).[27] This is how *Binah* – the Supernal Mother – is able to carry all of the seven lower *sefirot* within her and then during the emanation give birth to them all as seven individual *sefirot*. Thus, together they share her womb, but are able to be born as individual entities:

> Behold, as there is in the matter of the unification of a man and woman two aspects (*beḥinot*). The first is to impregnate anew and the second is to grow the shoots, that is in order that the offspring will exit. And so *Binah* and *Ḥokhmah*'s unification is not to be a renewed being, but rather to catalyze (*zeruzam*) being that they stand on their own character.

> Indeed, the mystery of the additional matter of the benefit of the children, as mentioned, is humility [. . .] And it ascended higher and higher for there is no commandment that will actually simulate the supernal copulation in all its aspects like this commandment. For the rest of the commandments of the Torah hint at the supernal image and likeness (*be-ṣelem ve-ha-demut*) to unite the *sefirot*; however, it is a very distant hint. But, the mystery of the male and female, they are really the mystery of the supernal *sefirot*, as he stated "Let us make man" and [in] their unification and copulation is hinted the supernal copulation [. . .] and when the lower male and female connect they will intend in

---

27 See also in his composition *Tefilah le-Moshe* ("A Prayer of Moses") 5b; R. Asher Ben David, *Sefer ha-Yeḥud* (Abrams ed., 127–131). See above Chapter 1, n. 100. Following Klein, Meltzer develops the concept of the mother's inner spaces and geographical zones. His ideas resonate with the description of maternal womb-chambers that appears in R. Moses Cordovero texts as well as in R. Isaac Luria derashot: "If [Freud] had just made this step [of developing the concept of an inner world] he could have leapt forward the way Melanie Klein's work leapt forward the moment she discovered that children were preoccupied with the inside of their mothers' bodies and that it was really a *place*, a world in which life was going on . . . But he seems somehow unable to come to any such conception at this point; that is, to take the primal scene and find a location for it by placing it inside. And I think the reason was that he just did not have that kind of mind; it took somebody like Mrs Klein, listening to little children talking about the inside of the mother's body with absolute conviction as if it were Budapest or Vienna as an absolutely geographical place, to realise that there really is an inner world and that it is not just allegorical or metaphorical, but has a concrete existence – in the life of the mind, not the brain." Meltzer, The Kleinian Development, 97–8.

actuality on the bound and unification of the supernal *RM"H* in *RM"H*, as actual binding of flesh with flesh. And he will intend on the mystery of the supernal unification.

For within this tract it is clarified with the explanation that there is no diadem (*aṭarah*) for the unification of son and daughter [. . .] if there is not in the time of the unification of *Ḥokhmah* and *Binah*. And since their unification is perpetual (*temidi*), the diadem will be on the children in the time of need [. . .] for the matter of this diadem and fancy garb, discussed in this tract, are from the side of the mother, and that is precisely in the cause of the unification of the father with her, for from there is the root (*iqar*) of the good oil mentioned in this tract.

The love of the Holy One, blessed be He, for the souls [of Israel] is more than his loves for the world, all the angels, and all created entities (*ha-nimṣa'im*), for they are the offspring of his intestines.

Chapter 8
Redemption as Birth, Birth as Redemption

> The consummation of the messianic era is the aspect of the birth and revelation of the light of the Lord in the depths of man's heart. –R. Schneur Zalman of Liadi, *Torah Or* 55:2

What does birth have to do with redemption? In this last and summative chapter, I suggest that the birth experience, due to the force of the metaphor of birth and the tangibility of the pain that birth entails, is often compared to the process of redemption. Anticipation of redemption is the focal point of Biblical verses, Rabbinic expositions, and the Kabbalistic and Hasidic literatures. The hope to extricate the Israelite nation and the individual from their harsh situation reflects the depths of their existential crisis and the longing for change and for a better future.[1] Some sources emphasize the historical significance of redemption, viewing it as occurring on a temporal axis. Others see it as mythos, bursting forth full-blown onto the scene and demolishing the laws of nature. The desire to hasten the Redemption contains individual, national, and historical aspects together with the supratemporal mythical element with which the Messianic idea is charged.[2] In addition, the Jewish philosophical literature raises questions concerning the connection between redemption and the World to Come and the standing of law and nature in the Messianic era. In addition, shared symbols and characterizations appear in late antiquity in the context of Jewish-Christian dialogue and polemic.[3]

Catastrophic perceptions of the present time foster apocalyptic representations of the Messianic era that are expressed in eschatological depictions of war, upheaval, and the emergence of a "new Torah."[4] The pre-redemptive period represents the end of suffering. Ephraim Urbach puts it thusly: "The magnitude of the degeneration, anarchy, and sufferings heralding the Messiah will be matched by the brilliance and glory of the Days of the Messiah."[5] These images of the lead-up to the Messiah's arrival are countered by restorative descriptions of the Redemption, with changes occurring mainly in the national and political realm, in the spirit of the Rabbinic dictum embraced by Maimonides:

---

1 Urbach, *Sages*, 585–623.
2 Mowinckel, *He That Cometh*, 1956. See also Baras, *Messianism and Eschatology*; Klausner, *Messianic Idea*.
3 Schäfer and Cohen, *Toward the Millennium*; Flusser, "Reflection."
4 Scholem, "Redemption through Sin"; Idel, "Torah Ḥadashah."
5 Urbach, *Sages*, 610.

"This world differs from that of the time of the Messiah only in respect to servitude to foreign powers."[6] It seems that the more extreme the perception of reality, the harsher the representation of the Messianic era, while harmonious conceptions of the present paint the time of the Messiah as the uninterrupted continuity of the existing reality.[7] This also pertains to the image of the Redeemer and his attribution to the Davidic line or other "redemptive" lineages.[8] On the one hand, he is presented as "a pauper riding on an ass," and, on the other, as an angel who descends from heaven with the Clouds of Glory; as one who comes in a generation that is either altogether righteous or one altogether wicked; as a suffering figure; and as one ready at any moment to be called to his mission and who therefore sits among the lepers at the Roman gate.[9] The Redeemer, like the idea of the Redemption, develops in the literature as a desire that we endlessly distance without bringing to fruition, for its realization would reveal its failure. As Gershom Scholem stresses: "Galut and redemption are not historical manifestations peculiar to Israel, but manifestations of all being, up to and including the mystery of divinity itself."[10]

The cyclical relationship between exile and redemption echoes the recurring nature of birth and death. While the term "rebirth" focuses on the process undergone by the individual, the terms "exile" and "redemption" reflect hope for the collective salvation of the nation. The pain of birth mirrors the power of the Redemption and the wish to survive its "birth throes."[11] Seemingly, birth and redemption are to be found at the diametric poles of existence: birth is aligned with the Creation, while redemption is aligned with the End of Days. However, there is a circular relationship between these concepts. Just as birth is comparable to redemption, redemption is akin to birth and creation. Birth is closer to death than it seems, and is the essence of redemption. Each of these two events symbolizes the quality of human potential and the limits of its realization. Like every meaningful creation, the end of the world is inherent in its beginning, and birth is redemption. The moment a person is born, the countdown of life begins, and he or she begins to die. At the same

---

[6] BT Sanhedrin 99b; Maimonides,*Mishneh Torah*, Hilkhot Melachim 12:2, Hilkhot Teshuva 9:2, and more.
[7] Scholem, "The Messianic Idea in Kabbalism"; idem, "The Crisis of Tradition in Jewish Messianism."
[8] On the Davidic Messiah, see Liver, *The House of David*; Kaniel, *Holiness and Transgression*; idem, *The Feminine Messiah*. For other examples, see Liebes, "The Messiah of the Zohar"; Idel, *Messianic Mystics*.
[9] BT Sanhedrin 98a.
[10] Scholem, "The Messianic Idea in Kabbalism," 48.
[11] On *hevlei leidah* and *hevlei geula*, birth and redemption "pangs," see Newman, "The Birth of the Messiah"; Preuss, *Medicine*, 114, 394–395.

time, redemption is the great alternative to death, the possibility of an "other" existence, an upward path that has reached its end goal: hope for living without the burden of an awareness of death's terror.

1 Redemption as Birth

Numerous eschatological depictions in the Bible compare redemption to birth. At the core of these descriptions are terms taken from actual birth, such as the "pangs" of redemption, as mentioned in Isa. 26:17: "Like a woman with child, who writhes and cries out in her pangs, when she is near her time, so were we because of you, O Lord." The fear of God's power and His appearance is likened to a woman in labor:

> Who has heard such a thing? Who has seen such things? Shall a land be born in one day? Shall a nation be brought forth in one moment? For as soon as Zion was in labor she brought forth her sons. Shall I bring to the birth and not cause to bring forth? says the Lord; shall I, who causes to bring forth, shut the womb? says your God.[12]

As a woman waits nine months for the embryo to come to fruition, God's might is revealed in His ability to bide His time and to wait for the right time to bring redemption: "The Lord goes forth like a mighty man, like a man of war he stirs up his fury [. . .] For a long time [. . .] I have kept still and restrained myself; now I will cry out like a woman in travail, I will gasp and pant" (Isa. 42:13–14). Significant to our discussion is the birthing technique revealed in these verses, which includes short and fast breaths, and is, as Mayer Gruber notes, comparable to physiological birth.[13]

The identification of redemption and birth is prominent in Second Isaiah, with its numerous portrayals of God as a feminine figure and as a mother who bears the people in her womb, and then nurses and nourishes them until they are grown: "But Zion said, 'The Lord has forsaken me, my Lord has forgotten me.' Can a woman forget her suckling child, that she should have no compassion on the son of her womb? Even these may forget, yet I will not forget you, you shall be comforted in Jerusalem" (Isa. 49:14–15); "and you shall suck, you shall be carried upon her hip, and dandled upon her knees. As one whom his mother comforts, so I will comfort you" (Isa. 66:12–13).[14] In these passages,

---

12 Isaiah 66:8–9. See Trible, "Depatriarchalizing in Biblical Interpretation," 33.
13 Gruber, "The Motherhood of God in Second Isaiah."
14 Rubin, *Beginning of Life*, 33; Gruber "The Motherhood of God in Second Isaiah." Gruber suggests that Second Isaiah (40–66) tends to stress positive feminine images such as motherhood and

birth is transformed into a metaphor containing both positive and negative features. It expresses extrication and overcoming difficulty while concurrently being based on the conception of birth and redemption as a source of anxiety and terror. This anxiety is associated with the suffering of exile, apocalyptic struggles, and darkness, all of which intensify as the Redemption draws near: "And they will be dismayed. Pangs and agony will seize them; they will be in anguish like a woman in travail" (Isa. 13:8); "trembling took hold of them there, anguish as of a woman in travail" (Ps. 48:6). Birth represents a liminal and dangerous moment with scant distance between life and death; successfully crossing it is a triumph.[15] These parallels imply that redemption, like birth, entails both pain and ensuing calm and serenity. As it is in birth that humankind is closest to divinity, these biblical depictions use birth as an unerring metaphor for redemption.

The catastrophic and apocalyptic attributes of birth are writ large to intensify the positive aspect of birth while also attesting to the powerful symbolism of birth and to the fears associated with the feminine body: blood, the face distorted by pain, the contorted form. Every physical birth recalls the Creation of the world in the Book of Genesis and the birth of the nation in the Book of Exodus. As Ilana Pardes explains, motifs exemplifying birth – such as the sea splitinto two and the blood smeared on the lintel – are highlighted in the Exodus from Egypt.[16] Inspired by Genesis and Exodus, the Redemption to come is presented in imagery which recreates the rescue from the surging sea and the defiance of the peril of annihilation. In psychological terms, the servitude in Egypt symbolizes a threat to life itself even before it has emerged. Just as the individual must overcome conditions that work against birth (like the royal command to cast all the Israelite sons into the Nile), so too the nation will need to encounter darkness and terror before it will bask in the salvation of the Redemption.

Similarly, descriptions of the advent of the Messiah are associated with the act of giving birth. Like a potentate in the ancient Near East, the Messiah is perceived as the son of God who comes forth from His womb.[17] The birth of the Messiah links the beginning and Creation with the end. God says to the Redeemer "Today I have begotten you" (Ps. 2:7), but this day also relates to the future and to the moment when the task of salvation is conferred upon him:

---

birth, unlike Ezekiel and Jeremiah, which present the Jewish nation as a harlot, who caused an increase in idolatry.

15 See also Isaiah 37:3; Hosea 13:13.
16 Pardes, *The Biography*, Chapter 1; Kessler, *Conceiving Israel*, 2–8.
17 Ps 2:7; 110:3; Isa. 9:5. Schneider, "Son of God"; Liebes, "Christian Influences;" Knohl, *The Messiah before Jesus*.

"And authority has settled upon his shoulders" (Isa. 9:5). The regularity of the pain and suffering, so characteristic of birth pangs, will reign also during the throes of the Redemption, since these are inevitable,[18] as can be seen from the discussion in BT Sanhedrin 98b on questions of the Messiah and salvation, which explicitly link birth and redemption:

> The Gemara clarifies: What is the meaning of the phrase "I see *kol gever*"? Rava bar Yitzḥak says that Rav says: It is a reference to *He Whom all strength is His* [even God will suffer like a woman in labor due to the troubles of salvation]. "And all faces turned green"? R. Yohanan says: The reference is to the heavenly entourage above, i.e., angels, and the earthly entourage below.

Earlier in this Talmudic passage, Ulla and Rabbah, like other sages, voice their apprehension concerning the birth pangs of redemption and their wish not to be alive upon the advent of the Messiah, declaring: "Let him come, but let me not see him." The Sages ask them "What is your reason? Shall we say, because of the birth pangs [before the advent] of the Messiah?", thus revealing their fear of the pain of birth.

In order to describe unbearable pain, R. Yohanan cites Jer. 30:6: "Why then do I see every man [*gever*] with his hands on his loins like a woman in labor? Why has every face turned pale?" According to R. Yohanan, in the Messianic era, pain will intensify to such a degree that men's faces will turn pale out of their efforts to bring forth life. This view is reminiscent of Hosea 13:13: "Pangs of childbirth assail him, and the babe is not wise – for this is no time to survive at the birthstool of babes." Israel's failure to "survive at the birthstool of babes" provides an ironic picture in comparison with the woman about to give birth, again and again. The exposition teaches that this difficulty is not restricted to human men: the male Holy One, blessed be He, "Him to whom all might [*gevurah*] belongs," too, will struggle to withstand these terrific birth pangs.[19]

It is unclear who in this exposition the owner is and who the borrower is. Does God take the imagery of birth from the woman, or does the woman borrow this imagery from God (since her ability to give birth comes from Him)? She derives the right to create life from Him, just as He creates *ex nihilo*. When Eve says that she created a man with God (see Gen. 4:1), she acknowledges her standing as a creature secondary to God by alluding to having given birth as one who learns this ability from Him, following His example in creating. The

---

18 According to the *Apocalypse of Baruch*, at the time of the Redemption women would not suffer birth pangs. See Klausner, *Messianic Idea*, 275.
19 Liebes, *God's Story*, 86–87.

woman shares with God the gift of birth, but she must travel a tortuous path to attain it as punishment and as a compromise in the wake of her sin.

Moreover, the woman learns from God the meaning of birth, since, as Phyllis Trible shows, "in the Hebrew Scriptures the wombs of women belong to God [. . .] [He] alone decides the meaning of the womb [. . .] The deity prepares the organ for the birth, does the birthing, and then receives the infant out of the mother."[20] He knows better than any human the pain of birth, which He experienced during the Creation. Consequently, only He will be able to experience it in the eschatological future. Thus, the "throes of the Messiah," which precede the Redemption in the Bible, are a concrete expression of birth pangs. Through the divine act of Creation and through the verses of the promised Redemption, man learns the nature of birth and of redemption, and woman learns of the pain that she must bear.

Countering the assumption that the male, and even God, learn the nature of birth from the woman, the picture is reversed in Trible's reading. We learn that pain is a consequence of the processes of beginning and end in the Godhead. The throes of the Redemption are not a pale reflection of the tangible, feminine experience, but rather their source.

In the mythic conception, the Redemption is the consummation of human history, and the Messiah compiles the totality of all souls, which he incorporates within his, as is indicated by the Rabbinic dictum: "The son of David will not come until all the bodies in *Guf* [the 'treasury of souls'] will have been disposed of."[21] An additional midrash in BT Ta'anit 2a presents three keys that were given to the Holy One, blessed be He, and not to man: "the key of rain, the key of childbirth, and the key of the resurrection of the dead." This Talmudic passage brings into sharp focus the connection between birth, which entails the opening of the female womb, and the Redemption, which means the future opening of the tombs of Israel.

The oxymoronic phrase "In its time I will hasten it" (Isa. 60:22) presents the proper relationship between birth and redemption: they cannot be advanced, but the moment that they come, speed and urgency are their necessary attributes. This combination demonstrates the difficulty of facing the unknown. The body undergoes its slow and mysterious processes, which cannot be hastened, while, on the other hand, from the moment that labor begins, the birth becomes "active" and occurs with uncontrollable speed. Accordingly, the skill required for bringing life is control and retention, coupled with release and forgoing knowledge. Birth is the ability possessed by God, since He is willing to gaze upon the finitude that springs

---

[20] Trible, *God and the Rhetoric of Sexuality*, 34–35.
[21] BT Yevamot 62a, 63b; BT Niddah 13b.

forth from within His infiniteness, just as the female body is willing to waive certain and absolute knowledge in order to create new life.

2 The "Constriction" and "Blockage" of the Gazelle and the Psychoanalytical Third

The similarity of redemption to birth is developed in the Kabbalistic literature, where their psychological meanings also acquire greater depth. This emerges from the myth of the gazelle who has difficulty in giving birth due to her narrow womb and who almost dies, but is saved in the end by a snakebite to her womb at the precise moment of the birth. This bite enables her to relax the muscles of her womb and bring life into the world. This short Talmudic myth becomes a central symbol in the Kabbalistic literature of the redemption of Israel, and is the subject of much scholarly attention. Here, I wish to examine the gazelle's constricted and "blocked" condition at the moment she is about to give birth.[22]

This begins with a brief account in BT Bava Bathra 16b: "This gazelle has a narrow womb. When she crouches to deliver, I prepare for her a serpent to bite her at the opening of the womb, and she will be relieved of her severe throes. Were it a second too early or too late, she would die." This is all the information that the Talmud gives us. Already at this stage, however, we have a mythological portrayal of the dramatic relationship between the serpent and the gazelle. The serpent – the legendary *drakon* (lit., "dragon") – inflicts pain on the gazelle, but also saves her life and that of her fetus. The depiction of the woman in labor as a gazelle is influenced by the Platonic conception of the female womb as an independent creature, a sort of unpredictable animal.[23] The gazelle represents purity and beauty while the serpent, in contrast, represents the forces of evil and any number of demonic and dangerous animals. A closer look, however, discloses greater complexity in the latter: the serpent represents phallic masculinity, but its molting also is reminiscent of periodic changes in the feminine body, and its slithering alludes to archetypical feminine dancing; it symbolizes healing and recovery and is identified with the god of medicine Asclepius – but it also causes harm and (often) death. According to Rabbinic midrashim, the primeval serpent

---

[22] On this myth, see Liebes "Two Young Roes of a Doe"; Carmeli, "Dead Mother." For an expanded bibliography, see Kaniel, "Gazelle and the Serpent."
[23] Barkai, *Science*, 45.

looked like an upright, haughty creature capable of speech, unlike the lowly creature that slithers in the dirt that we know today.[24]

These opposing features serve the complex nature of the myth from its very inception. In the exposition of the *Zohar* in *Beshelah*, the Israelites, who are confined between the raging sea and the pursuing Egyptians, find themselves in a state of perilous birth that could end in death. Israel needs the venom of the serpent (= Pharaoh) in order to survive:

> Come and see: When Israel encamped by the sea, they saw many troops, many armies, many camps, from above to below – all assembled against Israel. In their distress, they began praying. At that moment, the Holy Ancient One appeared and favor became manifest in all those upper worlds. Then radiance of all lustered. [. . .] Rabbi Shim'on said, "There is one doe on earth, and the blessed Holy One does so much for her. When she cries out, the blessed Holy One hearkens to her anguish. And when the world is in need of mercy, for water, she cries aloud and the blessed Holy One listens and then feels compassion for the world, as is written: 'As a hind longs for streams of water (Psalms 42:2)'. When she needs to give birth, she is totally constricted; then she puts her head between her knees, crying out and screaming, and the blessed Holy One feels compassion for her and provides her with a serpent who bites her genitalia, opening and tearing that place, and immediately she gives birth." Rabbi Shim'on said, "Concerning this matter, do not ask and do not test God so it is precisely."[25]

The Zoharic exposition highlights the intrinsic tension and dialectic in the birth experience: hunger and thirst, death and pain, along with the desire for life, the closing and opening of the womb, cries and hope, and the ever-intensifying stages of the birth process. Here, the *Zohar*'s association of the gazelle's giving birth with the splitting of the Reed/Red Sea (*Yam Suph*) facilitates understanding of the terror of birth and the salvation following the splitting, as the sea was split by the rod of Moses. Parallel expositions on the gazelle (*ayalah*) in the *Zohar* show that this is *ayelet ha-shahar*, the morning star, whose light bursts forth every morning; and the water that comes from the morning star / gazelle's womb parallels the fetus that comes forth with the help of the serpent's bite.[26]

In another exposition, two serpents accompany the gazelle in every birth, the "elusive" (or "tortuous") serpent Aklaton and the "fleeing" serpent Bariah. In this exposition in the *Zohar*, the serpent bites the gazelle twice.[27] This notion, as David Biale comments, overturns the natural order of human birth: first the blood that

---

24 On the shamanic and healing qualities of the serpent, see Eliade, *Rites and Symbols of Initiation*, 96–99. See the latter also on mythologies of/about snakes, sexuality and birth, such as the wish of man to be swallowed in the womb of the great mother, or the fear of the *vagina dentata* (51).
25 *Zohar* 2:52b (Matt, 4, 266).
26 Ibid., 2: 219b; *Zohar* 3:68a.
27 Ibid., 239a–b.

feeds the forces of the *Sitra Ahra* (the embodiment of all evil) appears, and only then does the water, signifying salvation and redemption, materialize.[28]

The gazelle in this exposition also fills a double role: as the *Shekhinah*, she is identified with the son, the people of Israel, crying and moaning to be extricated from her womb; and as the mother giving birth, she is torn asunder and saves the fetus from her birth canal.[29]

God, who sends the serpent to "[tear] that place," is presented in this myth in a dual role, as being in need and as savior. In the *Sefirah* of *Tiferet*, he strives with all His powers for this redemption, which reaches to the summit of the Sefirotic tree and which needs the help of *Atika Kadisha*, the Ancient Holy One. The *Zohar* states explicitly that the role of savior extends beyond this animal to all humankind.

Merav Carmeli examines the relationship between this exposition and the stages of physical birth, and shows how the dismay felt by the Israelites right before the splitting of the sea matches the secretion of oxytocin and adrenaline that aids in overcoming contractions and the emergence of the physical newborn. In her interpretation, the Ancient Holy One parallels the transition from the neocortex (which controls higher brain functions) to the hypothalamus (which controls more fundamental functions), which enables the woman to actualize the physical knowledge connecting this physiological event with the highest Kabbalistic level of *Ein-Sof*, which is meant for that rare moment of birth.[30]

For R. Isaac Luria, as Yehuda Liebes notes, the staff and the serpent represent disparate facets of a different order: states of *katnut* and *gadlut*, namely, sexual immaturity and adult male potency.[31] Luria reveals to his disciples that the serpent is not merely a harmful force it also is the male who couples with the gazelle for the birth of the Redeemer. This esoteric knowledge, called "the Seventh Day of Passover," erotically charges the encounter between the gazelle and the serpent. This reading offers an additional aspect of the imagery of redemption as birth in light of the perception that it is as difficult for God to pair Israelites as it was for him to split the sea (BT Sotah 2a). The serpent, therefore, fills a diverse range of tasks. He is perceived as father, male, enticer, a harmful yet beneficial element, a cause of suffering, a base animal, and the mythical creature who reveals consciousness and sexuality to Adam and Eve (Gen. 3:5).

---

28 Biale, *Blood and Belief*, 92 n. 40. On Jewish-Christian polemics regarding the motif of blood (blood of birth, menstruation, and circumcision) as opposed to the motif of water (baptism), see 95–107. See also Wolfson, *Venturing Beyond*, 136–142, 151–165.
29 In Hebrew, *Mizraim* ("Egypt") alludes to the birth canal and to the word "straits" *(mei'zarim)*.
30 Carmeli, "Birthing Hind."
31 Liebes, "'Two Young Roes of a Doe.'"

As I demonstrated in previous research, the serpent not only represents a sexually mature state that destroys or assists, it also represents the states of *katnut* of the Son/ Messiah and the fetus within the gazelle. The serpent accordingly reflects the myth of the "eternal youth," the *puer aeternus* (divine child), alluded to in the prophetic visions and various psychoanalytical theories.[32]

The masks worn by the serpent in this myth help us to see it as "the third" in the plot, similar to the analytical space that helps to provide a way out from situations in which there is no exit, such as the blockage of the gazelle. Relational approaches refer to the "third," that is, the entity who rescues the "couple" (the therapist and the patient), who are structurally and inevitably "stuck." The third provides them with potential space and creative freedom. In his attempt to encounter mental anguish, the therapist has the patient confront that pain while concurrently enabling the latter to lower his defenses and to bear the suffering that life entails.

In psychoanalytic theory, "the third" expresses varying roles: he is one of the triad, the moral third; the third who witnesses the trauma and verbalizes it; the harmonious and rhythmic third; the stranger who is close; the dyad that is aware of its separateness; the mother who identifies with the infant but also remains external to his situation, holding and containing him; and more.[33] This model reflects a person's relationships with another and the moments of imprisonment and captivity that occur within any dyadic dynamic. The gazelle's obstructed condition mirrors man's blocked state in the processes of his own birth, and the blockage of both the gazelle and the fetus who are trapped together, with no way out. The gazelle myth stresses the need of every individual for redemption and the consequential need for the "snakebite" – an external factor that aids in releasing familiar patterns and neutralizing the bonds of inner imprisonment.

The blockage of the gazelle, which finds itself at an impasse, does not only emulate the inner world of the fetus in the womb, it also mirrors the mother's condition. This is the dominant physical experience that emerges from women's testimonies: the anxiety, which appears at the end of the transitional stage, that the baby will not come out, that its head is too big. It is the terror of removing one body from within another – actually, it is terror of removing one *soul* from within another. The Kabbalistic literature portrays the woman in labor with the closed (i.e., final) letter *mem*, which opens after the birth. In Christian interpretation, the closed *mem* alludes to the immaculate conception of Mary

---

32 Isaiah 11:8. See Jung and Kerenyi, *Essays*; Benarroch, *Sabba and Yanuka*.
33 Ogden, "Analytic Third;" Benjamin, "Beyond Doer"; Gerson, "The Relational Unconscious";　Aron, "Analytic Impasse."

and the virginal birth of Jesus.[34] This transition is also deemed in Jewish sources to be a Messianic process, to which the verse of redemption in Isaiah 9:6 alludes ("abundant authority"), which Kabbalistic, Sabbatean, and Hasidic exegeses all understand as referring to the Redeemer.[35]

Blockage is connected with trauma, incomprehensible and unresolved pain, the foreboding of annihilation, and the fear of death. The *Zohar* associates the trauma of birth with the Exodus from Egypt. This is a bursting forth from the womb of the world, from the great and perilous (Reed/Red) sea, and it hints at blood and harsh judgments. All these motifs represent educational, "necessary," and unavoidable humanizing trauma.[36] Birth is a sundering, a "catastrophic change" capable of bringing forth remedy; it is rescue intertwined with harm.[37]

The memory of the singular experience of birth remains imprinted in one's flesh, and the body records it in two main ways. The first, primal and direct, is movement outward from within. The second, ceremonial and cyclic, occurs in the opposite direction, from without inward. Every person stores within their body the memory of their emergence from the other body, their mother's, even if this recollection is dim and hazy. A recurring and second imprint is performed in adulthood, in the reproductive organs of the man and woman, and attests to our having come from the same place. The singular ritual of piercing the hymen repeats the woman's own birth, but this time her body is pierced from the other side.[38] The fetus enables the mother to become a mother and to be reborn. The man, in contrast, is imprinted in the circumcision ceremony, with the *periah* (uncovering the corona) restoring the birth memory and seemingly unraveling (*pare'ah*) the body backward to the unformed world from which it came. This process concludes when the son, who is circumcised when eight days old, becomes an adult man, who himself is capable of creating life. The process has now come full circle, after beginning with blockage (in the mother's womb), continuing with opening (with the female's own birth and the male's circumcision), and concluding with an additional closing of imprinting and memory together with a taste of redemption. BT Niddah 30b speaks of this cyclical nature of life and death, of giving birth and entering the covenant of

---

34 Liebes, *The Secret of the Sabbatean Faith*, 166–179; idem, "'Two Young Roes of a Doe,'" 175; idem, "Christian Influences in the Zohar"; Wolfson, *Language*, Chapter 6; Kauffman, "Two Tsadikim."
35 The *mem* in *le-marbeh* is final ("closed"), despite being in the middle of the word.
36 Laplanche, "Seduction."
37 Bion, "Catastrophic Change"; Aharoni and Bergstein, "91–93"; Bergstein, "Beyond the Spectrum."
38 Freud, "The Taboo of Virginity."

circumcision as follows: "As soon as it sees the light of day, the closed [organ] opens, and then open, closes, for if this were not so, it could not live even a single hour."

As we have seen, it was commonly believed in antiquity that the sperm originated in the head, traveling from there, through the male's body, to create the "white" in the body of the fetus.[39] The movement of the sperm matches the fetus's exit from the mother's body. This memory begins with the physical birth, the tearing of one body from another, and ends with redemption and going forth to freedom from life's distressing "constricted places." Birth, then, is not merely being cast forth from the Garden of Eden, it also is a bridge, a connection, and an opportunity to repair the unraveled ends of human existence.

3 Birth Pains and Redemption in the Teaching of R. Nahman of Bratzlav

In one of his well-known dicta, R. Nahman declares that stories have the power to heal barren women: "[All] the world says that tales cannot bring about pregnancy. But I said that barren women will be visited [i.e., by God, who releases them from their barrenness] and will become pregnant" (*Hayyei MoHaran* 25). This statement is joined by numerous teachings that discuss various aspects of birth and being born, such as his pronouncement that stories clothe a person who has lost "his countenance" with a new face, which is like ending infertility.[40] These statements not only attest to R. Nahman's experience as a *tzaddik* who was troubled by the distress of barren women, they also demonstrate the centrality of birth imagery in his mystical and poetical thought, which I will now discuss in brief.[41]

R. Nahman examines the birth experience in the various genres of his works: the tales, *hanhagot* (rules of conduct), sermons and homilies, and teachings (*torot*). His teachings are based on the relationship between the pangs of birth and those of redemption; depictions of the creation of man and woman in Rabbinic midrashim; the gazelle myth in all its variations, from the Rabbinic literature to the Zoharic and Lurianic Kabbalah; and more. I will discuss several

---

39 *Leviticus Rabbah* 14:6; Liebes, "Sections of the Zohar Lexicon," 252–254; Biale, *Blood and Belief*, 88–93; Tamari, "Human Sparks," 159–169.
40 R. Nahman of Bratzlav, *Likutei MoHaran*, 1:60; see also 2:4.
41 On other Hasidic leaders who "help" women to give birth in the Habad movement today, see Kauffman, "Two Tsadikim"; Bilu, *With Us More Than Ever*, 197–204.

teachings in which he directly discusses birth and a prominent tale in which birth functions as an archetypical image for mystical cognition and rebirth.[42]

In R. Nahman's teachings, conception and birth are essential metaphors for a spiritual process and growth; nonetheless, the presence of the female body and the psychophysical connection transfers birth from being just a metaphor to a tangible concept. These expositions voice the cries of the woman in labor and the prayers of the woman on the birthstool. The force of the female body that gives birth and is torn asunder is evident – the body whose pain is capable of mitigating harsh judgments, of turning blood into milk, of delivering the infant so that it is born healthy and not stillborn. The imagery of miscarriage and premature birth concerned R. Nahman, and is at the center of his twentieth teaching (2:20):

> Because of controversy, people become famous before their time [. . .] This brings death to those involved in the controversy, or, when the damage is of a lesser order, it brings on poverty. This secret is thus explained in the Torah: "When two men quarrel and strike a pregnant woman, and her foetus is aborted" (Ex. 21:22). He who sets out upon a new path is like a pregnant woman; he has to remain hidden, just as the foetus is hidden until birth. This path which has not yet been known to the world is in a state of gestation, as Scripture says: "I have taught you the path of Wisdom" (Prov. 4:11). Such a person has to warm himself, like the foetus in the womb, before the time comes for him to expose his path to daylight. If he emerges [into the public eye] before his time, controversy may be said to have brought on a miscarriage.

This discourse begins with the directive to every individual to undergo the processes of impregnation that are sufficiently lengthy to give birth to proper thought and wisdom that "is fit to be born." It continues by discussing people who "become known prematurely," so that the Torah that they teach is lost and "is stillborn with them." Here, as well, the physical experience is central, to the extent that the metaphor seems to overpower all else: the imagery of people who are punished and are miscarried is stronger than the underlying message of the teaching. This reversal is striking in the continuation of the discourse:

> As with a pregnant woman, who is struck until she miscarries, there are two aspects: at times she loses the stillborns themselves, whom she miscarries by their being delivered before their time. At other times the pregnant woman herself is harmed by this and passes away.[43]

The tragedy of the loss of wisdom is made tangible and becomes a concrete experience thanks to the portraits of miscarriage and the death of the fetus and

---

42 Mark, *Mysticism and Madness*, 205–211; Pedaya, *Psychoanalysis and Kabbala*, 258.
43 *Likutei MoHaran* 2:20. See Green, *Tormented Master*, 113–115.

the pregnant mother. Pregnancy symbolizes the infinite potential of life and the redemption inherent in the wisdom to be uncovered and realized in the future. In contrast, the loss of the fetus and the woman seems cruel and unjust, as a reflection of the enigma of death that follows, according to the Biblical narrative, from needless violence between two men who cannot bring life and whose struggle reaps only ruin.

R. Nahman's personal experience as one imprisoned between contradictory self-images and who loses ("miscarries") his teaching due to the battles that raged around him might be behind the imagery of the pregnant woman. On the one hand, he views himself as a great innovator, *tzaddik ha-dor* (the outstanding Hasidic leader of his time) and a Messianic figure, one far above and beyond many other leaders of the Hasidic world. R. Nahman claimed that at the age of thirteen he already had reached the level of his grandfather the Baal Shem Tov, an assertion that aroused the ire of his generation. When his parents suggested that he visit the grave of the Baal Shem Tov, he responded: "If my grandfather wishes to see me, let him come here."[44] In addition to his awareness of his own greatness, he also battled with various figures, especially with the Hasidic leader known as the Saba (*zeide*) of Shpola – a disagreement which led to his becoming widely known as a *tzaddik* at an early age – with his arresting self-image as suffering from "torments the like of which were never known in the world."[45] R. Nahman might have felt that his teachings suffered due to his premature revelation at such an early age, and even identified with the stillborn (*nefel*) or the fetus that is harmed, due to his bitter struggles and freely traded insults with the Rabbinic world,[46] and to his battle with (and attraction to) the Sabbatean-Frankist world.[47]

Joseph Weiss portrays R. Nahman as one "dedicated to death," and who amplifies the fear of finitude in his thought like a sacrificial victim who gives his life in martyrdom for his faith.[48] To the fear of death evident in this teaching, we can also add the fear of life, which comes from what I called in Chapter 1 "the fear of not being born." Self-sacrifice is required not only for dying; it also

---

[44] Rapoport-Albert, "Hasidism after 1772," esp. n. 9; Green, *Tormented Master*, 111.
[45] *Shivhei Haran* 24; Green, *Tormented Master*, 95–130; Weiss, *Mehkarim Behasidut Braslav*, 8–26. Weiss explains R. Nahman's suffering in psychological terms: "The very structure of Nahman's personality led him directly into his sufferings and travails [. . .] he continually created and destroyed heretical worlds [. . .] in accordance with the ebbs and flows of his own sick soul" (42–57, 150–171).
[46] Green, *Tormented Master*, 114 n. 58.
[47] Kauffmann, *The Reborn Father*, 177–219.
[48] Weiss, *Mehkarim Behasidut Braslav*, 172–178; Liebes, *The Secret of the Sabbatean Faith*, 238–261.

is necessary for birth and realizing one's potential. The cost of the loss of many lives and stillborns occupied R. Nahman no less that the existential challenge of death. Furthermore, R. Nahman's doubt regarding his own self-worth and mission in this world and his lifelong sense of shame and anguish reinforced his self-perception as a nursing and vulnerable infant.[49]

On the mystical plane, this discourse, like most of R. Nahman's teachings, contains a Messianic desire. In *Likutei MoHaran* 2:20, the fetus within his mother's womb represents the future, hope, and redemption, while death represents the destruction of the anticipation of salvation.[50] This homily is based on the dramatic event portrayed in Exod. 21:22, wherein the consequences are laid out for anyone who should assail a pregnant woman. The circumstances in which the pregnant woman would be struck and harmed highlight the random and vague nature of loss caused by the struggle between two individuals. Since the mother, in this scenario, would remain alive, the Bible says "if there is no fatal injury [to the woman]," but R. Nahman identifies the tragedy in the harm to potential life, just like he does in his tale "The Rabbi's Son," which, too, presents a situation in which redemption – in the form of birth – almost arrives. Due, however, to a disruption – presumably marginal, but dramatic in the cosmic sense – the opportunity for redemption is just missed.

Ada Rapoport-Albert suggests that R. Nahman's hyperbole regarding the sublimity of his hidden Messianic capacity was not an attempt to deprive the other *tsaddikim* and righteous of his generation: "these exaltations of R. Nahman's unique messianic mission were never meant to undermine the position of other zaddikim in the hasidic leadership of his generation. On the level of sober consciousness he recognized his overt position in the reality of pre-messianic existence as the obverse of his messianic status, which was to remain concealed for the time being."[51]

This teaching might possibly disclose the tension between *malkhut be-itkasia* (the "concealed kingship") and *malkhut be-itgalya* (the "revealed kingship"). A hidden and "double" life, a sense of pregnancy in danger, and the gap between the revealed reality and the covert inner world could produce a powerful interpretation of the Biblical scene in Exodus on the consequences of the violence that occurs in the external world and that prevents life (or lives) from entering it.

---

49 On the self-perception of R. Nahman as a martyr, a sacrifice, and an unborn baby, see also *Likutei MoHaran* 1:26 on the chicken that dies inside his egg. See also Green, *Tormented Master*, 162, n. 48; on the motif of "returning from death," as the Messiah son of Joseph, see Green, *Tormented Master*, 196–198.
50 Jung and Kerenyi, *Essays*, 9–86.
51 Rapoport-Albert, "Hasidism after 1772," 113.

Along with the symbolic dimension of stillbirth, the experience of actual loss was not foreign to R. Nahman. He blames himself for the death of his son, and even compared himself to R. Isaac Luria, who lost a son because of some esoteric knowledge that he uncovered. R. Nahman, in contrast, revealed many such secrets – and not just one – to his disciples.

Likutei MoHaran 2:20 reflects the desire to be one "faithful of spirit" and remain protected as a fetus within the mother until the end of the allotted time to be revealed. R. Nahman identifies here with both the mother and the stillborn infant. He expresses, in his poetic and forceful way, the experience of loss and missed opportunity. As Arthur Green writes: "Nahman not only *was* a figure who personified the crisis [of faith] of his age and who fought internally with issues that his contemporaries had not yet learned to articulate, but also *was conscious* of his role as such a figure and sought the words to assert such a claim for himself."[52]

In contrast with this teaching, on the longing for fulfillment and the need to wait and prepare oneself until the time is right to be born, in *Likutei MoHaran* 1:21 R. Nahman focuses on the experience of the woman about to give birth. The discourse begins with a quotation from *Sifra de-Tzniuta* (*Zohar* 2: 176b–179a), that is, with the phrase "the concealed and hidden one," alluding to the hidden state of the *Sefirot* of the beginning of the process of emanation as parallel to human pregnancy. The emergence of the *sefirot* from the depths of their hidden source is expressed in the process of emanation, which at any moment possesses a closed dimension and the hope of bringing redemption.

R. Nahman's words imply that the cries of the mother giving birth are those of the *Shekhinah*, as is also indicated by *Likutei MoHaran* 1:89: "Behold, it is known that whatsoever a person lacks, whether spiritually or physically – that want is in the Divine Presence, which is the aspect of *Elohim* (the Lord). This is: 'But you made him wanting – [This want] is certainly 'slightly [wanting] from *Elohim*.' In other words, the want is certainly 'from *Elohim*' – i.e., in the Divine Presence." As he stresses in *Likutei Moharan* 1:21, all of our deficiencies – especially the pain of a life bursting forth and the cry of the woman in labor – attest to a deficiency in the *Shekhinah*:

> And at times the *moḥin* and the divine life-force are hidden, in the aspect of "fetal existence." And then "it is good for a person to cry out," whether in prayer or in Torah, when his *mochin* are concealed, for that concealment – i.e., that "fetal existence" – is in the aspect of "the Rock who has borne you, you have forgotten" [. . .]And with a person's outcry in his prayer and in his Torah, when his *mochin* are absent, he is in the aspect of

---

[52] Green, *Tormented Master*, 19.

3 Birth Pains and Redemption in the Teaching of R. Nahman of Bratzlav — 211

"fetal existence" – those outcries are the aspect of the outcry of the woman giving birth [. . .] And the revelation is the aspect of "birth."[53]

This discourse is based on the gazelle myth and its elaborations in the *Zohar* and the Lurianic Kabbalah. It links the gazelle's narrow womb with the cries of the *Shekhinah*, who is in a difficult labor and makes seventy sounds (as reflected in the seventy words in Psalms 20, which explains its use as an aid for women experiencing difficult labor). The cries of the woman in labor (a *hayah* – lit., an "animal" – in the Rabbinic sources)[54] graphically illustrate the physical experience of the woman who wants to put an end to her pains and hasten salvation.[55]

An additional association between birth, crying out, and redemption appears in *Likutei MoHaran* 1:60, in which R. Nahman connects depictions of the Creation with the awakening from (spiritual) sleep and the finding of a new countenance. This teaching returns to the narrative of the creation of the woman and its embellishments in Rabbinic midrashim. In the Rabbis' exegesis of the wording, "[God] built [*va-yiven*]" the structure (*mivneh*) of the woman's body purposefully; it is like an *otzar* ("treasury," in both the spiritual and physical sense) in which fruits can be kept.[56] The Sages portray God as constructing the woman in His image so that she will be able to give birth as He does. Then God connects her to Adam and acts as a matchmaker to bring them to the wedding, so that the two will bear offspring. Thus the Lord becomes a partner in reproduction and in the first wedding ceremony held after the "sawing apart" of the male and female. Based on this discourse, R. Nahman offers a mythological reading of birth, namely, that a person's every day begins with a scream – like the infant's cry as he emerges from the womb. At the beginning of his day (and life), a person feels limited ("restricted above"). Afterward, the day expands like a *shofar*, and he brings forth spiritual offspring, which is "expansive below," just like the female body.

This reading is influenced by the *Idrot* literature, which speaks of the sundering apart of the male and the female, for "all judgments deriving from the Male are harsh at the beginning and calm at the end, whereas all those deriving from the Female are calm at the beginning and harsh at the end."[57] As is his way, R. Nahman transfers this interpretative structure to spiritual birth and the notion of the *Shekhinah*, which is the soul associated with the attribute of awe.

---

[53] *Likutei MoHaran* 1:21.7. See Mark, *Mysticism and Madness*, 210. On crying, weeping, and screaming in R. Nahman's homilies, see Roi, "The Shout"; Mark, *Mysticism and Madness*, 135–145.
[54] See Chapter 4, n. 34.
[55] See *Zohar* 3:249b; 2:255b; Mark, *Mysticism and Madness*, 181–325.
[56] Trans. Kaplan, *Living Torah*, 8.
[57] *Zohar* 3:142b (Matt, 5, 438); Asulin, "Stature."

Our days are built, so he maintains, like the woman's uterus (*bet ha-rehem*, the two words, separately, meaning "house of the womb"), thereby enabling ongoing processes of being born. This connects the Rabbinic midrash to everyday reality. As Zvi Mark puts it: "'Rebirth' and making a completely new beginning comprise one of the central ways of being in Bratslav Hasidism. [. . .] every day a person falls to 'smallness' and begins his way from nothingness."[58] In the continuation of the discourse, barrenness is presented as comparable to sleep and blindness. Overcoming this condition is parallel to awakening, which in turn means finding the countenance that a person has lost. R. Nahman asserts that only stories have the power to extricate us from *hester panim*, the "hiding of God's face," and rescue us from our deep sleep.

In 1806, R. Nahman turned his hand to tales. It was around that time that his Messianic hopes were dashed, having suffered severe crises, including the deaths of his son and his wife and the fire that consumed his synagogue on Yom Kippur. Thirteen of his major tales were written between 1806 and his death in 1810, when he was only 39 years old. Green writes of this turn to storytelling: "Having failed to bring about the redemption by means of direct agitation, Nahman now expresses his longings through the medium of these fantastically elaborated stories."[59] In a Jungian reading, Haviva Pedaya proposes that R. Nahman's tales seek "to push the reader to the liminal moment of the loss of countenance" that represents the ego; and when the reader is naked, stripped of everything they own, "to clothe him with an ancient and lofty countenance," leading to the arousal of the consciousness.[60]

One of the most arousing tales, which has been given numerous interpretations and analyses with regard to its midrashic foundation, is that entitled "The Seven Beggars." I will examine one thread related to the myth of birth and redemption. The tale is related as a story within a story, which itself is set within a broader story as an expression of the *mise en abyme* literary technique. The blind beggar is the first to bless the young couple. Support for his declaration, "I am extremely old, but I am completely young. I have not yet begun to live," is given in the name of the Great Eagle: "This is not merely my own opinion; I have also the word of the Great Eagle." The tale later relates: "In the midst of this, the Great Eagle came and knocked on the tower. 'Stop being poor! Return to your treasures! Make use of your treasures!'" He then told them to leave the tower in order of their age, with the oldest going out first. In the frame story, the Great Eagle represents both the

---

[58] Mark, *Mysticism and Madness*, 208.
[59] Green, *Tormented Master*, 224.
[60] Pedaya, *Psychoanalysis and Kabbala*, 225–227; Ankori, *And This Forest Has No End*, 66.

beggar-narrator and R. Nahman himself, who calls upon his disciples to return to the tales, to the Torah, and to their primeval infancy.[61] The character of the old man is like the ancient Eagle, and he sees from one end of the world to the other, while at the same time he is, like a fetus, not yet living. This figure is reminiscent of the Jungian myth of the old man (*senex*) and the youth (*puer*); the latter is the Zoharic *yanuka*, who, as Jonathan, son of R. Asher ben Jehiel (the Rosh), elaborated, is reflective of the figure of the old man in the *Zohar*.

Additionally, Bratzlav tradition understands the tale as addressing the esoteric knowledge of *shiur komah* (the "measure" of the body of God) and the blind beggar as representing the uppermost *sefirah*. According to R. Nahman of Tcherin, the blind man is R. Nahman himself, who is also the deaf man, the stutterer, the hunchback, and so on – the unification of the sum total of the deficiencies within every *tzaddik*. R. Nahman, according to Joseph Dan, is the hero of all that happens in the tale, thereby expressing the ideas of correction and redemption.[62]

It is noteworthy that the deep connection between old age and pre-birth emerges from the initial scene, in which a group of survivors from the storm gather in the high tower in which they find all they need. Then each is invited to "tell an ancient story involving his earliest memory. Each one would tell what he remembered from the time that his memory began." In my interpretation, this is an invitation to dramatize the moment of impregnation (*ibbur*) and the most primal experience of existing. The recollections of the survivors are not concerned with realistic pictures; rather, they immediately delve into mental and spiritual symbolism and portraits of the two parents coupling and, in their fantasy, becoming a combined parental figure.

The two paradoxical axes are associated here with the mystery of birth: the motif of blindness (which actually represents in-depth vision and hidden perceptions) and that of memory (meaning the ability to forget and then to remember "absolutely nothing," which is actually the aspect of being nothing before being).[63] The blind beggar can himself "remember *absolutely nothing*" – and thereby understands the beginning of the beginning of everything. R. Nahman patently seeks to touch upon the elusive experience of impregnation (*ibbur*) and subthalamic memory and the body's coming into contact with the materials from which life is created: smell, sight, color, form, and taste. The seed and the fruit

---

[61] As Liebes, Green, and others have noted, the treasure that R. Nahman alludes to here is also the Book of the *Zohar*.
[62] Dan, *The Hasidic Story*, 161.
[63] On the phrase "I do not know" (which resonates with the idea of "absolutely nothing") in Rabbi Nahman's thought, see Mark, *Mysticism and Madness*, 209–210 and, generally, the work of Pedaya, Ankori, Liebes, Pachter, Green, Weiss, Rapoport-Albert, and others (see bibliography).

symbolize sexual and erotic elements, the seed as sperm and the fruit as the fetus within its mother until the moment of caesura and the severance of the umbilical cord, as the Great Eagle explains when leaving the tower (an action that is also compared to birth).

The tale alludes to the root of the soul with the picture of the burning candle, the tree, and the strata of *nefesh-ruach-neshamah* (all usually translated as "soul"),[64] and the early connection of the root to the branch, in the frequent Kabbalistic imagery of the beginning of the divine emanation. The reconstruction of the Creation process returns, step by step, to the primeval *tohu ve-vohu* ("formlessness and void") and the earliest memories of the universe. The storm and the sinking ships hint at the myth of the Edomite kings and the processes of *tzimtzum* ("constriction") and the "breaking of the vessels" that occurred within the Godhead when its *kelipot* ("husks") and *sigei din* ("judgments") were cast out.[65] The wise men, who "discovered the seed," depict the notion of the sperm that descends from the mind and the *Sefirah* of *Hokhmah*. Additionally, as the Eagle explains further on, the ships are the bodies that "were shattered, but they will be rebuilt."

The imagery of the body as a ship, already present in the *Zohar*, emphasizes the role of the *tzaddik* as connecting the worlds with the body and the soul.[66] The souls of the *tzaddikim* understand the ritual and cyclical nature of life and death, and link the infinite world with the finite one. The tale teaches us that "the action in the end begins with thought" and that the order of the fetus's creation begins with the thought that originates in *Ayin*. This Kabbalistic-Hasidic depiction moves from the concrete physical expanse to the spiritual and mystical realm, and assumes a legendary guise that is meant to remove us from our state of mental and spiritual barrenness. The old blind man and the Great Eagle, symbols of the lofty soul and ancient wisdom, come to aid us in shedding our husks, and to make use of the true treasures within us. Only then will we be able to be truly born, and this will be followed by collective redemption, which the tale yokes together with rescue from death and drowning in the stormy sea.

This tale is based on Zoharic poetics and especially on the eschatological and mystical picture painted in the exegesis of R. Metivta in *Zohar, Shelah Lekha*. R. Nahman's tale touches upon the above-mentioned quality or measure called *Ayin* in which fear and pleasure are intermingled, together with an

---

[64] Aryeh Kaplan, *Rabbi Nachman's Stories*, translates *nefesh* as "soul," *ruach* as "spirit," and *neshamah* as "essence."
[65] Ankori, *And This Forest Has No End*, 200–203; Dan, *The Hasidic Story*, 152–161.
[66] On the perception of the body and the tongue in R. Nahman's writings, see Ankori, *And This Forest Has No End*, 203.

awareness of the "Nothingness" that preceded it. Before a person is a composite of his parents' sperm and ovule, they were an aspect of the divine *Ayin*, which is both a self-negating and empowering consciousness, since it enables the memory of the oceanic state of inclusion within the Godhead through which the key to redemption can be comprehended.[67]

An additional metaphor of birth as redemption appears in *Likutei MoHaran* 2:4. R. Nahman, following the Rabbis, states that the annals of the *tzaddikim* are their meritorious deeds, especially charitable giving. But unlike the Rabbis, who compare their good deeds to the progeny they bring into the world, R. Nahman speaks of the birth process itself, beginning from the actuality of the pain of the first birth, when the womb is narrow, and comparing this to the initial difficulty of opening one's hand to give charity. R. Nahman devoted special attention to the essence of physical birth as the spiritual birth of the *tzaddik* as such, who has the power to bring redemption to himself and to his followers.

R. Nahman bases his description of the difficulty in the commandment to give charity on the imagery of the ravens who are commanded to feed Elijah (1 Kgs 17: 6–7). He asserts that this commandment is meant to destroy the cruelty in man's psyche, similar to the change in the symbol of the ravens, which go from cruel animals to nourishing and giving ones. The person who gives charity opens his hand and becomes compassionate (*rahman*) – that is, one who possesses a fertile *rehem* ("womb") and brings life. Elijah the Prophet, too, undergoes a psychological transformation in the Book of Kings, going from a zealot certain of his truth who must subject himself to hunger and thirst, to the vagaries of nature, and to the unknown and endure in the great revelation the lack of sound, voice, color, and form in order to bring within the "still, small voice."[68]

Unlike the cruelty of the ravens, there is also another cruelty, that of the birthing mother who, due to the pain of birth and the tearing asunder of her body, wants to cast away the newborn and dispatch it to oblivion. This is the moment that is not controlled by logic, when the mercies of heaven are needed. It is there that God sends the dragon to save the newborn the very second before its death. By associating the ravens with charity and birth, R. Nahman states clearly that every birth requires the almost impossible overcoming of basic egotism, which is the essence of human nature. As the mother finds redemption by giving life to the fetus that emerges from her womb, so too the giver of charity finds redemption by giving life (charity) to the pauper before him.

---

67 Magid, *Hasidism Incarnate*, 31–50.
68 On the figure of Elijah from the midrash to the Kabbalistic literature, see Yisraeli, *Temple Portals*, 78–100.

The womb of the first-time mother is narrow, like that of the mountain goat and the gazelle (both mentioned in the exposition in BT Bava Bathra 16b), which intensifies the difficulty of giving birth, and thereby resembles the act of charity, whose beginning is "hard and very burdensome." In conclusion, R. Nahman implies that "before giving birth to the newborn" the mother gives birth to herself and the very ability to rend her body and soul. He declares in this discourse that the rectification of all the moral attributes consists of bringing about birth, which is the Redemption. For the person who finds it hard to extend his fingers to give charity – like the woman who has difficulty in releasing the fetus when in labor or who seeks to kill it in her great pain and suffering – the solution lies in reversal. Like the woman in labor who goes out to the field to be alone, an instinct found in animals and at times in women about to give birth, R. Nahman proposes that every person act thusly: a person's every good act, everything learned and every commandment performed, is not of the aspect of birth, it is actual birth, which requires the release of inner constraints.

It is worthwhile comparing these teachings with the argument by Tsippi Kauffmann that in most Hasidic stories "the *tzaddik* who aids in the birth pushes the woman and the birth event offstage. In actuality, the birth serves merely as a pretext or catalyst for the appearance of the *tzaddik*, who performs miracles on the stage [. . .] The story focuses on the *tzaddik*, and not on the mother-to-be."[69] This is not the case here. In addition to the generic differences between R. Nahman's discourses and the Hasidic *shevahim* ("hagiography") literature, R. Nahman makes a remarkably singular attempt to generate identification and empathy with the feminine figure of the woman giving birth. He views the pregnant mother as a subject, and compares actual birth to the processes of redemption. The birth metaphor therefore reinforces the actual experience felt by the Hasidic student. The pains and cries of the woman in labor take center stage in R. Nahman's discourses, and not the *tzaddik* who rescues her in some magical or mystical way. The drama of these discourses plays out in the female body, the womb in particular. All humans are born of woman, R. Nahman declares, and accordingly we are all the midwives of the Torah and the Redemption.

4 Redemptive Birth in Kabbalah and in Psychoanalysis

The metaphor of birth as redemption is developed to such an extent in the Kabbalah and in Hasidism that at times we can hardly discern who is the one

---

69 Kauffmann, "Birth," 75.

giving birth: the man or the woman, mother or father, a divine or human figure, one individual or a collective. As was mentioned in Chapter Six, at the time of birth the mother reveals her male countenance. The *Zohar* calls the *Sefirah* of *Binah* "the male world," specifically at the time of birth. The *Shekhinah* is also frequently revealed through male figures, such as King David and R. Shimon bar Yohai. These gender reversals display the revolutionary position of the Kabbalists, who joined the act of giving birth and the maternal role with the male Godhead while also ascribing male actions and figures to the feminine Godhead, when the latter symbolized a transformative process of donning garments, *hitlabshut* ("enclothing"), meant to bring about the Redemption.

Underlying these reversals is a polemical stance that sought to address rigid conceptions of sex and gender in other schools within Judaism and in the surrounding society. Moreover, gender reversals and notions of fluid identity that emerge within the contexts of birth and redemption reflect the centrality of fertility in the psyche of the Kabbalists. They thought of birth as a redemptive act and as a focal point of their mystical and theurgic experience. Such identity games are a means of liberation, with the aim of creating a *communitas* in which the accepted hierarchies are torn down and the psyche is transformed.

The gender reversals and reshuffling of roles attest to the richness of the experiences of giving birth and being born, and how they permeated the Kabbalistic concepts of sex and gender while undermining and deconstructing them. In the Kabbalistic system of *sefirot*, all procreate and are born one within the other, in cyclical and continual fashion. As the *Zohar* explains: "This king, although He is Supreme King, is female in relation to the supernal point, concealed of all. But even though He is female, He is male in relation to the king below."[70]

The conception of birth as redemption challenges our understanding of the possibility of "giving birth" and of "being born," redefining them as phenomena that cross and rebuild gender and sexual identity, along with the expanses of time and place. To be born is to be redeemed, while redemption has the depth of the birth experience, with its terror and grandeur. This idea teaches us that birth was understood as a cosmic event that connects end and beginning, the Redemption and the Creation. As we have seen, in addition to birth being an individual, physical female experience, the Kabbalistic world transforms it into a powerful metaphor that documents two central processes in the Godhead: that of divine emanation and the Redemption. Each of these realms emphasizes the symbolic perception of birth that occurs in different strata and in different *sefirot*, male and female. This foundational metaphor represents the

---

[70] *Zohar* 2:4a (Matt, 4, 14–15).

Godhead, which agonizes over the "birth pangs" that round out the concept of the "birth pangs of the Redemption" for the Creation of the world and its eschatological salvation. This theme from the Kabbalistic literature was developed in the world of Hasidism, and it resonates in the consciousness of agency and healing that underlies psychoanalysis.

Analogous to the Kabbalistic world, the world of psychoanalysis, too, sees the desire to redeem and be redeemed as representing the universal, and primal, longing that uncovers man's most profound deficiencies and existential crises. It is the motive force driving analysis. This process is based on the hope of mending and on the belief in the possibility of healing, even when a miraculous transformation is required just to bridge the gap between what is desired and what is the case in reality.[71] Many psychoanalytical schools believe that change is possible, that reality can be alleviated, and that destructive psychological patterns can be altered. A successful course of treatment seeks to give the patient the opportunity for birth – a second birth, a rebirth – and redemption. The analyst encounters every fundamental point of crisis and serves as the "mother," seeking not to fail in the places where the actual mother stumbled.

More than other psychoanalysts, Wilfred Bion stressed that the hope for changing reality and the birth of new thought is the underpinning of analysis, which is capable of effecting rebirth: "In psychoanalysis [. . .] we can help the soul or psyche to be *born* even, and help it to continue to develop after it is born."[72] His approach is reminiscent of the Kabbalistic conception of redemption. It seeks the idea that will stimulate the "soul or psyche," and facilitate its blossoming and growth. The belief in the power of analysis to bring about "redemption" does not only speak to the patient and analyst as individuals. It also addresses all those participating in the psychoanalytical field, who together form a sort of broad collective of believers. This is the great message of psychoanalysis, the gift it bestows on humankind: "The Messianic idea betrays itself in the supposition that the individual patient is worth the analyst's very considerable devotion; as also in the view, sometimes openly expressed, that as a result of psychoanalytic work a technique will be perfected that will, ultimately, save mankind."[73]

---

[71] Abrams, *Female Body*; Winnicott, "Ego Distortion"; Starr, *Repair of the Soul*; Ghent, "Masochism, Submission, Surrender," esp. 109 n. 2 on the connection between holiness, making whole, and healing.
[72] Eschel, *The Emergence of Analytic Oneness*; Bion, *Bion in New York and São Paulo*, 95.
[73] Bion, *Experiences in Groups*, 176.

Epilogue

Throughout this book, I have examined birth as a singular, one-time event that constitutes an individual's consciousness of self. At the same time, I also have sought to view birth as a cyclical and circular ritual, an ongoing occurrence that takes place time and again. It continues to be desired, the object of yearning, while it has already happened. This is an event that occurs once, but is also eternal, as Søren Kierkegaard explains:

> But he who does not comprehend that life is a repetition, and that this is the beauty of life, has condemned himself and deserves nothing better than what is sure to befall him, namely, to perish [. . .] When one has circumnavigated existence, it will appear whether one has courage to understand that life is a repetition, and to delight in that very fact. He who has not circumnavigated life before beginning to live will never come to the point of living [. . .] he who chooses repetition really lives.[1]

My starting assumption, which is at the core of the entire book, is that man is a born creature, who is conscious of his birth. This led me to devise an existential model of birth and being born, which rests on linkages between an exegetical and mystical perspective and psychoanalytical thought. These connections were meant to show the amplitude of the birth experience that is embedded in the human body, and specifically in the female body.

We saw how birth is not only that primal, one-time occurrence, but an expansive metaphor that relates to various aspects of the individual's developmental processes. Many metaphorical births occur during our lives, but the force of the actual, initial birth leaves an indelible mark on human life, specifically because it happens only a single time in a person's life and because it is compulsory. As the Rabbis declare: "You were created against your will, and against your will you will be born and come forth into the world." Unlike the Rabbis, Winnicott argues that actual birth expresses the infant's free will and desire to live. At the moment of his birth, a person chooses life, and does not merely respond to the physical and mental pressure his environment exerts on him. Resulting either by circumstance or by choice, the primal birth is a unique, decisive fact, while the second and all succeeding births are "optional," a possibility, conditional.

Birth might infuse our lives with confidence just because of its singularity. In his book *On Certainty*, Ludwig Wittgenstein corresponds with the British philosopher George Edward Moore, as he presents the question of birth and death as the thresholds of our existence. The fact that once, before being born, we did

---

1 Kierkegaard, *Repetition*, 34.

not exist, just as we finite creatures move inexorably toward our deaths, influences the ability of human cognition to grasp any certain datum. We have no way of knowing what came before us. Yet it is because of the very singularity of the threshold experiences of birth and death that people enjoy complete certainty regarding human cognition and existence.[2]

The book depicts birth as a potential expanse, the place where the mother manifests herself as a playground, in which the infant is found after hiding for so long. In birth, the mother symbolizes in Dana Amir's terms the emergent principle and the continuous principle of the self, as well as the lyrical dimension of soul.[3] She is the corporeal and the flesh, the platform of life, the soul that creates substantiality. She connects reality and fantasy, language and prelanguage, nature and culture, wakefulness and the dream state. During birth, the mother transitions between states of being. She moves between the effort to retain the fetus within her – controlling muscles, pushing, deep breathing – and releasing the infant from her body, freeing herself from pain and fear. She moves between innate thought and the "unthought known," between "alpha function" and "beta elements," between conceptions and that which precedes them, between emotional impregnation and complete unraveling.

The infant, too, undergoes many states of actuality. He shifts from a state of "not being" to one of "being," from "not breathing" to "breathing," from the danger of annihilation and the fear of death to the joy of existence and the tension of life. He passes between heat and cold, anxiety and crying, to the delight of discovering a new world, a new contact, an enveloping other, compassion, and being seen; from being contained to the beginning of his transformation into container, in his body and in his thought processes.

Giving birth, like "being born," is the apex of human creativity.

The encounter with Eros in its deepest sense, as the love of life, as choosing life over all the rest, is the underpinning of the adult aesthetic experience and desire. We all return again and again to the same Eden, which we choose from anew, to the same primal womb to which we are led, repeatedly, by the search throughout life – the totality of our longings. All the maternal and human signs of desire return there.

The memory of melding returns there.

Birth precedes the dyadic mother–child unit, and is present beyond time.

There is no blurring of "self"-"not self," but rather the emanated departure from the Godhead.

---

[2] Wittgenstein, *On Certainty*, § 84, 92, 178, 182, 233, 407.
[3] Amir, *On the Lyricism*.

The Kabbalistic action of striking, *butzina de-kardinuta* ("a spark of impenetrable darkness"; *Zohar* 1:15a), the black light, resembles the quill that writes. It is also the head that strikes the membrane of the mother's uterus at the beginning of life. The child toys with the thought that he can go forth to exist in his own right. The mother toys with the thought that within her is a striking and kicking unknown, which possesses will – a will that is not her own.

> Our birth is but a sleep and a forgetting:
> The Soul that rises with us, our life's Star,
> > Hath had elsewhere its setting,
> > And cometh from afar:
> > Not in entire forgetfulness,
> > And not in utter nakedness,
> But trailing clouds of glory do we come
> > From God, who is our home:
> Heaven lies about us in our infancy!
> > > –William Wordsworth

Bibliography

Abrams, Daniel. "Eimatai Hubberah ha-Haqdamah le-Sefer ha-Zohar?" *Asufot* 8 (1994): 211–226.
Abrams, Daniel. *The Female Body of God in Kabbalistic Literature: Embodied Forms of Love and Sexuality in the Divine Feminine*. Jerusalem: Magnes Press, 2004. [Hebrew].
Abrams, Daniel. "The Invention of the Zohar as a Book." *Kabbalah* 19 (2009): 7–142.
Abrams, Daniel. *Ten Psychoanalytic Aphorisms on the Kabbalah*. Los Angeles: Cherub Press, 2011.
Aeschylus. *Eumenides*. Trans. Alan H. Sommerstein. Cambridge, MA: Harvard University Press, 2008.
Afterman, Adam. "From Philo to Plotinus: The Emergence of Mystical Union." *Journal of Religion* 93, no. 2 (2013): 177–196.
Aharoni, Hagit. "Hidden Secrets: Between an Attentive Ear and Containing Mind." *Sihot* 19 (2005): 159–168.
Aharoni, Hagit. "Brit bein ha-Betarim." In Wilfred R. Bion, *Caesura*. Trans. Hagit Aharoni and Avner Bergstein. Tel Aviv: Tolaat Sefarim, 2012, 99–142. [Hebrew].
Aharoni, Hagit, and Avner Bergstein. "Looking at the Future Born: An Introduction to the Hebrew Translation of A. Piontelli." In Alessandra Piontelli, *From Fetus to Child: An Observational and Psychoanalytic Study*. Ben Shemen: Modan, 2001, 12–20.
Aharoni, Hagit, and Avner Bergstein. "Introduction." In Wilfred R. Bion, *Caesura*. Trans. Hagit Aharoni and Avner Bergstein. Tel Aviv: Tolaat Sefarim, 2012, 7–25. [Hebrew].
Alvarez, Anne. *Live Company: Psychoanalytic Psychotherapy with Autistic, Borderline, Deprived and Abused Children*. London: Karnac Books, 1992.
Amir, Dana. *On the Lyricism of the Mind: Psychoanalysis and Literature*. London: Routledge, 2015.
Ankori, Micha. *And This Forest Has No End*. Tel Aviv: Tel Aviv University Press, 1990.
Anzieu, Didier. *The Skin-Ego*. Trans. Naomi Segal. London: Routledge, 2016.
Arberry, Arthur J. *The Koran Interpreted*, Vol. 1: *Suras I–XX*. London: George Allen & Unwin, 1955.
Aristotle. *The Nicomachean Ethics*. Trans. W. D. Ross. Oxford: Oxford University Press, 2020.
Aron, Lewis. "The Internalized Primal Scene." *Psychoanalytic Dialogues* 5, no. 2 (1995): 195–237.
Aron, Lewis. "Analytic Impasse and the Third: Clinical Implications of Intersubjectivity Theory." *International Journal of Psychoanalysis* 87, no. 2 (2006): 349–368.
Aron, Lewis. "Black Fire on White Fire: Resting on the Knee of the Holy and Blessed One." *Contemporary Psychoanalysis* 43, no. 1 (2007): 89–111.
Aron, Lewis. "'With You I'm Born Again': Themes and Fantasies of Birth and the Family Circumstances Surrounding Birth as These Are Mutually Evoked in Patient and Analyst." *Psychoanalytic Dialogues* 24, no. 3 (2014): 341–357.
Aron, Lewis, and Karen E. Starr. *A Psychotherapy for the People: Toward a Progressive Psychoanalysis*. New York: Routledge, 2013.
Artman, Tali. "The Tale Type of the Repenting Prostitute: Between Rabbis and Church Fathers." *AJS Review* 42, no. 1 (2018): 1–20.
Ashur, Dorit. "To Read and Write as If Your Life Depended on It: Personal Voices in American Feminist Writing on Literature in the 1970s and 1980s." PhD diss., Hebrew University, 2005. [Hebrew].

Ashurst, Pamela. *Understanding Women In Distress*. London: Tavistock, 1989.
Asulin, Shifra. "The Stature of the *Shekhinah*: The Place of the Feminine Divine Countenance (Parzuf) in *Idra Rabbah* and *Idra Zuta*." In Howard Kreisel, Boaz Huss, and Uri Ehrlich (eds.), *Spiritual Authority: Struggles over Cultural Power in Jewish Thought*. Beer Sheva: Ben-Gurion University of the Negev Press, 2009, 103–182. [Hebrew].
Asulin, Shifra. "The Flaw and Its Correction: Impurity, the Moon and the Shekhinah: A Broad Inquiry into Zohar 3: 79(Aharei Mot)." *Kabbalah* 22 (2010): 193–251. [Hebrew].
Atlas, Galit. *The Enigma of Desire: Sex, Longing, and Belonging in Psychoanalysis*. London: Routledge, 2015.
Balant, Michael. *The Basic Fault: Therapeutic Aspects of Regression*. London: Tavistock, 1979.
Bar-Asher, Avishai (ed.). León, Moses de, *Sefer Mishkan ha-Edut: Critically Edited, Introduced and Annotated*. Los Angeles: Cherub Press, 2013. [Hebrew].
Bar-On, Yaara. Seeing with Foresight: Birth and Newborns in the Modern Age. Haifa: University of Haifa Press, 2000. [Hebrew].
Balaskas, Janet. *New Active Birth: A Concise Guide to Natural Childbirth*. London: Thorsons, 1991.
Baras, Zvi (ed.). *Messianism and Eschatology*. Jerusalem: Zalman Shazar Center, 1983. [Hebrew].
Barkai, Ron. *Science, Magic and Mythology in the Middle Ages*. Jerusalem: Van Leer Institute, 1987. [Hebrew].
Bassin, Donna, Margaret Honey, and Meryle Mahrer Kaplan (eds.). *Representation of Motherhood*. New Haven, CT: Yale University Press, 1994.
Bataille, Georges. *Death and Sensuality: A Study of Eroticism and Taboo*. New York: Ayer Company, 1962.
Beauvoir, Simone de. *The Second Sex*. New York: Vintage Books, 1989.
Ben-Amos, Dan, and Jerome Mintz. *In Praise of the Baal-Shem Tov: The Earliest Collection of Legends about the Founder of Hasidism*. Lanham, MD: Rowman and Littlefield, 2004.
Benarroch, Jonatan. *Sabba and Yanuka: God, the Son, and the Messiah in Zoharic Narratives*. Jerusalem: Magnes Press, 2018. [Hebrew].
Benayahu, Meir. *Sefer Toldot ha-Ari: Its Editions and Historical Development*. Jerusalem: Makhon Ben Tzvi, 1967. [Hebrew].
Benjamin, Jessica. *The Bonds of Love: Psychoanalysis, Feminism, and the Problem of Domination*. New York: Pantheon Books, 1988.
Benjamin, Jessica. "An outline of intersubjectivity: The Development of Recognition." *Psychoanalytic Psychology* 7 (1990), 33–46.
Benjamin, Jessica. "Beyond Doer and Done To: An Intersubjective View of Thirdness." *Psychoanalytic Quarterly* 73, no. 1 (2004): 5–46.
Bergstein, Avner. "Transcending the Caesura: Reverie, Dreaming and Counterdreaming." *International Journal of Psychoanalysis* 94, no. 4 (2013): 621–644.
Bergstein, Avner. "Beyond the Spectrum: Fear of Breakdown, Catastrophic Change and the Unrepressed Unconscious." *Rivista di Psicoanalisi* 60, no. 4 (2014): 847–868.
Bergstein, Avner. "Emotional Truth beyond Words." *Sihot* 30 (2015): 29–42.
Berman, Nathaniel. *Divine and Demonic in the Zohar and Kabbalistic Tradition: The "Other Side" of Kabbalah*. Leiden: Brill, 2018.
Biale, David. "The God with Breasts: El Shaddai in the Bible." *History of Religions* 21 (1982): 240–256.
Biale, David. *Eros and the Jews: From Biblical Israel to Contemporary America*. New York: Basic Books, 1992.

Biale, David, "Counter-History and Jewish Polemics against Christianity: The *Sefer Toldot Yeshu* and the *Sefer Zerubavel*." *Jewish Social Studies* 6, no. 1 (1999): 130–145.

Biale, David. *Blood and Belief: The Circulation of a Symbol between Jews and Christians*. Berkeley: University of California Press, 2007.

Bick, Esther. "The Experience of the Skin in Early Object Relations." *International Journal of Psychoanalysis* 49, no. 2–3 (1968): 484–486.

Bilu, Yoram. *With Us More Than Ever: Making the Absent Rebbe Present in Messianic Chabad*. Stanford, CA: Stanford University Press, 2020.

Bion, Wilfred R. *Experiences in Groups and Other Papers*. London: Tavistock, 1961.

Bion, Wilfred R. *Learning from Experience*. London: Tavistock, 1962.

Bion, Wilfred R. "Catastrophic Change." *Scientific Bulletin of the British Psycho-Analytical Society* 5 (1966): 13–24.

Bion, Wilfred R. *Attention and Interpretation*. London: Tavistock, 1970.

Bion, Wilfred R. "Emotional Turbulence/On a Quotation from Freud." In P. Hartocollis (ed.), *Borderline Personality Disorders: The Concept, the Syndrome, the Patient*. New York: International Universities Press, 1977, 3–13; 511–517.

Bion, Wilfred R. Two Papers: "The Grid" and *"Caesura."* London: Karnac Books, 1977.

Bion, Wilfred R. *Clinical Seminars & Other Works*. London: Karnac Books, 1979.

Bion, Wilfred R. *Bion in New York and São Paulo*. Ed. Francesca Bion. Perthshire, UK: Clunie Press, 1980.

Bion, Wilfred R. *A Memoir of the Future*. New York: Routledge, 1991.

Bion, Wilfred R. *The Italian Seminars (Rome 1977)*. London: Karnac Books, 2005.

Bion, Wilfred R. *Second Thoughts: Selected Papers on Psycho-Analysis*. London: Heinemann, 1967.

Bion, Wilfred R. *Caesura*. Trans. Hagit Aharoni and Avner Bergstein. Tel Aviv: Tolaat Sefarim, 2012. [Hebrew].

Biran, Hanni. *The Courage of Simplicity: Essential Ideas in the Work of W. R. Bion*. London: Routledge, 2015.

Bloom, Harold. "Freud and Beyond." In *Ruin the Sacred Truths: Poetry and Belief from the Bible to the Present*. Cambridge: Harvard University Press, 1987, 143–204.

Bollas, Christopher. "The Transformational Object." *International Journal of Psychoanalysis* 60, no. 1 (1979): 97–107.

Bollas, Christopher. *The Shadow of the Object: Psychoanalysis of the Unthought Known*. New York: Columbia University Press, 1987.

Boyarin, Daniel. *Carnal Israel: Reading Sex in Talmudic Culture*. Berkeley: University of California Press, 1993.

Breen, Dana. *The Birth of a First Child*. London: Tavistock, 1975.

Britton, Ronald. "Subjectivity, Objectivity, and Triangular Space." *Psychoanalytic Quarterly* 73, no. 1 (2004): 47–61.

Brodsky, Hilit. "Secrets that I Don't Even Tell Myself." *Sihot* 27 (2012): 49–55.

Bromberg, Philip. "Standing in the Spaces: The Multiplicity of Self and the Psychoanalytic Relationship." *Current Psychoanalysis* 32, no. 4 (1996): 509–535.

Bromberg, Philip. *Standing in the Spaces: Essays in Clinical Process, Trauma, and Dissociation*. Hillsdale, NJ: Analytic Press, 1998.

Bromberg, Philip. "One Need Not Be a House to Be Haunted." In *Awakening the Dreamer*. Mahwah, NJ: Analytic Press, 2006, 153–173. https://www.amazon.com/Awakening-Dreamer-Clinical-Philip-Bromberg/dp/0415888085

Bynum, Caroline Walker. *Jesus as Mother: Studies in the Spirituality of the High Middle Ages.* Berkeley: University of California Press, 1982.

Bynum, Caroline Walker. *Fragmentation and Redemption: Essays on Gender and the Human Body in Medieval Religion.* New York: Zone Books, 1992.

Campbell, Joseph. *The Power of Myth.* New York: Doubleday, 1988.

Carmeli, Merav. "Ma Osot haya'alot baleilot: The Myth of the Birthing Hind and the Serpent in Parasht Beshalah in the Zohar." *Kabbalah* 23 (2010): 219–247.

Carmeli, Ronnie. "On Being Cut Out of the Dead Mother." *Psychoanalytic Psychology* 32, no. 1 (2015): 173–190.

Cassuto, Umberto. *A Commentary on the Book of Genesis. Part I: From Adam to Noah. Genesis I–VI:8.* Trans. Israel Abrahams. Jerusalem: Magnes Press, 1961.

Chasseguet-Smirgel, Janine. *Creativity and Perversion.* London: Free Association Books, 1985.

Chodorow, Nancy. *The Reproduction of Mothering: Psychoanalysis and the Sociology of Gender.* Berkeley: University of California Press, 1978.

Chodorow, Nancy. *Feminism and Psychoanalytic Theory.* New Haven, CT: Yale University Press, 1989.

Chodorow, Nancy. "Gender, Relation, and Difference in Psychoanalytic Perspective." In Claudia Zanardi (ed.), *Essential Papers on the Psychology of Women.* New York: New York University Press, 1990, 420–436.

Chodorow, Nancy, and Susan Contratto (eds.). *The Fantasy of the Perfect Mother.* New Haven, CT: Yale University Press. 2002.

Cixous, Hélène. "Portrait of Dora." *Diacritics* 13 (1983): 2–36.

Cixous, Hélène. *Coming to Writing and Other Writings.* Ed. Deborah Jenson. Cambridge, MA: Harvard University Press, 1991.

Cixous, Hélène, and Catherine Clément. *The Newly Born Woman.* Translated by Betsy Wing. Minneapolis: University of Minnesota Press, 1986.

Cixous, Hélène, Keith Cohen, and Paula Cohen. "The Laugh of the Medusa." *Signs* 1, no. 4 (1976): 875–893.

Cohen, Seymour (trans. and ed.). *The Holy Letter: A Study in Medieval Jewish Sexual Morality, Ascribed to Nahmanides.* New York: Ktav, 1976.

Cohen-Shabot, Sara. "Constructing Subjectivity through Labour Pain: A Beauvoirian Analysis." *European Journal of Women's Studies* 24, no. 2 (2015): 128–142.

Cohen-Shabot, Sara. "Making Loud Bodies 'Feminine': A Feminist-Phenomenological Analysis of Obstetric Violence." Human Studies 39 (2016): 231–247.

Cohen-Shabot, Sara. "Domesticating Bodies: The Role of Shame in Obstetric Violence." *Hypatia* 33, no. 3 (2018): 384–401.

Coltart, Nina. *The Baby and the Bathwater.* London: Karnac Books, 1996.

Dan, Joseph. *The Hasidic Story.* Jerusalem: Keter, 1975. [Hebrew].

Deutsch, Helene. *The Therapeutic Process, the Self, and Female Psychology.* New Brunswick, NJ: Transaction Publishers, 1992.

Dinnerstein, Dorothy. "Sometimes You Wonder if They're Human." In Claudia Zanardi (ed.), *Essential Papers on the Psychology of Women.* New York: New York University Press, 1980, 401–419.

DiQuinzio, Patrice. *The Impossibility of Motherhood: Feminism, Individualism and the Problem of Mothering.* New York: Routledge, 1999.

Douglas, Mary. *Purity and Danger: An Analysis of Concepts of Pollution and Taboo.* London, UK: Routledge and Kegan Paul, 1966.

Duncan, Patrick. "Immortality of the Soul in the Platonic Dialogues and Aristotle." *Philosophy* 17, no. 68 (1942): 304–323.
Edmundson, Mark. *The Death of Sigmund Freud*, London: Bloomsbury, 2007.
Ehrenreich, Barbara, and Deirdre English. *Witches, Midwives, and Nurses: A History of Women Healers*. New York: Feminist Press, 2010.
Eigen, Michael. *Psychic Deadness*. Northvale, NJ: Jason Aronson, 1996.
Eigen, Michael. *The Psychoanalytic Mystic*. London: Free Association Books, 1998.
Eigen, Michael. *Toxic Nourishment*. London: Karnac Books, 1999.
Eigen, Michael. *The Sensitive Self*. Middletown, CT: Wesleyan University Press, 2004.
Eigen, Michael. *Feelings Matter*. London: Karnac Books, 2007.
Eigen, Michael. *Madness and Murder*. London: Karnac Books, 2010.
Eigen, Michael. *Kabbalah and Psychoanalysis*. London: Karnac Books, 2012.
Eliade, Mircea. *The Myth of the Eternal Return*. Princeton, NJ: Princeton University Press, 1954.
Eliade, Mircea. *Rites and Symbols of Initiation: The Mysteries of Birth and Rebirth*. New York: Harvill Press, 1958.
Elior, Rachel. *Unity of Opposites: The Mystical Theosophy of Habad*. Jerusalem: Mosad Bialik, 1992.
Elqayam, Abraham. "As a Lily among Thorns: The Secret of the Rose as the Image of All Images in the Zohar." In Avi Elqayam and Shlomy Mualem (eds.), *Kabbalah, Mysticism and Poetry: The Journey to the End of Vision*. Jerusalem: Magnes Press, 2015, 121–241.
Eschel, Ofra. *The Emergence of Analytic Oneness into the Heart of Psychoanalysis*. London: Routledge, 2019.
Ettinger, Bracha L. *The Matrixial Borderspace: Essays from 1994–1999*. Minneapolis: University of Minnesota Press, 2006.
Ettinger, Bracha L. "(M)Other Re-spect: Maternal Subjectivity, the Ready-Made Mother-Monster and the Ethics of Respecting." *Studies in the Maternal* 2, no. 1 (2010): 1–24
Ettinger, Bracha L. "Demeter-Persephone Complex, Entangled Aerials of the Psyche, and Sylvia Plath." *ESC: English Studies in Canada* 40, no. 1 (2014): 123–154.
Faimberg, Haydée. *The Telescoping of Generations: Listening to the Narcissistic Links between Generations*. London: Routledge, 2005.
Feldman, Yael. "And Rebecca Loved Jacob, but Freud Did Not." In Peter L. Rudnytsky and Ellen Handler Spitz (eds.), *Freud and Forbidden Knowledge*. New York: NYU Press, 1994, 7–25.
Felman, Shoshana. *What Does a Woman Want? Reading and Sexual Difference*. Baltimore: Johns Hopkins University Press, 1993.
Fenton, Paul B. "Head between the Knees: Meditation Position in Jewish and Islamic Mysticism." *Daat* 32–33 (1993): 19–29.
Ferenczi, Sándor. "The Unwelcome Child and His Death-Instinct." *International Journal of Psychoanalysis* 10 (1929): 125–129.
Ferenczi, Sándor. "Confusion of the Tongues between the Adults and the Child – The Language of Tenderness and of Passion." *International Journal of Psychoanalysis* 30 (1949): 225–230.
Fine, Lawrence. *Physician of the Soul, Healer of the Cosmos: Isaac Luria and His Kabbalistic Fellowship*. Stanford, CA: Stanford University Press, 2003.
Fishbane, Eitan. "The Scent of the Rose: Drama, Fiction, and Narrative Form in the Zohar." *Prooftexts* 29, no. 3 (2009): 324–361.

Flusser, David. "The Reflection of Jewish Messianic Beliefs in Early Christianity." In Zvi Baras (ed.), *Messianism and Eschatology*. Jerusalem: Zalman Shazar Center, 1983, 103–134. [Hebrew].

Fonrobert, Charlotte Elisheva. *Menstrual Purity: Rabbinic and Christian Reconstruction of Biblical Gender*. Stanford, CA: Stanford University Press, 2000.

Fraiberg, Selma, Edna Adelson, and Vivian Shapiro. "Ghosts in the Nursery: A Psychoanalytic Approach to the Problems of Impaired Infant–Mother Relationships." *Journal of the American Academy of Child & Adolescent Psychiatry* 14, no. 3 (1975): 387–421.

Freud, Sigmund. "Delusion and Dream in Jensen's Gradiva." In James Strachey and Anna Freud (eds.), *The Standard Edition of the Complete Psychological Works of Sigmund Freud*, Vol. 9 (1906–1908): *Jensen's "Gradiva" and Other Works*. London: Vintage, 2001, 7–95.

Freud, Sigmund. "The Taboo of Virginity." In *Collected Papers*. Trans. Joan Riviere. New York: Basic Books, 1959 [1918], 217–235.

Freud, Sigmund. "A Special Type of Object Made by Men (Contributions to the Psychology of Love I)." In James Strachey and Anna Freud (eds.), *The Standard Edition of the Complete Psychological Works of Sigmund Freud*, Vol. 11 (1910): *Five Lectures on Psycho-Analysis, Leonardo da Vinci and Other Works*. London: Vintage, 2001, pp. 163–176.

Freud, Sigmund. "Beyond the Pleasure Principle." In James Strachey and Anna Freud (eds.), *The Standard Edition of the Complete Psychological Works of Sigmund Freud*, Vol. 18 (1920–1922): *Beyond the Pleasure Principle-Group Psychology and Other Works*. London: Vintage, 2001.

Freud, Sigmund. "Civilization and Its Discontents." In James Strachey and Anna Freud (eds.), *The Standard Edition of the Complete Psychological Works of Sigmund Freud*, Vol. 21 (1927–1931): *The Future of an Illusion, Civilization and Its Discontents and Other Works*. London, Vintage, 57–146.

Freud, Sigmund. "Constructions in Analysis." In James Strachey and Anna Freud (eds.), *The Standard Edition of the Complete Psychological Works of Sigmund Freud*, Vol. 23 (1937–1939): *Moses and Monotheism, An Outline of Psycho-Analysis and Other Works*. London: Vintage, 257–269.

Freud, Sigmund. "Inhibitions, Symptoms and Anxiety." In James Strachey and Anna Freud (eds.), *The Standard Edition of the Complete Psychological Works of Sigmund Freud*, Vol. 20 (1925–1926): *An Autobiographical Study, Inhibitions, Symptoms and Anxiety, Lay Analysis and Other Works*. London: Vintage, 87–174.

Freud, Sigmund. "Mourning and Melancholia." In James Strachey and Anna Freud (eds.), *The Standard Edition of the Complete Psychological Works of Sigmund Freud*, Vol. 14 (1914–1916): *An Infantile Neurosis and Other Works*. London: Vintage, 2001, 239–258.

Freud, Sigmund. "On Transience." In James Strachey and Anna Freud (eds.), *The Standard Edition of the Complete Psychological Works of Sigmund Freud*, Vol. 14 (1914–1916): *An Infantile Neurosis and Other Works*. London: Vintage, 2001, 303–307.

Freud, Sigmund. "Three Essays on the Theory of Sexuality." In James Strachey and Anna Freud (eds.), *The Standard Edition of the Complete Psychological Works of Sigmund Freud*, Vol. 7 (1891–1905): *A Case of Hysteria, Three Essays on the Theory of Sexuality, and Other Works*. London: Vintage, 2001, 123–246.

Freud, Sigmund. "The Interpretation of Dreams." In James Strachey and Anna Freud (eds.), *The Standard Edition of the Complete Psychological Works of Sigmund Freud*, Vol. 4 (1900): *The Intrepretaiton of Dreams (The First Part)*. London: Vintage, 2001.

Freud, Sigmund. "Why War?" In James Strachey and Anna Freud (eds.), *The Standard Edition of the Complete Psychological Works of Sigmund Freud*, Vol. 22 (1932–1936): *New Introductory Lectures on Psychoanalysis and Other Works*, 195–216. London: Vintage, 2001.

Freud, Sigmund, and Jacob Breuer. *Studies in Hysteria*. New York: Penguin Books, 2004 (1895).

Fuchs, Esther. *Sexual Politics in the Biblical Narrative*. Sheffield, UK: Sheffield Academic Press, 2003.

Galen. *On the Usefulness of Parts of the Body*, Vol. 2, Book 14. Trans. Margaret T May. Ithaca, NY: Cornell University Press, 1968.

Gamlieli, Dvorah Bat-David. *Psychoanalysis and Kabbalah: The Masculine and Feminine in Lurianic Kabbalah*. Los Angeles: Cherub Press, 2006. [Hebrew].

Garb, Jonathan. *Manifestation of Power in Jewish Mysticism*. Jerusalem: Magnes Press, 2004. [Hebrew].

Garb, Jonathan. *Yearnings of the Soul: Psychological Thought in Modern Kabbalah*. Chicago: University of Chicago Press, 2015.

Gay, Peter. *Freud: A Life for Our Time*. London: Norton Press, 1988.

Gerson, Samuel. "The Relational Unconscious: A Core Element of Intersubjectivity, Thirdness and Clinical Process." *Psychoanalytic Quarterly* 73, no. 1 (2004): 63–98.

Ghent, Emmanuel. "Masochism, Submission, Surrender." *Contemporary Psychoanalysis* 26, no. 1 (1990): 108–135.

Gikatilla, Joseph. *Sha'arei Orah*. Jerusalem: Y. Ben Shlomo, 1981.

Gilbert, Sandra M. and Susan Gubar. *The Madwoman in the Attic: The Woman Writer and the Nineteenth-Century Literary Imagination*. New Haven, CT: Yale University Press, 1979.

Giller, Pinchas. *The Enlightened Will Shine: Symbolization and Theurgy in the Later Strata of the Zohar*. Albany: SUNY Press, 1993.

Giller, Pinchas. *Reading the Zohar: The Sacred Text of the Kabbalah*. Oxford: Oxford University Press, 2000.

Giller, Pinchas. *Shalom Shar'abi and the Kabbalists of Beit El*. New York: Oxford University Press, 2008.

Gilligan, Carol. *In a Different Voice: Psychological Theory and Women's Development*. Cambridge, MA: Harvard University Press, 1982.

Gottlieb, Ephraim. *Studies in Kabbalistic Literature*. Ed. Joseph Hacker. Tel Aviv: Rosenberg, 1976. [Hebrew].

Green, Arthur. *Tormented Master: The Life and Spiritual Quest of Rabbi Nahman of Bratslav*. Tuscaloosa: University of Alabama Press, 1979.

Green, Arthur. "Shekhinah, the Virgin Mary, and the Song of Songs: Reflections on a Kabbalistic Symbol in Its Historical Context." *AJS Review* 26, no. 1 (2002): 1–52.

Grof, Christina, and Stanislav Grof. "Spiritual Emergency: The Understanding and Treatment of Transpersonal Crises." *ReVISION* 8, no. 2 (1986): 7–20.

Gruber, Mayer. "The Motherhood of God in Second Isaiah." *Revue Biblique* 90, no. 3 (1983): 351–359.

Hallamish, Moshe. *The Kabbalah in Liturgy, Halakhah, and Custom*. Ramat Gan: Bar Ilan University Press, 2000. [Hebrew].

Har-Shefi, Avishar. *The Myth of the Edomite Kings in Zoharic Literature*. Los Angeles: Cherub Press, 2015. [Hebrew].

Haskell, Ellen D. *Suckling at My Mother's Breasts: The Image of a Nursing God in Jewish Mysticism*. Albany: SUNY Press, 2012.

Heidegger, Martin. *Being and Time*. Trans. Joan Stambaugh. Rev. Dennis J. Schmidt. Albany: SUNY Press, 2010.
Hellner-Eshed, Melila. "Rabbi Moshe Cordovero's Mythical Midrash on the Fashioning of Ornaments." In Howard Kreisel (ed.), *Study and Knowledge in Jewish Thought*. Beer Sheva: Ben Gurion University Press, 2006, 207–222. [Hebrew].
Hellner-Eshed, Melila. *A River Flows from Eden: The Language of Mystical Experience in the Zohar*. Trans. Nathan Wolski. Stanford, CA: Stanford University Press, 2009.
Hellner-Eshed, Melila. *Seekers of the Face: Secrets of the Idra Rabba (The Great Assembly) of the Zohar*. Stanford, CA: Stanford University Press, 2021.
Hellner-Eshed, Melila. "Engravings and Rollers: Jewelry Design in the Work of Rabbi Moshe Cordovero." In Haim Kreisel (ed.), *Learning and Knowledge in Jewish Thought*. Beer Sheva: Ben Gurion University Press, 2005, 207–222. [Hebrew].
Hesiod. *Theogony*. Ed. Martin L. West. Oxford: Oxford University Press, 1966.
Hirsch, Marianne. *Family Frames: Photography, Narrative, and Postmemory*. Cambridge, MA: Harvard University Press, 1997.
Hoffman, Irwin. "At Death's Door: Therapists and Patients as Agents." *Psychoanalytic Dialogues* 10, no. 6 (2000): 823–846.
Holmes, Helen. *Seeing God in Our Birth Experiences*. New York: Routledge, 2020.
Horney, Karen. *Feminine Psychology*. New York: W. W. Norton, 1967.
Idel, Moshe. *Kabbalah: New Perspectives*. New Haven, CT: Yale University, 1988.
Idel, Moshe. "In the Light of Life: A Study of Kabbalistic Eschatology." In Isaiah M. Gafni and Aviezer Ravitzky (eds.), *Sanctity of Life and Martyrdom: Studies in Memory of Amir Yekutiel*. Jerusalem: Zalman Shazar Center, 1992, 191–211. [Hebrew].
Idel, Moshe. "On the Concept of Zimzum in Kabbalah and Its Research." In Rachel Elior and Yehuda Liebes (eds.), *Lurianic Kabbalah*. Jerusalem: Magnes Press, 1992, 59–112.
Idel, Moshe. *Hasidism: Between Ecstasy and Magic*. Albany: SUNY Press, 1996.
Idel, Moshe. *Messianic Mystics*. New Haven, CT: Yale University Press, 1998.
Idel, Moshe. "The Interpretations of the Secret of the 'Arayyot in Early Kabbalah." *Kabbalah* 12 (2004): 93–103. [Hebrew].
Idel, Moshe. *Enchanted Chains: Techniques and Rituals in Jewish Mysticism*. Los Angeles: Cherub Press, 2005.
Idel, Moshe. *Kabbalah and Eros*. New Haven, CT: Yale University Press, 2005.
Idel, Moshe. *Ben: Sonship and Jewish Mysticism*. New York: Continuum, 2007.
Idel, Moshe. "The Womb and the Infinite in the Kabbalah of R. Moshe Cordovero." *Peamim* 148 (2016): 41–64. [Hebrew].
Idel, Moshe. "Torah Ḥadashah: Messiah and the New Torah in Jewish Mysticism and Modern Scholarship." *Kabbalah* 21 (2010): 57–109.
Idel, Moshe. "Androgynes: Reflections on the Study of Religion." In Grazia Marchianò (ed.), *Labirinti della mente*. Siena: Società Bibliografica Toscana, 2012, 17–47.
Idel, Moshe. *The Privileged Divine Feminine in Kabbalah*. Berlin: De Gruyter, 2018.
Irigaray, Luce. *Speculum of the Other Woman*. Ithaca, NY: Cornell University Press, 1986.
Irigaray, Luce. *Je, Tu, Nous: Towards a Culture of Difference*. New York: Routledge, 1990.
Isaac Ben Samuel, of Acre. "Commentary on a Book of Creation." In *A Book of Creation with a Precious Light: Interpretation from the Ramak*. Jerusalem 1988.
Jacobson, Yoram. "The Aspect of the 'Feminine' in the Lurianic Kabbalah." In Joseph Dan and Peter Schäfer (eds.), *Gershom Scholem's Major Trends in Jewish Mysticism 50 Years After*. Tübingen: J. C. B. Mohr, 1993, 239–255.

James, William. "The Will to Believe." In *The Will to Believe and Other Essays*. London: Longmans, Green, and Co., 1897, 1–32.
James, William. *The Varieties of Religious Experience: A Study in Human Nature*. London: Longmans, Green, and Co., 1902.
Jung, Carl Gustav. *Psychology and Religion*. New Haven, CT: Yale University Press, 1938.
Jung, Carl Gustav. *The Practice of Psychotherapy: Essays on the Psychology of the Transference and Other Subjects*. London: Routledge, 1954.
Jung, Carl Gustav. *Memories, Dreams, Reflections*. Ed. Aniela Jaffé. Trans. Richard Winston and Clara Winston. New York: Vintage, 1965.
Jung, Carl Gustav, and Carl Kerenyi. *Essays on a Science of Mythology: The Myth of the Divine Child and the Mysteries of Eleusis*. Princeton, NJ: Princeton University Press, 1973.
Kaniel, Ruth Kara-Ivanov. "Eve, the Gazelle, and the Serpent: Narratives of Creation and Redemption, Myth and Gender." *Kabbalah* 21 (2010): 255–310. [Hebrew].
Kaniel, Ruth Kara-Ivanov. "Birth – From Metaphor to Reality in Psychoanalysis and Jewish Mysticism." *Psychoanalytic Dialogues* 24, no. 3 (2014): 374–386.
Kaniel, Ruth Kara-Ivanov. "Between Kabbalah, Gender and Law: Sexual Ethics in the Zohar." *AJS Review* 39, no. 1 (2015): 14–51.
Kaniel, Ruth Kara-Ivanov. "'The Impressive Caesura' and 'New Beginning' in Psychoanalysis and Jewish Mystical Experience." In Libby Henik and Lewis Aron, (eds.), *Answering a Question with a Question: The Tradition of Inquiry in Contemporary Psychoanalysis and Jewish Thought*. New York: Routledge, 2015, 40–64.
Kaniel, Ruth Kara-Ivanov. *Holiness and Transgression: Mothers of the Messiah in the Jewish Myth*. New York: Academic Studies Press, 2017.
Kaniel, Ruth Kara-Ivanov. "To Write or Not to Write" In Jonatan Benarroch, Melila Hellner-Eshed, and Yehuda Liebes (eds.), *The Zoharic Story*. Jerusalem: Yad Yitzhak Ben Zvi, 2017, 238–315. [Hebrew].
Kaniel, Ruth Kara-Ivanov. "Gender, Identity, and Fluidity in the Zohar: The Figure of Sarah as a Test Case." *Jerusalem Studies in Hebrew Literature* 31 (2020): 1–49. [Hebrew].
Kaniel, Ruth Kara-Ivanov. *The Feminine Messiah: King David in the Image of the Shekhina in Kabbalistic Literature*. Leiden: Brill, 2021.
Kaniel, Ruth Kara-Ivanov. "Matriarchs and Patriarchs as Sefirot – Multiple Self in Kabbalistic Literature", *Peamim* 157 (2019): 135–175.
Kaplan, Aryeh (ed.). *The Living Torah: The Five Books of Moses and the Haftarot*. Brooklyn, NY: Moznaim, 1981.
Kaplan, Aryeh (ed.). *Rabbi Nachman's Stories: The Stories of Rabbi Nachman of Breslov*. Brooklyn, NY: Breslov Research Institute, 1983.
Kauffman, Tsippi. "Two Tsadikim, Two Women in Labor, and One Salvation: Reading Gender in a Hasidic Story." *Jewish Quarterly Review* 101, no. 3 (2011): 420–438.
Kauffmann, Tsippi. "Birth in Hasidic Literature: Gendered Readings." *Jerusalem Studies in Jewish Literature* 27 (2014): 67–101. [Hebrew].
Kauffmann, Tsippi. *The Reborn Father, Rabbi Nahman of Bratslav and the Baal Shem Tov: Influence and Construction*. Jerusalem: Magnes Press, 2020. [Hebrew].
Kelly, Kathleen Coyne. *Performing Virginity and Testing Chastity in the Middle Ages*. London: Routledge, 2000.
Kierkegaard, Søren. *Repetition: An Essay in Experimental Psychology*. Trans. Walter Lowrie. New York: Harper & Row, 1964.

Kessler, Gwynn. *Conceiving Israel: The Fetus in Rabbinic Narrative*. Philadelphia: University of Pennsylvania Press, 2009.

Klausner, Joseph. *The Messianic Idea in Israel: From Its Beginning to the Completion of the Mishnah*. New York: Macmillan Company, 1955.

Klein, Melanie. "The Importance of Symbol Formation in the Development of the Ego." *International Journal of Psychoanalysis* 11 (1930): 24–39.

Klein, Melanie. "A Contribution to the Theory of Anxiety and Guilt." *International Journal of Psychoanalysis* 29 (1948): 112–123.

Klein, Melanie. "Infantile Anxiety Situations Reflected in a Work of Art and in the Creative Impulse." In Roger Money-Kyrle, Betty Joseph, Edna O'Shaughnessy, and Hanna Segal (eds.), *The Writings of Melanie Klein*, Vol. 1: *Love, Guilt and Reparation, and Other Works 1921–1945*. New York: The Free Press, 1975, 210–218.

Klein, Melanie. "Envy and Gratitude." In Roger Money-Kyrle, Betty Joseph, Edna O'Shaughnessy, and Hanna Segal (eds.), *The Writings of Melanie Klein*, Vol. 3: *Envy and Gratitude and Other Works, 1946–1963*. New York: The Free Press, 1975, 176–235.

Klein, Melanie. "Some Theoretical Conclusions Regarding the Emotional Life of the Infant." In Roger Money-Kyrle, Betty Joseph, Edna O'Shaughnessy, and Hanna Segal (eds.), *The Writings of Melanie Klein*, Vol. 3: *Envy and Gratitude and Other Works, 1946–1963*. New York: The Free Press, 1975, 61–92.

Klein, Melanie. "Weaning." In *Love, Guilt and Reparation: And Other Works 1921–1945*. New York: Delacorte Press, 1975, 290–305.

Knohl, Israel. *The Messiah before Jesus: The Suffering Servant of the Dead Sea Scrolls*. Berkeley: University of California Press, 2002.

Kohlenberger, John R. (III) (ed.). *The Parallel Apocrypha*. New York: Oxford University Press, 1997.

Kohut, Heinz. *The Analysis of the Self*. Chicago: University of Chicago Press. 1971.

Kohut, Heinz. *The Restoration of the Self*. New York: International Universities Press, 1977.

Kohut, Heinz. *How Does Analysis Cure?* Chicago: University of Chicago Press, 2013.

Koren, Sharon. "Immaculate Sarah: Echoes of the Eve/Mary Dichotomy in the Zohar." *Viator* 41, no. 2 (2010): 183–201.

Koren, Sharon. *Forsaken: The Menstruant in Medieval Jewish Mysticism*. Waltham, MA: Brandeis University Press, 2011.

Kristeva, Julia. *Powers of Horror: An Essay on Abjection*. New York: Columbia University Press,1982.

Kristeva, Julia. *In the Beginning Was Love: Psychoanalysis and Faith*. Eugene, OR: Wipf and Stock Publishers, 1987.

Kristeva, Julia. *Black Sun: Depression and Melancholia*. New York: Columbia University Press, 1989.

Kron, Tamar. *Women in Pink*. Tel Aviv: Am Oved, 1989. [Hebrew].

Kushelevsky, Rella. *Penalty and Temptation: Hebrew Tales in Ashkenaz Ms. Parma 2295 (de-Rossi 563)*. Jerusalem: Magnes Press, 2010. [Hebrew].

Lachower, Fischel, and Isaiah Tishby (eds.). *The Wisdom of the Zohar: An Anthology of Texts*, Vol. 1. Trans. David Goldstein. Oxford: Littman Library of Jewish Civilization, 1989.

Lachter, Hartley. *Kabbalistic Revolution: Reimagining Judaism in Medieval Spain*. New Brunswick, NJ: Rutgers University Press, 2014.

Laplanche, Jean. "Seduction, Persecution, Revelation." *International Journal of Psychoanalysis* 76 (1995), 663–682.

Levi-Strauss, Claude. *The Elementary Structures of Kinship*. Boston: Beacon Press, 1969.
Levinas, Emmanuel. "The Trace of the Other." In Mark C. Taylor (ed.), *Deconstruction in Context: Literature and Philosophy*. Chicago: University of Chicago Press, 1986, 345–359.
Levinas, Emmanuel. *Otherwise than Being, or Beyond Essence*. Pittsburgh: Duquesne University Press, 1998.
Lieberman, Saul. *Tosefta ki-Feshutah: A Comprehensive Commentary on the Tosefta*, 10 Vols. New York: Jewish Theological Seminary, 1955–1988. [Hebrew].
Liebes, Yehuda. "Sections of the Zohar Lexicon." PhD diss., Hebrew University, 1976. [Hebrew].
Liebes, Yehuda. "The Messiah of the Zohar: The Messianic Character of R. Shimon bar Yohai." In *The Messianic Idea in Israel: A Study Conference in Honour of the Eightieth Birthday of Gershom Scholem*. Jerusalem: Israel Academy of Sciences and Humanity, 1982, 87–236. [Hebrew].
Liebes, Yehuda. "Zohar ve'Eros." *Alpai'im* 9 (1984): 67–119.
Liebes, Yehuda. "'Two Young Roes of a Doe': The Secret Sermon of Isaac Luria before his Death." *Jerusalem Studies in Jewish Thought* 10 (1992): 113–169. [Hebrew].
Liebes, Yehuda. "Christian Influences in the Zohar." In Arnold Schwartz, Stephanie Nakache, and Penina Peli (trans.), *Studies in the Zohar*. Albany: SUNY Press, 1993, 139–161.
Liebes, Yehuda. "Myth vs. Symbol in the Zohar and Lurianic Kabbalah." In Lawrence Fine (ed.), *Essential Papers on Kabbalah*. New York: New York University, 1995, 212–242.
Liebes, Yehuda. *The Secret of the Sabbatean Faith*. Jerusalem: Mosad Bialik, 1995. [Hebrew].
Liebes, Yehuda. *Ars Poetica in Sefer Yetzira*. Jerusalem: Schocken, 2000.
Liebes, Yehuda. "Indeed, the Shekhinah is a Virgin? On the Book by Arthur Green." *Pe'amim: Studies in Oriental Jewry* 101–102 (2005): 303–313. [Hebrew].
Liebes, Yehuda. "The Zohar and the Tiqqunim: From Renaissance to Revolution." In Ronit Meroz (ed.), *New Developments in Zohar Studies*. Tel Aviv: Chaim Rosenberg School of Jewish Studies, 2007, 251–302. [Hebrew].
Liebes, Yehuda. *The Words of God: The Jewish Myth, Essays and Studies*. Jerusalem: Karmel, 2008. [Hebrew].
Liebes, Yehuda. "A Bride as She Is: On R. Moshe Cordovero, *Ma'ayan Ein Ya'aqov*." *Massekhet* 9 (2009): 191–198. [Hebrew].
Liebes, Yehuda. *God's Story: Collected Essays on the Jewish Myth*. Jerusalem: Carmel Press, 2009. [Hebrew].
Liebes, Yehuda. "Pool and Full of the Bright Book: A Reconsideration." *Kabbalah* 21 (2015), 121–142. [Hebrew].
Little, Margaret. "On Basic Unity." *International Journal of Psychoanalysis* 41 (1960): 377–384.
Little, Margaret. *Psychotic Anxieties and Containment: A Personal Record of an Analysis with D. H. Winnicott*. Northvale, NJ: Jason Aronson, Inc., 1977.
Liver, Jacob. *The House of David from the Fall of the Kingdom of Judah to the Fall of the Second Commonwealth and After*. Jerusalem: Magnes Press, 1959 [Hebrew].
Loewal, Hans W. "On the Therapeutic Action of Psycho-Analysis." *International Journal of Psychoanalysis* 41 (1960): 16–33.
Lorberbaum, Yair. *In God's Image: Myth, Theology, and Law in Classical Judaism*. Cambridge: Cambridge University Press, 2015.
Magid, Shaul. *From Metaphysics to Midrash: Myth, History, and the Interpretation of Scripture in Lurianic Kabbala*. Bloomington: Indiana University Press, 2008.

Magid, Shaul. *Hasidism Incarnate: Hasidism, Christianity, and the Construction of Modern Judaism*. Stanford, CA: Stanford University Press, 2014.

Mahler, Margaret. "A Study of the Separation-Individuation Process and Its Possible Application to Borderline Phenomena in the Psychoanalytic Situation." *Psychoanalytic Study of the Child* 26 (1971): 403–424.

Mahler, Margaret. "Rapprochement Subphase of the Separation Individuation Process." *Psychoanalytic Quarterly* 41, no. 4 (1972): 487–506.

Mahler, Margaret. "Symbiosis and Individuation: The Psychological Birth of the Human Infant." *Psychoanalytic Study of the Child* 29 (1974): 89–106.

Maiello, Suzanne. "The Sound-Object: A Hypothesis about Prenatal Auditory Experience and Memory." *Journal of Child Psychotherapy* 21, no. 1 (1995): 23–41.

Maimonides. *The Code of Maimonides: Book Eleven – The Book of Torts*. Ed. Julian Obermann. Trans. Hyman Klein. New Haven, CT: Yale University Press, 1954.

Margolin, Ron. *Inner Religion: Phenomenology of Inner Religious Life and Its Reflection in Jewish Sources*. Ramat Gan: Bar Ilan University Press, 2011. [Hebrew].

Margolis, Gerald J. "Secrecy and Identity." *International Journal of Psychoanalysis* 47 (1966): 517–522.

Mark, Zvi. *Mysticism and Madness: The Religious Thought of Rabbi Nachman of Bratslav*. London: Continuum, 2009.

Marmorstein, Arthur. *The Old Rabbinic Doctrine of God*. New York: Ktav, 1968.

Martin, Emily. *The Woman in the Body: A Cultural Analysis of Reproduction*. Boston: Beacon Press, 1987.

Mayer, Yakov Z. "The Introduction to the Zohar: Text, Structure and Editing." *Kabbalah* 33 (2015): 153–181. [Hebrew].

Matt, Daniel (trans.). *The Zohar*. Stanford, CA: Stanford University Press, 2004–2017.

McDougall, Joyce. *Theaters of the Mind: Illusion and Truth on the Psychoanalytic Stage*. New York: Basic Books, 1985.

Meltzer, Donald. *The Kleinian Development*, London: Karnac Books, 1978.

Meltzer, Donald. *The Claustrum: An Investigation of Claustrophobic Phenomena*. Perthshire, UK: Clunie Press, 1992.

Meltzer, Donald, and Meg Harris Williams. *The Apprehension of Beauty: The Role of Aesthetic Conflict in Development, Art, and Violence*. London: Karnac Books, 2008.

Meroz, Ronit. "Redemption in the Lurianic Kabbalah." PhD diss., Hebrew University of Jerusalem, 1988. [Hebrew].

Millett, Kate. *Sexual Politics*. London: Virago, 1971.

Milner, Marion. "The Communication of Primary Sensual Experience (The Yell of Joy)." *International Journal of Psychoanalysis* 37 (1956): 278–281.

Mitchell, Stephen. *Hope and Dread in Psychoanalysis*. New York: Basic Books, 1993.

Moi, Toril. "Representation of Patriarchy: Sexuality and Epistemology in Freud's Dora." In Charles Bernheimer and Claire Kahane (eds.), *In Dora's Case: Freud – Hysteria – Feminism*. New York: Columbia University Press, 1985, 181–199.

Montanari, Franco. *The Brill Dictionary of Ancient Greek*. Ed. Madeleine Goh and Chad Shroeder. Washington, DC: Center for Hellenic Studies, 2013.

Mopsik, Charles. *Sex of the Soul: The Vicissitudes of Sexual Difference in the Kabbalah*. Los Angeles: Cherub Press, 2006.

Mowinckel, Sigmund. *He That Cometh: The Messianic Concept in the Old Testament and Later Judaism*. Oxford: Basil Blackwell, 1956.

Naeh, Shlomo. "On Two Hippocratic Concepts in Rabbinic Literature." *Tarbiz* 66, no. 2 (1997): 169–185. [Hebrew].
Neumann, Erich. *The Great Mother an Analysis of the Archetype*. Princeton, NJ: Princeton University Press, 1991.
Newman, Hillel. "The Birth of the Messiah on the Day of the Destruction of the Temple: Historical and Anti-Historical Notes." In *Studies in the History of Ancient Israel Submitted to Uriel Rapoport*, ed. Menachem Mor. Jerusalem: Zalman Shazar Center, 2005, 85–110. [Hebrew].
O'Brien, Mary. *The Politics of Reproduction*. London: Routledge, 1981.
Ogden, Thomas. *The Primitive Edge of Experience*. Northvale, NJ: Jason Aronson, 1989.
Ogden, Thomas. "The Analytic Third: Implications for Psychoanalytic Theory and Technique." *The Psychoanalytic Quarterly* 73 (2004): 167–195.
Ortner, Sherry B. "Is Female to Male as Nature to Culture?" In *Women, Culture, and Society*, ed. Michelle Zimbalist Rosaldo and Louise Lamphere. Stanford, CA: Stanford University Press, 1974, 67–87.
Ostow, Mortimer. *Ultimate Intimacy: The Psychodynamics of Jewish Mysticism*. London: Karnac Books, 1995.
Pachter, Mordechai. "Katnut ('Smallness') and Gadlut ('Greatness') in Lurianic Kabbalah." *Jerusalem Studies in Jewish Thought* 10 (1992): 171–210. [Hebrew].
Palgi-Hacker, Anat. *Mother in Psychoanalysis: A Feminist View*. Tel Aviv: Am Oved. 2005. [Hebrew].
Pardes, Ilana. *Countertraditions in the Bible: A Feminist Approach*. Cambridge, MA: Harvard University Press, 1992.
Pardes, Ilana. *The Biography of Ancient Israel: National Narratives in the Bible*. Berkeley: University of California Press, 2000.
Pedaya, Haviva. *Nahmanides: Cyclical Time and Holy Text*. Tel Aviv: Am Oved, 2003. [Hebrew].
Pedaya, Haviva. *Expanses: An Essay on the Theological and Political Unconscious*. Tel Aviv: Hakibbutz Hameuchad, 2011. [Hebrew].
Pedaya, Haviva. "The Great Mother: The Struggle between Nahmanides and the Zohar Circle." In Sílvia Planas i Marcé and Lídia Donat Pérez (eds.), *Temps i Espais de la Girona Jueva*. Girona, Spain: Patronat Call de Girona, 2011, 311–328.
Pedaya, *Walking through Trauma: Rituals of Movement in Jewish Myth Mysticism and History*. Tel Aviv: Resling, 2011. [Hebrew].
Pedaya, Haviva. *Psychoanalysis and Kabbala*. Tel Aviv: Yediot Aharonot, 2015.
Pedaya, Haviva. "'Possessed by Speech': Towards an Understanding of the Prophetic-Ecstatic Pattern among Early Kabbalists." *Tarbiz* 65, no. 4 (2016): 565–636.
Pelikan, Jaroslav. *Mary through the Centuries: Her Place in the* History of Culture. New Haven, CT: Yale University Press, 1996.
Philo. "That the Worse Is Wont to Attack the Better." In Francis Henry Colson, George Herbert Whitaker, and Ralph Marcus (eds.), *Philo . . . in Ten Volumes*, Vol. 2. London: Heinemann, 1929.
Piontelli, Alessandra. *From Fetus to Child: An Observational and Psychoanalytic Study*. London: Routledge, 1992.
Plato. *Plato with an English Translation*. 12 Vols. Trans. Harold North Fowler. London: Heinemann, 1982.
Plotinus. *Enneads*. Trans. A. H. Armstrong. Cambridge, MA: Harvard University Press, 1978–1988.

Rank, Otto. *The Trauma of the Birth*. New York: R. Brunner, 1957.
Preuss, Julius. *Biblical and Talmudic Medicine*. New York: Sanhedrin Press, 1978.
Rank, Otto. *The Myth of the Birth of the Hero*. New York: Vintage Books, 1959.
Rapoport-Albert, Ada. "Hasidism after 1772: Structural Continuity and Change." In Ada Rapoport-Albert (ed.), *Hasidism Reappraised*. Oxford: The Littman Library of Jewish Civilization, 1996, 76–140.
Rich, Adrian. *Of Woman Born*. New York: W. W. Norton, 1986.
Róheim, Géza. "Fairy Tale and Dream." *Psychoanalytic Study of the Child* 8, no. 1 (1953): 394–403.
Roi, Biti. "The Shout in the Theology of Rav Nachman of Breslav." MA thesis, Hebrew University, 1999 [Hebrew].
Roi, Biti. *Love of the Shekhinah: Mysticism and Poetics in Tiqqunei ha-Zohar*. Ramat Gan: Bar Ilan University Press, 2017. [Hebrew].
Rojtman, Betty. *The Forgiveness of the Moon: Essays on Biblical Tragedy*. Jerusalem: Carmel Publishing, 2008. [Hebrew].
Rosen-Zvi, Ishay. "The Evil Impulse, Sexuality and Yichud: A Chapter of Talmudic Anthropology." *Theory and Criticism* 14 (1999): 55–84. [Hebrew].
Rosenzweig, Franz. *The Star of Redemption*. trans. Barbara E. Galli. Madison: University of Wisconsin Press, 2005.
Rubin, Nissan. *Beginning of Life: Rites of Birth, Circumcision and Redemption of the Firstborn in the Talmud and Midrash*. Tel Aviv: Hakibbutz Hameuchad, 1995. [Hebrew].
Rubin, Steffi. "*Sefer Yetsirah* and the Grammar/Physics of the Divine *Logos* as Noun/Matter *Ratso va-Shov* as Verb/Energy." Master's thesis, Townson University, 2009.
Sachs-Shmueli, Leore. "Seder Gan Eden – Critical Edition and Study (with Annotations by Gershom Scholem)." *Kabbalah* 28 (2012): 191–299.
Sack, Beracha. *The Kabbalah of Rabbi Moshe Cordovero*. Beer Sheva: Ben Gurion University Press, 1995.
Sack, Beracha (ed.). *R. Moshe Cordovero, Ma'ayan Ein Ya'aqov: Ha-Ma'ayan ha-Revi'i me-Sefer Elemah*. Beer Sheva: Ben Gurion University Press, 2009. [Hebrew].
Sacks, Jonathan (trans. and comment.). *The Koren Siddur*. Jerusalem: Koren Publishers, 2009.
Sadler, Michelle, Mário J, Santos, Dolores Ruiz-Berdún, Gonzalo Leiva Rojas, Elena Skoko, Patricia Gillen, and Jette A. Clausen. "Moving beyond Disrespect and Abuse: Addressing the Structural Dimensions of Obstetric Violence." *Reproductive Health Matters* 24, no. 47 (2016): 47–55.
Santner, Eric L. *On the Psychotheology of Everyday Life: Reflections on Freud and Rosenzweig*. Chicago: University of Chicago Press, 2001.
Scarry, Elaine. *The Body in Pain*. New York: Oxford University Press, 1985.
Schachter-Shalomi, Zalman (trans.). *The Open Siddur Project*. https://opensiddur.org/prayers/solilunar/shabbat/erev-shabbat/patah-eliyahu-began-saying-that-we-might-pray-well-from-the-tikkunei-zohar-trans-rabbi-zalman-schachter-shalomi (accessed April 9, 2021).
Schäfer, Peter. *Mirror of His Beauty: Feminine Images of God from the Bible to the Early Kabbalah*. Princeton, NJ: Princeton University Press, 2002.
Schäfer, Peter, and Mark R. Cohen (eds.). *Toward the Millennium: Messianic Expectations from the Bible to Waco*. Leiden: Brill, 1998.
Schneider, Michael. "The Angelomorophic Son of God, Yehoel and the Prince of Peace." *Kabbalah* 21 (2010): 143–254. [Hebrew].

Schneider, Michael. *The Appearance of the High Priest*. Los Angeles: Cherub Press, 2012. [Hebrew].
Scholem, Gershom. *Major Trends in Jewish Mysticism*. New York: Schocken, 1941.
Scholem, Gershom. "Redemption through Sin." In *The Messianic Idea in Judaism*. New York: Schocken, 1971, 78–141.
Scholem, Gershom. "The Crisis of Tradition in Jewish Messianism." In *The Messianic Idea in Judaism*. New York: Schocken, 1971, 49–77.
Scholem, Gershom. "The Messianic Idea in Kabbalism." In *The Messianic Idea in Judaism*. New York: Schocken, 1971, 37–48.
Scholem, Gershom. *Sabbatai Sevi: The Mystical Messiah, 1626–1676*. Princeton, NJ: Princeton University Press, 1973.
Scholem, Gershom. *On the Mystical Shape of the Godhead*. New York: Pantheon Books, 1991.
Scholem, Gershom. *Origins of the Kabbalah*. Princeton, NJ: Princeton University Press, 1991.
Scholem, Gershom. *Mehkarei Kabbala*. Tel Aviv: Am Oved, 1998.
Scholem, Gershom. *Tagebücher: Nebst Aufsätzen und Entwürfen bis 1923. Halbbd 2, 1917–1923*. Ed. Karlfried Gründer, Friedrich Niewöhner, and Herbert Kopp-Oberstebrink. Frankfurt on the Main: Jüdischer Verlag, 1995.
Scholem, Gershom. *Devils, Demons and Souls: Essays on Demonology*. Jerusalem: Ben Zvi Institute, 2004. [Hebrew].
Schwab, Gabriele. "Replacement Children: The Transgenerational Transmission of Traumatic Loss." *American Imago* 66, no. 3 (2009): 277–310.
Scott, Joan W. "Gender: A Useful Category of Historical Analysis." *American Historical Review* 91, no. 5 (1986): 1053–1075.
Showalter, Elaine. "Feminist Criticism in the Wilderness." *Critical Inquiry* 8, no. 2 (1981): 179–205.
Smith, Geoffrey (trans.). *Valentinian Christianity: Texts and Translations*. Oakland, CA: University of California Press.
Sobol, Neta. *Transgression of the Torah and the Rectification of God*. Los Angeles: Cherub Press, 2017.
Sokoloff, Michael. *A Dictionary of Jewish Palestinian Aramaic of the Byzantine Period*. Ramat Gan: Bar Ilan University Press, 1990.
Spero, Moshe Halevi. "The Civilization of Discontent Notes on the Hidden Sources of Unbehagen in Freud's Analysis of Civilization." *The Psychoanalytic Study of the Child* 61, no. 1 (2008): 221–253.
Spezzano, Charles. "A Home for the Mind." *Psychoanalytical Quarterly* 76 (2007): 1563–1583.
Sprengnether, Madelon "Enforcing Oedipus: Freud and Dora." In Charles Bernheimer and Claire Kahane (eds.), *In Dora's Case: Freud – Hysteria – Feminism*. New York: Columbia University Press, 1985, 254–275.
Starr, Karen E. *Repair of the Soul: Metaphors of Transformation in Jewish Mysticism and Psychoanalysis*. New York: Routledge, 2008.
Stein, Ruth. "The Enigmatic Dimension of Sexual Experience: The 'Otherness' of Sexuality and Primal Seduction." *The Psychoanalytic Quarterly* 67, no. 4 (1998): 594–625.
Stein, Ruth. "The Otherness of Sexuality: Excess." *Journal of the American Psychoanalytic Association* 56 (2008): 43–71.
Stern, Daniel N. *The Interpersonal World of the Infant: A View from Psychoanalysis and Developmental Psychology*. New York: Basic Books, 1985.

Tamari, Assaf. "Human Sparks: Readings in the Lurianic Theory of Transmigration and Its Concept of the Human Subject." MA thesis, Tel Aviv University, 2009. [Hebrew].
Tamari, Assaf. "The Discourse of the Body in the Lurianic Kabbalah." PhD diss., Ben Gurion University, 2016. [Hebrew].
Tanna de-Ve Eliyahu: The Lore of the School of Elijah. Trans William G. Braude and Israel J. Kapstein. Philadelphia: Jewish Publication Society of America, 1981.
Thorne, Barry and Marilyn Yalom (eds.). *Rethinking the Family: Some Feminist Questions*. New York: Longman, 1982.
Tishby, Isaiah. *Hekrai Kabbalah ve-Shelukhoteihah* [Studies in Kabbalah and Its Branches], Vol. 1. Jerusalem: Magnes Press, 1982. [Hebrew].
Tishby, Isaiah. *The Wisdom of the Zohar*, Vol. 2. Oxford: Littman Library of Jewish Civilization, 1989.
Tishby, Isaiah. *The Doctrine of Evil and the "Kelippah" in Lurianic Kabbalism*. Jerusalem: Magnes Press, 1992.
Trible, Phyllis. "Depatriarchalizing in Biblical Interpretation." *Journal of the American Academy of Religion* 42, no. 1 (1973): 30–48.
Trible, Phyllis. *God and the Rhetoric of Sexuality*. Philadelphia: Fortress Press, 1985.
Turner, Victor. *The Ritual Process: Structure and Anti-Structure*. Chicago: Aldine, 1969.
Tustin, Frances. "Psychological Birth and Psychological Catastrophe." In *Autistic States in Children*. London: Routledge, 1981, 96–110. https://www.amazon.com/Autistic-States-Children-Frances-Tustin/dp/0415081297
Urbach, Ephraim E. *The Sages: Their Concepts and Beliefs*. Trans. Israel Abrahams. Cambridge, MA: Harvard University Press, 1975.
Urbach, Ephraim E. *The World of the Sages: Collected Studies*. Jerusalem: Magnes Press, 1988. [Hebrew].
Valabregue-Perry, Sandra. *Concealed and Revealed: Ein Sof in Theosophic Kabbalah*. Los Angeles Cherub Press, 2000.
Van Gennep, Arnold. *The Rites of Passage*. Chicago: University of Chicago Press, 1960.
Weinstein, Ronnie. *Break the Dishes: Jewish Kabbalah and Modernity*. Tel Aviv: Tel Aviv University Press, 2011.
Weiss, Joseph. *Mehkarim Behasidut Braslav*. Jerusalem: Mosad Bialik, 1974.
Weiss, Tzahi. *Cutting the Shoots*. Jerusalem: Magnes Press, 2015.
Wilheim, Joanna. "The Trauma of Conception: Cellular Memory." Paper presented at the Brazilian Psychoanalytical Society of São Paulo, October 2005.
Winnicott, Donald W. "The Theory of the Parent–Infant Relationship." *International Journal of Psychoanalysis* 41 (1960): 585–595.
Winnicott, Donald W. "A Personal View of the Kleinian Contribution." In *The Maturational Processes and the Facilitating Environment*. New York: International University Press, 1965, 171–178.
Winnicott, Donald W. "Ego Distortion in Terms of True and False Self." In *The Maturational Process and the Facilitating Environment: Studies in the Theory of Emotional Development*. New York: International Universities Press Inc., 1965, 140–152.
Winnicott, Donald W. *The Maturational Processes and the Facilitating Environment: Studies in the Theory of Emotional Development*. New York: International University Press, 1965.
Winnicott, Donald. W. "The Use of an Object." *International Journal of Psychoanalysis* 50 (1969): 711–716.
Winnicott, Donald W. *Playing and Reality*. London: Tavistock, 1971.

Winnicott, Donald W. *The Child, the Family, and the Outside World*. London: Penguin Books, 1973.
Winnicott, Donald W. "Fear of Breakdown." *International Journal of Psychoanalysis* 37 (1974): 386–388.
Winnicott, Donald W. "Birth Memories, Birth Trauma and Anxiety." In *Through Paediatrics to Psycho-Analysis*. London: The Hogarth Press, 1975, 173–192.
Winnicott, Donald W. *Through Paediatrics to Psycho-Analysis*. London: The Hogarth Press, 1975.
Winnicott, Donald W. *Babies and Their Mothers*. Cambridge, MA: Perseus Publishing, 1987.
Winnicott, Donald W. *Human Nature*. London: Free Association Books, 1988.
Winnicott, Donald W. *Psycho-Analytic Explorations*, London: Karnac Books, 1989.
Wittgenstein, Ludwig. *On Certainty*. Ed. G.E.M. Anscombe. Trans. Denis Paul. Oxford: Blackwell, 2008.
Wolfson, Elliot (ed.). *The Book of the Pomegranate: Moses de Leon's Sefer ha-Rimmon*. Atlanta: Scholars Press, 1988.
Wolfson, Elliot. *Through a Speculum That Shines: Vision and Imagination in Medieval Jewish Mysticism*. Princeton, NJ: Princeton University Press, 1994.
Wolfson, Elliot. *Circle in the Square: Studies in the Use of Gender in Kabbalistic Symbolism*. Albany: SUNY Press, 1995.
Wolfson, Elliot. *Language, Eros, Being: Kabbalistic Hermeneutics and Poetic Imagination*. New York: Fordham University Press, 2005.
Wolfson, Elliot. *Venturing Beyond: Law and Morality in Kabbalistic Mysticism*. Oxford: Oxford University Press, 2006.
Yassif, Eli. *The Tales of Ben Sira in the Middle Ages: A Critical Text and Literary Studies*. Jerusalem: Magnes Press, 1985. [Hebrew].
Yerushalmi, Yosef Hayim. *Freud's Moses: Judaism Terminable and Interminable*. New Haven, CT: Yale University Press, 1993.
Yisraeli, Oded. *Interpretation of Secrets and the Secret of Interpretation*. Los Angeles, Cherub Press, 2005. [Hebrew].
Yisraeli, Oded. *Temple Portals: Studies in Aggadah and Midrash in the Zohar*. Jerusalem: Magnes Press, 2013. [Hebrew].
Zalman, Shneur. *Likutei Amarim – Tanya*. London: Kehot Publication Society, 1981.

Index

*The encounter between Kabbalistic sources and psychoanalysis stands at the center of this work. Thus, contemporary psychoanalytic thinkers will be mentioned in the Index, as they serve as objects of study, as opposed to scholars of Kabbalah, Talmud, and the Bible, who are mentioned throughout the book and in relevant footnotes.

Aaron 178
abandonment, maternal abandonment 29, 55, 63, 81, 101, 149
abjection 88, 155–156
Abraham 181
Abraham, Carl 69
Abulafia, Abraham 25, 86
abyss 20, 31, 34, 68, 72, 75, 114, 128, 139
Adah 112
Adam 3, 82, 84–89, 104, 140–141, 203, 211
adrenal gland 96
adrenaline 96, 203
aesthetic conflict (Meltzer) 50–52, 124
agency 60, 72, 98, 184
aggressiveness 5, 21, 39–42, 54–55, 59, 117, 142, 173
aggressiveness, anger, damage 40, 55, 81, 102–104, 172
Aharoni, Hagit 68, 76
air 28, 33–34, 91, 138
allegory and symbols 1–2, 13, 24, 26, 35–36, 43, 45, 47, 59, 63, 67, 77, 80, 83–84, 88, 91–92, 94, 99, 101, 103, 105–106, 108, 112–115, 124–128, 135–140, 142–145, 151–152, 166–169, 174–178, 182, 184, 188, 193, 195–196, 198, 201, 208, 210, 213–215, 217, 220
– allegory of ravens and charity 215–216
– allegory of souls and ships 214
– allegory of the animal 110
– allegory of the artist 13
– allegory of the boiling pot 24
– allegory of the bucket 167–169
– allegory of the nut 121
– allegory of the purse 24, 97, 101–103, 110, 125
– allegory of the womb as a prison 11, 24, 97–103, 106, 168

– baby as guest and mother as master of the house 186
– miscarriage 30
– Parable of the Barriers and Walls 160
– Plato's allegory of the Cave 160
– the parable of the fox in the vineyard 116
– the *tsela*, allegories of the creation of the female 84
– thighs and legs 74, 108, 111, 176, 186
alpha function and beta function 18, 172, 220
Alvarez, Anne 81
Amir, Dana 34, 220
androgynous 82–83, 85–87, 131, 141, 144, 164–165
– spiritual androgynous (androgynous soul) 85, 87
angel 15, 85, 109, 118–120, 136, 194, 196, 199
– Angel of Death 109
animal 89, 102–103, 110, 175, 186, 201, 211, 215–216
annihilation 19, 23, 28–29, 32, 38–39, 81, 112, 155, 159, 167, 190, 198, 205, 220
anxiety 21, 28–29, 41, 46, 69, 74–75, 93, 103, 117, 156, 161, 173, 204
– birth as the source of anxiety 39, 69, 104, 198, 220
– death anxiety 12, 17, 36, 38, 41, 103
– anxiety of not being 17–19, 23, 29–30, 32, 34, 41, 208
apocalypse 195, 198
Arikh Anpin ("the Great Countenance") 172, 187
Aristotle 11, 122, 154
Aron, Lewis 9, 42, 144, 181
as a home 114
Atlas, Galit 75
authority, struggle for authority 9, 108, 199, 205

Index

Baal Shem Tov 17, 32, 160, 208
baby 1, 3, 5, 23, 33, 40, 42–43, 49–51, 69, 75–76, 78, 84, 101, 103, 111, 114, 122, 124, 166, 186–188, 204, 209
– *puer aeternus* 204
back to back (*ahor be-ahor*) 27, 82–84, 87–88
Balaskas, Janet 96, 98
Balint, Michael 9, 35, 59, 69, 140, 190
bar Yohai, Shimon 139, 172, 217
basic fault (Balint) 45
Bataille, Georges 50
Bathsheba 52
beast 100, 102, 110–111, 142
beauty 50, 101, 103, 186
becoming O (Bion) 3
beginning V, 3, 8, 11–12, 16, 21, 33, 36, 38–42, 47, 49, 58–59, 62, 64, 71, 73, 77, 88–89, 93, 105, 108, 114, 118, 127, 129–131, 135, 137–141, 145, 147–148, 152, 159, 161–162, 166–168, 177, 187, 190, 196, 198, 200, 205, 210–211, 213–217, 219–221
– beginning of emanation 145
Benjamin, Jessica 9, 77, 161, 188
Bergstein, Avner 68, 73, 76
Bernard of Clairvaux 176
be-rosh hurmanuta de-malka (At the head of potency of the king) 129, 137–141
Binah 7, 14, 17, 19–20, 22–24, 26, 36, 48–49, 52–56, 60–63, 117, 128–137, 141–143, 153, 165, 167–168, 171, 173–175, 177–178, 181–188, 192–194, 217
– as great mother 14, 23, 56, 62, 165–167, 174, 185, 202
– as repentance 167
– as Supernal Mother 134, 136
– as the "World to Come" 167
– as the hidden world 63
– as the source of judgments 167, 177
– as the Supernal Mother 24, 52–53, 55–56, 62, 168, 185–186, 193
– relationship to the *Shekhinah* 54, 129–130, 137, 171, 174, 189, 183–184

Bion, Wilfred 3, 5, 16, 18–19, 32–34, 40–43, 56, 58, 68, 73, 77, 90, 98, 117, 119, 123, 138, 144, 161, 187, 218
birth V, 1, 3–4, 5, 8, 11–20, 22–49, 51, 53–56, 5961, 73, 75–79, 81–82, 86–90, 92–94, 96–99, 101–116, 118, 120–131, 134–135, 137–142, 144–148, 150, 153–155, 157–160, 163–166, 168–175, 180, 182–193, 195–207, 209–213, 215–221
– and death 16–17, 24, 28, 31, 36, 46, 61, 65, 69, 74, 97, 104–108, 110, 112, 114–115, 155, 158, 184, 186, 188–189, 196, 202, 219
– as a metaphor 25, 99, 106, 158, 166, 195, 198, 207, 215–217
– as redemption 99, 180, 186, 195, 197–199, 201–203, 205–206, 209, 211–212, 215–217
– as the source of anxiety 29
– birth of the hero 124
– birth throes 196
– birthing technique 47, 58, 197, 218
– danger 29, 69, 100, 106–107, 112, 186, 198, 220
– ethics of birth 46, 66–67
– first cry, birth cry 93
– male birth, paternal birth 131, 140–141
– medicalization of birth 70, 169
– metaphorical 43, 118, 124, 219
– non-birth 23
– pain 105
– pangs 56, 74, 96, 98–99, 105–107, 109, 112, 127, 199–200, 206, 218
– psychological 78, 81, 87, 190
– rebirth 19, 26, 41, 43, 45, 155, 167, 169, 182, 196, 207, 218
– stillbirth 30, 207–210
birth instruments
– forceps 169
– vacuum 169
bisexual 83
blending, merging, fusion 6, 32, 38, 51, 66, 79, 83, 85–86, 88–89, 147
blessing 24, 88, 106, 111, 132, 153, 170, 175–178

– Gomel [bestows good on the unworthy] 177
blindness 116, 161, 212–214
blood 24, 36, 44–45, 47–49, 61, 63, 65, 77, 92, 94, 102, 105, 109–110, 113–114, 116, 122, 125, 150–152, 157, 177, 188–189, 198, 202, 205, 207
Bohu 30, 94
Bollas, Christopher 19, 31, 42, 49, 51, 121
bowels 33, 100–101
breach 7
breakdown, breakthrough, break in unity 6, 23, 41, 75–76, 115
breaking of the vessels 51, 159, 214
breastfeeding [nursing] 16, 26, 48–49, 75, 103, 110, 141, 170, 172–178, 180–183, 185–186, 189–190, 209
– as allegory 48, 170–171, 173–176, 178, 180
breasts 48–50, 90, 101, 103, 141–142, 170–173, 176–179
– Eldad and Medad and Moses and Aaron as breasts 177
– good breast and bad breast 21, 29, 49, 173–174, 179
– right breast as *Hesed* and left breast as *Din* 49
Bromberg, Philip 6, 9
Buber, Martin 56
butzina de-kardinuta (a spark of impenetrable darkness) 221
Bynum, Caroline 141

caesura 33, 56, 68–69, 71–73, 75–78, 81–82, 86–88, 90, 93, 98–99, 111, 115, 187, 190, 214
Campbell, Joseph 124, 169
Cassuto, Umberto 46
Castile Kabbalah 19, 167
catastrophe 74, 85
– catastrophic change 16, 205
– catastrophic threat 34
chaos 138–139, 147
charity 215–216
Chasseguet-Smirgel, Janine 20
Chodorow, Nancy 60, 163

Christianity 3, 9, 11, 41, 44, 54, 104–105, 124–125, 141, 146, 151–152, 195, 203–204
– asceticism, abstinence 45, 151–152
– confession and atonement 109, 114
– immersion, baptism 32, 203
– myths about birth 41, 124
circumcision 8, 203, 205
Cixous, Hélène 46, 124
Closed *Mem* (ם) and an Open *Mem* (מ) 163–164, 166, 204
Cohen, Hila 81
Cohen Shabot, Sara 70
Combined Parental Figure 141–145, 213
communitas 174–175, 217
complex 5, 9, 34, 39, 43, 60, 63, 67, 78, 108, 118, 161, 177, 202
– Oedipus complex 42–43, 148, 182
conception, preconception 9, 19, 26, 28–29, 32, 41, 48–51, 60, 62, 66–67, 72, 76, 81, 85, 90–92, 94, 99, 106, 115, 118, 123–126, 140, 149, 152–153, 160, 170, 178, 186, 198, 200–201, 204, 207, 217
concession 14, 20–21, 57, 116
congeal 91, 94
conscious, unconscious 1, 4–6, 7, 13, 16, 32, 43–44, 52, 62, 70, 72–73, 76–78, 81, 119, 121, 126, 138, 140, 144–145, 147, 164, 168–169, 180–190, 203, 210, 212, 215, 218–219
– unrepressed unconscious 138
consciousness 96
continuity of being (Winnicott) 180
contractions 34, 96, 188, 203
– harsh contractions 96, 186
conversion, converts, souls of the converts 27–28, 174
Cordovero, Moses 25–26, 97, 132, 136, 147, 175–176, 180, 191, 193
cosmology, cosmogony 91
counter-transference 5
Couvade Syndrome 105, 140
creation 33, 35, 89, 91, 127, 140, 180, 186, 196, 198, 217
creation from the void 138
creation of the world 16, 24, 139, 198

crisis 23, 36–37, 41, 53, 73–76, 115, 121, 135, 179, 186, 195, 210, 212, 218
crying, weeping, tears 30, 109, 115, 120, 132, 179, 197, 203, 210–211

de Beauvoir, Simone 60, 103, 111, 153
de Leon, Moses 22, 24, 165
death 1, 7, 9, 11–12, 13, 14, 16–19, 23–24, 28–32, 36–42, 45–46, 59, 61, 64–65, 69, 73–74, 81, 90, 93, 96–97, 100, 103–116, 120, 148, 154–155, 158, 165, 173, 179, 182–184, 186–190, 196–198, 201–202, 205, 207–210, 212, 214–215, 219–220
– desire for death 96
– of the Edomite kings 31, 71, 148
– of the fetus 28, 207
decoration, adornment 84–85, 88, 133–135, 181
dependence 34, 47, 56, 58, 87, 94, 161
depression 7, 21, 39
– depressive position 7, 21, 39
– postpartum 56, 105, 109, 112, 183, 189
despair 57, 74, 96, 111
destruction 21, 30, 32, 34, 55, 57, 70, 117, 148, 156, 178, 204, 208, 215
Deutsch, Helene 54
Din (judgment) 7, 20, 60–61, 91–92
Dinnerstein, Dorothy 60
DiQuinzio, Patrice 64
dissociation 6, 120
divine countenances, faces (*partzufim*) 13, 25, 27, 82, 153, 172, 183–187, 199
divine providence 28, 108, 171
Divinity
– Divinity in human form 147, 149
Douglas, Mary 152
dreams 150–151, 157
Duncan, Patrick 12
du-partzufim (double faces) 82–83
Devekut (cleaving or communion with God) 51, 175
dyad/symbiosis 5, 16, 22, 43, 49–51, 56, 60, 67, 70, 76–77, 79, 82, 87–89, 132, 146, 162, 168, 175, 186, 188, 204, 220

eagle 212, 214
Egypt 9, 27, 179, 186, 198, 203, 205

Ehyeh (name of God, *Ehyeh Asher Ehye*, *Binah*) V, 177
Eigen, Michael 9, 19
El Shaddai (God with Breasts) 48, 177–178
Eldad and Medad 177–178
Eliade, Mircea 16, 106, 144
Elijah 21, 215
Elkanah 112
Elohim 133, 141, 177, 210
– as designation for *Binah* 130–131, 134
– commentaries on "*bereshit bara et Elohim*" 131
emanation 16, 23, 93, 123, 131, 146, 153, 168, 180, 190, 210, 214, 217, 220
emergent/continuous principle of the self (Amir) 220
empathy 60, 216
enclothing, garments 16, 53, 107–108, 133–137, 183, 217
endorphins 97
Ephraim of Sudilkov 160
eros 1–2, 4, 26, 38–39, 61, 83, 86, 103, 131–132, 136, 140, 149, 153–154, 171, 173, 214, 220
Esther 106, 141
eternity/eternal 11, 13–15, 24, 36, 42, 59, 62, 204, 219
euphoria 97
Eve 46, 83–89, 104–106, 109, 140–141, 199, 203
Existentialism, existential 1, 11–13, 16–17, 23, 31, 35–36, 41, 88, 104, 111, 195, 209, 218–219
extraction 98, 167, 169
eyes 3, 47, 113, 127, 129, 132, 143, 159–160, 171–172, 181

face to face 27, 62, 87–88, 168
faith 3, 5, 12, 47, 49, 81, 96, 208
falling 15–16, 41, 66, 75, 87–88, 100–101, 151, 183, 192
false/true self (Winnicott) 19, 83
family 31, 56
– divine family 142
– family romance 44
– Holy Family 45

– relations between Divine and humans as family 56
fatherhood 1, 8–9, 15–16, 20, 26, 29, 42, 46–47, 55, 67, 91–92, 102, 116, 123, 125–126, 128–129, 131, 137, 140–145, 147, 165, 175, 185, 194, 203, 217
fear 12, 16–17, 18, 19, 23–24, 29–30, 33–34, 36, 38–41, 60–61, 73, 76, 96–97, 101, 113, 115, 119, 124, 126, 143, 147, 150, 152, 154, 197–199, 202, 204–205, 208, 214, 217, 220
– of not being born 19, 38
– thalamic fear 33–34
feminine internal organs 183
feminism 10, 44–45, 58, 60–62, 70, 76, 124, 163, 169, 184
Ferenczi, Sándor 45, 69, 81
fertility 25–27, 44, 47–48, 87, 100, 112, 135, 154, 183, 215, 217
fetus 3, 5, 13, 15, 26, 28, 31, 33–36, 44, 50, 57, 64–71, 73, 76–77, 87, 89–91, 96–103, 105, 108, 110, 112, 115–116, 118–121, 123–125, 150, 154, 158, 162–163, 165–166, 169–170, 172, 175, 185–188, 190, 201–207, 209–210, 213–216, 220
first dot/first point 139, 144–145, 170
flame, flame arising from the ember 148
flood 32, 57, 75
forbidden sexual relationships 143
forgetting 15, 37–38, 43, 117–119, 121, 197, 213, 221
free will 16, 219
Freud, Sigmund V, 3, 5–6, 7, 8, 9, 23, 28–29, 38–39, 41–45, 49, 68, 81, 117, 124, 138, 140, 148, 150, 169, 179, 182, 187, 189, 193
Fuchs, Esther 152

Galen 92
Gaon, Saadia 85
Garden of Eden V, 15–16, 27, 85, 97, 104, 116, 118–119, 206, 220
garment 16, 53, 107–108, 133–137, 183, 217
gazelle/doe 102, 175, 184, 201–206, 211, 216

gender 1, 4, 9, 36, 49, 63, 85, 94, 97–99, 128, 130, 134, 146, 153, 156, 164, 174, 186, 217
– gender theories 4
genitalia 20, 47, 149, 202
geographical confusion (Meltzer) 51–52
Gevurah (attribute and *sefirah*) V, 7, 61, 171, 187
ghost 31, 181
ghosts, ancestors (Loewald) 73, 181
Gikatilla, Joseph 154, 167–168, 173
Girona, Kabbalah of Girona 19, 157–158
Gnosticism 146–147, 157–158, 169
grave 113
Great Mother 14, 19, 23, 56, 62, 124, 166–167, 174, 185, 202
Greenacre, Phyllis 69–70
Gruber, Mayer 197
guilt 21, 54, 61, 96, 101–102, 104–106, 109, 114, 117
gynocritics 131

Habad Hasidism 17, 59, 159, 206
Hannah 112
harsh judgments 24, 176, 205
head 15, 34, 62, 64–65, 70, 72, 96, 118, 120, 123, 128–132, 137–138, 140–141, 144–145, 151, 163, 165, 171, 174, 187, 202, 204, 206, 221
health 6, 44, 55–56, 58–59, 77, 80, 84, 102, 142, 144, 181, 207
Heidegger, Martin 12
Hesed (*sefirah*) 7, 20, 49, 60, 91–92, 138, 177, 187
Hesiod 122
Hippocrates 92, 98
hitpashtut (spreading) 27, 117, 160
Hod (*sefirah*) 186
Hoffman, Irwin 9
Hokhmah (*sefirah*), father, beginning, will 20, 22, 55, 128, 130, 137–139, 141–142, 167–168, 170, 181–182, 185–187, 214
Holmes, Helen 5
Homer 122
hormenuta 139
Horney, Karen 123

hypostasis 22
hypothalamus 96, 203

ibbur (impregnation) 3, 26–27, 32, 41, 45–46, 74, 123, 145, 150, 153, 175, 178, 180–185, 191–193, 207, 213, 220
– virginal conception 124
identification
– projective identification 40
idolatry 198
Idra, Idra literature 53, 171–172, 175, 187
image of God 13, 41, 46, 63, 87, 89
impurity 7, 106, 111, 157
incest 5, 22, 124, 143, 145
incorporation 10, 21
individuation 78–79, 83–84, 103, 135, 156
infancy 1, 3, 5, 18, 21–22, 24, 26, 28–31, 34, 36, 39–44, 46, 48–51, 55–67, 69–72, 75–80, 82–83, 86–90, 92–94, 96, 98–99, 101, 107–108, 110–111, 115, 117–121, 126, 137, 140, 144–145, 159, 161–164, 166, 170–176, 178–180, 200, 204, 207, 209–211, 219–220
infertility 206
Infinity (*Ein Sof*) 14, 16, 19, 20, 132, 137, 139, 147, 159, 162, 203
initiation 44, 106, 172
integration/disintegration 7, 41, 58, 75–76, 142, 144, 168
internal world 142
intestines (as a metaphor for womb) 185, 194
intuition V, 33, 68, 119
– embryonic intuition 33, 119
Irigaray, Luce 60, 76, 89, 162
Isaac of Acre 148
Isaac the Blind 148

Jacob 111, 153, 181
jealousy 21, 29, 39, 45, 57, 83, 103, 110, 117, 123–124, 126, 142, 178
Jerusalem 197
Jesus 29, 41, 176, 205
Joseph 182
Joshua ben Samuel Nehemia 150
Jubilee 52–53
Jung, Carl 22–23, 103, 169, 212–213

kelipot (husks) 14, 93, 190, 214
Kernberg, Otto 9
Kessler, Gwynn 125
Keter 137, 139, 145, 147, 167–168, 171, 192
Kierkegaard, Søren 219
King David 134, 163, 200, 202, 217
Kings of Edom, death of the Kings 30
Klein, Melanie 5, 7, 9, 21, 23, 28, 39, 42, 45, 49, 68–69, 141–142, 148, 170, 173–174, 178, 181, 189, 193
Kohut, Heinz 6, 9, 43, 80
kotel (shared wall) 62
Kristeva, Julia 49, 138, 152, 155–156

Laplanche, Jean 49–50
Leah 52
leap 151
– leap of faith 151
Levinas, Emmanuel 11, 66–67
light
– illumination 1, 47, 91–92, 94, 159–160, 172, 181, 186
Lilith 84–85, 156
Little, Margaret 59, 190
Loewald, Hans 43, 181
Lorberbaum, Yair 13
love 7, 13, 17–18, 21, 24, 27, 29, 40, 47, 55, 62, 81, 83, 85, 103, 115, 127, 142, 151, 157, 173, 178, 194, 220
– love and hate (Klein) 21, 157, 173
Luria, Isaac 3, 24, 26, 30–31, 34, 55, 58, 62, 87–89, 109, 161, 173, 175–178, 180–191, 193, 203, 206, 211
Luzzatto, Moshe Hayyim 62
lyrical dimension (Amir) 220

magic 144, 216
Mahler, Margaret 78, 80, 88
Maiello, Suzanne 42
Maimonides 65, 195
Makom, Makor (divine source) 47, 80, 149
Malkhut 20, 24, 26, 52–53, 54, 55, 88, 90, 132–137, 142–143, 153, 167, 174–175, 185, 191–192
marriage 16, 42, 62, 73, 90, 124, 150–151, 153–154, 158, 211
Martin, Emily 70, 98

martyrdom 26, 136, 180, 188, 208–209
Mary 41, 44, 105, 112, 125, 204
masochism 38, 156
McDougall, Joyce 7
mehabbalta, appellation for birther 107–108
Meltzer, Donald 5, 9, 42, 49–51, 141–142, 144, 148, 181, 193
memory 2, 30–33, 35–37, 43, 53, 70, 72–73, 76, 80, 99, 117, 120–122, 136, 169, 191, 205–206, 213, 215, 220
- birth memory 205
- fetal memory 32, 68, 73, 98
menstruation 110, 156, 203
Messiah
- mother of the Messiah 41
Messiah, Redeemer 41, 99, 125, 195–196, 198–200, 203, 205, 209
- as the son of God 125, 198
- pangs of 99, 199–200
messianism 127, 175, 195, 218
Mi (name for Binah) 132–133, 177
midrashim on birth
- hayetha, mehabbalta, mitbara 107–108
- the life of the mother has priority over the fetus 64
- May He who answered you mother answer you 106
- the Holy One, fashions a form of a fetus 13
- There are three keys maintained 114
- This world is like a vestibule before the World to Come 16
- Those who have been born [are destined] to die 115
- three partners in man 46
- three voices that are never lost 115
- three within three 183
- what was closed is opened 35
- Without your consent you were born 14, 116
midwife 96, 122, 124
milk 45, 75, 110, 117, 124–125, 170–172, 174–179, 188–189, 207
- blood into milk 207
Millett, Kate 152
mind 5, 68, 73, 82, 92, 121–123, 126, 175, 189, 193, 214
mirroring 6, 45, 66, 92, 204

miscarriage 207
misogyny 98, 102, 152, 155
Mitbara (appellation for birther) 107
Mitchell, Stephen 6, 9
moḥin (consciousness, lit. brains) 26–27, 140, 180–187, 210
Moore, George Edward 219
Moses 7, 9, 25, 29, 48, 124, 130, 178, 180, 182, 191, 202
mother 1, 3, 5, 9, 13, 15, 18, 21–22, 24, 28–29, 33–36, 39–67, 69–72, 75–83, 86–89, 91–94, 96, 98–116, 118, 120, 122–126, 128–131, 133–137, 141–145, 147, 149–153, 155, 157–158, 161–166, 168–180, 183–190, 193–194, 197, 200, 203–206, 208–210, 214–218, 220–221
- blame of the mother 104
- Lost mother 51, 155
- maternal matrix 20, 45
- Mother as a beacon 79
- Mother as a screen or partition 33, 71, 89
- mother as a threat 60, 91
- mother as subject 1, 44, 163
- motherhood and God 46, 48–50, 56
- perfect/ideal mother 61
- multiple self; multiplicity of the self (Bromberg/Mitchell) 6, 22, 144, 166, 184
- multiplicity of source 146–151
mutual recognition (Benjamin) 49, 77
mysticism/mystical experience 2–3, 4, 7, 16, 22, 26, 43, 46, 49, 51, 61–62, 79–80, 87–88, 118, 128, 130, 132, 137–138, 140–142, 147–148, 154, 157, 162, 169, 171, 174–175, 180, 182–183, 190, 206–207, 209, 214, 216–217, 219

Nahmanides 19, 154, 167
Narcissism 155
nefilat apayim, (ritual of "falling on the face") 183
negative capability (Bion) 138
neocortex 96, 203
Neoplatonism 47, 93, 131, 137, 146–147, 157–159

Netsaḥ (sefira) 186
Neumann, Erich 103
new beginning (Balint) 16, 93, 140, 190, 212
nine months of pregnancy 182, 185, 192, 197
Niqqudim 183
nuclear self 89
nullification of thought 148, 169
nurse 16, 26, 48–49, 75, 110, 141, 170–178, 180–182, 185–186, 189–190

O'Brien, Mary 47
object 3, 21, 34, 36, 40, 42–44, 50–52, 58, 69, 76, 114, 126, 140, 142, 152, 155, 168, 173, 179, 189–190, 219
ocean
– oceanic feeling 3, 43
ocean/sea 15, 33, 53, 135, 174, 198, 202
Oedipus 3, 9, 29, 42–43, 143, 148, 171, 182
Ogden, Thomas 19
old age 213
ontogenesis 148
opening V, 36, 47, 53, 77, 96, 100, 113–114, 128–131, 145, 150, 164, 180, 200–202, 205, 215
order of the fetus's creation (Seder Yetzirat ha-Valad) 15, 85, 119, 214
otherness
– great other 50
oxytocin 96, 203

pain V (intro.), 16, 32, 70, 186, 188, 198, 205, 211
palace 15, 30, 79, 100, 130, 143
Pappenheim, Bertha 58
Pardes, Ilana 46, 48, 198
parents 22, 32, 55, 58, 90, 128, 141–145, 179, 181, 213
– supernal parents 26, 186
Parmenides 14
passion 151
Patriarchs 134, 154, 177–178, 181
Philo 83, 92, 123, 126
philosophy 1, 10–12, 13, 37, 44, 47, 67, 85, 121–124, 126, 146
pinkas (writing tablet) 118–119
Piontelli, Alessandra 3, 42, 71, 76, 98

placenta 28, 33, 35, 44, 63, 89, 93, 96, 101, 155, 162
Plato 11–12, 14, 83, 86, 118–119, 121, 123, 126, 160, 201
Plotinus 146–147
prayer 21, 27, 86, 88, 105, 107, 109, 140, 175–178, 180, 185, 202, 207, 210
pre-Socratic 14, 93
primal scene 43, 142–144, 148, 193
primary maternal preoccupation 23, 59
psychoanalysis 1–2, 3, 4, 5, 6, 7, 8, 9, 10, 20, 22–23, 42–45, 57, 63–64, 69, 71, 89, 95, 111, 147–148, 154, 157, 161–162, 189–190, 204, 216, 218–219
psychosis 23, 78, 82, 144, 190
psychosomatic 2, 51, 72
psychotic 23, 144, 190
purity 109, 114, 201
– family purity 109
Pythagoras 14

R. Metivta (section in the Zohar) 130, 175, 178, 214
R. Nahman of Bratzlav 190, 206–216
Rachel 52, 106, 111–112, 188
rahmana 47
Rank, Otto 29, 42–43, 124, 148
rapprochement (Mahler) 78–79
ratzo ve-shov (running and returning) 79–81
ratzon (will) 79
reading of the Shema 183, 185–186
Rebekah 52, 111–112
reclamation (Alvarez) 81
redemption 58, 60, 174, 178, 180, 195–196, 198, 205, 216–218
– pangs of redemption and birth (hevlei geula & leidah) 56–57, 74, 98–99, 105–107, 109, 196–200, 206, 218
regression 6, 38, 43, 59, 140, 144, 172, 182, 190
reincarnation 14, 24, 150, 183
repentance (*teshuva*) 116, 152, 167
repressed aspects and layers 7–8, 22, 42, 45, 60, 98, 117, 121, 124, 138, 144, 152, 169

reshimu (divine presence) 32, 36, 70, 76, 136
resurrection of the dead 81, 111, 114, 200
return of the repressed 49
reverie 18
Rich, Adrienne V, 60, 70, 98, 105, 111, 153
righteous 17, 25, 27, 120, 158, 182, 184, 188, 191, 196, 206, 208, 213–216
ritual 7, 11, 44, 88, 105, 128, 132–133, 135, 147, 156, 178, 183, 205, 214, 219
river of milk 171
Rodef (persecutor, pursuer) 64–67
Rome 44, 87, 124–125, 196
rose 129, 132, 135, 156, 165
Rosenzweig, Franz 12
Rosh Hashanah (Jewish New Year) 88

Saba de-Mishpatim (section in the Zohar) 24, 130
Sabbateanism 4, 205, 208
Sabbath 27, 109, 113
sacrifice 16, 48, 84, 108, 166, 208–209
Sarah 52, 125
sawing (*nesirah*) 27, 50, 62, 82–85, 86, 87, 88, 89, 110, 116, 119–120, 125, 151, 185, 187, 211
schizo-paranoid position (Klein) 7
Schneur Zalman of Liadi 17, 159–160, 195
Second Isaiah 47, 197
secret concealment, 2–3, 7, 13, 25, 36, 42, 44, 50, 54, 58, 60, 63, 74, 113, 126–128, 131–133, 136–137, 139, 142–144, 150–152, 154, 159–160, 162, 167, 175–177, 180, 185–186, 191–193, 196, 207, 209–210, 213, 217
Sefer ha-Bahir 164–165
Sefer Yetzirah 80, 138, 148
sefirot 3, 5, 7, 14, 17, 19–21, 22, 23, 24, 26–27, 30–31, 49, 52, 54–55, 62–63, 80, 88, 90, 127–129, 131–141, 167, 170, 174, 178, 182–183, 185–187, 190, 192–193, 210, 217
– birth of the *sefirot* 14
– *sefirot* as essence or vessels 5, 22
– *sefirot* as family 128, 142
self in relations (Chodorow) 49
selfobject (Kohut) 2, 6

semiotic 2, 91, 137–138
separateness 20–22, 32, 49, 56, 62, 71, 77–78, 84, 86, 129, 142, 152, 155–156, 161–162, 167–168, 185, 204
Seven Blessings (of the Shekhinah) 88
sexuality 1–2, 8, 15, 25, 27, 41, 44–45, 49–50, 85–86, 90, 104–105, 131, 142–143, 147, 149–154, 156, 176, 180, 182, 184, 202–203, 214, 217
shadow 22, 30–31, 33, 120
shame 54, 109, 152
shattering of the vessels 190
Shavuot 53
Shekhinah 17, 20, 25, 27, 52, 60, 62, 130, 133–134, 150, 154, 156, 183–184, 188
– as the mother 48, 52, 56, 63, 164, 175, 179
– As the revealed world (olam ha-gilui); world of separation (olam ha-pirud) 20, 54
– as Upper Daughter 137
– has nothing of her own (*leit la-mi-garmah kelum*) 175
shibboleth 148
shiur komah (the measure of the body [of God]) 25, 149, 213
shofar 211
Silberg, Jules 9
sin 16–17, 22, 57, 104–105, 109–110, 133–134, 143
Sitra Ahra 7, 22, 26, 91, 94, 203
skin 2, 18, 91, 115, 135
– Skin-Ego 136
Slavin, Malcolm 9
sleep 57, 87–88, 118–119, 171–172, 211–212, 221
smallness (*qaṭnut*) 182–183, 185, 212
snake 102, 105, 115, 184, 201–203
Socrates 11, 122–124
Solomon 53
Sophia 158
Soranus 92
soul V, 1–2, 3, 4, 6, 11–16, 19, 23–24, 26, 35, 46, 63, 69, 72, 76–77, 79, 81, 84–87, 93–94, 98, 101, 108, 115, 118–123, 125, 152, 158, 163, 180, 182, 188, 204, 208, 211, 214, 216, 218, 220–221

– descent of the soul into the world 14, 16
– root of the soul 80, 214
souls 14, 26, 28, 47, 85, 88, 103, 107–108, 119, 122, 133, 136–138, 156–158, 167, 182, 184–186, 188, 194, 200, 214
sparks 26, 137, 139, 159, 187
sperm 25, 32, 91–92, 131, 175, 179, 206, 214–215
splitting/division 5–7, 20–24, 29, 51–52, 73, 80, 82–83, 85, 94, 114, 117, 131, 137, 143–144, 153–155, 157, 172–173, 202–203
– vertical/horizontal splitting 6
Stein, Ruth 9
Stern, Daniel 89, 162
stones (*ovnayim*, birthing stool) 74, 93, 106–108, 111, 186
sublimation 143
sun 25, 93, 157–160, 162
surgery 65, 83
sweetening 176, 186
symbiosis 16, 79, 87, 89, 162–163, 173, 188
symbol 45, 97, 123, 129, 141
Symposium 83, 86, 122

taboo
– totem and taboo 9
tearing 16, 36, 62, 69, 98, 202, 206–207, 215
Thales 93
Theaetetus 122
theurgy 54, 154, 158
– negative theurgy 54, 143
Tiferet 20, 26, 55, 62, 88, 90–91, 141–143, 172–173, 177, 181–182, 185, 192, 203
tikkun (repair) 2, 7, 20, 23, 60, 62, 81, 88, 152, 165, 182, 186, 190, 192, 216
Tikkunei ha-Zohar 21, 58, 128–129, 132, 136, 192
tohu 30, 94, 214
tomb 31, 96–97, 106, 200
– burial 33, 108, 117, 120
Torah 15, 24–26, 28, 35, 40, 53, 65, 91, 102, 118, 139–140, 152, 171–172, 175–176, 178, 180, 184, 188–189, 193, 195, 207, 210, 213, 216

toxic nourishment (Eigen) 179
transference 5, 57, 88
– counter-transference 57
trauma 8, 32, 35, 121, 204–205
– birth trauma 31, 34, 42–43, 69–70, 76, 186
– humanizing trauma 31, 205
– transmission of trauma 31
Tree of Knowledge 109
Tree of Life 158
Tree of the *Sefirot* 52
Trible, Phyllis 48, 114, 200
Turner, Victor 174
Tustin, Frances 19, 69
twins 71–72, 83, 193
tzela (side, rib) 84–85, 88
Tzimtzum ("constriction") 34, 51, 58, 71, 160–162, 214

uncanny (*unheimliche*) 37, 95, 112, 126
uninvited guest from the past 31
union 21–22, 34, 51, 53, 58, 85, 88, 142, 186, 193–194, 213
Upper Mother 19, 62, 130, 168
urge/drive/inclination 8, 21, 29, 37–41, 55, 60, 71, 86, 154
– death drive 23, 28, 38–40, 81, 120, 155, 173
– evil inclination 16
– libido 38
– life drive 38–39, 55

van Gennep, Arnold 105
vengeance 136
vessel, woman as a vessel 22, 94, 114, 135, 140, 167–169, 187
vessel/container 14, 18, 22, 25, 40, 59, 77, 86, 90, 94, 114, 135, 140, 159, 161–162, 167–169, 172–174, 182, 185, 187–188, 190, 220
virgin 41, 45, 67, 125, 135, 152, 205
Vital, Hayyim 183
voices 27, 43, 63, 115, 120, 139, 157, 174, 199, 207, 215
– voices that are never lost 115

war 39, 195
waste 66, 91–94, 100, 117, 156

water V, 32–33, 35, 59, 90–94, 101, 114, 116–117, 121, 163–164, 166–169, 174, 202–203
– creation from water 93
– embryonic fluid 93
– muddy water 93
– myths 90
Wilheim, Joanna 32, 42
Winnicott, Donald 23, 34, 40, 42, 54–56, 72, 76, 78, 98, 161, 170, 180, 190, 219
Wittgenstein, Ludwig 219
womb 3, 14–15, 18, 20, 23–24, 28–29, 31–33, 35–39, 42, 44–45, 47, 50, 53, 55–59, 62–64, 66, 68–72, 76–78, 83, 87, 89, 91–93, 95–103, 105–106, 109–116, 118–123, 125–126, 129–130, 136, 138, 140–142, 145, 150–151, 153, 157, 159, 161–165, 167–169, 172–173, 175–176, 180, 183, 185–193, 197–198, 200–205, 207, 209, 211–212, 215–216, 220
– and *Rahamim* 47
– as a boiling pot 24
– as a grave 24, 100, 111–113, 151
– as a home 95
– as a prison 11, 24, 97–103, 106, 168
– as a purse 24, 97, 101–103, 110, 125
– as a source 23, 44, 105, 110, 113, 118, 159
– as a tomb 31, 97, 106
– bad womb 103
– divine womb 137
– hysteria (Greek: *hystera*) 95
– rooms/chambers/doors of the womb 37, 109, 191, 193–194
– *vagina dentata* 202
womb and the 248 limbs (*RaMaH eivarim*) 191
Woo, Rose 42
world of the male (Olam ha-Zachar, "the masculine world") 61, 134, 164–165, 186, 217

Yerushalmi, Yosef Hayim 8
Yesod (sefira, "basis," "foundation") 134, 153, 174, 185–186, 191
YHWH (Tetragrammaton) 52, 84

Ze'ir Anpin (Small Countenance) 172, 176, 181–182, 184–185, 187–188
Zillah 112
Zohar V, 3, 14–15, 16, 19, 21, 24–25, 27, 31, 36, 49, 52–53, 55, 58, 62, 83–87, 90–94, 99, 115–116, 127–145, 149, 153–154, 156–158, 165, 167, 170–174, 178, 181–182, 184, 186–187, 202–203, 205–206, 210–211, 213–214, 217, 221

www.ingramcontent.com/pod-product-compliance
Lightning Source LLC
Chambersburg PA
CBHW020226170426
43201CB00007B/331